DEVELOPING THEORIES OF MIND

Edited by

Janet W. Astington
Ontario Institute for Studies in Education

Paul L. Harris
University of Oxford

David R. Olson
Ontario Institute for Studies in Education

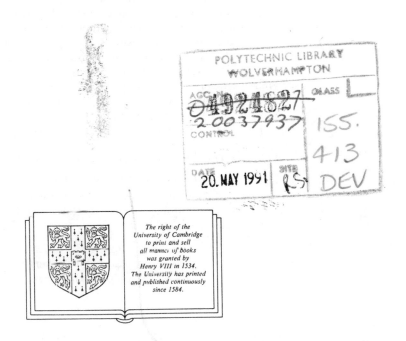

The right of the
University of Cambridge
to print and sell
all manner of books
was granted by
Henry VIII in 1534.
The University has printed
and published continuously
since 1584.

CAMBRIDGE UNIVERSITY PRESS

CAMBRIDGE

NEW YORK   PORT CHESTER   MELBOURNE   SYDNEY

Published by the Press Syndicate of the University of Cambridge
The Pitt Building, Trumpington Street, Cambridge CB2 1RP
40 West 20 Street, New York, NY 10011 USA
10 Stamford Road, Oakleigh, Melbourne 3166, Australia

First published 1988
First paperback edition 1989

Printed in Canada

Library of Congress Cataloging-in-Publication Data
Developing theories of mind.
Papers from the International Conference on
Developing Theories of Mind, University of Toronto,
May, 1986, and the Workshop on Children's Early Concept
of Mind, St. John's College, Oxford, June, 1986.
1. Cognition in children – Congresses. 2. Children
– Attitudes – Congresses. I. Astington, Janet W.
II. Harris, Paul L. III. Olson, David R. IV. Inter-
national Conference on Developing Theories of Mind
(1986 : University of Toronto) V. Workshop on Children's
Early Concept of Mind (1986 : St. John's College
University of Oxford)
BF723.C5D468   1988   155.4'13   87–34141

British Library Cataloguing in Publication Data
Developing theories of mind.
1.   Children. Mental development
I.   Astington, Janet W. II. Harris, Paul L.
III. Olson, David R.
155.4'13

ISBN 0 521 35411 0 hardcovers
ISBN 0 521 38653-5 paperback

Contents

v

Preface

In this book psychologists are developing theories to account for children's developing theories of mind. Its neatly ambiguous title, for which we thank Alison Gopnik, comes from the International Conference on Developing Theories of Mind, organized by Janet Astington, Lynd Forguson, Alison Gopnik, and David Olson through the McLuhan Program in Culture and Technology at the University of Toronto in May 1986. Many of the contributors to that conference subsequently participated in the Workshop on Children's Early Concept of Mind, organized by Paul Harris at St. John's College, Oxford, in June 1986. Both conferences generated an excellent set of papers, a very high level of constructive discussion, and an enormous amount of excitement and enthusiasm. The similarity of theme, participants, and goal was so great that the papers were combined into this single volume, jointly edited from Toronto and Oxford. In the year following the conferences, drafts and revised drafts of the papers were exchanged among the authors, as can be seen in the numerous arguments and agreements to which they refer in the published chapters. The result is much more than a set of conference proceedings: It is a coherent, sustained attack on a set of fundamental issues in developmental psychology and cognitive science. The volume, therefore, should be of interest to academics, researchers, graduate students, and advanced undergraduates who are interested in the nature and development of children's understanding of mental life.

We would like to acknowledge the support provided to the Toronto conference by the Connaught Foundation through a grant to the McLuhan Program. We are also grateful for support provided by the Faculty of Arts and Science, the Division of Life Sciences of Scarborough College, the Department of Psychology, and University College, all of the University of Toronto, and by Field Services and Research of the Ontario Institute for Studies in Education. In Oxford, support and hospitality were provided by St. John's College. We would like to thank all those who participated in the conferences, both those who contributed papers to the volume and all the other participants, including Inge Bretherton, Jerome Bruner, Susan Carey, Colin McGinn, and Andrew Woodfield. We also take this opportunity to thank Sylvia Wookey for ensuring that the Toronto conference ran smoothly, and Denese Coulbeck for secretarial assistance during preparation of the manuscript for publication. Finally and especially, we would like to thank Helen Wheeler, editor at Cambridge University Press, for her advice and guidance, and for expediting publication of the volume.

J.W.A.
P.L.H.
D.R.O.

Contributors

JANET W. ASTINGTON, Ontario Institute for Studies in Education

CAROLE R. BEAL, Dartmouth College

GARY BONITATIBUS, Saint Anselm College

MICHAEL CHANDLER, University of British Columbia

CAROL FLEISHER FELDMAN, New York University

JOHN H. FLAVELL, Stanford University

LYND FORGUSON, University of Toronto

ALISON GOPNIK, University of Toronto

DANA GROSS, University of Minnesota

PAUL L. HARRIS, University of Oxford

JÜRGEN HOGREFE, University of Salzburg

CARL NILS JOHNSON, University of Pittsburgh

ALAN M. LESLIE, MRC Cognitive Development Unit, University of London

DAVID R. OLSON, Ontario Institute for Studies in Education

JOSEF PERNER, University of Sussex

DIANE POULIN-DUBOIS, Concordia University

JAMES RUSSELL, University of Cambridge (previously University of Liverpool)

MARILYN SHATZ, University of Michigan

THOMAS R. SHULTZ, McGill University

BEATE SODIAN, University of Munich

MARJORIE TAYLOR, University of Oregon

HENRY M. WELLMAN, University of Michigan

HEINZ WIMMER, University of Salzburg

ILAN YANIV, University of Michigan

1

Introduction

DAVID R. OLSON, JANET W. ASTINGTON, and
PAUL L. HARRIS

Sometime after they learn to talk but before they begin formal schooling,
children come to display a new understanding of perception, action, and
talk that is symptomatic of a new sensitivity to the life of the mind. Children begin to recognize themselves and others as "things which think," as
things which *believe, doubt, wonder, imagine,* and *pretend.* This, in itself, is a
remarkable achievement as it marks their coming to make a systematic
distinction between the world and *mental representations* of the world. But
perhaps even more remarkable, the achievement of this new understanding of mind appears to spill over into a number of apparently unrelated
domains, including children's understanding of the distinction between
appearance and reality, and their understanding of the relation between
an utterance and its interpretation. Indeed, the repercussions are sufficiently
broad that it is not misleading to think of children's new understanding of
mind as constituting a new stage or level of intellectual development.

To characterize just what is achieved and how it is achieved is the
major focus of this volume. Although accounts vary somewhat, there is
agreement that this development does not consist simply of the addition
of a new piece of knowledge. Rather, it involves a fundamental alteration
or shift in children's orientation to their knowledge. Their mental representations cease to be transparent and invisible. Instead, they become
opaque. Children begin to recognize mental states in themselves and
others; they come to recognize beliefs as beliefs, desires as desires, and intentions as intentions. That recognition reflects children's acquisition of a
theory of mind, a set of explicit and interconnected concepts for representing
those representational states; that is, it involves the development of a set of
meta-representations. The chapters of this volume examine young children's
acquisition of this theory of mind, the impact of its acquisition on children's
understanding of their own and others' behavior, its role in their consciousness of their own mental states, and its role in their ascription of mental
states to others. As such, these chapters represent a state-of-the-art report

This chapter was written collaboratively; order of authorship indicates successive contributions.

I

on the conceptual and empirical advances being made in an important new area of research on children's cognitive development.

As the evidence for the impact of children's acquisition of a theory of mind on their talk, action, and interaction mounts, a number of related questions comes to the fore. Primary among them is how best to characterize this achievement. Is the development a matter of acquiring a general capacity for recursion, for embedding relations within higher-order relations? Is it a matter of acquiring a set of quasi-theoretical concepts for interpreting behavior? Is it a matter of becoming self-conscious, of learning to think about representations instead of thinking about the world? Or is it a matter of coming to understand the various causal connections between states of the world and intentional states of the mind such as thinking, knowing, and believing?

A second set of questions revolves around how we are to explain this remarkable achievement, the acquisition of a theory of mind. Is the explanation to be found in some fundamental and endogenous reorganization of the child's cognitive processes? Or is it to be found in the socializing practices of adults who impart a particular way of talking and thinking about language and action?

A third set of questions concerns the epistemological status of the child's theory of mind. Do children, irrespective of culture, discover a set of intrinsic and universal properties of the mind? Alternatively, have they acquired a "folk theory," a set of concepts about mental life that is culturally transmitted, just as any other set of beliefs is, whether true or not? The appeal to mental acts and mental states, that is, to *intentionality*, in cognitive psychology is one of the vexed problems in the cognitive sciences. On the one hand theorists such as Fodor (1981), Pylyshyn (1984), and Searle (1983) defend the view that beliefs, desires, and intentions are essential to psychological explanation. On the other, theorists including Quine (1960), Dennett (1978b), Churchland (1984), and Stich (1983) maintain that psychological explanation cannot be based on the ascription of intentional states and that meta-representations are at best part of a "language game," a social psychology, or a "folk psychology" that will sooner or later fall to the advance of a realist, empirical cognitive theory. This volume will not, of course, resolve that issue. But a careful examination of children's acquisition of a set of concepts for representing their own mental states and those of others, and the dramatic effect that such an achievement has on their behavior, may permit us to see the problem from a fresh perspective.

Acquisition of a theory of mind

Why can this accumulation of achievements be deemed the acquisition of a *theory* of mind? A theory, as Wellman (Chapter 4) reminds us, consists of a referential domain, that is, the set of events to be explained and predicted, an interrelated set of concepts that make up the theory, and a set of rules for using the theoretical concepts to explain and predict events in the referential domain. Consider, briefly, what is involved in having a theory of planetary motion. The events referred to are the orbital motions of a set of heavenly bodies, the theoretical terms are *planets*, *gravity*, and *centripetal force*, and the theoretical concepts can be used to explain and predict events, such as orbital planetary motion. If the theory successfully explains the events, the entities or forces identified by the theoretical terms – planets, gravity, and centripetal force – are treated as real entities.

So what is a theory of mind? The events to be explained and predicted are talk and action (some would say behavior). The theoretical concepts are those of *belief*, *desire*, *intention*, and *feeling*. And, third, these concepts may be used to explain and predict the events in the referential domain, namely, talk and action. Finally, if the theory provides the best explanation and prediction of the events in the referential domain, the entities specified by the theoretical terms may be treated as real entities.

Children sometime between their second and sixth years, at least children in western cultures, acquire such a theory. They begin to acquire the relevant set of mental predicates or concepts, beginning with *pretending* in their second year, as Leslie (Chapter 2) shows, and they quickly acquire the lexical terms for a set of mental concepts including *know*, *think*, *remember*, *forget*, *dream*, *pretend*, and the relations among those theoretical terms, as Wellman (Chapter 4) shows. Then they begin to understand, predict, and explain their own and others' talk and action by means of the concepts expressed by those mental terms, as Perner (Chapter 8), Wimmer, Hogrefe, and Sodian (Chapter 9), Flavell (Chapter 13), and others show. These meta-representational concepts are also theoretical in that they represent states that are not directly observable but inferred from overt action and speech and used to understand some properties of talk and action. In acquiring these meta-representational concepts, children are acquiring a "folk psychology," part of what Forguson and Gopnik (Chapter 12) refer to as the commonsense view of the world. It is these concepts that permit children to reflect on their own and others' mental states. It is important to stress that having a theory of mind goes beyond merely possessing such states. It involves the possession of concepts of those states. Because these concepts represent such states as beliefs, desires, intentions, and feelings, they constitute representations of representations and in this sense constitute a recursive or meta-representational system.

Premack and Woodruff (1978) were among the first, at least in recent times, to ask whether a theory of mind is the unique possession of human beings. They claimed that the behavior of chimpanzees could be most perspicuously explained by allowing that they imputed wants, beliefs, and intentions to others, that is, that they possessed a theory of mind. However, critics such as Dennett (1978a) noted that the training required to test the hypothesis that chimpanzees have beliefs about beliefs in others, could engender beliefs and habits that in themselves could explain the behavior of the animals without appealing to beliefs about beliefs.

Children, of course, are immature members of a different species, as Chandler (Chapter 20) points out, and they may have a theory of mind as part of their native endowment. Moreover, unlike chimpanzees, children are linguistic creatures, and, exercising some ingenuity, one can ask them about their own and others' mental states and so determine if they possess the relevant concepts and make the relevant distinctions. Further, by experimentation one can determine if and when they use a theory of mind in predicting and explaining the talk and action of themselves and others. Indeed, this volume consists of reports of ingenious devices that researchers have used to examine children's explicit concepts about their own and others' minds, and their recourse to such concepts in explaining and predicting what they or other people might do or say.

In arguing that it is helpful and appropriate to think of children's acquiring a theory of mind, we should underline certain caveats. First, in claiming that children have a theory of mind, we do not intend to suggest that they have a theory in which the referential domain is the mind itself. We mean only that in their explanation and prediction of talk and action, children have recourse to mental constructs. Thus, their theory, strictly speaking, is of action and talk; the mind enters as a theoretical construct, not as a domain requiring explanation. Similarly, it can be misleading, strictly speaking, to describe Newton as advancing a theory of gravity, if by that phrase one implies that the referential domain was gravity. Rather, Newton advanced a theory of planetary motion and of falling bodies, in which gravity served as a theoretical postulate. He explicitly avoided advancing an explanation of gravity itself.

A second caveat concerns the importance of explicit talk about the mind as opposed to predictions that appear to presuppose the mind. When children appear to take a given entity into account in making a prediction, we are not thereby entitled to infer that children do actually deploy that entity as a theoretical construct. Consider, for example, Piaget's observation of infants in the first year of life (Piaget, 1937/1954). In attempting to catch sight again of a rapidly moving object, they frequently anticipate where the object will have fallen and scan the floor. In some sense, they appear to take the consequences of gravity into account. Yet we clearly would not wish to assert that infants employ gravity as a theoretical construct on the basis of such observations. Similarly, from the mere fact that children appear to take beliefs into account in predicting behavior, we are not thereby entitled to infer that children employ beliefs as a theoretical construct in their predictions. However, children offer us much more evidence for their theory of mind than simple prediction. They make explicit reference to the theoretical entities that motivate their predictions. Thus, they refer explicitly to what they or others *know*, *think*, and *pretend*. As various authors show (Wellman, Chapter 4; Harris & Gross, Chapter 15), children are often capable of backing up the judgments and predictions that they make by reference to the relevant mental states. We cannot rely just on children's use of mental terms, as Perner (Chapter 14) emphasizes; it is the converging evidence from prediction and explanation that strengthens our conviction that children do indeed adopt a theory of mind.

The empirical findings reported in this volume and the interpretations of these findings are far too rich to summarize briefly. Yet there is enough agreement between both the data presented and the authors' interpretations to state the primary achievements involved in developing a theory of mind. First, children achieve some means for disconnecting – "decoupling," as Leslie (Chapter 2) describes it – representations from the things they are representations of. Sometime in their second year these detached representations become embedded in representational functions such as pretending. Second, children acquire a set of concepts for representing mental activities such as *thinking*, *dreaming*, *imagining*, and *pretending*, and the terms for referring to these concepts, sometime between their second and fourth years. Third, they become skilled in using these concepts for predicting and explaining actions premised on false beliefs, present beliefs discrepant from prior beliefs, appearances discrepant from reality, intentions discrepant from actions, utterances discrepant from beliefs and intentions, and facial expressions discrepant from actual feelings. This third achievement, the use of mental concepts to understand and predict what is said and done, begins, at least for children in our cultures, when they are about 4 years of age. Some would argue that only when these concepts function in the theoretical way just mentioned, can the child be credited with a theory of mind. Even then it will be some time before children are sufficiently skilled in using that theory of mind to understand such issues as perceptual and linguistic ambiguity, and the relativity of knowledge.

How are we to account for these relatively systematic changes? A number of factors are implicated. The swift and regular emergence of children's understanding of their own and others' minds between 2 and 4 years of age suggests that the development is, at least in part, maturational, that children at that age become capable of recursive operations enabling them to represent the contents of an earlier or nonveridical representation. Second, the fact that children have recently become language-using creatures when they begin to form meta-representations, such as those implicated in pretend play, suggests that language or a more general symbolic capacity may be an important element in the development of this understanding. Third, the fact that children are acquiring a mentalistic vocab-

ulary about this time suggests that the particular concepts represented
by that vocabulary play an important role; they appear to serve as a distinctive set of predicates for the formation of embedding (and embedded)
assertions, such as "John *pretends* that the banana is a telephone" or "John
thinks that the chocolate is in the cupboard." The extent to which language
in general, and such distinctive predicates in particular, are relevant to
the achievement of a theory of mind remains an important but unresolved
issue.

A brief overview of the volume

The acquisition of a theory of mind is not a simple matter but involves a
number of achievements. The early steps, taken in the second and third
year of life, are discussed in Part I. Thereafter, the child elaborates the
basic theory in a variety of domains. Two domains in particular have been
fruitful for empirical research: the child's understanding of the relationships among perception, knowledge, and reality (considered in Part II),
and the child's understanding of the relationship between minds engaged
in various types of dyadic interaction (considered in Part III). Further
implications of children's acquisition of a theory of mind are discussed in
Part IV. Below we give a brief overview of the child's initial theory, and its
subsequent elaboration.

I. Developmental origins of children's knowledge about the mind

The first and perhaps the most important step in the development of a
theory of mind is the ability to form meta-representations. This ability
requires that children isolate, or "decouple," as Leslie calls it (Chapter 2),
primary representations of the world from their normal input–output
functions. In pretend play, for example, a banana that in its primary representation is something to eat, comes to be represented in a secondary
way as, say, a telephone. How can the secondary representation be formed
without confusing the child about the intrinsic properties of bananas? To
resolve that predicament, Leslie proposes that representations are "decoupled" from the things they are representations of and so become eligi-
ble for a secondary representation that can violate the normal reference,
truth, and existence properties of the primary representation. Secondary
representations with these properties, Leslie calls "meta-representations,"
and they are expressed by such predicates as *pretend* and *think*. Leslie suggests that this meta-representational ability provides the basis for the
child's acquisition of these mentalist terms.

Not only do children begin to show evidence of a new ability to operate
on their representations, as suggested by their pretend play, they also

begin to report on their own mental states and on the general properties of these states, as Johnson (Chapter 3) and Wellman (Chapter 4) point out. Johnson argues that a primary source for such mental concepts is children's conscious experience of their own thoughts, dreams, and feelings, and that the theory of mind provides an expression for these conscious experiences. As Johnson points out, such experiences are rich and comprehensible. His claim that they are an adequate source for a theory of mind provides a possible counterargument to the claims of Sellars (1963), Nisbett and Wilson (1977), Quine (1960), and others, to the effect that people have little or no direct introspective access to higher mental processes and that what passes for introspection is often a retrospective interpretation along commonsensical or "folk theory" lines.

Wellman shows that 3-year-olds have an explicit understanding of the distinction between real objects and events and decoupled representations such as dreams, thoughts, and images. They have also mapped out some of the interdependencies among these concepts. It seems clear that children by this age possess the concepts needed for a theory of mind, but the fact that they cannot use these concepts to understand cases in which action is premised on a false belief, for example, suggests important limitations to that theory.

Unlike decoupled representations, the creation of primary representations depends upon appropriate perceptual access. Children's ability to assess another person's knowledge must depend, in part, on their awareness of whether or not that person had the appropriate perceptual access. Yaniv and Shatz (Chapter 5) show that even 2½- to 3-year-olds are aware of the conditions affecting perceptibility: seeing, hearing, smelling, and touching. From these observations they infer that young children have theories about perceptual access and its relation to mental processes. Although the latter part of this claim is still open to question because Wimmer, Hogrefe, and Sodian (Chapter 9) show that 3-year-olds are uncertain of what others know on the basis of what the other sees and hears.

Children must also understand the concept of intention if they are to predict and explain behavior, since a person's action is dependent not merely on what he knows or believes but also on what he desires or intends. Poulin-Dubois and Shultz (Chapter 6) review research on children's attribution of intentions to others, showing the beginnings of this ability in children as young as 2½ to 3 years of age. Even younger children show some knowledge of others' agency, if not of their intentionality, and Poulin-Dubois and Shultz discuss how children's understanding of the concept of intention may arise out of their concept of agency.

These cognitive achievements are reflected in children's linguistic ones; if children can embed mental representations in other representations, they can also do so in language, as Feldman shows (Chapter 7). Indeed,

Feldman suggests that the linguistic device for turning predicates into subjects, a fundamental recursive procedure that she observes in young children's language, may be the device for turning representations into meta-representations. In this way a mental attitude, treated as an object of discourse, acquires the status of a mental state.

II. Coordinating representational states with the world: Understanding the relationships among perception, knowledge, and reality

Somewhat later, roughly in their fifth year, children begin to ascribe false beliefs to other people, in the attempt to predict and explain their behavior. In an important paper, Wimmer and Perner (1983) reported that between 4 and 6 years of age children come to anticipate that others will act in accordance with the beliefs they hold, even if they are false, rather than in accordance with the way things are in the world. In the current volume, they take their initial findings in somewhat different directions.

For Perner (Chapter 8), the crucial new competence at this stage is the ability to represent the process of representation, and Perner would not apply the term "*meta*-representational" to children's abilities until this stage is reached. Two-year-olds can form representations, including hypothetical and counterfactual representations, and can compare these models to the world (that is, to their model of the world) so that they can enter a pretend scenario and can tell you that dreams are not real. However, 2-year-olds cannot represent the process of modeling whereas 4-year-olds can represent that process. Only then can they understand that someone entertaining a false belief takes it to be a true representation of the real world, and is the world in which he will act, even though it *mis*represents the actual situation.

An alternative proposal for what changes between the beginnings of meta-representations in the 2-year-old and the management of false belief by the 4-year-old is that the child acquires a new understanding of the sources of information about the world. Wimmer, Hogrefe, and Sodian (Chapter 9) show that the older, but not the younger, children recognize the role of perception and communication in the acquisition of beliefs, and suggest that children's success with false belief and appearance–reality tasks is a manifestation of their new understanding of informational conditions. Younger children, by contrast, failing to grasp this relation, discount the fact that the protagonist in a false belief story has not had perceptual access to the true state of affairs. Wimmer et al. also show that by 6 years of age children come to understand inference as a source of information. They emphasize that perception, communication, and inference function as informational sources for even the youngest children tested; what is gained between 4 and 6 years is an understanding of these processes.

About the time they begin to ascribe false beliefs to others in the attempt to predict and explain behavior, children begin to acknowledge their own prior false beliefs, as Astington and Gopnik (Chapter 10) report. The fact that false beliefs are recognized in others at the same time, or indeed even earlier, than in themselves again raises questions as to the origin of this knowledge. Does it arise from the introspection of conscious experience, or does it arise from social interaction with others? The fact that such understanding applies equally to self and other again suggests the theoretical nature of this new understanding. Astington and Gopnik argue that it reflects a profound conceptual change which occurs at this time.

Equipped with a theory of mind, the child is in a better position to assess what others will see and know in ambiguous perceptual situations, as Taylor (Chapter 11) points out. However, not until children are 6 or more years of age do they come to recognize that someone lacking a piece of knowledge or holding different beliefs from their own will see things differently from the way they themselves do. Incidentally, Perner's suggestion (Chapter 8), that these role-taking tasks are more difficult than false belief tasks because young children have more experience with evaluation of representations than with interpretation of them, is supported by the data from Taylor's training study. After being given the experience of interpreting ambiguous pictures, 4-year-olds performed as well as untrained 6-year-olds in a subsequent role-taking task.

Forguson and Gopnik (Chapter 12) trace the development in children of the commonsense view of the world, which uses beliefs and desires to predict and explain behavior, and which includes the assumption that there is a mind-independent reality. Underlying this view is the ability to form meta-representations and to distinguish between representations and reality. Forguson and Gopnik argue that a crucial step is taken at about 4 years of age when children not only are able to distinguish pretending, dreaming, and imagining from reality, but are aware that real objects are also mentally represented, that is, 4-year-olds develop a representational model of the mind. This achievement underlies 4-year-olds' ability to understand representational diversity (false belief), representational change, and the distinction between appearance and reality.

Flavell (Chapter 13) surveys a wide set of tasks that exhibit a marked developmental change and presents both empirical and theoretical arguments suggesting that children come to realize that objects, events, and, indeed, meanings may be represented in multiple ways. They can then understand that different people may have contradictory representations of the same content, and can disregard their own beliefs while predicting the actions of another person who holds different beliefs, or can acknowledge that one and the same object may have the appearance of one thing but in reality be another, or are able to understand that the same utterance can be intended to convey one meaning but actually convey another. These abilities all reflect what Flavell has previously referred to as "Level 2" understanding.

III. Further development of a theory of mind: Understanding mental states in social interaction

Whereas Part II focuses on the child's understanding of the knowing, perceiving subject and the relationship of that subject to the world, Part III is more obviously concerned with certain types of dyadic relationship, in which the actual or possible mental states of one member of the dyad must be seen as part of the intentional mental states of the other member. Thus, children come to understand that one person wants another person to believe something, or that one person may have a false belief about another person's current belief. Keeping track of these dyadic relationships, these representations about representations, requires a second-order, recursive ability that begins to emerge at around 5 or 6 years and upward.

Perner (Chapter 14) explicitly describes how certain types of social judgment can be made only when children master second-order representations. Thus, they begin to distinguish a lie from a joke on the basis of whether the speaker intended the listener to believe the false statement, and they assign responsibility for accidents on their assessment of the knowledge of the protagonists about one another's knowledge.

Similarly, Harris and Gross (Chapter 15) argue that children understand deceit in the form of misleading displays of emotion only when they can appreciate how people can deliberately seek to mislead observers about their real emotional states. Thus, 6-year-olds appreciate that a protagonist may deliberately look happy or sad in order to engender a false belief in onlookers about his or her emotional state.

Another indication of children's developing understanding of the mental states of others comes from research on children's understanding of communication failures. Beal (Chapter 16) points out that young children fail to distinguish the effect the speaker intended to have on the mind of the listener and the actual effect of the message, and thus fail to recognize that misunderstanding can arise not from faulty intentions but from faulty utterances. She shows that they find it particularly difficult to assess the actual effect of the message when they know the effect the speaker intended. This is a problem that arises in a number of symbolic domains.

Taking a similar line of argument, Bonitatibus (Chapter 17) shows that children who are told that speakers may have more than one intention find it easier to detect ambiguity in a message. However, this does not increase children's attention to the actual wording of the message. Bonitatibus sees attention to the words of a message as a skill that may be tied to literacy.

IV. Further theoretical implications of children's concept of mind

The authors in Part IV examine a variety of issues raised by considerations of children's acquisition of a theory of mind.

Shultz (Chapter 18) shows that computational modeling, one of the more powerful tools of cognitive science, can usefully be applied to the study of children's developing concepts of mind. Shultz's model determines whether the outcome of an action was intended or not, using the same heuristic procedures that children are presumed to use. A major contribution of Shultz's chapter is a methodological one: Because computational modeling demands the detailed specification of mechanisms, it forces a move from a level of general description to one of greater precision.

Russell (Chapter 19) outlines some of the conditions necessary for one to acquire a sense of oneself as a thinking subject. These conditions include recognition of the effects of agency on perception, recognition of failed expectations, recognition of the asymmetry between things and representations of things, and recognition of perceptual experience as intermediate between things and representations of things. These are not simple achievements, and Russell argues that they emerge over a relatively long period. He examines children's limited understanding of some of these conditions, even after 4 years of age, showing, for example, that they tend to treat *de dicto* representations as if they were *de re* ones, that is, they treat intensional contexts as if they were extensional ones. Put in the language of the other authors, children tend to ignore the fact that the appropriate description of what another person would say or do depends on that person's beliefs, not on the objective properties of the situation.

Like Russell, Chandler (Chapter 20) argues that the development of a theory of mind begins well before 4 years of age and continues long after that. Chandler denies that there is the watershed in development at about age 4, which many other authors are seeking to explain. He argues that the ability to understand that another's behavior may be premised on a false belief does not imply that the child has a truly constructivist theory of mind. Indeed, not until the early school years are children aware that different people may interpret the same stimulus differently, depending on their background knowledge. But even then, children believe that one of these interpretations must be the true one. Not until adolescence do they realize that knowledge acquisition is inherently subjective, that there may be no objective facts to appeal to. Chandler claims that this realization is a crucial part of the adult theory of mind.

Olson (Chapter 21) examines the relations between children's acquisition of a theory of mind and recent developments in the philosophy of mind. He asks what the status of that acquisition is. By the time children enter school they share with adults the Cartesian view of human talk and action;

they explain talk and action in terms of desires, beliefs, and intentions. But is that theory a true theory? Or is it merely a "folk theory," a set of beliefs, similar to beliefs in ghosts and demons, that children acquire in the course of growing up in a particular culture. Although this issue deeply divides such antimentalists as Quine, Stich, and Churchland, as well as such "instrumentalists" as Dennett, from such intentionalists as Fodor, Pylyshyn, and Searle, Olson suggests that this new work on developing theories of mind permits us to formulate a developmental alternative to the categorical ones just mentioned. By acquiring the predicates that make up the theory, children acquire the cognitive machinery that makes intentional state ascriptions literally true of them. Put simply, the behaviorists are correct about young children while the intentionalists are correct about linguistically sophisticated older ones.

Unanswered questions

Despite the breadth and richness of research reported in this volume, key questions remain unresolved and to some extent unasked. We indicate two of these. First, we have as yet no consensus on the question of whether children are born with a theory of mind or slowly construct one in the course of development. Fodor (1987) makes the following suggestion:

Here is what I would have done if I had been faced with this problem in designing *Homo sapiens*. I would have made a knowledge of commonsense *Homo sapiens* psychology *innate*; that way nobody would have to spend time learning it. And I would have made this innately apprehended commonsense psychology (at least approximately) *true* ... The empirical evidence that God did it the way I would have isn't, in fact, unimpressive. (p. 132)

Few contributors to the present volume make such an unadorned plea for nativism. Johnson (Chapter 3) comes close, however. He argues not only that children apprehend objects and events, but that they also have direct awareness of various modes of apprehension such as seeing, imagining, and wanting. Given his emphasis on direct access to such phenomenal modes, Johnson effectively denies that young children need to engage in anything like theory construction. Wellman (Chapter 4) insists that children construct a theory of action couched in mentalistic terms but argues that key features of that theory are in place from a very early age. Thus, he shares with Johnson an emphasis on the essential continuity between the theory espoused by the 2- or 3-year-old child and the theory espoused by the adult. Several contributors to the volume are impressed by the fact that children exhibit a fairly orderly series of new insights into the life of the mind, especially between 2 and 5 years. Indeed, the evidence for those changes occupies many of the chapters. Some contributors suggest that such developments depend, at least in part, on maturational changes. They argue that children acquire a general capacity for decoupling and recursion. Specifically, children become capable of taking a proposition, decoupling it from its customary reality-oriented implications, and treating it instead as the embedded proposition within an intentional assertion. Other contributors argue that such developments depend, in part, on cultural indoctrination, that children learn a theory of mind by mastering the set of linguistic predicates for interpreting and predicting the talk and action of themselves and others. Taking an even longer view is Chandler (Chapter 20), who underlines several important discontinuities between the theoretical stance of the preschool child and that of the adult. Given his emphasis on discontinuity, it is not surprising that Chandler opts for a classical constructivist position, in which theory and experience clash and intertwine again and again.

A second and related question is whether or not children adopt a universal theory of mind, irrespective of the culture they grow up in. Contemporary studies by such anthropologists as Heelas (1981), Hardman (1981), Rosaldo (1982), Duranti (1985), and Feld and Schieffelin (in press) certainly suggest that there are important differences among societies in the way adults conceive the operations of the mind. We have as yet, however, little understanding of how that variation might influence the child. Cultural variation might make its mark in at least three distinct ways. First, the data confronting the child might vary from culture to culture; for example, depending on the emotional display rules that operate in the society, children might be confronted by adults who routinely mask any display of intense emotion. Conceivably, such experiences might retard or accelerate the child's understanding of the distinction between real and apparent emotion (Harris & Gross, Chapter 15). Second, certain psychological distinctions may be routinely marked in the language, even at the syntactic level. For example, in Turkish, speakers must choose between two past-tense morphemes when they encode past events, to indicate whether they know about the event directly through personal observation, or indirectly through inference or report by another person (Aksu-Koç & Slobin, 1986). Such syntactic marking might facilitate the child's understanding of the link between perception and belief as discussed by Wimmer, Hogrefe, and Sodian (Chapter 9). Alternatively, the child's production of such linguistic marking might emerge only after understanding of the link. Third, the explicit conceptualization of mental phenomena varies from culture to culture. Several societies, for example, take dreams to involve wanderings of the spirit to another realm, different but no less real than waking reality. If the distinction between subjective and objective phenomena is marked in a different way in such cultures, children growing up in them might reach different conclusions about them.

Our hunch is that although in the early years cultural differences may have some impact on the rate of development and on the degree of conceptual elaboration, they are unlikely to alter the fundamental character of meta-representational states. Thus, we anticipate that, irrespective of linguistic and cultural variation, children will come to understand the distinction between seeming and being, the predictive power of ascribing false belief, and the disguisability of intentional and emotional states in much the same way at much the same age. The limited amount of cross-cultural data currently available supports this conclusion (Harris, in press). Thus, despite the apparent diversity of characterizations of mind found in anthropological reports, we expect developmental research eventually to reveal a universal core to the theory of mind. Still, we do not yet understand just what is universal nor how that universal core is modulated by the different explicit conceptualizations that have been described by anthropologists and cultural historians. This is an important issue for further research.

REFERENCES

Aksu-Koc, A. A., & Slobin, D. I. (1986). The acquisition of Turkish. In D. I. Slobin (Ed.), *The cross-linguistic study of language acquisition*. Hillsdale, NJ: Erlbaum.

Churchland, P. M. (1984). *Matter and consciousness*. Cambridge, MA: Bradford Books/MIT Press.

Dennett, D. C. (1978a). Beliefs about beliefs. *The Behavioral and Brain Sciences, 1,* 568–570.

Dennett, D. C. (1978b). *Brainstorms: Philosophical essays on mind and psychology*. Montgomery, VT: Bradford Books.

Duranti, A. (1985). Famous theories and local theories: The Samoans and Wittgenstein. *The Quarterly Newsletter of the Laboratory of Comparative Human Cognition, 7,* 46–51.

Feld, S., & Schieffelin, B. (in press). Hard words: A functional basis for Kaluli discourse. In D. Tannen (Ed.), *Analyzing discourse: Talk and text*. Washington, DC: Georgetown University Press.

Fodor, J. A. (1981). *Representations*. Cambridge, MA: Bradford Books/MIT Press.

Fodor, J. A. (1987). *Psychosemantics: The problem of meaning in the philosophy of mind*. Cambridge, MA: Bradford Books/MIT Press.

Hardman, C. E. (1981). The psychology of conformity and self-expression among the Lohorung Rai of East Nepal. In P. Heelas & A. Lock (Eds.), *Indigenous psychologies: The anthropology of the self*. New York: Academic Press.

Harris, P. L. (in press). The child's theory of mind and its cultural context. In G. Butterworth & P. E. Bryant (Eds.), *The causes of development*.

Heelas, P. (1981). The model applied: Anthropology and indigenous psychologies. In P. Heelas & A. Lock (Eds.), *Indigenous psychologies: The anthropology of the self*. New York: Academic Press.

Nisbett, R. E., & Wilson, T. D. (1977). Telling more than we can know: Verbal reports on mental processes. *Psychological Review, 84,* 231–259.

Piaget, J. (1954). *The construction of reality in the child.* New York: Basic. (Originally published in French, 1937).

Premack, D., & Woodruff, G. (1978). Does the chimpanzee have a theory of mind? *The Behavioral and Brain Sciences, 1,* 515–526.

Pylyshyn, Z. W. (1984). *Computation and cognition: Toward a foundation for cognitive science.* Cambridge, MA: Bradford Books/MIT Press.

Quine, W. (1960). *Word and object.* Cambridge, MA: MIT Press.

Rosaldo, M. (1982). The things we do with words: Ilongot speech acts and speech act theory in philosophy. *Language in Society, 11,* 203–237.

Searle, J. R. (1983). *Intentionality: An essay in the philosophy of mind.* Cambridge University Press.

Sellars, W. (1963). Empiricism and the philosophy of mind. In *Science, perception and reality.* London: Routledge & Kegan Paul.

Stich, S. P. (1983). *From folk psychology to cognitive science.* Cambridge, MA: Bradford Books/MIT Press.

Wimmer, H., & Perner, J. (1983). Beliefs about beliefs: Representation and constraining function of wrong beliefs in young children's understanding of deception. *Cognition, 13,* 103–128.

PART I

Developmental origins of children's knowledge about the mind

2

Some implications of pretense for mechanisms underlying the child's theory of mind

ALAN M. LESLIE

Human beings possess several cognitive capacities that set them apart from other species. One of the most important is the power of the human mind to conceive of its own states and of the mental states of others. Recently, it has become clear that this power is established in the first few years of life. For example, 4-year-old children can understand how someone comes to have a mistaken *belief* about something. They can work out what that belief will be and what effect it will have on that person's behavior (Wimmer & Perner, 1983; Baron-Cohen, Leslie, & Frith, 1985). This remarkable fact needs a lot of explaining.

Figure 2.1 illustrates a simple experimental test of this ability. The child is shown a scenario involving two dolls, Sally and Anne. The first doll, Sally, hides her marble in a box, then goes away for a walk. While she is away, Anne transfers Sally's marble to a basket and hides it there. Sally then returns wanting her marble. The child is asked some control questions to make sure he or she has followed the events. Then the child is asked, "Where will Sally look for her marble?" If the child is able to understand that Sally will believe the marble is still in the box, then he or she should point to the box and not to where the marble *really* is.

Normal 3-year-olds mostly fail on such tasks (Perner, Leekam, & Wimmer, 1987). So, too, do most autistic children, even if they have mental ages of 7 years or more (Baron-Cohen, Leslie, & Frith, 1985). What autistic children and 3-year-olds do is predict the behavior of Sally in terms of the *actual* situation – where the marble *really* is and not where Sally should *think* it is – as if the marble itself will exert a causal influence on Sally's behavior.

The 4-year old has developed a theory of mind. She is able to infer unobservable mental states in herself and in others, and to use such attributions to explain and predict behavior. There are many other kinds of internal state – for example, being in pain, feeling angry, or being thirsty – which the child comes to understand but which we shall not discuss here. The mental states we are primarily interested in are distinguished by having a characteristic form. First and foremost, they

Figure 2.1. A false belief scenario (from Baron-Cohen, Leslie, & Frith, 1985).

have a *content* expressing what the state is *about*. Second, they report an *attitude* to the content – whether the content is believed, expected, hoped, feared, desired, and so on. And finally, there is the person who has the attitude to the content. So, for example, *Sally believes* (attitude) *that the marble is in the box* (content).

Notice that it doesn't matter from the point of view of explanation whether the marble really is in the box or not: It is Sally's *belief* that will *cause* her behavior. And it is this simple but subtle point that is crucial for the utility of "theory of mind" to explain and predict behavior.

It is perhaps astonishing that 4-year-olds, without schooling or special training, come to grasp such a difficult and unobvious idea as a contentful mental state. Whatever it is that normal 3-year-olds possess and autistic children lack, it puts the one on the threshold of a monumental discovery, while the other has to suffer a deep and long-lasting impairment of social competence.

My proposals for understanding these phenomena come down to two points: First, that the development of a theory of mind depends on *specific* innate mechanisms, and, second, that these mechanisms are at work very early in life generating *pretend* play.

A word is probably in order to the theoretically minded about how I shall discuss this topic. My approach to understanding these processing mechanisms makes certain assumptions about the nature of human cognition. These assumptions center on the hypothesis that human cognition involves *symbolic computations* in the sense discussed, for example, by Newell (1980) and particularly by Fodor (1976). The ideas discussed here – and in Leslie (1987) – could in part be seen as investigating such symbolist assumptions. What sort of internal symbol manipulating machinery is responsible for the development of the human capacity to form a theory of mind? What systematic properties of its internal representations are involved? How is this machinery related to the conceptual systems the child eventually builds? This notion of internal representation has to do with fundamental properties of a certain general class of computational system that underlies certain human cognitive powers (Fodor, 1987). Thus, I approach the cognitive capacities of infants and young children with the intention of exploring the assumption that they embody a formal symbolic system, which is used in perception and thought and which is specialized for describing the world (Leslie, 1982, 1986, 1987, in press; Leslie & Keeble, 1987): in short, that there is a language of thought.

Pretense and false belief

One possible way of explaining 4-year-olds' success on the false belief task is in terms of a fundamental *logical* ability, which they possess but which 3-year-olds lack. Wimmer and Perner (1983) suggest that the critical ability to be acquired is the capacity to appreciate simultaneously two alternative and contradictory models of reality. A number of others have advanced similar views (see, for example, Flavell, Chapter 13; Gopnik & Astington, 1988).

There is another task that requires the child to construct contradictory models of reality. This is where an object appears to be one thing but is really another. For example, children are shown a sponge that has been designed to look like a rock. The children are allowed to succumb to its rocklike appearance and then to discover that it is really a sponge. They are then tested to see if they can appreciate the simultaneous contrast between what the object *looks like* and what the object *really* is. Flavell, Flavell, and Green (1983) have tested children on this sort of problem. Again it appears that most 4-year-olds succeed whereas most 3-year-olds fail.

Something important, then, seems to develop between 3 and 4 years of age, something that has to do with the child's ability to infer another person's mental state or to work out the different ideas people may have about a situation. But is the ability to conceive of "alternative realities"

really absent in the 3-year-old? Is it this fundamental logical ability that
has to develop, or must we look elsewhere for an explanation?

Has Mother gone bananas?

Consider what is involved when a 2-year-old engages in pretend play. The
child is pretending that a banana is a telephone. The child sees an object
on a table and recognizes it as a banana. She gets the idea of a telephone –
perhaps because the banana shape reminds her of a receiver or perhaps in
some other way. She picks up the banana and holds it to the side of her
face. She begins to simulate talking.

The child can see what the banana really is and yet pretends that it
is a telephone. At one and the same time, the child is representing the
situation perceptually as one that contains a banana and pretendwise
as one in which the banana is a telephone. Isn't this child representing
alternative and contradictory models of the same situation?

Consider what happens a few moments later. The child's mother joins
in by pretending to undress and bath teddy. Mother meticulously removes
teddy's imaginary clothes, then places teddy in an imaginary bath and
rubs him all over with "soap." What is the child to make of this? What
Mother *actually and literally* does is to wiggle her fingers in the vicinity of
teddy, then lay teddy on the floor, making slurping noises and rubbing
him with a toy brick. This is what the child *actually* sees and hears. If
the child is not to be completely bamboozled by this display, she must
infer from what she sees and hears Mother doing to what Mother is
pretending.

The price of not being able to infer pretense in another person could be
very high for a young child. Consider our 2-year-old watching Mother
using a real telephone. Of course, the child does not really understand
what telephones are for, nor how they work. But still, storing away
information about what Mother does with these objects could provide
important and useful clues in the future for solving this particular problem
about telephones and the social activities of adults.

But now our 2-year-old is watching Mother pretending that a banana is
a telephone. What happens if the child treats this information in the same
serious way as before? Clearly, the child would end up with some very
strange ideas. An environment in which people pretend would threaten
the developing encyclopedic knowledge of a child who could not
understand pretense. The game continues. Mother says, "Here, take the
telephone," and hands the child the banana. Now language learning is
put in jeopardy as well.

Fortunately, pretending in the vicinity of 2-year-olds does not lead to
disaster. Instead, they readily and with obvious enjoyment enter into

shared pretense (Dunn & Dale, 1984). Very young children, then, do appear to understand the alternative "reality" of pretense, and are able simultaneously to relate it to the literal reality of what they see before them. So why is false belief not handled correctly for another two years?

Calculating alternative models

Appreciating alternative realities does not seem to be the critical change that allows 4-year-olds their new success in false belief tasks. But perhaps there is a change in the child's ability to *handle* contradictory models – to work out *precisely* what the alternative model should be. Let us consider this more closely.

In pretense, the alternative mental model is just stipulated or invented. It is just made up. But in the case of false belief, there is a right and a wrong answer. It has to be worked out. Even where the child has to work out what someone else is pretending, the pretense can simply be "read off" from what the other person is literally doing, or at least it is strongly suggested by it. When a very young child is involved, one takes pains to communicate clearly what the pretense is: by exaggerating one's actions, by repetitions and by *telling* the child. The difficulty of the inferences the child must make is thus kept to a minimum.

But things are quite different in the false belief situation. Here Sally's belief has to be worked out on the basis of what Sally did and did not see of the situation. The child must correctly identify, out of all the things that Sally did and did not see, just the right and relevant things. Then the child must work out what Sally will *do* on the basis of that belief. None of this is handed to the child on a plate. It needs to be calculated.

Clearly, there is extra difficulty in calculating the alternative model in false belief compared with pretense. Still, one may wonder if this is sufficient explanation for the long 2-year lag between solving these two types of problem. To be sure, the extra difficulty must be a factor to some extent, but does it really demand a doubling of mental age? This seems doubtful to me. For example, one might ask – in connection with Flavell's appearance–reality task – why the child, having worked out the reality, cannot just read off the appearance?

Or, to go back to the 2-year-old pretending: When a 2-year-old works out that *Mother is pretending that the banana is a telephone*, she is, in effect, attributing a mental state to mother. *Mother* is the agent who has the attitude of *pretending* to the content *that the banana is a telephone*. In other words, it has the characteristic form of the mental state attributions we are interested in. A 2½-year-old watches her father, who pretends to fill a cup with (pretend) water and who then upturns the cup over the head of a doll. When the child reaches for a cloth and pretends to dry the

doll, she shows us that she has worked out the consequences of an attributed pretense. In other words, she has "handled" and made precise
calculations within an alternative model of reality.

One thing at least ought to be clear by now: To make progress with
these questions we need something in the way of an explicit analysis of the
representations and mechanisms underlying early pretense. The analysis
I present here and in Leslie (1987) shows that being able to pretend and to
understand pretense in others requires mastery of exactly the same
"logical" structures as understanding mental states. One could say that
early pretend play is actually a primitive manifestation of the child's
theory of mind. More precisely, pretense emerges with a mechanism that
provides a specialized and powerful capacity to represent and manipulate
cognitive relationships to information. The significance of this mechanism
is that it constitutes a major part of the specific innate basis for the development of theory of mind. But it will also be important to understand
the limitations of this mechanism. For it is such limitations that bring into
a clearer light what else is required for the child to build this innate base
into a conceptual theory of mental phenomena.

Pretense from a mechanistic point of view

From a mechanistic point of view, pretense comes in three fundamental forms. First, there is *object substitution*, where the pretense is about
identities or types. For example, one might pretend that Mummy is daddy
or that one object (a banana) is another type of object (a telephone).
Second, there is *pretend attribution of properties*, where an object, event, or
situation is pretended to have properties it doesn't. For example, one
might pretend that the weather is fine today or that doll's face is dirty.
And third, there is *imaginary object* pretense, where one pretends that an
object exists where there is none. For example, I might pretend that there
is whiskey in this bottle or that this empty cup contains water.

These fundamental forms of pretense – object substitution, pretend
properties, and imaginary objects – seem to emerge together in the child
usually between about 18 and 24 months. It is generally assumed that
this development is the result of the infant's acquiring for the first time a
capacity for the mental representation of objects and events (Piaget, 1962;
Fischer, 1980; McCune-Nicolich, 1981). Although I very much doubt
whether representational capacity emerges *for the first time* in the second
year (see, e.g., Baillargeon, 1986; Leslie, 1987, in press; Leslie & Keeble,
1987), that is not really the point here. What is to the point is that there
are obvious evolutionary reasons why perception and thought require a
system that represents the world in a serious and literal way. I shall call
this basic kind of representation "primary representation" (Leslie, 1987).

The important question for us now is this: How can the same representational system be used both for representing the world in a serious, literal way *and* for representing the distorted world of pretense?

Figure 2.2 helps bring out part of the nature of this problem. How can an internal representation of telephones refer to a *banana*? Why should we even say that that representation is a representation of telephones if it can also represent bananas? How does the child's internal symbol system know anymore what the representation of telephones represents? Next time that representation is used (or abused), what will it mean? Telephones? Bananas? Boomerangs? Or what? Object substitution pretense is often said to be the result of a process of *internal definition*, such that, for example, **telephone = banana** (Piaget, 1962; Huttenlocher & Higgins, 1978; McCune-Nicolich, 1981). But we cannot take this suggestion at face value, even if only a momentary redefinition is envisaged. The concepts of *telephones* and *bananas* do not become synonymous for the child, even momentarily, as a result of pretense. The child does not pretend that this banana and telephones are indistinguishable; nor does she mistake this banana for a telephone. On the contrary, the child *pretends* that this banana is a telephone – something fundamentally different. The pretense relates to the actual situation in highly specific ways. But previous accounts leave us very much in the dark about what exactly this relation is.

The example in Figure 2.2 involves the reference of primary representations. But pretense distorts *truth* relations as well. How can an internal representation, **doll's face is dirty**, be used to represent a situation in which doll's face is seen to be clean? Why does the representational predicate, **is dirty**, not change its meaning? Somehow the normal truth implications have been suspended. But what sort of representational system would do a thing like that?

Finally, existence implications are also abused in pretense. How can a representation, **the empty cup contains water**, be applied to a cup the child knows is empty? Indeed, how can the child even begin to entertain a representation with such a blatant internal contradiction? What sort of mechanism is capable of *this* kind of thought? Does it mean, for example, that there is a multiplicity of codes and representational systems complete with attendant translation procedures?

Pretense and mental state reports: A deep isomorphism

Let us take stock for a minute. Pretense seems to distort the normal *reference, truth, and existence* relations of primary representations. The first thing we want to understand is why there are these three fundamental forms of pretense and why they emerge together in development. Then

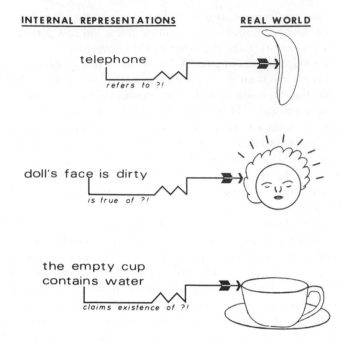

Figure 2.2. Some problems of representation in pretense: How do we account for the peculiar semantics of the internal representations underlying pretense?

perhaps these other questions will be put in perspective. I think that a vital clue lies in the highly similar semantic properties of certain kinds of expressions found in language. Interestingly enough, these expressions are principally *reports of mental states*.

Suppose John believes that *Ronald Reagan is a movie star*. Does it follow from this that John must also believe that *the President of the United States is a movie star?* Obviously not. But normally – if the propositions in italics were being considered on their own – one could simply say that because "Ronald Reagan" and "President of the United States" refer to the same person, then what's true of one must be true of the other. But when these propositions appear in a belief context, we cannot draw this inference. (John may not be aware of the equation). Put in a belief context, the terms have their normal reference suspended. We can no longer look through the terms to see what they refer to in deciding these matters of implication. Quine (1961) coined the term "referential opacity" for this.

Something similar happens to the truth implications of expressions in a mental state context. Compare: "John picked up the cat, *which was ill*" and "John believed that *the cat was ill*." The first sentence can be true only

Table 2.1. *An isomorphism*

Semantic properties of propositions expressing the content of mental states	The fundamental forms of pretense
1. referential opacity	1. object substitution
2. nonentailment of truth–falsehood	2. attribution of pretend properties
3. nonentailment of existence	3. imaginary object pretense

if the embedded italicized expression is also true, but the second sentence can be true (or false) regardless. Normal truth and falsehood implications are suspended by mental state contexts.

Finally, consider "The King of France is bald." Even taking this proposition as false, it still implies that there exists a king of France (who is not bald!). But "John believes that *the king of France is bald*" makes no such existence implication.

There is, then, a striking isomorphism between the semantics of mental state reports and the three fundamental forms of pretense (see Table 2.1). For each of the above semantic properties there is a corresponding form of pretense. First, corresponding to "referential opacity," there is the peculiar referential behavior of internal representations in object substitution pretense. Second, corresponding to the suspension of truth–falsehood implications, there is the attribution of pretend properties. And third, corresponding to the failure of existence implications, there is imaginary object pretense.

I don't think this isomorphism could be coincidental. Instead, I think it reveals that underlying these two seemingly unconnected cognitive phenomena – pretend play and reports of mental states – *there is a common form of internal representation*. This is the nub of what I have to say about pretense.

Modeling meta-representations

The next step is to think about how an insight into the above isomorphism might be exploited theoretically. One option is to go for the weak position of saying that mental state expressions simply provide a model for the representations underlying pretense. Another option is to pursue the stronger explanatory idea that both reporting mental states and pretending are activities that depend cognitively upon the same specialized form of internal representation and that *therefore inherit its semantic properties*.

In Leslie (1987) I develop this second option. Lack of space here prevents me from laying out the arguments in detail, so I shall just summarize some of the main points.

I shall use the term *meta-representation* and define it as an internal representation that consists of the following three parts:

Agent–informational relation–"expression."

The **agent** part will typically represent persons. Any primary representation can replace **expression**. The quotation marks signify that the enclosed piece of code has its normal reference, truth and existence relations suspended while so enclosed. I shall call such expressions "decoupled," to suggest that they have been removed from their normal input–output relations. I make an analogy with quotation in language because reported speech also shows the semantic properties discussed in an earlier section: for example, *John said, "The king of France is bald,"* does not imply there really is a king of France, and so on. The logician Carnap (1947) used this fact to develop his "quotation theory" of mental state expressions. For more recent discussions of similar ideas in a cognitive context, see Fodor (1982) and Jackendoff (1983).

The final part that makes up a meta-representation (as I define it) is the **informational relation**. Because decoupled expressions no longer automatically relate to the system of primary representation, they need to be specifically related to primary representations. Informational relations can be looked at as computational functions that perform this job, relating together agents, decoupled expressions, and primary representations. One such informational relation is PRETEND, another might be THINK. PRETEND and THINK will differ in terms of the relationship they specify between agents, decoupled expressions, and primary representations.

We also need to say something about the mechanism that would implement meta-representations and, in particular, generate pretense in the young child. Figure 2.3 specifies the general relationship between a decoupling mechanism and systems of primary representation. This mechanism constructs representations like, for example, I PRETEND **"this empty cup contains water."** Thus, the representations underlying the child's pretense are equivalent to *internal reports* of the child's own mental state.

The decoupling mechanism introduces new semantic properties into the child's representational system. This solution avoids having multiple specialized representational codes for specific contexts like pretending. The same representational code can be employed in perceiving a situation and pretending about a situation, while the special semantics of pretense is produced by the operation of decoupling. As Leslie (1987) points out, this not only is parsimonious but also captures important generalizations concerning what pretend representations and primary representations

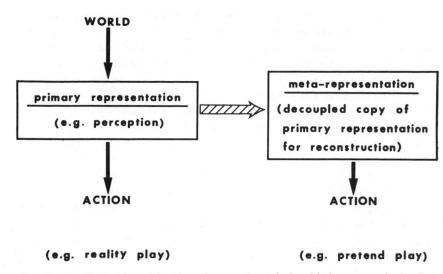

Figure 2.3. Illustration of the general processing relationship between a decoupling mechanism and the rest of the cognitive system. On this basis, the ability to pretend can be defined as the power to compute the function PRETEND **(Agent, "e_i," e_j)** where "e_i" is a decoupled representation and e_j a primary representation (of the currently perceived situation) (from Leslie, 1987).

have in common. When a child perceives a telephone and pretends something is a telephone, there is not some merely *arbitrary* relationship between the two representations of **telephone** involved. What they have in common is captured in the meta-representational theory by the two cases sharing subexpressions: We do not have to have ad hoc translation procedures.[1]

Although this outline of the meta-representational theory of pretense is necessarily brief, we can already begin to account for why there are three fundamental forms of pretense, why these forms emerge together in development, and why there is an isomorphism between pretense and reports of mental states. We say that these are all reflections of the semantic properties of meta-representations.

But this account will also explain what is perhaps the most striking fact about the development of pretense: When the child acquires the ability to pretend herself she simultaneously acquires the ability to understand pretense in others. So long as one thinks about pretense as the creation of subjective and egocentric symbols (Piaget, 1962), this must remain something of a mystery. But if pretense depends upon meta-representation in the sense I propose, then exactly the same mechanism will account for both the ability to pretend oneself and the ability to understand pretense in others. When the child, in the course of shared pretense, constructs representations like **Mother** PRETEND **"the banana is a telephone"** or **Father** PRETEND **"the empty cup contains water,"** she is exploiting the same representational resources as when she generates **I** PRETEND **"..."**

In summary, the meta-representational theory defines the ability to pretend (and understand pretense in others) as the power to compute a three-term function PRETEND **(a, "e_i", e_j),** where **a** ranges over agents, **"e_i"** is a decoupled expression and **e_j** a primary representation (e.g., of the current perceived situation to which **"e_i"** is related).

Before returning to consider the developmental relation between pretense and false belief, let us consider a possible objection to what I have proposed. It might be thought that the notion of decoupling is unnecessary and that really the expression embedded within the pretend representation is simply marked as "false." Thus, for example, **Father** PRETEND **(the empty cup contains water)$_{false}$** where the parentheses enclose the bit that is marked as false. The hope would be that this avoids the problems of representational abuse.

Actually, this proposal is no better than that pretend representations are marked as "true." Let's take reference first. The child infers that **Mother** PRETEND **(this banana is a telephone)$_{false}$.** Mother then offers the child the banana and says, "The telephone is ringing." The child represents this as **Mother** PRETEND **(the telephone is ringing)$_{false}$.** What telephone? *True or false,* the representation **telephone** does not have its normal reference here – instead it "refers" to the banana that mother is holding! Saying the telephone is *not* ringing makes no difference to this. The assumption of marking as false offers no account of the suspension of normal reference. Extra machinery would have to be brought in to accomplish this.

Now consider truth-falsehood implications in the "mark as false" model. Mother PRETEND **(this empty cup contains water)$_{false}$** implies that **Mother** PRETEND **(this empty cup does not contain water)$_{true}$.** But we do no want this implication! Normally such an implication would hold. What blocks it in pretense? The "mark as false" account offers no explanation for this. Again extra machinery would have to be imported for this purpose.

Next consider existence implications in the "mark as false" account. The child generates, **I** PRETEND **(this empty cup contains water)$_{false}$.** The child then upturns the cup, leading to **I** PRETEND **(the water has made the table wet)$_{false}$.** But what water? There should be no such existence implication from this pretend representation. What blocks this implication if the pretend representation is marked as false? Again extra machinery would have to be dragged in to block these implications.

So we would require extra machinery to suspend the normal reference of primary representations, to suspend their normal truth–falsehood implications and to suspend their normal existence implications. In short, we end up having to smuggle decoupling in again by the back door!

One final point on this. There is no reason in principle why one cannot pretend that *p*, when *p* is true. Vygotsky (1967) discusses just such an example. I have myself seen a child (2 years 6 months) do the following: (pretend to) fill an empty cup with (pretend) water, (pretend to) pour the water out, say "Allgone!" then proceed (to pretend) to fill it up once more. In pretending the cup is empty again, the cup really *is* empty. Thus to pretend that *p* when *p* is the case may not be so unusual as one might think at first blush. But a "mark as false" account rules this out as *logically impossible*! Clearly, marking the pretend representation as false does not even begin to capture the semantics of early pretense.

To sum up what I have been saying in this section: The ability to pretend emerges with a mechanism that can generate *meta-representations*. These are equivalent to internal reports of mental states in several important ways, including informational relations and the semantic properties of decoupling. Pretend play, then, does not, as is perhaps generally assumed, reflect a more advanced level of understanding objects and events as such. Instead, it is actually an early manifestation of the nascent ability to understand cognition. Whether shared with others or carried out in isolation, pretense inherently involves characterizing and manipulating attitudes to information.

Limitations on mechanisms underlying early pretense

The postulated decoupler mechanism has significant but nevertheless limited powers. I should like to highlight two different areas in which it is restricted. The first has to do with the circumstances under which the mechanism can be engaged, while the second has to do with limitations on the expressive power of the meta-representations it generates.

It appears that there are certain specialized "mannerisms" that are important and perhaps critical for engaging early shared pretense. These mannerisms include "knowing looks and smiles," a kind of melodic intonation, and highly exaggerated gestures (Piaget, 1962; Rosenblatt, 1977; Bretherton, O'Connell, Shore, & Bates, 1984). These have often been referred to in the literature but seldom described or studied in detail. Bateson (1955) discussed this kind of behavior as "metacommunication" – as the signaling of pretense to the other person. From the present point of view, such a specialized behavioral morphology functions as a meta-communication by engaging the child's pretend decoupling mechanism. There may be other aspects of social context that facilitate or hinder the engaging of this mechanism, such as familiarity with and friendliness of the co-pretender. These things seem to be important for the early sharing of pretense and therefore for children showing competence in an experimental setting. Interestingly, just telling children to pretend something does not seem to be an effective way of getting them to pretend (at least in the preschooler) and seems to produce serious nonpretend actions instead (Malvestuto-Filice, 1986).

The second limitation I want to consider is brought out nicely by Wellman's work with 3-year-olds (1985; Chapter 4). Wellman argues that the 3-year-old already shares with the adult the fundamentals of the "basic belief – desire – intention framework" for understanding human acts. For example, the 3-year-old already seems to understand something of the ontological difference between a concrete object and a thought (one can be touched, the other not, and so on). That these children perform well in Wellman's tasks implies that they can already handle the notions *the thought of* x and *thinking that* p. But understanding notions like this cannot be supported by the meta-representations we argued for earlier.

According to the present theory, the meta-representations generated by the pretend decoupler mechanism have the form: **agent–informational relation–"expression."** This is required to account for pretense and understanding pretense in others. If a variety of informational relations are available to the child (e.g., THINK, DREAM and so on), then these different mental states will also be representable. This provides a framework for investigating the properties of early concepts of different mental states (cf. Johnson, Chapter 3).

But meta-representations in this form will not allow the representation of *encyclopedic knowledge* about mental states and about "mentalistically entrenched" acts like pretense. There are important differences between the following representations: **Mother PRETEND "this banana is a telephone"; (the) PRETENSE (that) "this banana is a telephone" (... is fun)**; and **PRETENDING "this banana is a telephone" (... is fun)**. The latter two forms underwrite a notion of pretense as respectively an entity or an activity (which can then be "commented" on).

To account for 3-year-old thought it seems we need to postulate a family or package of *systematically related* meta-representational forms: **I PRETEND "e," (the) PRETENSE "e" and/or PRETENDING "e"; I THINK "e," (the) THOUGHT "e," and/or THINKING "e"**; and so on. (Although it is an analogy that should not be pushed too far, there are sets of sentence surface forms in English – such as *John refused the offer, John's refusal of the offer, John's refusing the offer* – whose underlying syntax reveals complex systematic relations [Chomsky, 1972].) So I suggest that the cognitive mechanisms that form the basis of the child's capacity to construct a theory of mind exploit the systematic formal relations that hold between sets of meta-representational expressions in the language of thought.

Although many details of the child's abilities are still unknown, the general idea behind this suggestion is supported at several points by present knowledge. It may be that the subtle conceptual relations and distinctions between the notions *I am thinking about a banana*, *the thought of a banana*, and *thinking about a banana* are grasped easily and spontaneously by the child because of the systematicity of his meta-representational machinery. This same representational package may also partially underwrite the comprehension, decoding, and acquisition of the relevant natural language expressions.

Understanding false belief: Linking meta-representations with causality

What my analysis of pretense shows is that even very young children can handle the basic "logic" required for understanding mental states. Despite this, children fail in false belief tasks until about 4 years of age. Why?

So far, I have suggested only that it is too complex a task for the child to work out what belief will result from a given exposure to a situation. A recent study by Perner et al. (1987) sheds some more light on this. Perner and his collaborators took a group of twenty-nine 3-year-olds and gave them the following false belief task. The children were shown a well-known confectionery box (Smarties – the U.S. equivalent being M&M's) and asked what they thought it contained. All the children answered "Smarties," as expected. Then they were shown that in fact the box contained only a pencil and no Smarties. After this the box was closed again with the pencil still inside it. The children were then asked three further questions. The first was to check that the children could remember correctly what was actually inside the box. In the second the child was asked, "What did you think was in here when you first saw it?" And finally, the child was asked to predict what his friend (who was waiting outside) would think was in the box if he saw it as it was now, that is, closed up. Most of the children (16) failed to predict their friend's false belief and most of those who succeeded were the older ones between 3½ and 4 years. These results with a new task support the general finding that false belief understanding develops around 4 years.

But the most intriguing aspect of these results concerned 9 of the 16 who failed. These children were able to tell the experimenter correctly that they had thought the box contained Smarties, and that they were wrong. Nevertheless, when asked what their friend would think was in the box, they answered, "A pencil"!

Despite the ability to *report* their false belief, these 3-year-olds could not understand where that false belief had come from (cf. Wimmer, Hogrefe, & Sodian, Chapter 9). Despite the fact that they themselves had just undergone the process of getting that false belief, the children were quite unable to understand and reconstruct that process, and thus unable, minutes later, to predict what would happen to their friend.

There is other evidence from an intensive study of a single child by Shatz, Wellman, & Silber (1983) and by Wellman (1985) that shows that the 3-year-old can verbalize with full syntactic elaboration his own previous false beliefs and that he recognizes them as false. Yet presumably such a child would still fail the prediction-from-false-belief task.

One might have been tempted to dismiss this evidence as relating only to a single solitary child but the findings of Perner et al. (1987) must dissuade us from this. Indeed, even a study by Gopnik & Astington (1988), which concluded that prediction from false belief in someone else is a slightly easier task than reporting one's own previous false belief, nevertheless seemed to find examples of children who, like those in the Perner et al. (1987) study, reported their own previous false belief but were unable to predict the same for someone else.

Of course, there are many reasons why a 3-year-old might *not* be able to report a previous false belief – for example, it may be immediately overwritten in memory or access to it blocked by the current belief. And *reconstructing* the belief from the primary representations of the events themselves would require the very abilities the child apparently lacks and that are required to pass the prediction of false belief task.

We need to pay close attention to the conditions under which 3-year-olds will meta-represent their own mental states. Little or nothing is known about this, but one thing is obvious: Meta-representing one's own mental states can be neither an automatic nor a routine process in memory for events. We simply have too many mental states too fast for this to be practical. A major advantage of having a theory of mind is that it allows a principled way of identifying circumstances under which one should calculate meta-representations of others (and one's own) mental states and of integrating them meaningfully as part of the episode. Without this, meta-representing beliefs, like pretense, must remain a specialized ability.

Until more is known about the special conditions under which young children will meta-represent their own beliefs about events, claims such as Gopnik and Astington's to have controlled these conditions experimentally will unfortunately remain moot.

The theoretical significance of the existence of a group of children who can access their own previous (false) belief about a situation but fail in a related prediction task must therefore be emphasized. Accessing his or her own false belief does not inevitably allow the child to predict that the same belief will arise for someone else under the same circumstances. It is even more revealing to consider that this does not prevent the child from confidently predicting a belief in someone else that, if it did arise, would be quite simply miraculous. This provides an important clue: Miraculous knowledge, like any other miracle, is something that arises *outside of the causal order.*

We can now appreciate that the child's problem is not with representing a false belief as such. Pretense shows that the child has long had the power to represent beliefs, and, indeed, the child soon acquires and (sometimes) uses the language forms needed to talk about false beliefs. It seems instead that what the child has yet to understand is how beliefs relate *causally* to situations in the world.

The reality of mental states

As adults, we often attribute "mental states" to things like machines, plants, and the weather. We do this because although we may not understand much about how these things really work, we still want to be able to explain and predict their behavior. Dennett (1971, 1981) calls this "taking the intentional stance." For example, I say that my central heating system *knows* when it's cold and *wants* to keep the house warm. Sometimes (when I have Scottish visitors) I trick the system by holding my hand over its thermostat and waiting till I hear the boiler go out. Then I say to myself (and to my visitors) that the central heating *thinks* the house is warm. But I do not imagine for a moment (and neither do my visitors) that my central heating system has thoughts or anything like thoughts. I am attributing "mental states" in a purely formal sense for strictly utilitarian purposes.

Could the 3-year-old child be attributing "mental states" to people in a similar way? Perhaps, under certain circumstances and for special purposes, very young children will use their meta-representational capacity to generate attributions and use these to handle situations like pretense or reporting changes in one's knowledge, but without regarding these mental states as *things that really exist.*

To put this another way: It may not occur to the 3-year-old that mental states are actually *caused* by things – by *concrete events* – and that they are, in turn, the *cause* of other concrete things – behavior.

Wellman (1985; Chapter 4) shows that 3-year-olds already have clear ideas about the way mental states exist. The children understand that although a banana may be eaten, the thought of a banana may not! When explaining these things, they use mentalistic language and locate states in the head: "It's in his head, it's only pretend." Indeed, it is striking how often they seem to qualify mental states with "just" – "just pretending" – or "only" – "only a dream." The force of this qualification seems to be to *contrast* mental states with concrete things.

This focus upon mental states' abstractness and lack of materiality may exact a price on 3-year-olds' conceptualization. It may make it more difficult for them to grasp the idea that although not concrete and material themselves, mental states can nevertheless be both the *effect and the cause* of things that *are* concrete and material. And that therefore, in just this way and for just this reason, mental states must be real. Before this insight, there will be no particular reason to look closely at situations and people's exposure to them with a view to working out what mental state will result. But following this insight, the child can be systematically curious about how concrete events are related to mental states. *Now* the inferential problem can rear its head. I submit that these are the main intellectual developments, taking place between 3 and 4 years, that lead to success on false belief tasks.

Forging links

My suggestion, then, is that children have to forge a link between their understanding of cause and effect in the physical world and their capacity to represent mental states. By 3 and 4 years, they have grasped many of the fundamentals of physical mechanics (Bullock, Gelman, & Baillargeon, 1982; Shultz, 1982) building upon foundations that are evident in infancy (Baillargeon, 1986; Leslie, 1986, in press; Leslie & Keeble, 1987). One aspect of the preschoolers' causal view is revealed in their understanding of when people are and are not in a position to see and hear things – what Flavell (1978) called Level 1 understanding. For example, there are striking similarities in the demands of a "line of sight" task (e.g., Hughes & Donaldson, 1979) and in working out, for example, whether a given candle could be blown out by a certain hair dryer (Shultz, 1982): Both require ascertaining if an unblocked "line of transmission" exists through space connecting source and target. Yaniv and Shatz (Chapter 5) have studied the child's understanding of perception in a number of other source–target causal problems.

Perhaps a conceptual bridge is needed to link children's causal view of the concrete world with their more abstract understanding of the mental world. The child's understanding of perception could provide such a bridge. How would this work in terms of the false belief and appearance–reality tasks we have discussed?

First, consider the false belief scenario of Figure 2.1. Here the child has to realize that Sally's exposure to the marble in the box will *cause* her to believe that the marble is in the box. Notice that the content of this belief will reflect its cause. Sally's view of the object's subsequent change of position, however, is blocked. Her nonexposure to this leaves her belief unchanged. It is this unchanged belief, then, that will determine what Sally does when she returns to the situation. In the "Smarties" scenario,

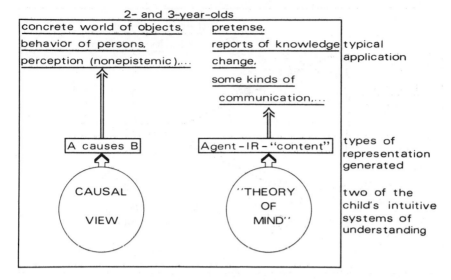

Figure 2.4. Two- and 3-year-olds: The independence of the causal view and "theory of mind."

my friend's exposure to the closed box will *cause* him to believe that it contains Smarties, while his nonexposure to what it really contains will leave that belief unchanged. This unchanged belief will then determine what he *says*.

Likewise, understanding appearance—reality requires the child to figure out what belief would be *caused* in someone who was exposed to only some of the visual properties of an object. The child can in a certain sense just "read off" the appearance of the object, and indeed did read it off when it was first presented. But what mental state, what belief, would such an appearance cause in someone who does not know what the object really is — that is, in someone who had not been exposed to the other perceptible properties as well? This is what provides the insuperable problem for the 3-year-old who does not place belief states in a causal framework (cf. Wimmer, Hogrefe, & Sodian, Chapter 9).

Figures 2.4 and 2.5 summarize the ideas being put forward concerning the relationship between the 2-year-old pretender and the 4-year-old false belief understander. Figure 2.4 suggests that very young children can take a causal view of the world. As far as the behavior of people is concerned, they include as possible causes of behavior only concrete objects and events (but also possibly "internal states" like hunger, which can be dealt with as essentially complex causal properties of animate objects). *Independently of this causal view*, these children can also formulate representations of mental states. This power develops in parallel with the

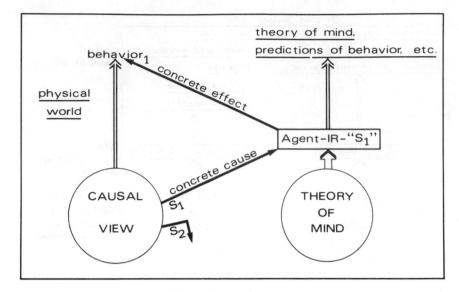

Figure 2.5. Four-year-olds: Their "theory of mind' gets linked to their causal view and becomes a theory of mind.

causal view but is used only in special circumstances, like pretense, reporting change of knowledge (and perhaps in formulating the goals of some complex communicative acts – see, e.g., Bretherton, McNew, & Beeghly-Smith, 1981).

Around 4 years of age, these two independent capacities are brought together; children enlarge their notion of "possible causes of behavior" to include mental states. From this point, mental states can be treated as both *causes* of behavior and *effects* of perceptual exposure to a situation. The contents of the mental states that are caused by perceptual exposure will reflect the situation that caused them. As a result of becoming part of the causal fabric of the world, mental states will become predictable, reliable, and *learnable about*. In short: For the child, mental states become real while remaining nonconcrete and immaterial.

Figure 2.5 illustrates how a 4-year-old deals with a false belief scenario. Sally is exposed to the situation (S_1) in which the marble is in the box. Because Sally is perceptually exposed to S_1 she will contract the belief *that S_1*: the child constructs the meta-representation, **Sally THINK "S_1."** Let us call the situation in which the marble is moved to the basket, S_2. Sally is not perceptually exposed to S_2, so she will not modify her *belief that S_1*, despite the fact that S_2 contradicts S_1. When Sally reappears it will be the belief that S_1 that will cause her behavior, B_1. And what is S_1 in the meta-representation, **Sally THINK "S₁"**? It is the child's own representation of that event as the child himself perceived it. This is a simple and reasonable, if ultimately limited, heuristic for the child to employ.

When development goes wrong: Childhood autism

Children who suffer from the syndrome of childhood autism show severe deficits in their social competence (Kanner, 1943; Wing & Gould, 1979; Rutter, 1983). Recently, we have obtained evidence suggesting that, even when they are not mentally retarded, autistic children do not develop a theory of mind normally. Baron-Cohen et al. (1985) tested a group of autistic children with borderline to average IQ (mean 82) on the false belief task outlined in Figure 2.1. Their performance was then compared with that of a group of Down's syndrome children who were younger and more severely retarded (mean IQ 64) and also with a group of clinically normal younger children (mean age 4 years 5 months). The Down's and the young normal children performed identically, with around 85% passing the test question. The autistic group, by contrast, fared very badly, with only 4 out of the 20 passing. The rest all failed by pointing to the object's actual location and not to where Sally should believe it to be. None of the autistic children failed the control questions, so they were quite capable of following the basic events of the scenario.

The same children were subsequently studied using a picture-sequencing task (Baron-Cohen, Leslie, & Frith, 1986). The picture sequences depicted three kinds of events: causal mechanical events involving both objects alone and people with objects; social behavioral events involving either one person acting alone or two persons interacting; and a third set that seemed to us to involve understanding the mental state of one of the protagonists. One of the mental state sequences, for example, depicts a boy placing a candy in a box, going outside, his mother eating the candy while he is outside, and the boy returning to look in the now empty box.

The autistic children performed very well on the first two types of event involving mechanical or social behavioral scenarios but scored only at chance level on the last event type involving mental states. This was a quite different pattern of performance from that shown by either the Down's or the normal children, as Figure 2.6 shows. The Down's children's performance, although fairly poor throughout, was above chance on all conditions and significantly better than the autistics' on the mental state condition.

Protocols were taken in response to the experimenter's request to the child to describe each scenario immediately following its sequencing. These were analyzed for linguistic expressions corresponding to the three

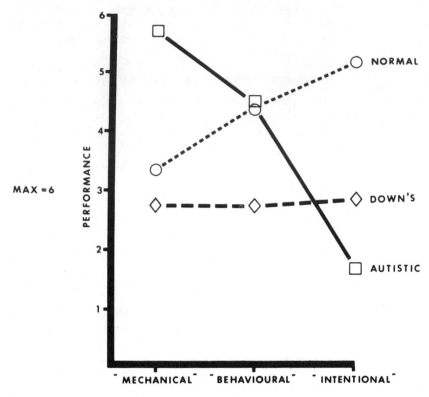

Figure 2.6. Autistic, Down's syndrome, and normal children's performance on a
picture-seqencing task (from Baron-Cohen, Leslie, & Frith, 1986).

event types: causal, descriptive, and mental state. The results here were
closely consistent with the sequencing data. The autistic children were
marked by a paucity of mental state language, as shown graphically in
Figure 2.7.

Autistic children, then, seem to be specifically impaired in their theory
of mind in a way accounted for neither by general mental retardation nor
by difficulties with understanding causality or social situations in general.
It is far too soon to say with any confidence what *is* wrong. We have a
number of studies under way that look at a variety of hypotheses concerning the nature of the underlying cognitive deficit. One thing, however, that suggests autistic children are not simply arrested at the normal
3-year-old level is the many reports of their highly abnormal development
in pretend play (Wing, Gould, Yeates, & Brierley, 1977; Rutter, 1978;
Sigman & Ungerer, 1981; Ungerer & Sigman, 1981; Wulff, 1985; Baron-
Cohen, 1987). Indeed, it may even be that autistics lack a capacity for

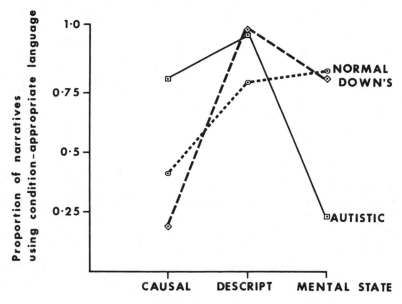

Figure 2.7. Protocol scores from Baron-Cohen, Leslie, & Frith's (1986) picture-sequencing task. Shown are the proportion of narratives for each clinical group using the most appropriate language for each condition (causal for mechanical condition, descriptive for behavioral condition and mental state for intentional condition). The complement of these proportions was descriptive for the mechanical and intentional conditions and mental state for the behavioral condition, with the sole exception in this last condition of an autistic child whose narrative was causal.

pretense altogether, although the proper experimental tools for answering this question definitively have yet to be developed (Leslie & Frith, 1987). This has now become a question with wide significance. If it turns out that autistics are fundamentally impaired in their capacity to pretend, it will suggest that they suffer a serious neurodevelopmental problem – one that tragically strikes at the innate basis of theory of mind (Leslie, 1987).

The meta-representational approach

As I explained earlier, the approach I am developing sets out to explore those aspects of cognitive development that result from the existence and functioning of mechanisms that manipulate systems of internal symbolic arrays. Many of the central ideas of such an approach can be summed up in the term *language of thought*. For anyone interested in exploring the idea of a language of thought, a basic question will be whether we need a notion rich enough for us to take seriously the *language* term or whether a more modest "*medium* of thought" would be more appropriate. I think that the sort of analysis developed here and in Leslie (1987) supports a rich interpretation of this idea, in terms both of showing an articulated and systematic formal structure and of having languagelike semantic relationships with the external world. In addition, this work suggests that a language of thought exists at latest by the end of infancy (but Leslie [in press] argues for much earlier) and that it plays a key role in cognitive development.

The theory I have outlined can help synthesize a number of current suggestions. It addresses the specific innate basis of theory of mind. This leads to an explanation not only of why Flavell's Level 1 – Level 2 distinction should be significant for descriptions of development, but also of why pretense is an exception to generalizations based on this distinction. For example, it becomes possible to explain why children's understanding of the pretend – real distinction develops much earlier than their understanding of the appearance – reality distinction (Flavell, Flavell, & Green, 1987; Flavell, Chapter 13). Understanding the former is an immediate consequence of the innate capacity to acquire a theory of mind, whereas the latter requires the formation of an appropriate causal theory.

Wellman's studies of 3-year-olds' conceptualization of mental states have a clear significance within the meta-representational framework. And finally, the co-opting by the child of meta-representations within his causal view of the world will also explain why, prior to this, the child has problems understanding *both* the sources of mental states, as Wimmer et al. (Chapter 9) argue, *and* their representational status, as Perner (Chapter 8) argues.

The meta-representational theory of pretense tries to explain how the normal child can develop, within 4 years of birth, something as exotic as a theory of mind. I have suggested at least four major developmental events that need to be considered. Meta-representations have a central role in each of these. First, there is the emergence of a meta-representational capacity itself, most dramatically signaled by the appearance of pretense in both its individual and its social manifestations. Second, there is the appearance of a package of related forms of meta-representation: **some- one PRETEND/THINK "e" – the PRETENSE/THOUGHT "e" – PRETENDING/ THINKING "e."** This package begins to go beyond specialized abilities and allows general knowledge about mental states to be represented. This system of meta-representation underwrites the next major event, which is the acquisition of the relevant natural language expressions. These three events prepare the child for a crucial and profound theoretical insight: The conceptualization of mental states within a causal framework.

This brings to bear a powerful inferential capacity that can incorporate meta-representations. With this the child tackles the intricacies of understanding the social world at a new conceptual level.

ACKNOWLEDGMENTS

Parts of this chapter are based on papers presented to the International Conference on Developing Theories of Mind, University of Toronto, May 1986, to the Oxford Workshop on Children's Early Concepts of Mind, University of Oxford, June 1986, and to the 8th Advanced Course on Symbolism and Knowledge, Fondation Archives Jean Piaget, University of Geneva, September 1986.

NOTE

1 Recent suggestions that there are no symbolic codes and therefore no symbolic processes in cognition (e.g., Rumelhart, Hinton, & McClelland, 1986) run into a similar dilemma in trying to account for these phenomena. First there is the need to keep serious and pretend related cognition apart (and also the need to keep apart my pretend from your pretend, my beliefs from your beliefs, my beliefs from my beliefs about my beliefs, and so on). Avoiding this horn of the dilemma will require functionally distinct networks. This immediately removes the possibility of accounting for why the "content" of the different networks are always systematically related to one another and never free to differ arbitrarily as distinct networks are. A meta-representational theory, by contrast, accounts in a principled way for both the differences and the similarities between these different classes of cognitive state in terms of systematic properties of the representations involved. For example, thinking **this cup is full of water** and thinking **I** PRETEND **"this cup is full of water"** are different states because of **I** **PRETEND** and decoupling but are related through sharing a sub-expression. Pylyshyn (1984, chap. 3) discusses a similar point.

REFERENCES

Baillargeon, R. (1986). Representing the existence and the location of hidden objects: Object permanence in 6- and 8-month-old infants. *Cognition, 23*, 21–41.

Baron-Cohen, S. (1987). Autism and symbolic play. *British Journal of Developmental Psychology, 5*, 139–148.

Baron-Cohen, S., Leslie, A. M., & Frith, U. (1985). Does the autistic child have a "theory of mind"? *Cognition, 21*, 37–46.

Baron-Cohen, S., Leslie, A. M., & Frith, U. (1986). Mechanical, behavioural and intentional understanding of picture stories in autistic children. *British Journal of Developmental Psychology, 4*, 113–125.

Bateson, G. (1955). A theory of play and fantasy. *A.P.A. Psychiatric Research Reports, 2*. Reprinted in G. Bateson, *Steps to an ecology of mind*. Aylesbury: Chandler, 1972.

Bretherton, I., McNew, S., & Beeghly-Smith, M. (1981). Early person knowledge as expressed in gestural and verbal communication: When do infants acquire a "theory of mind"? In M. E. Lamb & L. R. Sherrod (Eds.), *Infant social cognition*. Hillsdale, NJ: Erlbaum.

Bretherton, I., O'Connell, B., Shore, C., & Bates, E. (1984). The effect of contextual variation on symbolic play: Development from 20 to 28 months. In I. Bretherton (Ed.), *Symbolic play and the development of social understanding*. New York: Academic Press.

Bullock, M., Gelman, R., & Baillargeon, R. (1982). The development of causal reasoning. In W. Friedman (Ed.), *The developmental psychology of time* (pp. 209–254). New York: Academic Press.

Carnap, R. (1947). *Meaning and necessity*. Chicago: University of Chicago Press.

Chomsky, N. A. (1972). Remarks on nominalization. In N. A. Chomsky (Ed.), *Studies on semantics in generative grammar* (pp. 11–61). The Hague: Mouton.

Dennett, D. (1971). Intentional systems. *Journal of Philosophy, 68*, 87–106.

Dennett, D. (1981).Three kinds of intentional psychology. In R. Healey (Ed.), *Reduction, time and reality*. Cambridge University Press.

Dunn, J., & Dale, N. (1984). I a Daddy: 2-year-old's collaboration in joint pretend with sibling and with mother. In I. Bretherton (Ed.), *Symbolic play and the development of social understanding*. New York: Academic Press.

Fischer, K. W. (1980). A theory of cognitive development: The control and construction of hierarchies of skills. *Psychological Review, 87*, 477–531.

Flavell, J. H. (1978). The development of knowledge about visual perception. In C. B. Keasey (Ed.), *Nebraska symposium on motivation* Vol. 25. Lincoln: University of Nebraska Press.

Flavell, J. H., Flavell, E. R, & Green, F. L. (1983). Development of the appearance–reality distinction. *Cognitive Psychology, 15*, 95–120.

Flavell, J. H., Flavell, E. R., & Green, F. L. (1987). Young children's knowledge about the apparent–real and pretend–real distinctions. *Developmental Psychology, 23*, 816–822.

Fodor, J. A. (1976). *The language of thought*. Brighton: Harvester Press.

Fodor, J. A. (1982). Propositional attitudes. In J. A. Fodor (Ed.), *Representations: Philosophical essays on the foundations of cognitive science*. Brighton: Harvester Press.

Fodor, J. A., (1987). *Psychosemantics: The problem of meaning in the philosophy of mind*. Cambridge, MA: MIT Press.

Gopnik, A., & Astington, J. W. (1988). Children's understanding of representational change and its relation to the understanding of false belief and the appearance–reality distinction. *Child Development, 59*, 26–37.

Hughes, M., & Donaldson, M. (1979). The use of hiding games for studying the coordination of viewpoints. *Educational Review, 31*, 133–140.

Huttenlocher, J., & Higgins, E. T. (1978). Issues in the study of symbolic development. In W. Collins (Ed.), *Minnesota symposia on child psychology* (Vol. 11). Hillsdale, NJ: Erlbaum.

Jackendoff, R. (1983). *Semantics and cognition*. Cambridge, MA: MIT Press.

Kanner, L. (1943). Autistic disturbances of affective contact. *Nervous Child, 2*, 217–250.

Leslie, A. M. (1982). Discursive representation in infancy. In B. de Gelder (Ed.), *Knowledge and representation* (pp. 80–93). London: Routledge & Kegan Paul.

Leslie, A. M. (1986). Getting development off the ground: Modularity and the infant's perception of causality. In P. van Geert (Ed.), *Theory building in development* (pp. 405–437). Dordrecht: North Holland.

Leslie, A. M. (1987). Pretense and representation: The origins of "theory of mind." *Psychological Review, 94,* 412–426.

Leslie, A. M. (in press). The necessity of illusion: Perception and thought in infancy. In L. Weiskrantz (Ed.), *Thought without language.* Oxford University Press.

Leslie, A. M., & Frith, U. (1987). Metarepresentation and autism: How not to lose one's marbles. *Cognition, 27,* 291–294.

Leslie, A. M., & Keeble, S. (1987). Do six-month-old infants perceive causality? *Cognition, 25,* 265–288.

McCune-Nicolich, L. (1981). Toward symbolic functioning: Structure of early use of early pretend games and potential parallels with language. *Child Development, 52,* 785–797.

Malvestuto-Filice, G. R. (1986). *The development of the understanding of the intentional predicates "pretend" and "imagine."* Unpublished doctoral dissertation, University of Toronto.

Newell, A. (1980). Physical symbol systems. *Cognitive Science, 4,* 135–183.

Perner, J., Leekam, S. R., & Wimmer, H. (1987). Three-year-olds' difficulty with false belief: The case for a conceptual deficit. *British Journal of Developmental Psychology, 5,* 125–137.

Piaget, J. (1962). *Play, dreams and imitation in childhood.* London: Routledge & Kegan Paul.

Pylyshyn, Z. (1984). *Computation and cognition: Toward a foundation for cognitive science.* Cambridge, MA: MIT Press.

Quine, W. V. (1961). *From a logical point of view.* Cambridge, MA: Harvard University Press.

Rosenblatt, D. (1977). Developmental trends in infant play. In B. Tizard & D. Harvey (Eds.), *Biology of play* (pp. 33–44). London: Heinemann Medical Books.

Rumelhart, D. E., Hinton, G. E., & McClelland, J. L. (1986). A general framework for parallel distributed processing. In D. E. Rumelhart & J. L. McClelland (Eds.), *Parallel distributed processing: Explorations in the microstructure of cognition* (pp. 45–76). Cambridge, MA: MIT Press.

Rutter, M. (1978). Language disorder and infantile autism. In M. Rutter & E. Schopler (Eds.), *Autism: A reappraisal of concepts and treatment.* New York: Plenum.

Rutter, M. (1983). Cognitive deficits in the pathogenesis of autism. *Journal of Child Psychology and Psychiatry, 24,* 513–531.

Shatz, M., Wellman, H., & Silber, S. (1983). The acquisition of mental verbs: A systematic investigation of the first reference to mental state. *Cognition, 14,* 301–321.

Shultz, T. (1982). Rules of causal attribution. *Monographs of the Society for Research in Child Development, 47,* No. 1.

Sigman, M., & Ungerer, J. (1981). Sensorimotor skill and language comprehension in autistic children. *Journal of Abnormal Child Psychology*, *9*, 149–165.

Ungerer, J. A., & Sigman, M. (1981). Symbolic play and language comprehension in autistic children. *Journal of the American Academy of Child Psychiatry*, *20*, 318–337.

Vygotsky, L. S. (1967). Play and its role in the mental development of the child. *Soviet Psychology*, *5*, 6–18.

Wellman, H. M. (1985). A child's theory of mind: The development of conceptions of cognition. In S. R. Yussen (Ed.), *The growth of reflection in children*. New York: Academic Press.

Wimmer, H., & Perner, J. (1983). Beliefs about beliefs: Representation and constraining function of wrong beliefs in young children's understanding of deception. *Cognition*, *13*, 103–128.

Wing, L., & Gould, J. (1979). Severe impairments of social interaction and associated abnormalities in children: Epidemiology and classification. *Journal of Autism and Developmental Disorders*, *9*, 11–29.

Wing, L., Gould, J., Yeates, S. R., & Brierley, L. M. (1977). Symbolic play in severely mentally retarded and in autistic children. *Journal of Child Psychology and Psychiatry*, *18*, 167–178.

Wulff, S. B. (1985). The symbolic and object play of children with autism: A review. *Journal of Autism and Developmental Disorders*, *15*, 139–148.

3

Theory of mind and the structure of conscious experience

CARL NILS JOHNSON

> Either consciousness is nothing or it arises from original and specific
> categories which by their nature ignore material facts. These categories do
> exist.   (Piaget, 1968, p. 64)

What does it mean to say that children have a "theory" of mind? At best,
this characterization highlights positive features of early cognition: Children's understanding of human action is coherent, causal, and categorical
(see Wellman, Chapter 4). This likening of child thought to abstract
theory stands in sharp contrast to traditional depictions of child thought
as the very antithesis of rational thinking, that is, as preconceptual,
acausal, and adualistic.

Characterizing children's knowledge as theorylike is part of a broader
trend emphasizing that concepts are embedded in causal explanatory
frameworks (Murphy & Medin, 1985; Keil, 1986). Beyond this general
qualification, however, attributing a "theory" to young children is empty
at best and misleading at worst. It is empty of any specification of cognitive mechanisms: Causal-explanatory frameworks could be the consequence of a variety of very different cognitive systems. It is misleading to
the extent that the metaphor of a "theory" is taken literally (see Premack
& Woodruff, 1978).

The present chapter is an antidote to the theory metaphor. The point is
that young children do not really have anything like a theory. This is not
to deny the richness and power of early cognition. Young children are
not irrational, nor are they behaviorists. But neither are they theorists.
The guiding heuristic is that the seemingly theoretical characteristics of
children's understanding of human action can be explained in terms of
concrete, non-theorylike mechanisms.[1]

The trouble with attributing theory to young children is that it collapses
a useful distinction between theoretical and intuitive knowledge. Children's early understanding of human action will here be characterized as
"intuitive." Consistent with diSessa's (1985) description, intuitive knowledge, whether of physics, epistemology, or psychology, is a rich, systematic,
and causal "though hardly deductive or theorylike collection of knowledge

47

elements" (p. 99). Intuitive knowledge is distinctively marked by *first-order* conceptions, consisting of *primitive* elements that are self-explanatory. Such knowledge is *minimally abstract*, being closely tied to concrete experience, hence *phenomenological* in nature. And it is *local*, the link between knowledge and the situation being "essentially at the level of recognition; little or no justification for the application to the context can be provided" (p. 100).

What is confusing in the present volume is that terminology tradition-ally used to distinguish second-order conceptions is used to distinguish first-order knowledge. First-order knowledge about mental states is de-scribed as being inherently meta-representational, reflective, and theoreti-cal (see Leslie, Chapter 2; Wellman, Chapter 4; and Forguson & Gopnik, Chapter 12). Perceptions, emotions, or thoughts occurring within the stream of *action* are currently described as *representations* (Mandler, 1983). Hence, the *representation* of human experience and action is deemed a *meta-representation*. Unfortunately, this use of "meta-representation," distin-guishing the reflective *content* of knowledge, is easily confused with notions of "meta-conception" marking truly recursive *structure* (see Chi, 1987). Meta-representations are nothing more than first-order concepts of phenomenal experience (desires, beliefs, feelings, and the like): They are not second-order reflections on first-order conceptions.

As Wellman (Chapter 4) notes, young children do not really have a theory of mind at all: Understanding is limited to practical knowledge about human action. Take, for example, the knowledge that thoughts are not perceptible things. Characterizations of this achievement as "impres-sively conceptual, internal, inferred and abstract", entailing a "theory of reality" (Wellman & Estes, 1987; Wellman, Chapter 4) belie the fact it is a classic example of "minimally abstract" intuitive knowledge. Young child-ren are becoming aware of what they can and cannot do with thoughts and things: The thought of an ice-cream cone cannot be licked, served as a treat, or saved in the refrigerator, but this thought can be had at whim, in infinite quantity, and it never melts onto your hand. These are phenom-enological truths, not theoretical ones. Knowing that a thought is not a thing does not require an appeal to a theory, it is intrinsic to first-order knowledge of what thoughts and things are.

Characterizing young children's understanding as intuitive helps pre-serve what is fundamentally correct about Piaget's theory.[2] Piaget (1929/1979) acknowledged that young children have an intuitive understanding of psychology.[3] Like Wellman (Chapter 4), he argued that by about the age of 3 years children become consciously aware of "two orders of reality," the world of perceived reality and the world of imperceptible intentions, desires, and images (Piaget, 1932/1973, p. 234).[4] This con-scious awareness was seen to provide the foundation for the "principle categories of childhood thought," one focused on the external perceptible world and the other having an "intentionalistic origin" arising from "the conscious realization of psychological operations relative to intentions, and not from a mere observation of the world given in perception" (p. 236).

Although Piaget (1932/1973) recognized that young children have an intuitive understanding of human behavior that is pervasively, categorically, and causally "intentional," he equally claimed that they lack any ability to apply this understanding discriminately: The young child "does not think of ascribing intentions to definite 'I's' – but of intentions that are impersonal" (p. 235). Young children are thus described as indiscriminate mentalists, failing to distinguish their own psychological intuitions from other persons (egocentrism) as well as other things (animism).

Evidence reported in the present volume demonstrates that young children are far more discriminate in ascribing intentional states than Piaget supposed. Yet it is equally clear that young children's understanding is limited to first-order concepts: Recursive second-order concepts rarely appear before the classic 5- to 7-year age range (see Perner, Chapter 14). Apparently, young children do not need higher-order concepts, or theory, to understand intentional states discriminately. But how is this possible? How is it that young children not only have psychological intuitions, but discriminately ascribe such intuitions to definite "I's"? There are three parts to the story. First, experience is originally, prereflectively, structured to differentiate self and world. Children do not have to develop the knowledge that mental states are ascribed to definite "I's", this is given in experience itself. Second, this primitive structure is accessible to consciousness. The power and limits of this conscious access are seen to define the nature and development of intuitive psychology. Finally, a mechanism is proposed that extends the power of consciousness beyond first-person experience, to the prediction of the behavior of different people in different situations. By *simulating* the status of people in the world, children are able to make generative predictions from their own simulated states in the absence of any abstract theory.

The structure of experience

Why does children's understanding of human behavior take the form it does? Why are children intuitive mentalists and not intuitive behaviorists? Why are these mental intuitions so discriminately applied to subjects and not objects? Surely these characteristics cannot be explained as the mere acquisition of a cultural convention, a folk psychology. Intuitive psychology is no more the product of mere convention than is intuitive physics. The mentalism of children, like that of chimpanzees (Premack & Woodruff, 1978), must have its roots in the structure of experience itself.

Intuitive psychology, like folk psychology (see Heelas, 1981), rests upon basic capacities of the human organism to monitor its subjective status
in the world. Mechanisms for differentiating subjective from objective
states must be built into the structure of experience and action itself.
Imagine, for example, an infant who is truly "adualistic" or "egocentric"
with no mechanisms for distinguishing its action on the world from the
world itself. Such an organism would be unable even to begin to adapt to
reality and to organize actions. "Adualism" in this sense can only reflect
a nonfunctioning or malfunctioning representational system; it tells us
nothing of the necessary structure of the system itself (see also, Gibson,
1979; Harris, 1983b; Samuels, 1986).

The structure of experience is inherently dualistic. As Pribram (1986)
recently put it: "In the world of appearances there is no question but that
human mental experiencing can be distinguished sharply from the contents of the experience"(p. 510). This duality is not a matter of distinguishing the self as object in the world, but the self as a subject, the "I" as actor
and experiencer. This original sense of self, the "I" within the stream of
behavior, has been described as primitive, both philosophically (McGinn,
1982, 1983) and psychologically in the existence of subjective intentions
and experiences in infancy (Lewis & Brooks-Gunn, 1979; Damon & Hart,
1982; Harter, 1983).[5]

What kinds of self–world relations are specified in this primitive sense
of self? Consider that the human organism is built with a combination of
action and perceptual systems that in concert direct behavior toward
causally affecting the world to fulfill its needs and goals, while being appropriately affected by the world, responding to and anticipating its relevant
properties. To this end, the organism must be capable of distinguishing
between its intentions and actual states of affairs, its own efforts to causally
effect the world and effects of the world on itself. Moreover, these distinctions must be made locally, within each processing modality. For example,
there must be mechanisms within the visual system that enable the organism to distinguish its own movements from the perception of movements
in the world.

These basic characteristics of subjective experience and action appear
as defining elements in Searle's (1983) analysis of intentionality (in the
philosophical sense of term). Intentional states are described as psychological modes with properties of "direction of fit" and/or a "direction of
causality." The direction of fit has to do with whether the organism is
oriented toward adapting (fitting) the world to the goals of the mind, or
adapting the mind to the properties of the world. The causal directions
similarly go either from mind to world or from world to mind. In these
terms, intentional actions are mind-caused acts directed toward fitting the

world to the intentions of the organism, whereas perceptual modes, such as seeing, are world-caused experiences directed toward fitting the mind to real properties of the world.

There is good reason to suppose that these directional distinctions, causality and fit, are built into the operational design of the nervous system. The "fit" dimension is comparable to Piaget's distinction between assimilation and accommodation: The world is assimilated to the mind (world-to-mind fit), while the mind accommodates to the world (mind-to-world fit). Although generically accepting this division, Piaget failed to specify how it is built into the structure of subjective experience. On the present account, perceptual systems must be inherently oriented toward *accommodating* to information about the world. Action systems (motives, desires, intentions) in turn must be distinctly designed to direct the organism toward meeting its needs (fitting the world to the mind). Support for this position comes from current views of behavior in infancy as originally propelled by intentions (not reflexes), and from findings showing that perceptual knowledge develops quite independently from action schemes (cf. Harris, 1983b).

The causal dimension is equally fundamental. In order for an organism to get around in the world, it must distinguish between what it is trying to do (causes arising within the self) and what happens (causes arising outside the self). This division must be built into the very structure of afferent versus efferent functions. Such causal distinctions are documented in infancy (see Clark, 1983, p. 794), and appear to be universally marked in semantic distinctions between agent-caused actions (agent-action) and stimulus-caused experiences (stimulus-experiencer) (Brown & Fish, 1983). Heelas (1981) also takes this causal dimension to be a universal organizing principle across folk psychologies.

What is offered here is not a new set of distinctions but a way of interpreting these distinctions as the structural basis of intuitive psychology. The two dimensions, fit and causality, can be incorporated as axes in a semantic space (see Figure 3.1).[6] We can think of the placement of a given psychological category with respect to these two axes as providing an answer to two questions: First, does the cause of a given psychological state appear to lie within the self or does it appear to lie within the world? Thus, intentional acts appear to be caused by the self, whereas perceptions and emotional experiences by contrast typically appear as caused by the world. Second, is a fit between mind and world achieved by accommodating the mind to the world or by adjusting the world to fit the mind? Beliefs are directed toward fitting the world. Desires are directed toward fitting the world to the needs and goals of the mind.

Note that within the categories of action and perception, both axes are

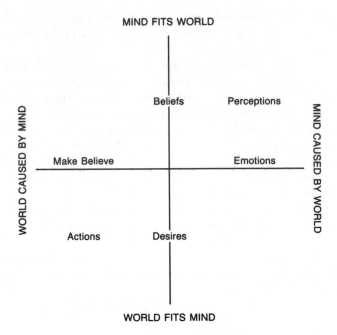

Figure 3.1. Dimensions of experience

relevant because the directions of fit and causality are conjoined: The perception of an object appears to be caused by the presence of the object and fits the properties of the object; an intentional act appears to be caused by the self and oriented toward fitting the goals of the self. Both axes are not always relevant, however, because they are separable. Intentional states exist outside the immediate context of perception and action. Beliefs, for example, like perceptions, are experienced as fitting the world, yet beliefs often appear to arise spontaneously (spawned by unconscious inferences or prejudices) with no direct causation in the world. Similarly, desires, like actions, are directed toward fitting the world to the mind, yet they can be triggered by unconscious causes lying either within or outside the self. In turn, make-believe is self-caused but is intentionally disconnected from any real fit in terms of purposive goals and objective reality (see Leslie, Chapter 2). Finally, emotions typically appear as a consequence of world-caused perception (objects and events "make us" afraid, happy, etc.), yet persist beyond perceptual contact and are directed toward fitting neither the mind to world nor world to mind.[7]

The structure of experience, thus described, provides a wealth of information for differentiating overt and covert intentional states, providing the basis for an intuitive psychology. In the next section, this structure will be interpreted as providing a basis for distinguishing between intuitive and nonintuitive concepts and hence between concepts that are readily acquired from those that pose greater difficulty. But first it is necessary to consider how this structure can be known; how properties inherent in action and experience become accessible to representation.

Conscious experience

Reflective consciousness is commonly recognized to be an adaptive design feature, marked by the capacity of an organism to access, recognize, and hence regulate its own processing states (cf. Johnson-Laird, 1983; Mackay, 1984; Mandler, 1984; Oatley, 1985; Kissen, 1986; Weiskrantz, 1986a,/ 1986b). Conscious representation in this sense is nothing more than a representation of a peculiar content. Just as the mind has access to information about the world, so too it has access to information about its own processing states.

Conscious access is a higher-order projection of information already available at lower levels of processing. At an unconscious level, action systems and perceptual systems must mutually inform one another of their ongoing status: Incoming information must be coordinated with outgoing intentions. At a conscious level, access enables the organism to recognize its own states and hence more flexibly direct behavior. In either case, access is adaptively limited to information that has a direct bearing on the *direction* of behavior. We have access to the mode and direction of processing, to *what* we see, think, desire, or will and *that* we think, desire, or will it, but not to the mechanisms that make these states possible. In other words, access is limited to episodic, intentional states and not available to procedural, nonintentional processes (cf. Kissin, 1986).

Although conscious access is strictly limited, its power should not be underestimated. Imagine an organism who intentionally perceives and acts on the world but lacks any conscious awareness of its perceptual states or behavioral acts. States like "seeing" and "looking" would be entirely subordinate to behavior directed toward acting on and accommodating to the world. Unable to assess consciously whether or not an object was seen, or a discrete behavior executed, the organism would be incapable of consciously directing its visual system or its movements. In other words, metacognitive experience and actions would be absent, forestalling the development of metacognitive knowledge (Flavell, 1987). Even more dramatically, there would be no capacity for conscious thought: no capacity to "internalize action," to think consciously about what objects look like or to plan how one might act.

Deficits in conscious awareness are evident not only in infancy (e.g., the inability of infants to direct visual searches consciously) but also in cases of neurological damage among adults. In the best-documented syndrome, "blind sight," neurological damage renders individuals incapable of conscious seeing in part of their visual field (Weiskrantz, 1986a, 1986b). Despite evidence that information is still processed in that part of the visual field, patients report no experience of seeing. Selective deficits of this type are not limited to vision. Cases have been reported of individuals who process tactile information yet do not experience touch, and of individuals who learn from experience but have no subsequent memory of that experience. Such evidence demonstrates both that access is a local design feature,[8] and that its destruction is no small handicap. As Weiskrantz (1986b) explains,

to be aware of a visual event is not only to be able to categorize it independent of retinotopic space, to deal with it in canonical form, but to be able to treat that event as an image, to compare it or contrast it with other images, in short to think visually, and to guide action relevant to such imagery. Similarly, to "remember" is to enable one to compare past with present, to reflect, to link separate past events, to order them, and to do so in relation to one's self as a coherent "thing." These capacities are precisely the ones that these patients lack. (p. 14)

Conscious access provides the basis for going beyond perceptual-motor action to the representation of action itself. Such a capacity is what Piaget (1932/1973) describes as "representation," and what is currently termed "meta-representation."[9] Whatever the terminology, the present task is to define how such representations are constrained by local data structures and the limits of conscious awareness, and how these constraints determine the developmental course of intuitive psychology.

The general constraints are classic: The data structures are presumed to be limited to information about the *mode* and *direction* of behavior. In turn, consciousness is focally limited to the sequential processing of directionally defined states.[10] These constraints define the first order conceptions or intuitions of the preschool period. During this period children are capable of differentiating a whole array of intentionally directed states, recognizing the directional effects of such states on behavior (see Figure 3.1). What is originally missing, however, is any recognition that the apparent direction of intentionality may in fact be governed by mental processes operating in an opposing direction. For example, young children have no awareness that "seeing" that appears as an accommodation to the world (mind-to-world fit), may in fact be due to assimilative processes (world-to-mind fit; see Figure 3.1). During the school years, children go beyond these first-order concepts to postulate the existence of underlying intentional processing. They recognize that perceptions and emotions are not just passively received by the mind but are actively mediated by mind-caused interpretation (Olson, Chapter 21); they conceive that intentional achievements that appear self-caused are codetermined by traits outside intentional self-control (cf. Dweck & Elliot, 1983). At this point, it can be said that children truly have a "theory of mind," a theory of mental processes as distinct from personal intentions. These processes, however, are still conceived in strictly intentionalist terms. Only in early adolescence do children begin to consider the role of nonintentional processes in behavior, and how a physical-causal system, the brain, is related to intentional, conscious experience. For the first time, the mind–body distinction becomes a problem with the full range of possible theoretical alternatives.[11]

The present account preserves the traditional claim that young children's cognition is limited to appearances; that understanding is initially limited to behavior, only later extending to mind. This characterization remains true once it is recognized that behavior "appears" not as mere overt movement but as intentionally directed overt and covert states. Although appearances provide a powerful understanding of discriminately animate behavior (see Gibson & Spelke, 1983), they provide no independent understanding of the processes of minds or nervous systems. To this extent, young children's understanding remains naive and magical. Action appears to be generated by mere spontaneous will; seeing appears as a passive consequence of orienting one's eyes; desires and beliefs can seem to arise mysteriously from nowhere. To avoid potentially magical extrapolations of these notions, children must develop a theory about how conscious intentional states are embedded in unconscious cognitive operations and neurophysiological processes.

Young children are also realists, not in the sense that they locate intentional states in the world, but in the sense that they fail to recognize that seemingly objective properties (fitting mind to world) can stem from a subjective source (world to mind). It is notable that of the three phenomena Piaget (1929/1979) originally studied thoughts, names, and dreams – only thoughts are intentional states (i.e., a name is not a psychological mode; dreams are not intentionally directed). And only in the case of thought was there no apparent confusion about the subjective source of the representation. The purported realism about thoughts was documented, not by ideas that thoughts come from the world, but by speculations that thinking is a form of speech. Whatever the questionable nature of these data (see Johnson & Wellman, 1982) they at least constitute an interpretation of thought as a potentially private (subvocal) intentional act. Dreams and names pose a different problem, however, because their subjective status is experientially ambiguous. Compare, for example, the experience of a dream with the experience of imagination. Whereas the latter state is consciously self-caused and disconnected from fit, dream experiences rarely appear to be under conscious control (seemingly arising outside the self) and often seem real within the dream, yet unreal outside it (i.e., not fitting the world). Similar ambiguity is apparent in the case of names. Unlike intentional states, which are attributes of subjects, names have a transpersonal identity associated with objects. Names are not just a matter of personal whim, they are something "out there" that must be accommodated to. On the other hand, names are evidently not perceptible properties of things (cf. Markman, 1976) and we can intentionally "call" something anything we please (i.e., disconnected from accommodating to the "real" name). As with dreams, young children have access to both seemingly objectlike and seemingly subjectlike properties of names. What children initially lack is a second-order account, or theory, about how these seemingly contradictory properties are in fact related, how seemingly external experiences can take place in the head, and how the real names of things can be merely what they are called.

Although children's intuitions about intentional states become increasingly differentiated during the preschool years, they remain nonetheless limited to first-order concepts. As Perner (Chapter 14) makes clear, second-order concepts remain the distinctive province of middle childhood. The latter concepts mark the beginning of not only interpsychic understanding, as Perner points out, but equally intrapsychic understanding. A qualitative change in children's understanding is marked by the realization that appearances that seem to be derived from outside the self are in part derived from the mind. During the school years, children come to recognize consciously that the same external-appearing object or event, name or message, under the same viewing conditions (i.e., the same viewer, with the same information), may be interpreted differently, resulting in different perceptions, beliefs, or emotions concerning that reality (cf. Chandler & Boyes, 1982; Harter, 1982; Harris, 1983a; Selman, Lavin & Brion-Meisels, 1982; Robinson & Whittaker, 1986). School-age children similarly come to recognize that seeming self-caused and self-motivated behavior may in fact be mediated by subpersonal abilities and traits that run counter to one's best efforts or desires (cf. Barenboim, 1981; Dweck & Elliot, 1983).

The constructed knowledge of middle childhood can be characterized as an intentionalist theory of underlying neuro–mental processes and traits. Children become aware of the existence of a level of mental–brain processing below the level of direct self-control and experience (see Johnson, 1982; Johnson & Wellman, 1982). Whereas young children deny that any such processing is needed simply to act or perceive, older children judge that the brain is necessary for these functions: The brain is needed to see and to walk because it "tells" you what you see and where to go. The brain is interpreted as a subpersonal homunculus, an internal intentional agent and experiencer with a mind of its own. Only later, during adolescence, do children become aware of the strictly neuro–physical functions of the brain, and hence more sharply distinguish the intentional processes of the mind from nonintentional processes of the brain (see Johnson, 1982). Now the real theoretical dilemma arises: How can phenomena that appear to be intentionally rooted in the self–mind be equally rooted in a physically causal brain?

Other minds

This chapter was originally proposed as an antidote to the suggestion that children have a theory of mind. What is perhaps most misleading about the theory metaphor is that it suggests children are approaching the problem of other minds from a third-person perspective, inferring the existence of abstract theoretical entities to explain the behavior of others. Although states such as desiring, thinking, and willing may seem like abstractions from the outside, they are the very substance of experience from the inside. The present chapter has emphasized this first-person alternative. The question remains, however, of how first-person consciousness can provide the foundation for knowledge about others. Given that children have access to their own intentional states, how is it that such states can be discriminately ascribed to other "I's" in the world?

It is, first of all, important to emphasize that there is nothing peculiarly subjective about children's knowledge of intentionality. Just as experience provides access to information about the structure of the physical world, so too it provides access to information about the structure of experience itself. That intuitions about experience are shared and generalizable is no more remarkable than the fact that intuitions about physics are shared and generalizable.

The second point is that conscious knowledge about the subjective "I" develops simultaneously with knowledge about how "I's" exist as perceptible objects, or objective selves in the world (see Lewis & Brooks-Gunn, 1979; Damon & Hart, 1982). In having experiences children can directly take note of the objective conditions under which such experiences occur. Children do not have to *infer* the existence of covert mental states from overtly behavioral criteria; they have direct access to invariant relationships between objective conditions and subjective experiences (cf. Kohler, 1930; Gibson, 1979). The organism is also undoubtedly set up to map its own experiences onto others as well as to take advantage of the joint sharing and labeling of experiences of others (Bretherton, McNew, & Beeghly-Smith, 1981).

In this light, conscious awareness of subjective states does not rise out of the blue but is the result of a developing capacity to locate the "I" as actor and experiencer within an objective self ("me") existing in space, time, and social context. The important point, however, is that children begin by representing intentional states of objective selves, not mental states of subjective minds. They are limited to representing "I's" as actors and experiencers in the context of the known objective world. To this extent, children have no representational access to intentional states other than their ability to imagine possible intentional states of persons in the world. In other words, children are not representing abstract states of mind but are representing concrete actors and experiencers in the world.

Just as intentional behavior is originally embedded in the world, so too first-order representations are embedded in representations of the world. Lacking any second-order concepts, children's representational access to intentional states is limited by their ability to imagine or simulate states of people in the world. As Gordon (1986) has recently argued, simulation offers an alternative to the view that commonsense psychology is a theory. Simulation avoids the need of a theory of mind by taking advantage of the structure of mind itself. It allows children to make efficient and adaptive use of their own conscious experience to understand the experience of others.[12]

It would be a mistake to underestimate the power of simulation. The play of children attests to a remarkable capacity for imagining different people in different roles and contexts, reading off the implications for behavior. This capacity is not a matter of consciously putting one's mind in someone else's shoes, but rather of putting one's "I" in someone else's shoes. It is, perhaps, young children's ignorance of minds that allows this transformation to be so readily engaged.

ACKNOWLEDGMENTS

Thanks to Paul Harris for many things: discussions, criticism, editing, and a marvelous sabbatical year. Thanks to John Flavell and Henry Wellman for many thought-provoking discussions. The original presentation of these ideas was given at the Workshop on Children's Early Concept of Mind, Oxford, June 1986.

NOTES

1 The idea that children can make seemingly abstract inferences about subjective states on a concrete basis is certainly not new. The role-taking literature is replete with descriptions of possible mechanisms, such as scripts, imagery, or social category knowledge (see Higgins, 1981). Such mechanisms, however, have typically been applied in a piecemeal fashion and fail to account for the seeming coherence and power of young children's understanding. The challenge is to explain this seeming theorylike quality.

2 Carey (1983) has insightfully pointed out that Piaget's developmental stages stand up well as an account of changes in metaknowledge, but fail when taken to be an account of changes in basic representational format.

3 In Piaget's (1929/1979) words: "There is present in the child a whole extremely
   delicate psychology, often very shrewd and pointing in every case to a keen
   appreciation of its affective life. In a preceding work [*Judgment and Reason*, chap.
   4, §1] we maintained that the child's efforts at introspection are extremely
   crude, but this does not in the least contradict the present contention. It is possible to feel acutely the results of a mental process (logical reasoning or affective reasoning) without knowing how such a result came about. This is precisely
   the case with the child and is what is meant when the child's 'intuition' is
   spoken of; a true perception of the contents of consciousness but no knowledge
   about how these contents were acquired, such is the paradox of 'intuition' "
   (p. 125).

4 Piaget (1932/1973) provides a remarkably insightful account of developmental achievement, anticipating much of the current literature: "At about 3 ...
   the imagined is something distinct from the real. According to Stern, this is the
   age when we first meet with such words as "perhaps," etc., which are precisely
   those which mark a divergence between the imagined and the real. Again, to
   quote Stern, there appear at the same date such verbs as 'to think,' 'to believe,'
   etc. ... It is at about the same period (2;9 and 3;10) that Scupin detected the
   earliest lies, or, as P. Janet has so excellently described them, "beliefs about the
   future" as opposed to beliefs about the present. ... Finally, it is also at about
   the age of three that grammatical accident makes its first appearance. Cases
   and tenses of a certain complexity, the simpler forms of subordinate preposi-
   tions – in a word, the whole necessary apparatus for the beginnings of formulated reasoning begins to be incorporated in the language of the subject. Now
   the function of this reasoning is to construct, over and above the immediate
   world of sensation, a reality supposedly deeper than the mere given world. And
   all these transformations have this fundamental trait in common, that they
   indicate an act of conscious realization. From now on the child distinguishes
   between the real as it appears immediately to his senses, and something which
   precedes events and underlies all phenomena. Let us describe this something
   by the very comprehensive term – intention" (p. 234).

5 It is now commonly acknowledged that the concept of self includes a developmentally primitive sense of self as subject, "the I," as distinct from a sense of
   self as object, the "me." The "I" is taken to be primitively given in the ongoing
   structure of experience and action, emerging with the organization of behavior
   in infancy. While recognizing the importance of this primitive sense of self, the
   current self-concept literature nevertheless reflects biases of the Piagetian tradition: (1) Attention given to the subjective "I" is almost exclusively focused on
   the sense of self as an agent to the neglect of the sense of self as an experiencer.
   (2) The basis of the subjective "I" has not been clearly defined with respect to
   actual processing mechanisms. (3) Research has focused predominately on the
   development of the objective sense of self to the neglect of the development of
   the existential, phenomenological sense of self (cf. Harris, 1983b, p. 747).

6 I am indebted to Paul Heelas (1981) for stimulating this idea with his proposal for a similar semantic space, describing the underlying structure of folk
   psychologies.

7 Note should be made of the two unfilled quadrants. The upper left quadrant,

defined by active creations of the mind that are directed toward fitting the world, would include imitations, drawings, hypotheses, and theories (thanks to Paul Harris and Colin McGinn for pointing these out). Less clear are categories falling in the lower right quadrant, defined as world-caused psychological states oriented to fit the objectives of the self.

8 As Sperry (1969) put it, "it is not merely the complexity of high order organization that ... endows a neural event with consciousness. It is rather the specific operational design of the cerebral mechanism for the particular conscious function involved" (p. 18).

9 While similarly recognizing the significance of conscious representation, Piaget's theory of its development differs in important ways from the one proposed here. The most serious difference surrounds Piaget's explanation of representation as a kind of literal internalization of action schemes via imitation. This model is cumbersome and implausible (cf. Kosslyn, 1980). In unduly focusing on motor action, Piaget neglected both the structure of experience and the potential for direct access to this structure. This bias left the Piagetian tradition open to a curious infusion of behaviorism. Lacking a direct awareness of experiences as attributes of subjects, children have been presumed to be aware of only the external, physical, behavioral features of the world: Mind is supposed to be constructed out of an initial awareness of external behavior (cf. Flavell, 1978). Once subjective experience is taken seriously, subjective states need not be inferred from overt behavior, they are intrinsic and accessible in behavior itself.

10 The idea that consciousness is limited to the sequential processing of isolated states not only is common in current cognitive theory but has a long history in the field of phenomenology. In the latter case, a distinction is drawn between prereflective and reflective consciousness (cf. Valle & King, 1978). Prereflectively, the mind and world are said to be co-constituted. In present terms, the mind fits and causes the world just as the world fits and causes the mind. But reflective consciousness inevitably splits experience into a subject–object dualism, forcing thought into a sequential causal analysis.

11 Obviously the development described here is not culture free. The underlying structure of experience is taken to be universal, but how this structure is exploited is culturally dependent (see Heelas, 1981). Although all children have the capacity to distinguish directions of fit and causality, and intuitively distinguish primitive psychological modes in the same way, different cultures may emphasize different aspects of experience, and may provide different higher-order theories integrating first-order notions. In any case, folk psychologies are not merely intuitive but commonly seek to go beyond intuitive consciousness to offer nonobvious explanations for how it is that intentions exist in the world, and postulate the existence of some kind of subpersonal processes to explain deviant behavior.

12 Lewis (1983) makes the same point: "Any private act is by its nature known by another only through the use of the self in imagining what one would feel, think, or experience in a similar situation. This extension of the self into another, the process of social cognition, is egocentric" (p. 169).

REFERENCES

Barenboim, C. (1981). The development of person perception in childhood and adolescence: From behavioral comparisons to psychological comparisons. *Child Development, 52,* 129–144.

Bretherton, I., McNew, S., & Beeghly-Smith, M. (1981). Early person knowledge as expressed in gestural and verbal communication: When do infants acquire a "theory of mind"? In M. E. Lamb & L. R. Sherrod (Eds.), *Infant social cognition.* Hillsdale, NJ: Erlbaum.

Brown, R., & Fish, D. (1983). The psychological causality implicit in language. *Cognition, 14,* 237–273.

Carey, S. (1983). Are children fundamentally different kinds of thinkers and learners than adults? In S. Chipman, J. Segal, & R. Glaser (Eds.), *Thinking and learning skills: Research and open questions.* Hillsdale, NJ: Erlbaum.

Chandler, M. J., & Boyes, M. C. (1982). Social cognitive development. In B. Wolman (Ed.), *Handbook of developmental psychology.* Englewood Cliffs, NJ: Prentice-Hall.

Chi, M. T. H. (1987). Representing knowledge and metaknowledge: Implications for interpreting metamemory research. In F. E. Wienert & R. H. Kluwe (Eds.), *Metacognition, motivation, and understanding.* Hillsdale, NJ: Erlbaum.

Clark, E. V. (1983). Meanings and concepts. In J. H. Flavell & E. M. Markman (Eds.), *Handbook of child psychology: Cognitive development* (Vol. 3, P. H. Mussen, General Ed.). New York: Wiley.

Damon, W., & Hart, D. (1982). The development of self-understanding from infancy through adolescence. *Child Development 53,* 841–864.

diSessa, A. (1985). Learning about knowing. *New Directions for Child Development, 28,* 97–124.

Dweck, C. S., & Elliot, E. S. (Eds.), (1983). Achievement motivation. In. E. M. Hetherington (Ed.), *Handbook of child psychology: Socialization, personality, and social development.* (Vol. 4, P. H. Mussen, General Ed.). New York: Wiley.

Flavell, J. H. (1978). The development of knowledge about visual perception. In C. B. Keasey (Ed.), *Nebraska symposium on motivation* (Vol. 25). Lincoln: University of Nebraska Press.

Flavell, J. H. (1987). Speculations about the nature and development of meta-cognition. In F. E. Weinart & R. H. Kluwe (Eds.), *Metacognition, motivation and understanding.* Hillsdale, NJ: Erlbaum.

Gibson, E. J., & Spelke, E. S. (1983). The development of perception. In J. H. Flavell & E. M. Markman (Eds.), *Handbook of child psychology: Cognitive development.* (Vol. 3, P. H. Mussen, General Ed.). New York: Wiley.

Gibson, J. J. (1979). *The ecological approach to visual perception.* Boston: Houghton Mifflin.

Gordon, R. M. (1986). Folk psychology as simulation. *Mind & Language, 1,* 158–171.

Harris, P. L. (1983a). Children's understanding of the link between situation emotion. *Journal of Experimental Child Psychology, 36,* 490–509.

Harris, P. L. (1983b). Infant cognition. In M. M. Haith & J. J. Campos (Eds.),

Handbook of child psychology: Infancy and developmental psychobiology (Vol. 2, P. H. Mussen, General Ed.). New York: Wiley.

Harter, S. (1982). A cognitive-developmental approach to children's understanding of affect and trait labels. In F. C. Serafica (Ed.), *Social-cognitive development in context*. London: Guilford Press.

Harter, S. (1983). Developmental perspectives on the self-system. In E. M. Hetherington (Ed.), *Handbook of child psychology: Socialization, personality, and social development* (Vol. 4, P. H. Mussen, General Ed.). New York: Wiley.

Heelas, P. (1981). The model applied: Anthropology and indigenous psychologies. In P. Heelas & A. Lock (Eds.), *Indigenous psychologies: The anthropology of the self*. New York: Academic Press.

Higgins, E. T. (1981). Role-taking and social judgment: Alternative developmental perspectives and processes. In J. H. Flavell & L. Ross (Eds.), *Social cognitive development*. Cambridge University Press.

Johnson, C. N. (1982). Acquisition of mental verbs and the concept of mind. In S. Kuczaj II (Ed.), *Language development: Syntax and semantics*. Hillsdale, NJ: Erlbaum.

Johnson, C. N., & Wellman, H. M. (1982). Children's developing conceptions of the mind and brain. *Child Development, 53*, 222–234.

Johnson-Laird, P. N. (1983). *Mental models*. Cambridge University Press.

Keil, F. (1986). The nonrepresentative nature of representational change: Some possible morals to draw from Nelson's *Making Sense*. *Cognitive Development, 1*, 281–291.

Kissen, B. (1986). *Conscious and unconscious programs in the brain*. New York: Plenum.

Kohler, W. (1930). *Gestalt psychology*. London: G. Bell.

Kosslyn, S. M. (1980). *Image and mind*. Cambridge, MA: Harvard University Press.

Lewis, M. (1983). The role of the self in the process of knowing. In L. S. Liben (Ed.), *Piaget and the foundations of knowledge*. Hillsdale, NJ: Erlbaum.

Lewis, M., & Brooks-Gunn, J. (1979). *Social cognition and the acquisition of self*. New York: Plenum.

McGinn, C. (1982). *The character of mind*. Oxford University Press.

McGinn, C. (1983). *The subjective view. Secondary qualities and indexical thoughts*. Oxford University Press (Clarendon Press).

Mackay, D. M. (1984). Mind talk and brain talk. In M. S. Gazzaniga (Ed.), *Handbook of cognitive neuroscience* (pp. 293–317). New York: Plenum.

Mandler, G. (1984). *Mind and body*. New York: Norton.

Mandler, J. M. (1983). Representation. In J. H. Flavell & E. M. Markman (Eds.), *Handbook of child psychology: Cognitive development* (Vol. 3, P. H. Mussen, General Ed.). New York: Wiley.

Markman, E. (1976). Children's difficulty with word-referent differentiation. *Child Development, 47*, 742–749.

Murphy, G. L., & Medin, D. L. (1985). The role of theories in conceptual coherence. *Psychological Review, 92*, 289–316.

Oatley, K. A. (1985). Animal awareness, consciousness and self-image. In K. A. Oatley (Ed.), *Brain and mind*. London: Methuen.

Piaget, J. (1968). *Experimental psychology: Its scope and method*. New York: Basic.

Piaget, J. (1973). *The language and thought of the child.* London: Routledge & Kegan Paul, 1932; New York: World.

Piaget, J. (1979). *The child's conception of the world.* London: Routledge & Kegan Paul, 1929; Totowa, NJ: Littlefield, Adams.

Premack, D., & Woodruff, G. (1978). Does the chimpanzee have a theory of mind? *The Behavioral and Brain Sciences, 1,* 515–526.

Pribram, K. H. (1986). The cognitive revolution and mind/brain issues. *American Psychologist, 41,* 507–520.

Robinson, E. J., & Whittaker, S. J. (1986). Children's conceptions of meaning– message relationships. *Cognition, 22,* 41–60.

Samuels, C. A. (1986). Basis for the infant's developing self-awareness. *Human Development, 29,* 36–48.

Searle, J. R. (1983). *Intentionality.* Cambridge University Press.

Selman, R. L., Lavin, D. R., & Brion-Meisels, S. (1982). Troubled children's use of self-reflection. In F. C. Serafica (Ed.), *Social-cognitive development in context.* London: Guilford Press.

Sperry, R. W. (1969). A modified concept of consciousness. *Psychological Review, 76,* 532–536.

Valle, R. S., & King, M. (1978). An introduction to existential-phenomenological thought in psychology. In R. S. Valle & M. King (Eds.), *Existential-pheno- menological alternatives for psychology.* Oxford University Press.

Weiskrantz, L. (1986a). *Blindsight: A case study and implications.* Oxford University Press (Clarendon Press).

Weiskrantz, L. (1986b). Some contributions of neuropsychology of vision and memory to the problem of consciousness. Unpublished paper, University of Oxford.

Wellman, H. M., & Estes, D. (1987). Children's early use of mental verbs and what they mean. *Discourse Processes, 10,* 141–156.

4

First steps in the child's theorizing about the mind

HENRY M. WELLMAN

When children understand *what* about the mind is a topic of classic as well as contemporary interest. Discussions about this topic, however, encompass several diverging positions. On the one hand, persons working with older infants (e.g., Bretherton, McNew, & Beeghley-Smith, 1981; Leslie, 1987) have argued that such young children have an implicit theory of mind. On the other hand, until 10 years ago it was believed that accurate verbalizable conceptions of the mind were beyond the grasp of children until age 6 or 7 (Piaget, 1929; Laurendeau & Pinard, 1962). Denial of an understanding of mental phenomena to young children also finds its advocates among more contemporary researchers (e.g., Broughton, 1978; Keil, 1979). However, recent research more generally, has demonstrated sophisticated verbalizable understanding of some important aspects of the mind – false beliefs, intention, mental terms, and the brain – in 4- and 5-year-olds (Johnson & Wellman, 1980, 1982; Shultz, 1980; Wimmer & Perner, 1983). Yet this newer research typically fails to show understanding of these matters in children aged 3 or younger.

I propose to consider some middle ground between these diverging positions and findings. *Descriptively*, I will focus on the early development of explicit knowledge of the mind in 2½- and 3-year-olds. I claim that this represents first achievement of a theory of mind, albeit an achievement with clear antecedents in earlier abilities. *Conceptually*, I will explore the notion of theory involved in the phrase "theory of mind." Can very young children legitimately be said to have *theories* and specifically theories of mind?

Theories

I start by identifying three features central to whether or not some body of knowledge is a theory. What constitutes a theory is itself an unresolved question in the philosophy of science (see e.g., Suppe, 1974). Thus, my analysis is intended to be utilitarian rather than definitive. I do not claim that the features I identify are necessary nor sufficient to define the notion of a theory. My point is only that we should take the theory metaphor seriously. In order to take it seriously, we must explicitly consider what it might mean, or ought to mean, to talk of someone's theory of mind. The three features I have outlined are a step in this direction. At the very least it would be informative to know if and when children's understanding in this domain is theorylike in these three senses.

To begin, imagine a continuum of the sorts of knowledge a person might possess. At one end is discrete, minimally connected knowledge about some set of things. For example, my knowledge of the names of state capitals, or since I am mythologically naive, my knowledge of mythical creatures such as dragons, gryphons, and unicorns. At the other end of the continuum imagine a scientific theory about some domain of phenomena. For example, imagine the knowledge of astronomy possessed by an expert astronomer. What features characterize knowledge at the theorylike end of this continuum?

First, as you progress along this continuum toward the theory end, knowledge gets more *coherent*. By *coherent* I mean that the concepts and terms of interest become embedded in one another, each providing necessary support for the rest. Indeed, in theories it becomes impossible to consider a single concept in isolation, because its meaning and significance are determined by its role in an interrelated web of other constructs and terms. The notion of a planet, for example, is a concept entrenched in a larger understanding of what a solar system is, what comets and asteroids are, and how bodies revolve around others because of differing mass and gravitational forces.

In the extreme, terms or concepts within a theory – theoretical terms – get their meaning simply via their interconnections with other terms in the theory; by virtue of their place in a context of theoretically cohesive terms and propositions. This seems mysterious at first. However, that certain ideas interconnect with sufficient coherence to mutually specify one another, and indeed that completely new terms can be understood simply by being embedded within this context, is a common phenomenon. David Lewis (1972) has made this clear in his discussion of theoretical identifications. Lewis asks us to imagine that:

We are assembled in the drawing room of the country house; the detective reconstructs the crime. That is, he proposes a *theory* designed to be the best explanation of phenomena we have observed: the death of Mr. Body, the blood on the wallpaper, the silence of the dog in the night, the clock seventeen minutes fast, and so on. He launches into his story:

"X, Y and Z conspired to murder Mr. Body. Seventeen years ago, in the gold fields of Uganda, X was Body's partner. ... Last week, Y and Z conferred in a bar in Reading. ... Tuesday night at 11:17, Y went to the attic and set a time bomb. ... Seventeen minutes later, X met Z in the billiard room and gave him the lead pipe. .... Just when the bomb went off in the attic, X fired three shots into the study through the French windows ..."

And so it goes: a long story.

The story contains the three names, "X," "Y," and "Z." The detective uses these new terms without explanation, as though we knew what they meant. But we do not. We never used them before, at least in the senses that they bear in the present context. All we know about their meanings is what we gradually gather from the story itself. (p. 250)

Yet, eventually, we know an extraordinary amount about X, Y, and Z simply because of their roles and relations within the detective's hypothetical account. This sort of interconnectedness, coherence, and mutual specification is typical of theories – hence Lewis's claim that X, Y, and Z are theoretical terms known by theoretical identification.

After coherence, a second important aspect of theories is that they include and rest upon specific *ontological distinctions* or commitments. Theories carve phenomena into different kinds of entities and processes; they specify, directly or indirectly, the kinds of things that there are in the relevant domain. Current understanding of astronomy, for example, specifies that stars are not pinpoints of light on a heavenly spherical screen at fixed distance from us, but are massive bodies each similar to the sun, coexisting and interrelating within an extended space–time continuum of immense extent. Very different perspectives on philosophy of science all agree that a theory is held together in part by an accepted conception of what it refers to (Carey, 1985; Churchland, 1984; Morton, 1980).

Third, a theory invokes and provides a *causal-explanatory framework* to account for, make understandable, and make predictable phenomena in its domain. Celestial mechanics, for example, provides explanations for days, seasons, tides, eclipses, and the observed movements of stars and planets, to name just a few. What counts as a possible explanation can differ across different theories, as can the specific causes and explanations posited – witness, for example, the differences between physics and economics. But *that* a theory revolves around a causal-explanatory scheme of some sort seems essential.

In total, subscribers to a theory share three things: a basic conception of what phenomena are encompassed by the theory; a sense of how these phenomena and propositions about them are mutually interdependent; and consequently, what counts as a relevant and informative explanation of changes and relationships among the various phenomena. To provide an example somewhat closer to home, consider the similarities and differences between behavioristic and Piagetian theories of behavior and development. Both offer coherent, causal-explanatory schemes based on distinctive ways for conceptualizing the domain of human action; they are cogent theoretical accounts. Of course, the ontological commitments (e.g., their focus on behavior vs. mental structures) and causal-explanatory workings of these two theories are quite different.

An obvious question, given this analysis, is whether adults possess a theory of mind. This is an intriguing question, indeed, a controversial one in current philosophy of mind (Morton, 1980; Stich, 1983). I wish to finesse this question, at least in part. I intend to assume that adults' understanding here is something theorylike and then ask whether the child's is too. But I offer two preliminary considerations to bolster this assumption. First, in current philosophy of mind a strong contender as a model for everyday, adult understanding of the mind is what Morton (1980) calls the "theory–theory." The theory–theory is the contention that our knowledge of the mental world – the realm of beliefs, desires, intentions, thoughts, and so on – is a theory (see also Churchland, 1981, 1984). It is a naive theory, not a developed or disciplined scientific theory, but a theory nonetheless.

Second, and related to the first, is that intuitively adults' knowledge of the mind can be characterized by the three theory-relevant features I have outlined. Thus, adults' understanding of mental terms and their related concepts seems like a coherent, mutually defining body of knowledge. If I try to define dreams for you, I will do so by referring to thoughts and mental images. If I try to define thoughts, I will mention dreams, memories, imagination, fantasies, and the like. Further, adults' understanding of the mind requires and is based on certain ontological understandings. One obvious ontological requirement concerns appreciation of a basic distinction between internal mental entities and processes versus physical objects and events. Mental entities and processes – such as thoughts and dreaming – are seen as categorically different sorts of things from external physical objects and events – such as rocks and thunderstorms – and from manifest, observable parts of the body and actions – such as the head and running (see Estes, Wellman, & Woolley, in press). An obvious index of the centrality of this ontological divide in our everyday thinking comes from simply considering the natural language contrasts we have available to refer to this distinction: idea-thing, psychological-physical, fantasy-reality, mind-body, mental-real.

Finally, adults' understanding of the mind is part and parcel of a causal-explanatory system. Indeed, a coherent conception of the mind is the central and essential component of our everyday explanation and prediction of human behavior, our naive psychology of human action and thought. This psychological theory is essentially mentalistic, not behavioristic. We explain actions in terms of the wishes, hopes, beliefs, plans, and intentions of the actor, and we feel that our own behavior is produced via related voluntary-mentalistic mediators. A shorthand description of this causal-explanatory system is that it is a belief–desire–intention framework for action. If John goes to the store to buy groceries, for example, this is explained, in essence, by appeal to something like John's *desire* to eat, his *belief* that he can buy food at the grocery store, and his forming an *intention* or plan to go to the store. Similarly, if I decide to go to the grocery store rather than to the drugstore, I do so because I desire to get food not pharmaceuticals, and I believe that food is best found at the grocery store.

In short, adults seemingly possess a theory of mind, manifest in a naive psychology. The notions invoked here – that is, notions such as thoughts, dreams, beliefs, desires, and intents – are an interconnected coherent body of concepts including theoretical terms; they rest on and define basic ontological conceptions; and the theory provides a causal-explanatory account of a relevant domain of phenomena – that is, human action and thought.

Children's early theory of mind

I believe that children too have a theorylike understanding of the mind by 2½ and 3 years of age. I wish to stake this claim, and to provide empirical support for it, but it is not yet possible to prove the claim definitively. The data I will appeal to in support of this claim come predominantly from 3-, 4-, and 5-year-olds. The 3-year-olds are focal, the 4- and 5-year-olds provide an appropriate interpretive context. Further, I believe that the same story will extend to cover children from about 2½ years on (see Shatz, Wellman, & Silber, 1983), but here the data are particularly preliminary and sparse.

Of the three features outlined above, my collaborators and I have the most data to offer on children's appreciation of the necessary ontological distinction. Specifically, we have investigated children's understanding of the distinction between a mental entity – for example, a thought about a chair – and a real physical object – for example, a chair. The studies were based initially on an intuitive analysis of criteria that adults can invoke to distinguish these very different sorts of things.

There are at least three such criteria (Wellman, 1985). First, real objects as opposed to their mental counterparts – that is, a chair versus a thought about a chair – afford *behavioral-sensory evidence*. You can see a chair, touch it, sit on it, break it up, and burn it, but you cannot do these things to an idea or to an image. Second, real things such as my furniture or the rooms of my house have a *public existence*. Other people can see and touch the walls, stand on the floor, sit on the bedroom chair. In contrast, a dreamed-of entity, a dreamed-of room, or a dreamed-of chair, for example, might seem to me as if I can see it and touch it while dreaming, but no one else experiences these things similarly. In general, mental entities lack the sort of public existence real objects possess. Third, a real object, for example, my bedroom, has a distinctive temporally *consistent existence*. Each morning when I wake up, there it is. Mental entities are not similarly consistent. Each night when I go to sleep I have different dreams, or my image of a chair can come and go simply by willing it, quite unlike a real chair.

Our first studies (Wellman & Estes, 1986) asked whether young children judge real and mental entities to be different in terms of these three criteria. The foil for these studies was Piaget's claim that young children are realists. In part he claimed that younger children do *not* honor a distinction between mental and real phenomena and hence think of mental entities as concrete physical ones: "The child cannot distinguish a real house, for example, from the concept or mental image or name of the house" (Piaget, 1929, p. 55).

The first of these studies involved a series of brief presentations, each of which contrasted two characters. For example, one presentation contrasted a boy who had a cookie and a boy who thought about a cookie. The child was asked which of these entities – the cookie or the thought – could be seen, touched, and manipulated (behavioral-sensory contact); which could be seen by someone else (publicness); and which could be manipulated in the future (consistency). Different types of mental-real contrasts were included involving four different verbs: *think, dream, remember,* and *pretend*.

The 3-, 4-, and 5-year-olds were all very good at these judgments. Even 3-year-olds were correct in ascribing behavioral-sensory, public, and consistent status to real objects but not mental entities 75% of the time, greatly in excess of chance. In addition, when children did make errors, they were as likely to ascribe not-real status to real items as they were to ascribe real status to not-real, mental items. Thus, even in the errors they made, young children did not display any systematic tendency toward realism – that is, to interpret mental entities as objective and real.

There was a problem with this first experiment, however. Suppose children tend to misinterpret presentations about mental entities to be merely specifying *nonpossession*. That is, they do not understand "thinking about a cookie" to specify a mental experience, but they nevertheless at times come up with a reasonable interpretation of such descriptions. Specifically, "This boy is thinking about a cookie" tends to be translated into "This boy hasn't got a cookie." If young children interpret mental terms in such a fashion, this would constitute a subtle but convincing form of realism.

This concern shaped the next study we conducted. In the second experiment (Wellman & Estes, 1986), we again presented mental versus

Table 4.1. *Items for Study 2 in Wellman & Estes (1986)*

Mental	Mental-explicit nonpossession	Possession	Nonpossession
Judy likes apples. She is thinking about an apple.	Judy likes apples. She doesn't have an apple. She is thinking about an apple.	Judy likes apples. She didn't have an apple. Then her mother gave her an apple.	Judy likes apples. She had an apple then she ate it. Now she doesn't have an apple.

real objects and had the child judge them on the basis of the three reality criteria. However, as shown in Table 4.1, several sorts of items were included.

Each item was a simple story about a single character. Sometimes the story depicted (a) simple mental experiences, sometimes (b) a mental experience coupled with explicit mention of nonpossession of the real object; for control purposes there were (c) simple possession and (d) simple nonpossession stories as well. If mental stories are sometimes translated into nonpossession stories – stories about real but absent objects – then this should happen more frequently when explicit mention of nonpossession was made along with use of the mental term. If this was the case, then we should be able to detect it by comparing the results for mental items, mental plus nonpossession items, and true nonpossession.

Children saw a picture of the character (with no objects depicted) as that character's experience was described. Following each presentation children were asked behavioral-sensory, publicness, and consistency questions about each character's experience. Responses in this study are shown in Figure 4.1. Consider first the top of the figure, where three hypothetical patterns of results are displayed. On the left is the case where children are realists in some strong and obvious sense. That is, children believe mental entities to be real physical objects. If they do, then only nonpossessed items should be judged as not visible, intangible, and so on, because possessed objects and mental objects are equally real. What about the subtle realism case where children at times judge mental items correctly, but only when they interpret talk about such items as talk about nonpossessed items? If this occurs, then results something like those in the upper right should obtain. Children would distinguish mental from possessed items, but would do so more and more clearly to the extent that the items specify nonpossession. Thus, some decreasing stair-step pattern should be apparent for their judgments of mental, mental-explicit non-possession, and nonpossessed objects. Finally, as presented in the middle of the figure, what if children understand the mental-real distinction?

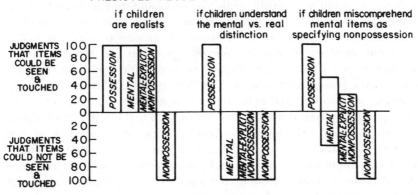

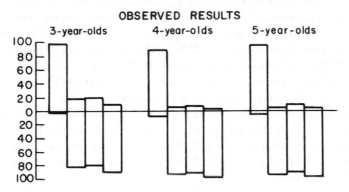

Figure 4.1. Judgments of mental and real entities with respect to several reality criteria. From Wellman & Estes (1986).

Then only possessed items should be judged visible and tangible.

As is clear from the data at the bottom of the figure, children at all ages correctly distinguished the real and mental items.

These early studies made clear that children were not ontological realists in the strong sense of equating mental entities – a thought about a dog – with their corresponding physical referents – a dog. And children are not prone to one sort of compelling but more subtle realistic confusion, thinking of mental entities as absent, nonpossessed entities. It is still possible, however, that children might hold other subtle realistic misconceptions. For example, ideas and dreams may indeed be conceived of as physical things but as special, insubstantial types of physical things, perhaps like smoke, or shadows, or air. Piaget (1929), in fact, quotes older preschoolers as saying that thoughts are smoke, air, shadows, lights, and external pictures seen with the eyes. As Keil (1979) expresses it, childhood realism "does not necessarily mean that ideas and dreams must have the properties of the things thought or dreamt about" but only means that children "think that all things are types of physical objects" (p. 128).

In our next set of studies therefore we addressed the question of whether young children are plagued with realistic confusions of these subtle sorts (Estes, Wellman, & Woolley, in press). In one study, for example, we had children make judgments about mental entities, about corresponding physical objects, and about such real but intangible things as sounds, smoke, shadows, and pains. In two other studies we had children judge their own mental images and, in comparison, make similar judgments about hidden objects and photographs. A brief description of one of these, a study of children's knowledge of mental images, will illustrate our methods and our findings.

We were interested in children's knowledge of their own mental images for several reasons. First, in the prior studies children judged others' mental entities. Asking them to judge their own mental images extends the findings from others to self. Second, note that all the judgments made by children of mental entities so far, have a consistent negative flavor to them. Mental entities are *not* real, *can't* be touched, *can't* be seen. There are two issues here, one substantive, one methodological.

Substantively, mental processes and thoughts have intriguing positive features as well. For example, one can imagine a light bulb turning on simply by thinking of it. Simply thinking will not turn on a real light bulb. Thus, we wanted to know if children are aware of certain positive aspects of mental entities.

Methodologically, what if children are not really reasonably knowledge-able about mental entities but simply have negative associations about them. Something on the order of "I don't really know what a thought is, I just know you can't do anything with it." In this case children might look more knowledgeable than they are by virtue of a negative response bias. In querying children about their images, however, we were able to devise questions about mental entities that were conceptually positive as well as negative.

Finally, we wanted to devise a conservative test of the realism position. Mental images are a lot like pictures. In this study, in fact, we termed mental images "pictures in your head" when talking about them to the children. We did so, first, in order to talk about images at all to young children. And we did so, second, because such terminology seems to be an open invitation to mistaken realism responses – talking and conceiving of images as if they were real pictures. In short, we hoped to show that children's understanding of the crucial distinction between objects and thought holds, even in a case that seems ripe for realistic confusions. If children maintain the mental-real distinction here, that would provide strong evidence of the robustness of their conceptions.

We asked children questions about three sorts of entities (1) a real object – for example, a deflated balloon; (2) a real object hidden, invisible, and inaccessible – for example, a deflated balloon hidden in a box; and (3) a mental image of a real object – for example, a mental image of a deflated balloon. For the mental image questions, we first showed the children the balloon, asked them to close their eyes and make a "picture of it in your head," then asked our questions about that "balloon in your head."

The top portion of Figure 4.2 shows the design of this study by depicting an idealized correct pattern of response. The questions we asked are shown along the horizontal axis. They were: That balloon in your head, can you *see* it with your eyes? Can you *touch* it with your hands? Can I see it with my eyes (the publicness question)? And (the transformation question), just by thinking about it, can you make it stretch out long and skinny? Note that correct judgment of images requires positive and negative responses; conversely, correct judgment of objects requires negative as well as positive responses. If children think images are real objects – for example, real concrete pictures – they should answer about images just as they do about objects. More subtly, if children think that images are real, but inaccessible, objects – literally a picture in your head – they should answer about images as they do about the hidden objects. Finally, if children simply have a general negative response bias, they would answer about images as they do about hidden objects, that is, say "no" to all the judgments.

I have labeled this response pattern an idealized one, and one point is obviously idealized. This concerns answers to the see-question for the image. It is somewhat imprecise but a perfectly acceptable way of talking to say that we see our images. Therefore, we did not actually expect children to deny consistently that they see their images. Note, however, that we phrased the see-question as "Can you see the item *with your eyes.*" Given that phrasing, we did expect children to affirm less often that they see their images with their eyes, than they affirm that they see real objects with their eyes.

The bottom part of Figure 4.2 shows the observed data from 24 children at each of the three ages. It is obvious, I think, that children appropriately distinguish between mental and real entities. Even 3-year-olds' responses conform in essence to the ideal pattern.

In these sorts of studies children's ability to distinguish between mental and real entities is also quite clear in their explanations. For example, if asked to say *why* they cannot touch a mental image versus why they cannot touch a hidden object, children's resulting explanations typically fall into one or the other of four large categories. These are:

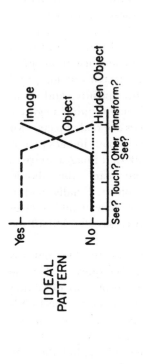

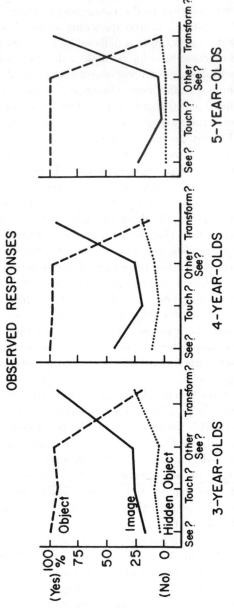

Figure 4.2. Judgments of images and objects with respect to several discriminative properties. From Estes, Wellman, & Woolley (in press).

1 *Mental identity*: Children say that the item is mental by using terms such as *dream, thought, imagination, pretend,* and *mind* or *brain.*

2 *Reality status*: Children appeal to the item's reality: "It's real"; "It's not real"; "It's not really anything."

3 *Location–possession*: Children talk about the object's location – here or away – or the character's possession or loss of the item: "It ran away"; "He has one."

4 *Physical ability–moral constraint*: Children talk about their physical ability or about moral and social constraints on action: "I'm big enough"; "My mom won't let me"; "It's not too hard."

Other sorts of explanations, and incomprehensible explanations, do occur, but these four broad categories encompass 85% of children's explanations.

We have compared children's explanations across different item types by means of star graphs (Anderson, 1960). Figure 4.3 shows nine such graphs. As an example, consider first the upper left-hand graph. The star has four arms. Each arm corresponds to one of the four categories of explanation and is marked off in percentages. The distance along an arm thus corresponds to the percentage of the children's total explanations that are of that one type. The plots along each arm are then connected together to form a graphical figure. The upper left-hand graph shows explanations from more than thirty 3-year-olds when asked to explain their judgments for real, physical items. When asked, for example, why they say a character can touch a real, physically present ball, 3-year-olds typically say "because he has hands" "because it's there," and every so often "because it's real." They never mention mental terms. The data for the other item types and for the other age groups are shown in the remainder of Figure 4.3.

Note first the similarity in explanations across the ages, that is, for the 3-, 4-, and 5-year-olds. Note next that the explanations characteristically and appropriately differ across the item types: real objects, mental entities, and real but absent or nonpossessed objects. Recall that children say that both mental and nonpossessed items cannot be touched. But why? Look at the graphs. Mental entities cannot be touched in part because they are not there, because they are not real, and because characters are not able to. In addition and essentially, mental entities cannot be touched because they are mental – just a dream, only pretend, only in his mind. In contrast absent, not-possessed real objects cannot be touched simply because they are gone away, they are not there.

The data discussed thus far show that children make appropriate onto-logical distinctions between physical and mental entities in their judg-ments and in their extended explanations. Three-year-olds are essentially as clear about this fundamental distinction as 4- and 5-year-olds, who are essentially at ceiling.

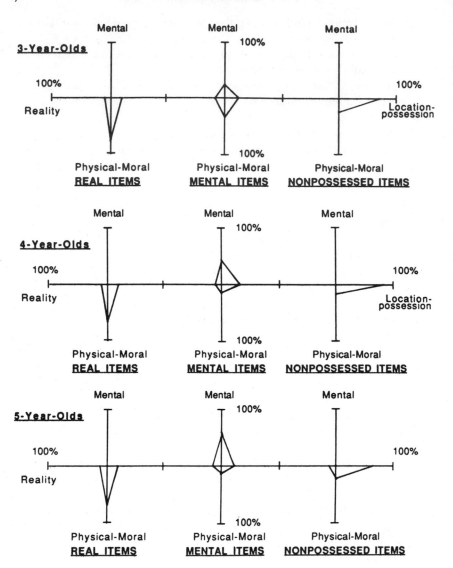

Figure 4.3. Star graphs of children's four major categories of explanation of various mental and physical items. Data compiled from Experiment 2 of Wellman & Estes (1986) and Experiment 1 of Estes, Wellman, & Woolley (in press).

Consider now the issue of coherence. Notice in Figure 4.3 that when asked to explain mental entities, subjects often respond by explaining them in terms of *other* mental entities. That is, mental terms are identified by appealing to their similarity to other mental terms. Here are some examples:

1 About a dream: "It's in his head, it's only pretend."
2 About a memory: "It's only in his head and he's imagining it."
3 About a mental image: "I could only touch it with my dream hands."
4 About a thought: "It's just thinking, people can't see my imagination."

These sorts of explanations would be unremarkable for an adult – they seem like straightforward attempts to define and refer to various mental phenomena in terms of each other. This is the sort of coherent talk about the mental world in which we all engage. Figure 4.4 shows some of this coherence graphically for children. These graphs capture the main features of the mental explanations of 30 to 50 children at each age, when questioned with respect to an average of four mental entities per child. These are the children's explanations following a judgment of a mental item in studies like those just described. The ovals represent the sorts of mental entities we were questioning children about – thoughts, dreams, memories, pretense. The arrows represent a type of explanation expressed in at least 10% of children's explanations. The boxes, as opposed to ovals, are terms and expressions that we never mentioned to children, even on some previous item. Thus, they represent some completely spontaneous expressions – "it's imagination," "it's not real," "it's in his mind." More of these spontaneous expressions were provided by children than those depicted here – for example, "it's just an idea," "it's only a wish," and the like – but the ones presented here occurred in at least 10% of all explanations. In fact, the average arrow in these graphs represents a link mentioned in 24% of all mental explanations in our samples of explanations.

Once again the data for 3- through 5-year-olds are similar. Further, these data straightforwardly document a reasonable degree of coherence in children's understanding of mental phenomena and their interconnected use of mental terms. Of course, the data here come from only a limited set of questions – questions about reality criteria – and for a limited set of entities – thoughts, dreams, memories, and pretend entities. Further, the data represent small samples of talk from many children summed up into a group composite. They are thus only indirectly related to the coherent network of concepts possessed by a single child. Still, the data clearly support the limited claim I wish to make. Young children's understanding of mental phenomena is appropriately interrelated, interconnected, and mutually self-defining – in short, coherent.

The final point to address, therefore, concerns young children's appreciation of a causal–explanatory theoretical framework. The general topic here concerns children's causal understanding of human action. Following from naive everyday psychology, the generation and interpretation of human action from a mentalistic point of view rests on the interplay

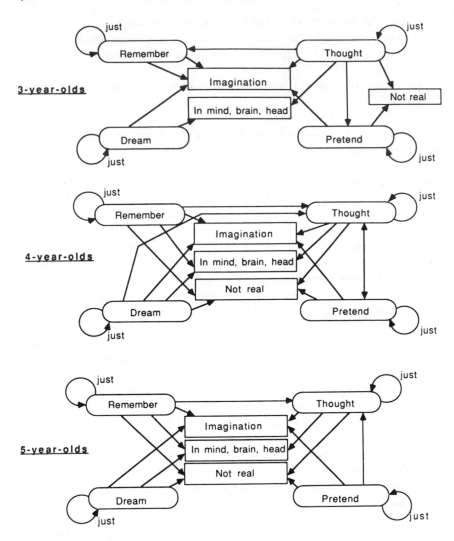

Figure 4.4. Analysis of children's explanations of mental phenomena depicting their interdependent use of mental terms and constructs to define and explain one another. Data compiled from Experiment 2 of Wellman & Estes (1986) and Experiment 1 of Estes, Wellman, & Woolley (in press).

between three interrelated constructs: a belief–desire–intention triad of factors. People's beliefs include their thoughts, knowledge, hunches, expectations, and the like. Their desires include the wanting of various positive outcomes and states and their wanting to avoid negative outcomes and states. *Hope, fear, wish, want, hate, love,* and so on are terms indicative, at least in part, of desires. Intentions include plans: plans for a single act (lifting a glass); plans for a desired outcome (drinking the juice); or plans consisting of a whole series of goals and subgoals (going to the store to buy juice to have it available to drink in a glass). These factors – beliefs, desires, intentions – intertwine and interpenetrate. Along with constructs such as feelings and emotions, ability and dispositions, reason and imagination, they form a coherent explanatory system for human action.

Children's understanding of this everyday psychological theory is both a topic that is well researched – witness the research on children's understanding of emotion, of story characters' actions, of moral versus immoral behavior, and so on – and a topic in need of research – the literatures just cited provide considerably less than a comprehensive perspective on children's understanding of psychological causation properly conceived. Nonetheless, it is clear, I believe, that from a young age children share much of our basic everyday psychological causal-explanatory framework for human action. To make this point, let me first cite some research with 4- and 5-year-olds, then work backward to 3-year-olds.

A litmus test for understanding psychological causality concerns understanding and predicting a person's actions that stem from false beliefs (Dennett, 1978). X is hungry for some chocolate. The chocolate is in the kitchen. X looks for the chocolate in the living room. Why? X *wanted* the chocolate but *believed*, falsely, that it was in the living room. In a series of studies Wimmer and Perner (1983) have shown intriguing, indeed sophisticated, abilities on the part of 4-year-olds in reasoning about false beliefs and in interpreting human action based on false beliefs. Indeed, in more than eight different conditions in four studies (as summarized in Perner, Leekam, & Wimmer, 1987) these researchers have found that 4-year-olds are correct between 50% and 80% of the time in judging how an actor will act (that is, incorrectly) given a mistaken belief, and in judging what an actor thinks (that is, the content of his mistaken belief) given that he has been deceived about or is unaware of some critical change in events.

Wimmer and Perner's work sheds light on children's understanding of everyday psychology by documenting children's understanding of belief. Shultz's work sheds light on the same topic but from a different direction: by concentrating on children's understanding of intention. Shultz (1980) has found that by 4 or 5 years of age children can clearly distinguish intended acts from mistakes, and from reflexive or passive behavior. Thus, for example, they distinguish the difference between jerking your knee because you wish to versus because someone has tapped it with a hammer, by claiming that only the former was done "on purpose." He has found that preschoolers can also distinguish intending a particular act from intending a consequence – for example, when executing an act that leads to their losing a competitive game, children say that they meant to engage in that act but meant to win not lose. Children at this age can also diagnose the intentions of others according to various inference schemes. A simple inference scheme of this sort is that if a person states an intention – for example, to hit a target – then (in the absence of deception) when he hits the target that is what he meant to do, but if he misses it, that is something he did not mean to do.

Given these sorts of abilities, then, it is not surprising that Stein and Trabasso have shown that 5-year-olds are quite good at understanding the psychological causality depicted in simple stories about human characters who want certain goals, possess certain beliefs, utilize the information in their beliefs to execute certain plans to overcome obstacles to their goals, and are appropriately happy or sad or angry when they have attained or failed to attain these goals (e.g., Nezworski, Stein, & Trabasso, 1982; Stein & Jewett, in press).

What about 3-year-olds? There is less research here. The existing data show that 3-year-olds are not as proficient at many of the psychological inferences required in these sorts of tasks as are slightly older children. For example, 3-year-olds regularly fail false belief tasks (Perner, Leekam & Wimmer, 1987). However, the basic question is not one of proficiency but whether such young children are engaged in the same enterprise at all. Do children at this age honor and appeal to a mentalistic psychological framework for the explanation of behavior, one that interprets human behavior in terms of desires, beliefs, and intentions? Or do they, perhaps, (1) interpret action behavioristically, conceiving only of stimuli and overt responses? Or do they (2) interpret it only mechanistically, viewing the movements of humans in terms similar to the movements of tricycles, balls, and rocking chairs? Or do they, perhaps, (3) act and interact with little if any conceptual understanding of human action?

I believe it is undeniable that by age 3, children are engaged in the same folk-psychological enterprise that adults are – understanding human behavior via the internal mental states of the actors, that is, via their beliefs, desires, and intentions. Specifically, although 3-year-olds' understanding of human action may not always or largely be accurate with respect to a comprehensive everyday psychological framework for action, it is nonetheless sensible with respect to that framework. Even when wrong, young children are in the same theoretical ballpark.

Perhaps the most obvious piece of evidence for this claim is that by the time they are 2½ and 3 years of age children engage in considerable conversation about mentalistic psychological states. Table 4.2 contains a sample of such conversations from a single child we studied (Shatz et al., 1983; Wellman, 1985). All the examples were taken within one month of the child's third birthday and obviously concern the beliefs, desires, and inten-

Table 4.2. *Children's conversations about beliefs and desires and plans*

1. Child: How long it's, how long . . .
   Other: What?
   Child: I said how long, uh, I said I wanted to play a game pretty soon and how long my, our game will be finished?
   Other: Uh. How long until the game's ready to play?
   Child: Yeah.

2. Child: I would like to eat something while I paint.
   Other: What would you like to eat?
   Child: I wanna eat pomegranates.
   Other: We're out of pomegranates.
   Child: I wanna see.

3. Child: I wanna take, I wanna take this [puzzles to the store].
   Other: Do you think you might lose them?
   Child: No, I think I'm gonna take them home again.

4. Child: I'm through [making a picture]. Hang this. No. This is not for the wall, this is for Daddy.
   Other: Why don't you make another for me?
   Child: No, I'm tired [of] making lots of pictures.

5. Child: I thoughted I will eat my cinnamon toast first. 'Cept I decided I will eat my banana first.

6. Mom: [To Dad] Did you see what child's-name made me?
   Dad: Wow, what a pretty picture.
   Child: I didn't made a picture for you for a surprise.
   Dad: You didn't?
   Child: No.
   Dad: I wish that you would make me a surprise.
   Child: When I make you surprise, I love you. When I don't make you a surprise, I don't love you.
   Dad: Don't you love me?
   Child: Yeah, I do. I will make you a surprise later. This time I will make my mommy and my daddy a surprise together.

7. Mom: Don't touch this cloth when your hands are dirty.
   Child: Do my hands look like they're dirty?
   Mom: Yes, they look very dirty.
   Child: Why I painted on them?
   Other: Why did you?
   Child: Because I thought my hands are paper!

8. [Child watering plants with a squirt gun]
   Dad: Did you squirt this one?
   Child: No, I'll squirt it now though . . . I already squirted that one.
   Dad: Are you going to squirt it again?
   Child: No. It don't need squirting again.
   Other: Did you squirt the candle?
   Child: No it wasn't thirsty. I didn't squirt the lamp because it wasn't thirsty either.

Table 4.2. *(cont.)*

Other: Oh, are the plants thirsty?
Child: Yeah, and I squirted them.

9. Child: I'm hungry, I'm hungry, Daddy.
Dad: What do you want to eat?
Child: I don't know . . . How about, how about, uh, I think how about, uh, uh, some, some . . . I deciding. I'm thinking. I'm thinking of something I like to eat.

10. Child: I want some candy. I want some candy, Mommy.
Other: You can't have any right now. You've got diarrhea and I don't think that you should eat any more candy.
Child: Now, I don't.
Other: I know. But we have to wait till tomorrow to see if your poo-poo gets hard again.

11. Child: When we played in the street Mommy got mad.
Dad: What happened?
Child: Mommy said "Hey wait. Did you cross the street all by yourself?" And I said yes.
Dad: Did you cross the street yourself?
Child: Yeah.
Dad: Well, you should wait for Mom.
Child: Her didn't come yet.
Dad: She didn't come, so you went by yourself?
Child: Yeah.
Dad: Well, you should wait for her. It's real dangerous so you should wait for us.
Child: I looked down the road and there was no cars coming.
Dad: You did look?
Child: Yeah, 'cept there was not cars.

12. Child: This don't have a hole in it yet. You're going to cut it. Okay?
Dad: Okay. Let me find some scissors.
Child: Scissors won't work.
Dad: What do you need.
Child: You get a little saw.
Dad: Oh. I'm not sure that'll work.
Child: I think with Mommy's scissors will be a good idea.
Dad: You think I need to use Mommy's scissors?
Child: Yeah. They will work pretty easy.

13. Dad: I don't guess we can make that into an ax.
Child: Yeah we could.
Dad: No.
Child: Yeah we could.
Dad: You can't make an ax out of a penis.
Child: This is not a penis.
Dad: Why do you pss-pss all the time for?
Child: Because I thought it was a penis.
Dad: You were pretending.
Child: Pss-pss [laughs]. Let's make an ax out of it.

Table 4.3.

Standard:	Sam wants to find his puppy. It might be hiding in the garage or under the porch. Sam thinks his puppy is under the porch. Where will Sam look for his puppy [garage or porch]?
Not:	Sam wants to find his puppy. It might be hiding in the garage or under the porch. Sam thinks his puppy is *not* in the garage. Where will Sam look?
Not-own:	Sam wants to find his puppy. It might be hiding in the garage or under the porch. Where do you think Sam's puppy is? [e.g., under the porch] But, *Sam* thinks his puppy is in the garage. Where will Sam look?
Change:	Sam wants to find his puppy. It might be hiding in the garage or under the porch. Sam thinks his puppy is under the porch. Where will Sam look? *But,* before Sam can look for his puppy, Sam's mom comes out of the house. Sam's mom says she saw his puppy in the garage. So now Sam thinks his puppy is in the garage. Where will Sam look?

tions of the participants. These sorts of conversations are not atypical; rather, they are typical of young 3-year-olds, as anyone who has worked with them is well aware. I submit that it would be impossible for children and adults to engage in such conversations at all unless they shared a common framework for interpreting behavior.

This sort of sensible, causal interpretation of human action is becoming apparent in certain experimental studies as well. Although it is true in Wimmer and Perner's work, for example, that 3-year-olds are confused about false beliefs, they nonetheless have a rudimentary understanding of ignorance (see Hogrefe, Wimmer, & Perner, 1986). They understand that X simply may not know where the candy is and thus that his beliefs can be distinguished from those of someone who does. Similarly, many of Shultz's (1980) investigations concerning understanding of intentions have included 3-year-olds. Such young children make at least some of the relevant distinctions. Finally, my collaborators and I have been investigating belief–desire reasoning in young children in the following fashion.

We start by telling children about a character who desires something – for example, "Sam *wants* to find his puppy." But "the puppy is lost, and it might be hiding in the garage *or* under the porch." Then the child is told about the character's belief. "Sam *thinks* his puppy is under the porch." Then the child is asked where Sam will look, in the garage or under the porch? This task requires the child to use information about the character's desire coupled with his belief to predict his action.

Let us call this the standard belief–desire task, as shown in Table 4.3. Unfortunately the child could make accurate predictions on this standard task without really knowing very much about beliefs and desires. For example, suppose the child just responds by predicting the last location mentioned. Because the last thing he or she is told is that "Sam thinks the puppy is under the porch," the child simply cites "the porch" as his or her prediction. To control for this possibility we have a second version of the task called the *not-version* (see Table 4.3). In this version the child is told "Sam thinks his puppy is *not* in the garage." The correct prediction is therefore the unmentioned location – that is, given Sam's belief that the dog is not in the garage, Sam should look under the porch.

Suppose by chance that our belief statements about the character "Sam thinks his puppy is under the porch" consistently coincide with the child-subject's own belief (the child thinks puppies will really hide under porches, not in garages). In that case, subjects might conceivably be correct not by understanding the belief–desire causation of action but simply by predicting what they themselves would do – "The puppy is lost, *I'd* look under the porch." To control for this possibility we have a third version of the task, the *not-own version*. In the not-own version the child is told that Sam wants to find his puppy and that the puppy might be in the garage or under the porch. At this point the child is asked, "Where do *you* think the puppy is?" After the child states her belief, she is told that the character in fact has the *opposite* belief. Thus, if the child says she thinks the puppy is under the porch, she is told, "Well, *Sam* thinks the puppy is in the garage." Then the child is asked to predict where *Sam* will go to look for the dog.

This not-own version of the task has some strong similarities to false belief tasks, although it is certainly not identical to such tasks. Specifically, there is a conflict between two beliefs, the child's own and another's, the child must ignore his or her own belief and predict the other's act on the basis of the *other's* belief.

Finally, we have a fourth version of the task called the *change version* (see Table 4.3). In the change version, the child is told about Sam's desire and Sam's belief and predicts Sam's action, just as in the standard version. At that point, however, the child is now told, for example, that "*before* looking under the porch Sam's mom comes out of the house. Sam's mom tells Sam she saw his puppy in the garage." "So now," the child is told, "Sam thinks his puppy is in the garage." That is, Sam now has the opposite of his prior belief and the child must predict again where Sam will look for his dog.

This change version of the task also has some intriguing and important features. If answered correctly, it shows that the child knows that beliefs can change and that the same desire coupled with two different beliefs leads to two *different* actions – this evidences the child's understanding of the independent contribution of belief as well as desire to the formulation of an action. Also, because Sam changes his belief before he looks for the dog initially, correct responses show that the child appreciates that beliefs do not just inevitably result in actions. In total, across all four versions of

Predicted Results

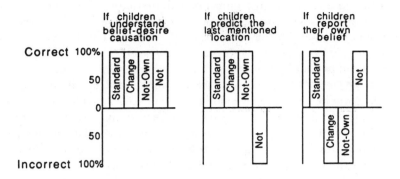

Observed Results

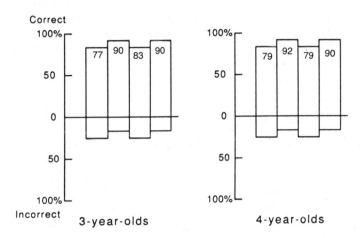

Figure 4.5. Children's prediction of the character's action across four types of belief–desire scenarios.

the task, correct responses require understanding that both beliefs and desires, as internal mental states, are partly independent of action and of fact. Still, they conspire together to provide the mental causation of action.

In a recent study of this sort (Wellman & Bartsch, in preparation) we presented 3- and 4-year-olds with 12 different belief–desire scenarios, three each in the *standard*, *not*, *not-own*, and *change* versions. The top portion of Figure 4.5 captures the design of the study and some of the relevant competing hypotheses. On the left, if children understand this basic sort of belief–desire causation, then they should be uniformly correct across all versions of the task, where correct means the straightforward prediction in the standard version, the unmentioned alternative in the not-version, the opposite of their own stated belief in the not-own version, and the subsequent changed belief rather than the original belief in the change version.

In the upper middle is a depiction of the results if children simply predict the act corresponding to the last-mentioned possibility. In this case they would get the not-version consistently wrong. The upper-right-hand graph depicts children's responses if they simply predict what they would do *and* their belief just happens to coincide consistently with the belief stated for the actor. In this case children would be coincidentally correct for the standard and not-versions, but incorrect on the change and especially the not-own versions.

At the bottom of Figure 4.5 the actual data from sixteen 3- and sixteen 4-year-olds are shown. As is clear from these data, even 3-year-olds are consistently correct across all versions of the task. They average 85% correct, greatly in excess of chance. Even on the not-own version 3-year-olds are 83% correct, where they have to predict the other's action on the basis of the other's belief that is the exact opposite of their own; 3-year-olds are also correct 90% of the time on the change version, where they first predict the character will do x, then predict he will do y upon hearing that this belief has now changed.

In short, I believe it is undeniable that by age 3 children are engaged in the same folk-psychological enterprise that adults are – understanding human action via the internal mental states of the actor, that is, via his or her beliefs and desires. There is obviously more that could be said and more that must be researched with respect to young children's developing appreciation of the rich and intricate causal understanding of human action captured in our everyday psychology. My claim is only that by ages 2½ and 3 children's understanding of human action shares a fundamental kinship to adult naive psychology. It shares, in principle if not in detail, the basic belief–desire framework for understanding human acts. Therefore, in total, I claim that by 3 years of age children possess a theory of mind. That is, they have explicit knowledge of the mind, obvious in their use and comprehension of mental terms such as *think*, *remember*, *know*, *wish*, *hope*, and *want*. Further, this knowledge is coherent, rests on and mandates crucial ontological distinctions, and is centrally tied to a causal-explanatory framework.

Qualifications and conclusions

To avoid misunderstandings about the nature of this claim, it is important to contrast 3-year-olds' understanding with older children's and adults'.

That is, it is important to describe the 3-year-olds' deficiencies as well as proficiencies in two respects.

First, although 3-year-olds can be seen as committed adherents to our everyday psychological theory of mind, they are novice not expert theorists. They are in the process of mastering the theory's central tenets and grasping its most obvious implications; fluency in the theory's workings and applications is still ahead of them, as is appreciating its nonobvious and even unexpected nuances.

Many of us have seen at first hand different levels of mastery of a theory when, for example, we have taught students about behaviorism or about Piaget's theory. It is easy to imagine, then, a person who upon exposure to the theory accepts it – considers himself a Piagetian, for example – and understands the basic workings of the theory, but who has not yet mastered the theory in any proficient sense. A person who, continuing the Piagetian example, has not yet confronted décalage and thus may believe that all concrete operational skills would be apparent in a child if any one was. A person who, for example, could not predict the theoretical relationship between imitation and play. In short, there obviously can be persons who would be ignorant of a great deal of the theory and who would mistakenly attribute to the theory certain simplistic predictions, but nonetheless persons whose understanding of the domain in question may well reflect the appropriate theoretical position. They could still appreciate the theory's essential distinctions – those between structures, contents, and processes, for example, or between sensorimotor versus symbolic versus operational thinking. They could evidence a coherent understanding of the basic set of theoretical terms and descriptions of the theory – for example, reflexes and schemes, concrete and formal operations, logicomathematical and physical experience, stages and structures. And they could appreciate in principle, if not in detail, the explanatory heart of the theory – an assimilation–accommodation structural-equilibration explanation of development. Thus, it is easy to imagine persons who have a sensible theoretical understanding of a domain of inquiry and yet are imperfect, limited, and even faulty in their predictions from and interpretations of the theory. Such, I claim, is the knowledge of the 3-year-old with respect to our everyday mentalistic psychology. The 3-year-old's theoretical commitment is clear, and a basic grasp of the theory's coherence, ontology, and explanatory system is in place, but little more.

Second, it is important to consider the notion of mind that does and does not characterize the young child's theorizing. In this regard I claim that children's theory of mind changes in an important and qualitative way from early preschool to later childhood because their notion of mind itself changes.

Consider two different senses for the term *mind*. One is the sense I have been emphasizing thus far: that is, the notion of mind required for a rudimentary but coherent mentalistic theory of human action. Notice that the focal phenomenon for theory construction here is human action. The phenomena of interest are not overt, manifest behaviors – forming the hand like so, or moving the body thusly – but actions described with respect to an actor's beliefs, desires, and plans. The mentalism entrenched in such a theory is of critical importance, but the notion of mind itself need not be fleshed out in any detail. In fact, it seems to me that young children could explain and predict much about human action by taking into account only two things about the mind. First, they must appreciate that mental entities and experiences are different from objective ones – that is, that the actor may be dreaming about x rather than seeing x. And, second, they must consider the propositional content of a person's mental states or attitudes – that is, that the actor believes x rather than y. These aspects of mind have direct and obvious implications for the actor's action, what he or she will do, but they do not require an elaborated notion of the mind itself and its workings; the requisite notion of mind need be nothing more than the repository of the sum of a person's mental attitudes and contents.

Contrast that concept of mind with a second one – one more like that underlying contemporary cognitive psychology. In this case the mind itself and its organized collection of processes becomes more focal. The mind not only "holds" beliefs, it perceives, construes, and interprets information about the world, then hypothesizes, conjectures, and reasons about this information. This results, at times, in decisions, beliefs, and knowledge and at other times in confusion, wonder, and misunderstandings. In this second sense, the mind is an intermediary that interprets and directs all perception and action – it is, in current terms, a central information processor.

Young preschoolers have a theory of mind in the first sense but not in the second. They have yet to achieve an understanding of the mind as an interpretive, executive, mediating entity. Carl Johnson and I provided some preliminary data for this claim in a study of children's conception of the mind and brain (Johnson & Wellman, 1982). In this research preschool children judged that the mind and brain were implicated in thinking, dreaming, and remembering – that is, in paradigmatic mental acts and states. They denied, however, that mentation was involved in walking or kicking or seeing or hearing. Only elementary school children claimed that the mind and brain were needed for those activities as well, explaining that "It tells your legs where to go" or "You have to think about what you're seeing." Similarly, if asked whether the mind helps your eyes or your ears, and conversely whether the eyes or ears help your mind, younger children judged that the mind and the sense organs were essentially autonomous. Only somewhat older children judged them to be interdependent – the mind interpreting sensation and directing the sense organs. In short, explicit consideration of the mind as a central information processor was notably absent in young preschoolers but became more and more apparent as children grew older.

These two notions of the mind – mind as the sum of one's thoughts versus mind as a processor and interpreter – are similar in one fundamental respect. Both honor the ontological distinction between thoughts and things, ideas and acts. Indeed, an early appreciation of this distinction engenders a later, more elaborated conception of mind. "Because thoughts and beliefs may be purposefully or accidentally different from what is so, some conception of what mediates these differences is necessary" (Wellman, 1985). Still, although very young children clearly grasp the distinction between thoughts, beliefs, and what is so, they have not yet unraveled the implications of this distinction. They do not yet conceive of a mind that mediates and construes.

If such a difference characterizes young preschoolers versus older children's theories of mind, then one place where it should make its presence felt is children's theories of knowing – their conception of how knowledge is formed and transformed, their epistemologies. I think that this difference in conception does evidence its existence in children's theories of knowing. Thus, something like Chandler's description of young children as having a copy theory of knowledge versus older children as having a constructivist theory of knowledge is on the right track (Chandler & Boyes, 1982; see also Chandler, Chapter 20, and Flavell, Chapter 13). I prefer to say that young children possess an encounter theory of knowledge. The younger preschooler can be described as believing that thoughts are substantially different from things, but as believing that thoughts are formed rather directly from one's experiential encounters with things and events. Such young children therefore appreciate only three things about how knowledge is formed: People (1) encounter things in the world and therefore know about them, and (2) fail to encounter things and therefore remain ignorant of them, and even (3) simply imagine or dream of nonexistent (unencountered) things. But the process of forming thoughts is an unspecified one, a form of direct cognition or simple apperception. "Knowing *that* one knows is possible in this context in ways that knowing *how* or in *what way* one knows is not" (Chandler & Boyes, 1982, p. 392).

In contrast, older preschoolers', older children's, and adults' conception of knowing progressively becomes that of a constructive, meaning-generating process. That is, knowing is understood in terms of construal, interpretation, conjecture, and hypothesis – those sorts of processes of cognition that variably and imperfectly turn an encounter into knowledge, belief, or illusion. From this perspective (but not from the earlier one) it becomes clear that a person may form two very different ideas about the same thing at different times or indeed even at the same time – a person may be "of two minds." Similarly, two persons might both encounter the same objective experience but form quite different thoughts and beliefs about it.

Little research exists as yet on children's theories of knowing – their conceptions of how knowledge is formed and transformed with or without the invocation of intervening mental processing of various sorts (but see Taylor, Chapter 11, and Wimmer et al., Chapter 9). Nonetheless, I predict that the child's theory of mind changes in a crucial way from a notion of mind as a repository of directly formed thoughts and desires to a notion of mind as a system of interpretive mental processes that indirectly produce not only thoughts, beliefs, and desires but hunches, conjectures, confusions, ambiguities, and subtle misconceptions as well.

In sum, therefore, I conclude that there is an important sense in which younger preschoolers do *not* possess a theory of mind. Specifically, they do not conceive of anything like a central information processor or an intermediating, interpreting mind. The later development of this sort of theory of mind is an important developmental step. There is another and crucial sense, however, in which preschoolers, even 2½- and 3-year-olds do possess a theory of mind. This is an impressive achievement and a critical first step. Such children's mentalistic folk-psychological understanding of human action entails and reveals a knowledge about the mind that is clearly theorylike in its coherence, ontological commitments, and causal-explanatory relevance.

ACKNOWLEDGMENTS

Support for this research was provided by a Research Career Development Award and by grant HD-22149, both from NICHD. Many of the ideas presented here stemmed from a series of talks and communications with Susan Carey, Carl Johnson, and David Estes. Parts of this paper were presented at the International Conference on Developing Theories of Mind, Toronto, Canada, May 1986, at the Workshop on Children's Early Concept of Mind, Oxford, England, June 1986, and at the meetings of the Society for Research in Child Development, Baltimore, April 1987.

REFERENCES

Anderson, E. (1960). A semi-graphical method for the analysis of complex problems. *Technometrics*, 2, 387–392.

Bretherton, I., McNew, S., & Beeghly-Smith, M. (1981). Early person knowledge as expressed in gestural and verbal communication: When do infants acquire a "theory of mind"? In M. Lamb & L. Sherrod (Eds.), *Infant social cognition*. Hillsdale NJ: Erlbaum.

Broughton, J. (1978). Development of concepts of self, mind, reality and knowledge.

In W. Damon (Ed.), *New directions for child development*. San Francisco: Jossey-Bass.

Carey, S. (1985). *Conceptual change in childhood*. Cambridge, MA: Bradford Books/ MIT Press.

Chandler, M., & Boyes, M. (1982). Social-cognitive development. In B. Wolman (Ed.), *Handbook of developmental psychology*. Englewood Cliffs, NJ: Prentice-Hall.

Churchland, P. M. (1981). Eliminative materialism and propositional attitudes. *Journal of Philosophy, 78*, 67–90.

Churchland, P. M. (1984). *Matter and consciousness*. Cambridge, MA: Bradford Books/MIT Press.

Dennett, D. C. (1978). Beliefs about beliefs. *The Behavioral and Brain Sciences, 1*, 568–570.

Estes, D., Wellman, H. M., & Woolley, J. D. (in press). Children's understanding of mental phenomena. In H. Reese (Ed.), *Advances in child development and behavior*. New York: Academic Press.

Hogrefe, G., Wimmer, H., & Perner, J. (1986). Ignorance versus false belief: A developmental lag in attribution of epistemic states. *Child Development, 57*, 567–582.

Johnson, C. N., & Wellman, H. M. (1980). Children's developing understanding of mental verbs: Remember, know and guess. *Child Development, 51*, 1095–1102.

Johnson, C. N., & Wellman, H. M. (1982). Children's developing conceptions of the mind and brain. *Child Development, 53*, 222–234.

Keil, F. C. (1979). *Semantic and conceptual development*. Cambridge, MA: Harvard University Press.

Laurendeau, M., & Pinard, A. (1962). *Causal thinking in the child*. New York: International Universities Press.

Leslie, A. M. (1987). Pretense and representation in infancy: The origins of "theory of mind." *Psychological Review, 94*, 412–426.

Lewis, D. (1972). Psychophysical and theoretical identifications. *Australian Journal of Philosophy, 50*, 249–258.

Morton, A. (1980). *Frames of mind*. Oxford University Press (Clarendon Press).

Nezworski, T., Stein, N. L., & Trabasso, T. (1982). Story structure versus content effects on children's recall of evaluative inferences. *Journal of Memory and Language, 21*, 196–206.

Perner, J., Leekam, S. R., & Wimmer, H. (1987). Three-year-olds' difficulty with false belief: The case for a conceptual deficit. *British Journal of Developmental Psychology, 5*, 125–137.

Piaget, J. (1929). *The child's conception of the world*. London: Routledge & Kegan Paul.

Shatz, M., Wellman, H. M., & Silber, S. (1983). The acquisition of mental verbs: A systematic investigation of the first reference to mental state. *Cognition, 14*, 301–321.

Shultz, T. R. (1980). Development of the concept of intention. In W. A. Collins (Ed.), *The Minnesota symposia on child psychology* (Vol. 13). Hillsdale, NJ: Erlbaum.

Stein, N. L., & Jewett, J. L. (in press). A conceptual analysis of the meaning of negative emotions. In C. E. Izard & P. Read (Eds.), *Measurement of emotion in children*. Cambridge University Press.

Stich, S. (1983). *From folk psychology to cognitive science*. Cambridge, MA: Bradford Books/MIT Press.

Suppe, F. (1974). The search for philosophic understanding of scientific theories. In F. Suppe (Ed.), *The structure of scientific theories*. Chicago: University of Illinois Press.

Wellman, H. M. (1985). The origins of metacognition. In D. L. Forrest-Pressley, G. E. MacKinnon, & T. G. Waller (Eds.), *Metacognition, cognition and human performance*. New York: Academic Press.

Wellman, H. M., & Bartsch, K. (in preparation). Young children's reasoning about beliefs.

Wellman, H. M., & Estes, D. (1986). Early understanding of mental entities: A reexamination of childhood realism. *Child Development, 57*, 910–923.

Wimmer, H., & Perner, J. (1983). Beliefs about beliefs: Representation and constraining function of wrong beliefs in young children's understanding of deception. *Cognition, 13*, 103–128.

5

Children's understanding of perceptibility

ILAN YANIV and MARILYN SHATZ

The general question of how children gain insight into the workings of their own and others' minds has been a focus of much research over the last decade. It is likely that such insight develops from experience and growing awareness of how one's own processes compare to those of others. In some domains information about the mental faculties of others may not be transparent to the child (or even to the psychologist, for that matter). For example, understanding of the factors affecting another's memory for events may not be easy to gain because it requires access to knowledge about the distribution of another's attention to the various aspects of the remembered event. That is, to know what someone else remembered implies knowing what they encoded, and such information can only be gained very indirectly.

In contrast, children have early and direct opportunities to experience similarities and differences between their own and others' perceptions. For example, children have daily experience with situations that allow or disallow perception. They find they can see in the day, but not at night when the lights are turned out. Their siblings whisper to each other, and they are not privy to the conversation. Such experiences are salient events suggesting to children that perceptions differ from situation to situation and person to person. Thus, children can discover both that perceptions are constrained by situational factors and that they are a source of knowledge. The reasonableness of a perceptual basis to knowledge or belief is recognized both in philosophy (e.g., Locke, Hume) and in common idiom ("Seeing is believing"). Indeed, some languages mark grammatically the evidentiary basis for an assertion, and children use such markings appropriately by the age of 4 to 4½ (Aksu-Koc & Slobin, 1986). Intuitively, then, it seems that a good area in which to examine children's understanding of mental capacities is the perceptual domain.

There has been only limited research addressing directly the acquisition of knowledge about perception. Early research on children's ability to infer how spatial layouts appear to others indicated that the ability to

This paper represents truly collaborative work. Order of authorship is arbitrary.

make accurate judgments of others' visual percepts is not fully developed until late childhood (Piaget & Inhelder, 1956; Flavell, Botkin, Fry, Wright, & Jarvis, 1968). However, there are other factors affecting perception besides visual perspective that may be easier to process and more accessible from a child's early experience. Indeed, research over the last decade has shown that some rudimentary knowledge about factors affecting perceptibility is available to children as young as 2½ and that young children of this age can use such knowledge to accomplish perceptual perspective-taking, that is, taking account of another's perceptual experience.

In a series of seminal studies, Flavell and his colleagues investigated the early knowledge about visual perception that young children display in perceptual perspective-taking tasks (Flavell, 1978). Two-and-one-half-year-olds take account of the effects of occlusion on the perceptions of others (Flavell, Shipstead, & Croft, 1978). By 4½ years of age, children consistently judge effects of distance on visual perceptibility (Flavell, Flavell, Green, & Wilcox, 1980), and at about the same age they begin to notice changes in projective size and shape with changes in distance and orientation both for themselves and for others (Pillow & Flavell, 1986). Understandings about the role of orientation on visual perceptibility vary with the task but in some cases are not consistently revealed until 5½ (Fishbein, Lewis, & Keiffer, 1972; Flavell, Flavell, Green, & Wilcox, 1981; Masangkay et al., 1974; Salatas & Flavell, 1976; Yaniv & Shatz, 1987).

There are other studies that suggest preschoolers can also use perceptual information to do conceptual perspective-taking, that is, taking account of another's state of knowledge. Maratsos (1973) showed that children asked to describe objects to blindfolded and nonblindfolded listeners adjusted their speech accordingly. Mossler and his colleagues showed that 4-year-olds recognized that their mothers, who had watched a videotape with the sound turned down, did not have access to the same information they themselves had heard earlier (Mossler, Marvin, & Greenberg, 1976). The same-aged children could also keep track of who had learned a "secret" depending on who was whispering to whom and whose eyes were covered in a three-person interaction (Marvin, Greenberg, & Mossler, 1976). Thus, children as young as 4 can recognize differences in knowledge and that such differences can be based on differences in the availability of perceptual experience.

Basic to such understandings is a reasonably sophisticated understanding of the factors affecting perceptibility. For example, if someone's vision is occluded with a blindfold, he or she cannot see what you see. In general declarative terms, a clear line of sight between object and eye is required for visual perception. If a speaker is whispering softly in your ear, even a bystander in the same room cannot hear what you hear. Again in general terms, the intensity of the sound and the distance from the source both affect auditory perceptibility. Children's ability to draw on such knowledge about the factors affecting perceptibility when considering others' perceptual experiences is a determinant of performance on perceptual perspective-taking tasks. Children must take into account not only the source of information available to the perceiver, but how those sources function in varying situations. Thus, the perceptual perspective-taking utilized in conceptual perspective-taking itself depends on the existence of and access to knowledge of conditions for perceptibility.

Analyzing perspective-taking tasks this way clarifies an important point: A child may fail to show conceptual perspective-taking in a given task for a variety of reasons other than the inability to make inferences about mental states. That is, failure in the system can occur earlier down the line. For example, if a child has difficulty computing orientation of objects in complex arrays, it will be impossible to assess consequent knowledge differences based on those orientations. Even adults' ability to take another's perspective can be degraded by difficult computational task demands. Adults regularly seem egocentric when they have to give directions to a stranger, and even referential communication tasks in the laboratory can induce problems if the target-distractor array is sufficiently complex (Freedle, 1972).

We propose that children's failures on both perceptual and conceptual perspective-taking tasks are often the result of failures earlier in the system, namely, their incomplete knowledge of factors affecting perceptibility or their difficulty in accessing their knowledge in particular circumstances. This proposal contrasts with a common view in the field that young children are incapable of making inferences about the mental states of others (e.g., Olson & Astington, 1987). There are several sources of support for our proposal. For one, the previously cited work by Flavell and his colleagues (1978) shows that even 2½-year-olds can do visual perspective-taking in simple situations when minimal computation is involved. Second, children before their third birthdays spontaneously make reference to the mental states of themselves and others in appropriate ways (Shatz, Wellman, & Silber, 1983). Finally, children of about the same age have been observed to lie (Shatz & Ebeling, in preparation). Such behavior suggests that children of this age know they can create a false belief in the mind of the lie's recipient. In short, currently available evidence suggests not that children cannot make the appropriate sorts of inferences, but that their inferences are only as good as the knowledge and the computational capacities on which they are based.

If our proposal is correct, then it is important to investigate more fully children's knowledge about the factors affecting perceptibility and the

conditions under which such knowledge is utilized. There has been virtually no work on modalities other than the visual one, or on the question of
whether children understand that a factor like occlusion or distance may
not operate in similar ways across modalities. Anecdotal evidence suggests
that children sometimes behave as though they do not understand modality
differences. Parents regularly report that children use demonstrative pro-
nouns when they call to a listener in another room or that when children
hide somewhere, they often giggle so loudly, they are discoverd. It is unclear whether these anecdotes reflect the norm or just momentary lapses
in the utilization of knowledge about perception. If we are to understand
what children can do versus what they sometimes actually do, we need to
investigate more thoroughly what they know about perceptual abilities
and the factors constraining them, as well as when they can call on such
knowledge.

In the present studies we explored children's understanding of how the
factors of distance, occlusion, and intensity of the stimulus (size or loudness) might affect vision, audition, smell, and touch. Because we did not
want children just to tell us what they were seeing (or hearing, etc.) at the
moment, we asked them to give judgments about another's perceptions.
By varying the location of a toy perceiver, the characteristics of the stimuli,
and the perceptual contexts, we could examine children's ideas about the
effects of the three factors on perception in the four modalities. We also
wanted to investigate what explicit theories children might have about perception and its feasibility under various circumstances. Therefore, we also
asked them to explain their judgments of perceptibility. The explanation
data in combination with the judgment data give us the opportunity to
consider whether the knowledge that children use to judge perceptibility is
readily available in general declarative form.

Pilot study

In a pilot study we askcd 44 children in four age groups (ranging from $2\frac{1}{2}$
to $5\frac{1}{2}$) two questions concerning the effect of distance on perceptibility.
Two identical stimuli, either two identical pictures or two identical ducks
that squeaked, were placed at varying distances from the toy perceiver,
one 6 inches away and the other 18 inches away; both stimuli were equi-
distant from the subject. The experimenter situated either the pictures or
the ducks and asked, "Which picture (duck) can Ernie see (hear) better?"

Ninety-one percent of the children indicated that the picture nearer to
Ernie could be seen better, and there were no differences among the age
groups. On the hearing question, 80% of the children indicated that the
nearer duck could be heard better. The three older groups answered
roughly equally well; the youngest group's performance was not different

from chance on the hear-question. However, the children's overall high performance convinced us that even the younger children were able to deal with an experimental setting involving a toy perceiver.

Main study

The purpose of this study was to obtain judgments of perceptibility in more situations and modalities and to explore children's ability to justify their judgments. The questionnaire in this experiment involved yes–no judgments about vision, audition, smell, and touch. In addition to variation in occlusion and distance, variation in loudness and size of the stimuli was also included. Unlike the pilot experiment, where the context provided was minimal, in the new situations the toy perceiver and the stimuli were placed in "richer" contexts including dollhouses and miniature pieces of furniture. We thought the more familiar context might facilitate elicitation of explanations and justifications.

Method

Subjects. Thirty-six children (evenly divided among males and females) were recruited through a university-run children's center. They were divided into three equal groups of 12, with mean ages and ranges 36 (30–40), 45 (41–50), and 56 (52–62) months.

Stimuli and procedure. All subjects were interviewed in individually administered sessions of 20 minutes each in a quiet test-room. The experimenter introduced the child to a setting that included two dollhouses (18" high), toy figures (2.5" high) known to all children from a TV show, a bell mounted on one of the houses, a cow (3" high), a pig (3" high) that squeaked, and miniature furniture items including a small vase of flowers made of paper (2" high), and a single small paper flower (.25" long). After subjects had identified all stimuli, they were asked four yes–no questions including "Can Ernie see the pig?" "Can Ernie hear the pig?" "Can Ernie smell the flowers?" and "Can Ernie touch the flowers?" in the following three situations: (a) *proximity*, in which the toy perceiver and stimulus source were placed near each other in the same room in one of the dollhouses; (b) *occlusion*, in which the perceiver and stimulus were the same distance as in (a) but were in two rooms of the dollhouse separated by a single wall; and (c) *distance*, in which the perceiver and stimulus were put in separate doll houses 7 feet apart, but with nothing but space separating them. The distance situation included two additional questions that were intended to test understanding of the effect of stimulus that represented a very low

Table 5.1. *Number of children producing "yes" responses (n = 12 per group)*

		Appropriate response	Age (in months)		
Situation	Modality		36	45	56
Proximity	See	Yes	12	12	12
	Hear	Yes	12	10	12
	Smell	Yes	12	12	12
	Touch	Yes	11	11	11
Occlusion	See	No	5	3	0
	Hear	Yes	9	11	11
	Smell	No	6	6	3
	Touch	No	2	2	0
Distance	See	Yes	10	11	8
	Hear	Yes	11	8	10
	Smell	No	6	3	2
	Touch	No	3	2	1
Low intensity	See	No	10	8	2
	Hear	No	9	6	0

level of intensity. The low-intensity stimulus corresponding to *see* was a tiny paper flower laid down on a toy table in one house. The stimulus corresponding to *hear* was a very soft squeak.[1] Thus, each child was asked 14 "Can ..." questions, 1 for each of the three situations and four modalities (see, hear, smell, and touch) plus the 2 extra questions concerning size and loudness variation. The order of the situations was balanced across subjects, as was the order of the questions within each situation.

Each yes−no judgment made by the child was followed by a request for explanation. The experimenter asked the child "why?" and then recorded the verbal explanation as well as any relevant nonverbal action behaviors.

Yes−no data

Data analysis. Table 5.1 presents the breakdown of "yes" responses by age, situation, and modalities. To evaluate children's understanding of a given factor, we examined the frequencies of "yes" responses to the various modalities. For example, if children are aware of the differential effects of occlusion on the various modalities, then the frequency of "yes" responses should be higher for the hear question than for the see and touch questions. Thus, it is the differential pattern of "yes" responses across all modalities in a given situation that is diagnostic of understanding. To determine statistical significance of the results, we employed the Cochran Q test (Siegel, 1956), which is suited for testing *within* subject response patterns. With this test, a significant Q value indicates that subjects respond differentially to the various questions. Pairwise comparisons (binomial test) were then performed to locate the source of the differences.

Proximity situation. In this situation the appropriate response to all four modalities was "yes." Inspection of Table 5.1 shows that children responded "yes" almost invariably. The results of this situation provide a baseline for assessing their perceptibility judgments in situations that constrain perception in a more complex manner.

Occlusion situation. Unlike the proximity situation, in this situation subjects had to differentiate among the modalities. The appropriate response was "yes" to the hear question and "no" to the see, smell, and touch questions.[2] Cochran Q statistics were computed on the data for each group to determine whether "yes" responses occurred with differential frequency in the four modalities. All three groups differentiated their responses by modality [$Q(3) = 9.4$, $p < 0.5$ for the youngest group; $Q(3) = 21.1$, $p < .01$ for the middle group; and $Q(3) = 27.0$. $p < .001$ for the oldest]. Pairwise comparisons of modalities were also made because for this situation, significant differences between the hear-question and the others imply an understanding that occlusion affects perception differently depending on modality. Binomial tests showed that the youngest group produced significantly fewer "yes" responses on only the touch-question compared to the hearing one. The two older groups significantly differentiated the see-, smell-, and touch-questions from the hearing one [$p < .05$].

Distance situation. The appropriate responses in this situation were "yes" for the see- and hear-questions, and "no" for the smell- and touch-questions. All three age groups tended to differentiate their responses by modality [$Q(3) = 7.7$, $p < .1$ for the youngest group; $Q(3) = 14.1$, $p < .05$ for the middle group; and $Q(3) = 11.0$, $p < .05$ for the oldest group]. Inspection of Table 5.1 will reveal that *see* was not different from *hear*, and *smell* was not different from *touch*. Thus the significant Q values were primarily due to differential responding to the see- and hear-questions versus the smell- and touch-questions. Pairwise comparisons revealed that the younger group produced significantly more "yes" responses on the see- and hear-questions than on the touch-question, while the middle and older groups produced significantly more "yes" responses on the see- and hear-questions over the smell- and touch-questions [$p < .05$].

Stimulus intensity. Because of the constraints of the testing situation, plausible variations of stimulus intensity could be made only for the auditory and visual modalities. The appropriate responses were "no" to both the see- and the hear-questions at low intensity. The oldest group performed reasonably well in both modalities, whereas the younger groups performed poorly. Significant age differences were found in both modalities [$X^2(2) = 7.33$, $p < .05$ for vision, and $X^2(2) = 13.97$, $p < .001$ for audition].

In summary, children at all age groups made meaningful judgments about the effects of occlusion and distance on perceptibility of stimuli to other perceivers. The youngest children understood the differential effects of occlusion on hearing versus touching. They also assessed correctly the effects of distance on hearing and seeing versus touching. Thus, they understood well that proximity was not necessary for vision and audition, and that hearing does not require a line of sight between the perceiver and the stimulus. The middle and older groups showed more clearly understanding of the differential effects of occlusion and distance on all modalities. In addition, the oldest group, in contrast to the two younger ones, consistently modified their responses to take account of variations in intensity (loudness and size) of stimuli.

Analysis of explanations

How well can children justify their perceptibility judgments? We analyzed the explanations that children gave for their yes–no judgments in terms of their form and the content expressed in them. Overall, children volunteered codable explanations 84% of the time (85%, 70%, and 96%, for the three age groups from youngest to oldest); the rest of the time they either said, "I don't know," or failed to respond to the "why" question at all. The following sections describe the coding system used to categorize the codable explanations and the results of this analysis.

Irrelevant explanations. We begin the discussion of the codable responses by describing three types of explanations that we have considered irrelevant: *action* responses, *affective* explanations, and *unrelated* explanations.

Action explanations occurred when the child acted upon the toys, for example, touching the doll to the flowers when asked to explain why the doll could smell the flower. We considered action responses irrelevant because the child, rather than pointing to the factors affecting perception in the situation, preferred to move the toys around to create a situation in which perception would be enabled. Action explanations were observed only in the youngest and middle groups' behavior (9% and 7% of codable explanations, respectively). This age trend is consistent with findings on the prevalence of action behaviors reported previously by Shatz (1978a).

The second category of irrelevant responses involved *affective* explanations such as, "He wants to," "He likes him," and "He's happy." The frequency of affective explanations also declined sharply with age (9%,

6%, and 0% for the three groups respectively). The third category of irrelevant responses called *unrelated* involved explanations that made no sense at all in the context of the experimental situation. Their frequency also decreased with age (12%, 2%, and 1%, respectively).

Relevant explanations. The majority of the codable responses were relevant explanations (70%, 85%, and 99% respectively for the three groups). We categorized them into five categories: simple, relational, conjunction, interaction, and conditional. The two most frequent categories, simple and relational, were then broken down further. In what follows, we describe first the five categories and then the ways the two major ones were further analyzed (see Table 5.2).

An explanation was coded *simple* if it referred to only one aspect of the situation, either the perceiver or the stimulus but not both ("He's there"). An explanation was coded *relational* if two aspects of the situation and the relation between them were mentioned ("The flowers are right in front of his nose") or if the relation between stimulus and perceiver was expressed with a spatial term ("Too far"). An explanation was coded *conjunction* if it consisted of a conjunction of two simple explanations ("Because he is upstairs and the pig has squeaky noise"). However, if it explicitly emphasized the interaction of two dimensions, such as distance and loudness, it was coded *interaction* ("He is way over there and it doesn't make much noise"). Explanations were coded *conditional* when children explained their "no" judgments by explicating the state of affairs that would have made perception possible ("If we hold it up").

In addition to the five categories, we further categorized simple and relational explanations in two important ways. First, they were both coded according to whether the spatial layout of the situation was mentioned or whether properties inherent to the perceiver or the stimulus were mentioned. Thus, *spatial* explanations referred to locations ("Ernie is in the house") or they contained spatial terms such as, *far, close,* and *right next to him. Inherent* explanations referred to properties of the perceiver ("He has nose"), or to properties of the stimulus ("It's squeaky"). Second, relational explanations were coded *explicit* if the perceiver and the stimulus were both mentioned explicitly; otherwise they were coded as *implicit.* For example, the explanation "The flowers are in front of his nose" is explicit, whereas "He's very close" is *implicit* because the relation between the perceiver is implied without the stimulus being mentioned.

Finally, simple explanations were also broken down a bit further. *Simple spatial* explanations were coded according to whether the perceiver ("Ernie is in the house") or the stimulus ("The flowers are there") was mentioned. They were coded *unknown* when the subject of the explanations could not be determined ("He is way there"). *Simple inherent property* explanations

Table 5.2. *Percent of the codable explanations that were relevant, by category*

Categories of relevant explanations and examples	Age (in months)		
	36	45	56
SIMPLE			
Spatial			
Perceiver	4	3	2
"Ernie is in the house."			
Stimulus	10	4	9
"The flowers are there."			
Unknown	18	4	1
"He's way there."			
Inherent properties			
Body parts	8	11	15
"He has nose."			
Perceptiveness	4	8	2
"He can touch it."			
Stimulus	6	2	1
"It's squeaky."			
Context	1	5	2
"They have light."			
RELATIONAL			
Spatial			
Implicit	13	28	24
"He's very close."			
Explicit	4	10	20
"The flowers are in front of his nose."			
Inherent			
Implicit	0	2	10
"When you squeak loud."			
Explicit	1	0	4
"The bell is ringing and Ernie can listen."			
CONJUNCTION	0	1	3
"Because he is upstairs and the pig has squeaky noise."			
INTERACTION	0	1	3
"He is way over there and it doesn't make much noise."			
CONDITIONAL	1	8	3
"Even if he was next to them."			

Table 5.3. *Percent of appropriate "no" responses
followed by appropriate explanations*

	Age (in months)		
	36	45	56
Occlusion	38	67	97
Distance	50	71	91

either mentioned a *body part* of the perceiver ("He has nose"), or included a statement about *perceptiveness* ("He can touch it") or a property of the *stimulus* ("It's squeaky"). An explanation was coded *context* if it referred to the surroundings ("They have light").

Table 5.2 presents the observed percentages of the various subcategories of the explanations. Several notable findings were revealed when we examined patterns in the most frequently occurring categories. About half the explanations (collapsed across simple and relational) were spatial (49%, 49%, and 56% for the three groups from the youngest to the oldest), whereas only about a quarter of the explanations were inherent (19%, 23%, and 32%). Second, the percentage of simple explanations dropped with age (51%, 37%, and 32%), whereas the percentage of relational explanations increased (18%, 40%, and 58%). In addition, spatial explanations were more likely than inherent explanations to be relational at all ages: 35%, 78%, and 79% of spatial explanations were relational, whereas only 5%, 9%, and 44% of inherent ones were. Finally, explicitness also increased with age: 41% of the oldest group's relational explanations were explicit, whereas only 28% and 25% of the younger groups' explanations were.

Children in all age groups drew on almost the entire range of possible explanations. Because each of the relevant dimensions mentioned in their explanations could be considered a necessary condition for perceptibility, it was difficult to assess systematically the appropriateness of the explanations that followed "yes" responses. An appropriate "yes" response can, in principle, be justified in a variety of ways (e.g., "He has nose," "He is near," etc.), whereas a "no" response requires more focused attention on the factor disabling perception. Therefore, we calculated separately the percentages of appropriate "no" responses that were followed by explanations mentioning explicitly the factor(s) that truly disabled perception in the situation.

As Table 5.3 shows, the younger the child, the less able she was to explain the "no" response that she had given. The youngest children's explanations often focused on irrelevant factors ("He has nose") or pro-

vided insufficient information ("He is there"), or were completely unrelated. The oldest children focused on the correct factor more than 90% of
the time (e.g., mentioned the wall in the occlusion situation, or that Ernie
was far away in the distance situation).

In summary, explanations with age became increasingly less affective,
more relevant, and more appropriate. Relevant explanations became more
relational and more explicit, and on occasion the older children revealed
more sophisticated reasoning by pointing to the interaction of two factors
such as distance and intensity. In general, children attended more to spatial
factors as determinants of perceptibility than to inherent properties of the
stimulus. This may partly explain the poor performance of the two youngest
groups on the two questions that involved low intensity stimuli. As Table
5.1 shows, they responded "yes" (incorrectly) to the low-intensity questions, almost as often as they did to the high-intensity questions. The explanation data suggest that this might be because first, they attended more to
spatial factors than to inherent factors and, secondly, when they did focus
on inherent factors they were more likely to consider perceiver characteristics than stimulus ones. By themselves, perceiver characteristics in our
situations did not provide an adequate basis for disabling perception.

Discussion

In the work that we have presented, we asked children different questions
with different response demands about perceptibility in various conditions.
Children in all age groups showed some understanding that the factors of
distance and occlusion operate differently depending on sensory modality,
although the youngest group was more error-prone. The youngest children
demonstrated an understanding that touch differs from hearing in the
occlusion case and from both seeing and hearing in the distance case. The
older groups revealed clear understanding of the differences among modalities. The oldest children also seemed to take into account intensity of the
stimulus in addition to distance and occlusion.

A developmental progression was also revealed in the explanation data.
The older children produced more sophisticated explanations for their
yes–no responses, which were also more appropriate than those of the
younger children. The latter, even after giving appropriate "no" responses,
were less able to point clearly to the factors disabling perception. This
suggests that the younger children's display of competence depended on
response mode.

Additional data from the pilot study mentioned in an earlier section
confirms the suggestion that younger children's performance is especially
sensitive to response mode. As in the main study, children had to indicate

whether or not a doll perceiver could hear and see various toys that were either occluded or not from the doll's point of view. A cardboard screen was positioned in front of the doll perceiver. Two seats were provided for a duck; one was occluded from the perceiver by the screen, the other was not. All aspects of the situation were visible to the child. The experimenter placed the duck once in each seat and asked in both cases, "Can Ernie see the duck?" and "Can Ernie hear the duck?"

Over all age groups, 89% of the subjects indicated that Ernie could not see the duck when it was occluded, but could see it when it was not. In response to the hear-questions, all children said that the toy perceiver could hear the duck regardless of whether the duck was occluded or not.

The children were also given a nonverbal version of the task. In this version, the experimenter handed the duck to the subject and said, "Put the duck so that Ernie can see (hear) it." All children placed the duck on the appropriate side of the barrier in response to the see-question. On the hear-question, children picked the occluded and nonoccluded locations about equally often. Thus, both verbal and nonverbal tasks reveal that most children in all age groups differentiated seeing from hearing with regard to the effect of occlusion.

A priori, it would seem that the two versions of the occlusion task were logically equivalent. Therefore it is striking that the youngest children's performance on the nonverbal "see" task was error-free, whereas on the verbal task, 4 of 11 children were incorrect. Apparently the response demands in the nonverbal task allowed access to their knowledge more readily. In a perspective-taking task with similar nonverbal response demands, Hughes and Donaldson (1979) also found good performance among the 3-year-olds.

It is possible that the need to compute some action response forced the children to attend more closely to the spatial relations in the nonverbal task, and hence to do the necessary computations of spatial relations required to determine the doll's perspective. However, it is also possible that the spatial computations were done in both cases, but that action response modes can better access the level of representation in which young children might store such information. Gallistel (personal communication) argues that the computation of spatial relations is a basic and necessary part of the encoding of any event, readily available to lower-order organisms. Possibly some of the young children's ability to perspective-take is based on reading off such basic computations, at least when response demands allow it. It may also be that children's preference for spatial explanations is a consequence of some rudimentary ability to access reflectively the representation of this spatial information. However, if verbal response modes require more general declarative representations as input, then young children would be disadvantaged either because they do not represent information so abstractly or because the burden of doing so when necessary sometimes produces too heavy a load on a fragile system.

We do not know what level of knowledge representation is required to do more demanding perceptual perspective-taking tasks, where task or response demands may require well-organized or speedily recoverable perceptual knowledge. Nonetheless, we suspect that much of the difficulty young children have in demonstrating their perceptual perspective-taking ability has to do with the limitations of their knowledge base and their difficulty in doing on-line complex computations, and not with a deficit or inability to reason about others' mental processes (Yaniv & Shatz, 1987; see also Shatz, 1978b, for a similar argument regarding communication skill).

Earlier we cited previous research supporting this claim. We believe the data we have just presented also support this position. Even 3-year-olds can do some perceptual perspective-taking involving a doll perceiver when response demands are not high. To do so, our young subjects had to agree to the conventions the experimenter set up. They had to suspend their belief that dolls do not really see or hear. They had to take the dollhouses, paper flowers, and other stimuli as representations of real-world situations. They had to ignore their own sensations. It is hard to imagine how the children could have done our task at all and kept from getting hopelessly confused if they did not at least have some way of creating possible worlds and keeping them separate from ongoing reality as they thought about them. It is even more impressive that when considering such possible worlds, they were still able to bring to bear knowledge they had gained about perceptibility in the real world.

Despite their impressive showing, the young children produced appropriate explanations infrequently, and even the oldest children had difficulty producing good interaction explanations for perceptibility under varying circumstances. This finding suggests that children's knowledge of the specific physical properties underlying perceptibility is still not readily available to them in general declarative form.

As for conceptual perspective-taking tasks, for example, those in Wimmer, Hogrefe, and Sodian (Chapter 9), similar arguments for a distinction between declarative and computational ability can be made. If, as Wimmer et al. argue, 3-year-olds do not relate perceptual experience to mental states as possible bases for them, this would be a deficit in declarative knowledge. On the other hand, 3-year-olds might have such knowledge but not access it readily. It would be interesting to see how 3-year-olds perform in a nonverbal task requiring the relation of perceptual experience to knowledge states. If their performance improved, then their difficulty with the Wimmer et al. task would be attributable to computational problems related to verbal responding and not to the lack of the declarative knowledge that perceptual experience can be a basis for a knowledge.

In summary, we have argued that previous work as well as our present study support the conclusion that by 2½ to 3, young children are indeed capable of thinking about others' mental processes, and that they have rudimentary theories about perception. Their inferences may sometimes be crude or even wrong because their knowledge about the way humans interact with a complex physical world is incomplete and because accessing the knowledge they do have may be difficult. To understand better why young children are often worse than older ones on tasks involving perspective-taking, we have to investigate not only whether children have theories of mind and what those theories are, but the state and accessibility of the knowledge on which they are based.

NOTES

1 In the proximity situation, the stimuli for the see- and hear-questions were the vase of flowers and a squeak of the pig, respectively. Pilot research showed that children uniformly agreed that objects could always be sensed by a perceiver in the same room with them, regardless of the size and loudness of the stimuli used. Because we were concerned about having an interview of reasonable length, we used only one stimulus value in the proximity situation.
2 Because the flowers represented a faint odor, the expected response to "Can Ernie smell the flowers?" in the occluded situation was "no".

REFERENCES

Aksu-Koc, A. A., & Slobin, D. I. (1986). The acquisition of Turkish. In D. I. Slobin (Ed.), *The cross-linguistic study of language acquisition*. Hillsdale, NJ: Erlbaum.

Fishbein, H. D., Lewis, S., & Keiffer, K. (1972). Children's understanding of spatial relations: Coordination of perspectives. *Developmental Psychology, 7*, 21–33.

Flavell, J. H. (1978). The development of knowledge about visual perception. In C. B. Keasey (Ed.), *Nebraska symposium on motivation, 1977* (Vol. 25). Lincoln: University of Nebraska Press.

Flavell, J. H., Botkin, P. T., Fry, C. L., Wright, J. W., & Jarvis, P. E. (1968). *The development of role taking and communication skills in children*. New York: Wiley.

Flavell, J. H., Flavell, E. R., Green, F. L., & Wilcox, S. A. (1980). Young children's knowledge about visual perception: Effect of observer's distance from target on perceptual clarity of target. *Developmental Psychology, 16*, 10–12.

Flavell, J. H., Flavell, E. R., Green, F. L., & Wilcox, S. A. (1981). The development of three spatial perspective-taking rules. *Child Development, 52*, 356-358.

Flavell, J. H., Shipstead, S. G., & Croft, K. (1978). Young children's knowledge about visual perception: Hiding objects from others. *Child Development, 49*, 1208–1211.

Freedle, R. (1972). Language users as fallible information processors. In R. Freedle & J. Carroll (Eds.), *Language comprehension and the acquisition of knowledge*. Washington, DC: V. H. Winston.

Hughes, M., & Donaldson, M. (1979). The use of hiding games for studying the coordination of view points. *Educational Review, 31*, 133–140.

Maratsos, M. P. (1973). Nonegocentric communication abilities in preschool children. *Child Development, 44*, 697–700.

Marvin, R. S., Greenberg, M. T., & Mossler, D. G. (1976). The early development of conceptual perspective taking: Distinguishing among multiple perspectives. *Child Development, 45*, 357–366.

Masangkay, Z. S., McCluskey, K. A., McIntyre, C. W., Sims-Knight, J., Vaughn, B. E., & Flavell, J. H. (1974). The early development of inferences about the visual percepts of others. *Child Development, 45*, 357–366.

Mossler, D. G., Marvin, R. S., & Greenberg, M. T. (1976). Conceptual perspective taking in 2- to 6-year-old children. *Developmental Psychology, 12*, 85–86.

Olson, D. R., & Astington, J. W. (1987). Seeing and knowing: On the ascription of mental states to young children. *Canadian Journal of Psychology, 41*, 399–411.

Piaget, J., & Inhelder, B. (1956). *The child's conception of space*. London: Routledge & Kegan Paul.

Pillow, B. H., & Flavell, J. H. (1986). Young children's knowledge about visual perception: Projective size and shape. *Child Development, 57*, 125–135.

Salatas, H., & Flavell, J. H. (1976). Perspective taking: The development of two components of knowledge. *Child Development, 47*, 103–109.

Shatz, M. (1978a). On the development of communicative understandings: An early strategy for interpreting and responding to messages. *Cognitive Psychology, 10*, 271–301.

Shatz, M. (1978b). The relationship between cognitive processes and the development of communication skills. In C. B. Keasey (Ed.), *Nebraska symposium on motivation, 1977* (Vol. 25). Lincoln: University of Nebraska Press.

Shatz, M., & Ebeling, K. (in preparation). Developing communication skills: Discourse agreement and disagreement in two year olds' speech.

Shatz, M., Wellman, H. M., & Silber, S. (1983). The acquisition of mental verbs: A systematic investigation of the first reference to mental state. *Cognition, 14*, 301–321.

Siegel, S. (1956). *Nonparametric statistics for the behavioral sciences*. New York: McGraw-Hill.

Yaniv, I., & Shatz, M. (1987). *Heuristics and analogical reasoning in children's visual perspective taking*. Unpublished manuscript, University of Michigan, Ann Arbor.

6

The development of the understanding of human behavior: From agency to intentionality

DIANE POULIN-DUBOIS and THOMAS R. SHULTZ

The last 15 years have witnessed concerted psychological efforts toward the study of the development of social understanding (see reviews by Forbes, 1978; Shantz, 1983). Progress has been made in the conceptualization of skills and knowledge required for understanding both the meaning of the behavior of others and others as persons. The child's growing understanding of intentional behavior is an area of inquiry that has recently received considerable attention.

This chapter considers the evidence for the concept of intentionality in infancy and early childhood and its origin in the concept of agency. The first section of the chapter summarizes recent efforts to examine the child's knowledge of intention per se and the inference rules that children use in judging the intentionality of action outcomes. The concept of intentionality in very young children viewed through the window of language and pretend play is considered in the second section. This research indicates some knowledge about others' psychological states in the toddler period.

Whether mental reference is expressed implicitly in infancy is the issue considered in the following section. It is suggested that intentional communicative acts observed in infants indicate at least some knowledge of people's agency if not of their intentions. What is currently known about young children's knowledge of independent agency is discussed. The results of a study that explores infants' distinction between animate and inanimate objects in terms of the concept of independent agency are reported. The chapter concludes with an attempt to summarize the current state of knowledge through the time of emergence of the major stages in the development of the concepts of agency and intentionality. Unresolved issues in the conceptualization of knowledge required to understand human behavior are discussed within this developmental framework.

Development of the concept of intention

Much of human behavior is considered to result from the enactment of intentions to perform the behavior (Hampshire, 1965; Harre & Secord, 1972; Irwin, 1971; Meiland, 1970; Miller, Galanter, & Pribram, 1960; C.

Taylor, 1964; R. Taylor, 1966). *Intention* refers to a mental state that guides and controls behavior (Shultz, 1980). Essentially, intention consists of a determination to act in a particular way or to bring about a particular state of affairs, even if that determination is not conscious. These behaviors are considered to be produced as the person's intention is set into motion.

Until about the last six years, the psychological study of intention concepts was restricted to their role in moral judgments. The major problem with using moral judgments to study the child's knowledge of intention is that it is too indirect. Typically, the moral-judgment researcher infers the children's use of intention information from the patterns of moral judgment alone. It may be that the child identifies the intention information correctly but fails to see its relevance to issues of moral responsibility. Also, many essentially nonmoral aspects of intentionality are not assessed within the moral judgment paradigm. Consequently, it has become necessary to examine knowledge of intention per se.

Perhaps the most central aspect of knowing about intentionality is the ability to distinguish actions that are intentional from those that are not intentional (i.e., accidents, mistakes, reflexes, and passive movements). Shultz, Wells, and Sarda (1980) found that 3-, 5-, and 7-year-olds were able to accurately distinguish intentional actions from mistakes emitted either by themselves or by someone else. Using game-playing situations, Shultz (1980) found that 3-year-olds could accurately distinguish between their own conditional and nonconditional intentions in that they were able to identify otherwise intended actions as mistakes when the intended condition was not satisfied.

Shultz and Wells (1985) examined the inference rules that children might use in judging the intentionality of action outcomes. The matching rule specifies that if there is a match between an intentional state and a behavioral outcome, then that outcome is intended. If there is not a match, then the conclusion is that the outcome is not intended. An interesting feature of the matching rule is that information regarding intentional states can be obtained either through direct subjective awareness (when judging oneself) or by processing objectively available evidence. The latter could occur when actors publicly state their intentions or when the context clearly prescribes a particular intention. Shultz and Wells (1985) found that children between 3 and 11 years used the matching rule to judge the intentionality of action outcomes whenever they had access to intentional states of mind, that is, in self-observation or when observing an actor whose intention was publicly stated. The computational model recently developed by Shultz (Chapter 18) shows how this matching process needs to be elaborated to take account of multiple descriptions of action, approximate matching, vaguely known plans, and the manner in which the outcome was caused.

Although the most direct assessment of intentionality is likely provided by the matching rule, a number of other rules are relevant to judging intentionality. These include discounting, valence, and monitoring, each of which operates on objective evidence equally available to observer and actor. The discounting rule, a variant of Kelley's (1973) discounting principle, specifies that internal causes such as intentions can be discounted to the extent that sufficient external causes are perceived to be operational. The valence rule specifies that outcomes that are positive for the actor are intended whereas outcomes that are negative for the actor are not intended. The monitoring rule specifies that an outcome is intentional insofar as the actor is observed to monitor, and thus presumably control, the relation between action and outcome. Evidence for the use of both of these rules by the age of 5 years has been presented by Smith (1978). However, monitoring and valence rules may not develop quite as early as the matching rule (Shultz & Wells, 1985).

Shultz and Wells (1985) found that when the matching rule was made to conflict with an objective rule such as discounting, monitoring, or valence, children between 3 and 11 years of age invariably used matching. Furthermore, they were more certain of intentionality judgments based on matching than of those based on the objective rules. It may be concluded that the matching rule not only appears early in development but is viewed as more essential than the various objective rules in judging intentionality. All of these heuristics and findings have been implemented in the computational model of judging intention developed by Shultz (Chapter 18).

The child's knowledge of intention as expressed in pretend play and language

Although considerable attention has focused on the development of what children know about other people's intentions, little is known about the beginnings of such knowledge. Many studies assessing the concept of intentionality in very young children have examined mental terms in naturally occurring speech. Terms applied to others and referring to volition were first observed around the age of 21 months, while those related to cognition were applied only to self and appeared later (Bretherton, McNew, & Beeghly-Smith, 1981).

Bretherton & Beeghly (1982) asked the mothers of 28-month-olds to report child utterances containing six categories of internal-state words (perception, physiology, affect, volition, cognition, moral development). Among the categories of internal-state words most frequently produced by children to refer to self and others was volition/ability. The words *want* and *need* were produced by 77% and 60% of the children respectively.

The above-mentioned studies seem to indicate that the ability to analyze the motives of others begins to be expressed verbally around the age of 21 months and is fairly well developed in the third year. However, the use of words referring to mental states does not necessarily imply an understanding of intentions and motives. They might be used as conventional pause-fillers not intended to make specific reference to the listener's knowledge state (Shatz, Wellman, & Silber, 1983).

The study of replica play has also been used as a source of knowledge about children's concepts of others. In replica play, children assume all the character roles and frequently assume the stance of a narrator who comments on or explains the actions of the individual figures. Wolf, Rygh, and Altshuler (1984) collected observations of nine children between the ages of 1 and 7 years as they engaged in play with small replicas. Episodes of replica play were scored for instances of the representation of human behavior on a 5-point scale (from treating a figure as a passive recipient to ascribing cognitions like thinking and knowing to the figures). When age of onset for each of the levels was examined, it was found that children began to ascribe intentions to the figures around the age of 31 months (see also Wolf, 1982). Moreover, the data provided strong longitudinal evidence that children first develop the capacity to ascribe perceptions or sensations (cf. Yaniv & Shatz, Chapter 5), then emotions and intentions, and finally cognition, to figures in replica play (see also Fenson, 1984).

In conclusion, findings obtained through the study of language productions and replica play suggest that early in their third year, children begin to represent internal experiences as a part of the human repertoire explicitly through language and gesture, and their combined use in play.

Concept of intentionality in preverbal infants

One central issue in the study of the development of children's concept of intention is whether mental reference is expressed implicitly before being represented in various symbolic forms. The literature is replete with claims about how infants are innately predisposed to engage in "proto-conversations" with their caretakers. For instance, infants appear to follow a biologically regulated cycle of attention and withdrawal of attention to social stimuli (Bateson, 1975; Brazelton, Koslowski, & Main, 1974). Another approach has focused on the structure of prelinguistic interactions between infants and parents in the first few months of life (Stern, 1977). The behaviors selected for study are those that will later figure in intentional communication, including vocalizations (Anderson,

Vietze, & Dokecki, 1977; Freedle & Lewis, 1977; Snow, 1977), mutual gaze (Collis & Schaffer, 1975; Scaife & Bruner, 1975; Stern, 1974), and facial expressions (Tronick, Als, & Adamson, 1979). The turn-taking structure of these exchanges between caretaker and infant is strikingly similar to adult dialogic interactions and has consequenctly been termed "protoconversation." Some researchers have proposed that this precocious type of communication implies mutual intentionality and interfacing of minds between mother and child (Trevarthen, 1977). To ensure a successful mutual regulation of behavior of both partners, the baby must: (1) understand his partner's communicative acts; (2) modify his own communicative behaviors as a function of the intention expressed by his partner; and (3) fulfill his own intentions (Tronick, 1981).

The attribution of knowledge about other people's intentions to babies in the first few months of life has been criticized on many grounds. To what extent are infants genuinely contributing to such interactions as opposed to having their behaviors appear to be contributions because of their mothers' sensitivity to timing and overlap (Golinkoff, 1982)? And more importantly, the behavior of very young infants simply does not appear to be motivated by a desire to produce a specific effect on the listener (Scoville, 1984).

A widely accepted hypothesis regarding the emergence of knowledge about others' intentions proposes that infants manifest this ability when they develop intentional communication for instrumental purposes during the last quarter of the first year (Bates, Camaioni, & Volterra, 1975; Bruner, 1975; Harding & Golinkoff, 1979; Lock, 1976; Sugarman, 1978). Intentional communication is operationally defined by the alternation of gaze between a desired object and the adult's eyes or by the use of gesture (e.g., pointing) with alternating eye contact and/or by infant behavior such as handing an object to the mother that functions as a request to operate it. Communicative intent is defined as a speaker's a priori awareness of the effect that the message is designed to have on the addressee (Bates et al., 1975). This definition implicitly ascribes to infants a capacity to impute at least some internal states, such as understanding and intention, to self and others (Bretherton & Bates, 1979). It is not assumed that infants can reflect on their own or others' inner states. An infant's ideas about mind remain implicit in behavior. The mastery of symbolic representation renders them increasingly observable and explicit.

We suggest that the presence of intentional communication, in which the infant seeks to influence the behavior of someone else, does not necessarily imply the existence of the concept of intentionality. It does, however, imply the ability to see people as potential agents, capable of serving as a means to an end (Golinkoff, 1981). Intentionality could perhaps be regarded as a more advanced and more refined analysis of how agents generate their own behavior. In this sense, a notion of intention would presuppose knowledge of agency, but the reverse would not necessarily hold.

Understanding human agency

Research about the child's developing knowledge of agency has focused almost exclusively on its expression in language and play. In language, the agentive case expresses the notion of an object initiating some action, as in *dog run* or *Mommy read*. There is an early and pervasive use of the agentive case by children beginning to speak (Bloom, Lightbown, & Hood, 1975; Bowerman, 1976). It is also well known that beginning speakers typically place animates that function as agents preverbally (Bloom, 1970; Bloom, Lightbown, & Hood, 1975; Bowerman, 1973). As mentioned, attribution of active agency to people (e.g., *Baby's drinking*) has also been observed as early as 20 months in the context of doll play (Fenson, 1984).

Further evidence related to the early understanding of agency has also emerged from recent studies of pretend and replica play. The growth of pretend action is characterized by decentration, which refers to the child's increasing tendency to incorporate objects other than self into play. Infants use agents in the following developmental sequence: (1) self as agent; (2) use of an object as a passive agent; (3) use of a substitute object as a passive agent; and (4) use of an object as an active agent (Corrigan, 1982; Largo & Howard, 1979; Lowe, 1975; Watson & Fischer, 1977; Wolf, 1982; Wolf, Rygh, & Altshuler, 1984).

All the above-mentioned studies seem to suggest that the grasp of the autonomy of other people emerges at the close of the second year in both language and play. But do infants show this conception of human beings in early behavior before these concepts are articulated in various symbolic forms? Agents appear to be a salient aspect of nonlinguistic stimuli. Robertson & Suci (1980) found that infants distribute their attention to an agent–action–recipient sequence in a characteristic manner. The results indicated that the infants attended to the agent actor during and after the action. Golinkoff (1975) and Golinkoff and Kerr (1978) showed films in which agents and recipients of actions reversed roles to infants between 14 and 24 months of age. They found that infants noticed when an actor changed to being the recipient of the action.

There is some evidence that young infants differentiate a key property of animate objects, namely, that they can act on their own. A study by Sexton (1983) examined 11- to 23-month-old infants' understanding of people as autonomous causal agents. Only at 17 months did babies begin to turn to people to request them to re-create an interesting event. Carlson (1980) taught 10-month-old infants to activate a manipulandum to create animate and inanimate events. Infants used the manipulandum to re-create the inanimate stimulus significantly more often compared to the animate stimuli, indicating that infants of that age know how animate versus inanimate objects are set in motion. Films in which inanimate and animate objects reversed roles in causal sequences were shown to 14- and 25-month-old infants (Golinkoff, 1975; Golinkoff & Kerr, 1978). Anomalous reversals did not receive more recovery (cardiac deceleration response) than plausible reversals. More recently, Golinkoff and Harding (1980) presented to 16- and 24-month-olds a real chair that seemed to move on its own. Infants' emotional and motor responses indicated that only the older children reacted to this anomalous event. The authors conclude that expectations of what an inanimate object can and cannot do are formed by the end of the second year.

The attribution of knowledge about other people's internal experience to children who display intentional communication is debatable. However, it seems reasonable to credit children capable of intentional communication with the concept of independent agency. That infants during the last quarter of the first year are observed to confine their communicative overtures to animate beings suggests they would know that people, unlike inanimate objects, are capable of moving and initiating actions without the impetus of any external force. The study reported in the section that follows was designed to test this hypothesis by systematically comparing infants' reactions to causal sequences in which the role of agent was played alternately by animate and inanimate objects.

The subjects were 31 infants, all from middle-class families, 15 boys and 16 girls, in two age groups. The first group consisted of sixteen 8-month-old infants and the second group consisted of fifteen 13-month-old infants. All subjects were from English- or French-speaking families living in Montreal

Upon coming to the laboratory, the infants participated in an experimental session that was videotaped and divided into two parts. In the first part, the infant's communicative abilities were assessed in a structured, naturalistic setting. In the second part, the habituation paradigm was employed to assess the child's reaction to animate and inanimate beings playing the role of agent. The entire session lasted approximately 45 minutes with the administration of the two experiments separated by a 10-minute pause. The communication task consisted of four episodes in which a specific procedure was adopted to increase the likelihood of observing communicative behaviors directed toward the mother (cf. Harding & Golinkoff, 1979). In two free-play episodes, the infant played with a toy (e.g., music box, xylophone) while his mother demonstrated its use and showed him that she could activate it. Each free-play episode was followed by a frustration episode in which the mother was directed to sit in front of the child for 40 seconds while the toy was visible but inaccessible or impossible to activate.

The general procedure followed throughout the administration of the agency task was to expose the infant to the same event for a series of 10 trials. Four events were presented to each child, who was seated on his or her mother's lap inside a cubicle. Each event was designed to assess the infant's discrimination between the capabilities of social and nonsocial objects to serve as agents (i.e., to be self-activated). In two conditions, an inanimate object appeared to move on its own or was involved as the agent in a causal sequence. In one instance, a chair wired with clear plastic strings was pulled forward from one side to the other side of the cubicle. The second event displayed a ball rolling along a groove and hitting a second ball, which in turn struck a wobbling doll. An animate being (a person) played exactly the same roles in the other two conditions (e.g., a female adult walking on her knees or pushing a ball). These control conditions were designed to determine the role played by novelty in the infant's reaction to inanimate objects acting as agents. The order of presentation of the four conditions was counterbalanced across subjects (see Poulin-Dubois & Shultz, 1987, for methodological details).

The data from the two frustration episodes of the communication experiment were analyzed using a time-interval sampling technique (Sackett, 1978). The behavioral categories scored were based on Sugarman's system of molecular notation (1978). Two judges observed the videotapes and noted which behavioral categories were displayed at least once during each interval (modified frequency) in response to recorded auditory signals at 3-second intervals. The mean interobserver reliability for the two groups was 85%. The total fixation time in seconds on each trial was the dependent variable in the causality tasks. Two observers recorded onset and offset of visual fixation. Intcrobserver reliability based on the independent observations of the first author and an assistant on the data from four children averaged 87%.

In order to test the hypothesis of a link between intentional communication and the ability to distinguish between animate and inanimate objects with regard to autonomous movement and agency, the children were divided into two groups: intentional or nonintentional communicators. To be classified in the first group, a child should have exhibited one of the following behaviors at least twice in one of the two episodes: points or reaches for the object in combination with gazing at the mother, using a linguistic symbol to request the object, or hands the toy to the mother. This rather stringent criterion was adopted because only such communicative behaviors involved a sequence of orientation to

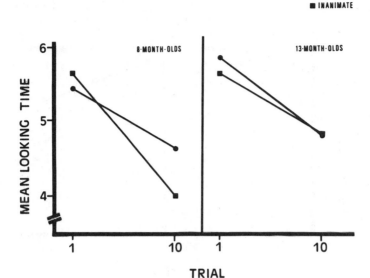

Figure 6.1. Mean looking time on first and last trials at each age in the person- and chair-autonomous conditions.

the object and ritualized signal addressed to the mother, or use of a conventional symbol or gesture. The application of this criterion resulted in the expected distribution of the infants into two groups. Indeed, all the 13-month-olds were classified as intentional communicators, whereas all the 8-month-olds failed to meet the criterion and fell in the other group.

The data from the causality tasks were analyzed by comparing fixation time on the first and last trials in each version of the two conditions (with animate and inanimate object) for each group. The comparison of the two groups' reactions to the autonomous movement of a chair and a person revealed that the 13-month-olds looked more at the stimuli than the 8-month-olds. An overall decrease of attention from the first to the last trial was also observed across age and type of object. The older group showed a greater decrease of attention when they looked at an animate object (from 5.82 sec to 4.80 sec) than when the same action was performed by an inanimate object (from 5.60 sec to 4.87 sec), as illustrated in Figure 6.1. In contrast, the younger group showed a larger decrease of attention from the first to the last trial when confronted with a chair moving on its own (5.65 sec and 4.02 sec respectively) than to a person in the same situation (5.36 sec vs. 4.62 sec).

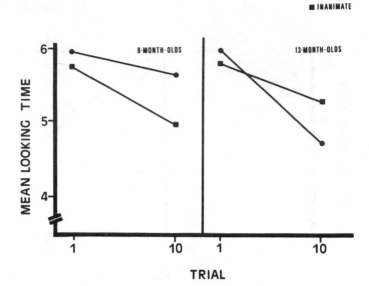

Figure 6.2. Mean looking time on first and last trials at each age in the person- and ball-as-agent conditions.

To assess potential differences in the reaction to animate and inanimate beings playing the role of agent in a causal sequence, fixation time on the first and last trials were compared in each group. The comparison of the first and last trials for each type of object and group separately revealed a pattern similar to the one observed in the first condition. As can be seen in Figure 6.2, the 13-month-old infants showed a clear decrease of attention over the 10 trials in the person-as-agent condition (from 5.97 sec to 4.73 sec). However, the same children did not show signs of habituation to a causal sequence in which an inanimate object, a ball, was the agent (5.81 sec vs. 5.31 sec). The results once again contrasted with the behavior exhibited by the 8-month-olds, who did not habituate in the person-as-agent condition (5.90 sec vs. 5.63 sec) but showed a decrease of attention in the ball-as-agent condition (from 5.73 sec to 4.90 sec). The analyses of the data of the two causality tasks with blocks of trials (N = 5) as the repeated measure replicated the results reported above with only two trials being considered.

Summary and conclusions

One building block, perhaps a cornerstone, of social cognition is the knowledge that human beings direct and control their behavior in accord

Table 6.1. *Steps in the development of the concept of agency and intentionality*

Description	Age of onset (in months)
1. Animate objects treated as passive recipients under the control of the child's behavior.	4
2. Independent agency attributed implicitly to animate objects.	9–13
3. Animate objects treated as passive recipients of action in replica play.	18
4. Animate objects treated as autonomous agents in replica play and language.	21–24
5. Production of linguistic terms to refer to the intentions of people or figures.	28–30
6. Distinction between intentional actions and accidents/ mistakes. Use of the matching rule to judge the intentionality of action outcomes.	36

with their own self-generated rules and plans. This understanding is only gradually constructed during the first three years of life. Taken together, the findings of the present research and previous work suggest a series of steps in the development of the concepts of independent agency and intentionality (see Table 6.1). From a concept of human beings as passive recipients of his or her own actions the child progresses to regarding them as independent actors. The infant's knowledge of others as independent agents manifests itself first in his differential emotional response (e.g., interest) to human beings as performers of overt actions that cause observable events. The separation anxiety exhibited by infants between 9 and 15 months can also be considered as evidence for the recognition that animate objects act unpredictably and are beyond the infant's control (Goulet, 1974; Zaslow, 1978). Similarly, the contemporaneous appearance of communicative appeals directed to adults for instrumental assistance reflects the infant's recognition of the power of animates (Bates, Camaioni, & Volterra, 1975; Harding & Golinkoff, 1979).

The concept of agency which is implicit in the infant's behavior is then encoded through both gesture and language. The explicit, verbally expressible concept of agency that begins to emerge around the age of 18 months follows the same developmental sequence as the implicit. In both replica play and language, animate objects are first considered as passive recipients before being treated as autonomous agents a few months later. The ability to speak about other people's intentions develops during the third year of life. This capacity to reflect on internal experiences has been documented in naturally occurring speech as well as in the context of doll play. In the last stage, children begin to assimilate information on

intention to causal schemes and to use inference rules in judging the
intentionality of action outcomes.

The empirical evidence for a clear developmental progression from
agency to intentionality can be complemented by a conceptual argument.
Intention is an elaboration of agency. Agency explains that a being moves
or behaves on its own. Intention elaborates on that explanation by
postulating an internal mental state that guides and controls the action.
That the two concepts are intertwined is illustrated by the fact that 3-
year-olds sometimes attribute mental states to inanimate objects that
move spontaneously (Bullock, 1985). Moreover, the idea that the concept
of autonomous agency is the antecedent of intentionality fits nicely with
the cognitive transformation that takes place between early and late
infancy, namely the progression from action to representation (Piaget,
1954).

Despite the recent research on young children's concept of intentionality, there are many gaps in our knowledge. The study of early
representation of human agency has revealed a developmental sequence
similar to that reported in the sensorimotor period. However, no *direct*
evidence is available for an implicit attribution of intentions to people by
infants. To what extent infants are aware of intentional states remains
an open question until appropriate methodologies are created. Many
researchers believe that children between 1 and 2 years build up an implicit understanding of internal experiences. It has been suggested that
intentional communication implies at least the understanding that people,
unlike inanimate objects, attend, hear, see, and understand (Bretherton &
Beeghly, 1982; Wolf, 1982). The observations of communicative overtures
toward inanimate objects with autonomous movement would be a way to
determine whether independent agency is sufficient for the attribution of
internal states.

Social referencing might be considered as indirect evidence for the
concept of intentionality in preverbal infants. Social referencing is defined as the deliberate search for emotional information in another's face,
voice, and gesture to help disambiguate uncertainties in the environment
(Klinnert, Campos, Sorce, Emde, & Svejda, 1983). Whether seeking out
and using the emotional expressions of others before deciding how to react
reflects a knowledge of the mental states underlying these external cues
remains an open question, however. It has been argued that the infant
must understand about the goals and strivings of others before he or she
can understand the elicitation of emotion in them (Trevarthen, 1979).

The empathetic offers of comfort and interest to others that are
observed during the second year have also been interpreted as evidence
that infants extrapolate from their own internal experience (Zahn-Waxler,

Radke-Yarrow, & King, 1979). However, newborns can respond in kind to the distress of another human (Martin & Clarke, 1982). As Hoffman (1978) has pointed out, it is possible in such cases that the child's feelings may not have been accompanied by any sort of mental representation. The study of infants' reactions to incongruence between emotional expressions and intentions in the context of dyadic interactions might be a promising line of investigation for future research.

Further developmental steps in the sequence of development of intentionality have yet to be unraveled. Judgments of intentionality may involve complex considerations of immediate and distant motives. The understanding of motives themselves may precede the ability to make intentional judgments that require complex motivational considerations (Berndt & Berndt, 1975). Similarly, how attribution of intentions to explain simple outcomes is related to attribution of a plan to achieve a goal remains unexplored. Although there has been considerable interest in the development of children's planfulness, no attention has been given to their knowledge of other people's plans (Pea, 1982).

In this chapter, we have addressed the issue of whether knowledge about the action power of human beings is a precursor of the attribution of intentions. The comparison of infants' reactions to self-propelled animate and inanimate objects has allowed us to demonstrate what seem to be the beginnings of the concept of independent agency. It first appears during the last quarter of the first year, much earlier than previous research had indicated, and at the same time as the child is acting with communication as a goal. Whether the development of the concept of agency facilitates the restriction of communicative overtures to animate beings or whether the failure of communicative bids toward inanimate objects helps to make this basic distinction, remain open for further investigation.

It might be legitimate to hypothesize that many months of experience using inanimate objects as instruments and observing animate beings moving without any external impetus culminates in the restriction of communicative overtures to human beings. The next task facing the infant is to understand that some of people's actions are instigated by their own inner intentions. Clearly, knowledge of the existence of intentionality must precede the full-fledged grasp of what makes an act intentional or unintentional. As Flavell (1985) has recently pointed out, before children can try to infer the presence and characteristics of psychological states in people on particular occasions, they have to become aware of the very existence of these states. What the present study shows is that one of the preconditions for the development of the awareness that people have intentions is present at a very early age. It provides the foundations for the acquisition of further knowledge about the physical and social world.

REFERENCES

Anderson, B., Vietze, P., & Dokecki, P. (1977). Reciprocity in vocal interactions of mothers and infants. *Child Development*, *48*, 1676–1681.

Bates, E., Camaioni, L., & Volterra, V. (1975). The acquisition of performatives prior to speech. *Merrill-Palmer Quarterly*, *21*, 205–226.

Bateson, M. (1975). Mother-infant exchanges: The epigenesis of conversational interaction. *Annals of the New York Academy of Science*, *263*, 101–113.

Berndt, T., & Berndt, E. G. (1975). Children's use of motives and intentionality in person perceptions and moral judgment. *Child Development*, *46*, 904–912.

Bloom, L. (1970). *Language development: Form and function in emerging grammars.* Cambridge, MA: MIT Press.

Bloom, L., Lightbown, P., & Hood, L. (1975). Structure and variation in child language. *Monographs of the Society for Research in Child Development*, *40*.

Bowerman, M. (1973). Structural relationships in children's utterances: Syntactic or semantic? In T. Moore (Ed.), *Cognitive development and the acquisition of language* (pp. 197–213). New York: Academic Press.

Bowerman, M. (1976). Semantic factors in the acquisition of rules for word use and sentence construction. In D. Morehead & A. Morehead (Eds.), *Normal and deficient child language* (pp. 99–179). Baltimore, MD: University Park Press.

Brazelton, T. B., Koslowski, B., & Main, L. (1974). The origins of reciprocity: The early mother–infant interaction. In M. Lewis & L. Rosenblum (Eds.), *The effect of the infant on its caregiver* (pp. 49–76). New York: Wiley.

Bretherton, I., & Bates, E. (1979). The emergence of intentional communication. In I. Uzgiris (Ed.), *Social interaction and communication during infancy* (pp. 81–100). San Francisco: Jossey-Bass.

Bretherton, I., & Beeghly, M. (1982). Talking about internal states: The acquisition of an explicit theory of mind. *Developmental Psychology*, *19*, 906–921.

Bretherton, I., McNew, S., & Beeghly-Smith, M. (1981). Early person knowledge as expressed in gestural and verbal communication: When do infants acquire a "theory of mind"? In M. E. Lamb & L. R. Sherrod (Eds.), *Infant social cognition* (pp. 333–373). Hillsdale, NJ: Erlbaum.

Bruner, J. S. (1975). The ontogenesis of speech acts. *Journal of Child Language*, *2*, 1–19.

Bullock, M. (1985). Animism in childhood thinking: A new look at an old question. *Developmental Psychology*, *21*, 217–225.

Carlson, V. (1980, March). *Differences between social and mechanical causality in infancy.* Paper presented at the International Conference on Infant Studies, New Haven, CT.

Collis, G., & Schaffer, H. (1975). Synchronization of visual attention in mother–infant pairs. *Journal of Child Psychology and Psychiatry*, *16*, 315–320.

Corrigan, R. (1982). The control of animate and inanimate components in pretend play and language. *Child Development*, *53*, 1343–1353.

Fenson, L. (1984). Developmental trends for action and speech in pretend play. In

I. Bretherton (Ed.), *Symbolic play* (pp. 249–270). New York: Academic Press.

Flavell, J. H. (1985). *Cognitive development.* Englewood Cliffs, NJ: Prentice-Hall.

Forbes, D. (1978). Recent research on children's social cognition: A brief review. In W. Damon (Ed.), *Social cognition* (pp. 123–139). San Francisco: Jossey-Bass.

Freedle, R., & Lewis, M. (1977). Prelinguistic conversations. In M. Lewis & L. Rosenblum (Eds.), *Interaction, conversation, and the development of language* (pp. 157–175). New York: Wiley.

Golinkoff, R. M. (1975). Semantic development in infants: The concepts of agent and recipient. *Merrill-Palmer Quarterly, 21,* 191–193.

Golinkoff, R. M. (1981). The influence of Piagetian theory on the study of the development of communication. In I. Sigel, D. Brodzinsky, & R. M. Golinkoff (Eds.), *New directions in Piagetian theory and practice* (pp. 127–142). Hillsdale, NJ: Erlbaum.

Golinkoff, R. M. (1982). Infant social cognition. In L. Liben (Ed.), *Piaget and the foundations of knowledge.* Hillsdale, NJ: Erlbaum.

Golinkoff, R. M., & Harding, C. G. (1980, March). *Infants' expectations of the movement potential of inanimate objects.* Paper presented at the International Conference on Infant Studies, New Haven, CT.

Golinkoff, R. M., & Kerr, J. L. (1978). Infants' perception of semantically defined action role changes in filmed events. *Merrill-Palmer Quarterly, 24,* 53–62.

Goulet, J. (1974). The infant's conception of causality and his reactions to strangers. In T. G. Decarie (Ed.), *The infant's reaction to strangers* (pp. 59–96). New York: International Universities Press.

Hampshire, S. (1965). *Thought and action.* London: Chatto & Windus.

Harding, C. G., & Golinkoff, R. M. (1979). The origins of intentional vocalizations in prelinguistic infants. *Child Development, 50,* 33–40.

Harre, R., & Secord, P. F. (1972). *The explanation of social behavior.* Oxford: Blackwell Publisher.

Hoffman, M. L. (1978). Empathy: Its developmental and prosocial implications. In C. B. Keasey (Ed.), *Nebraska symposium on motivation* (Vol. 25, pp. 169–217). Lincoln: University of Nebraska Press.

Irwin, F. W. (1971). *Intentional behavior and motivation: A cognitive theory.* Philadelphia: Lippincott.

Kelley, H. H. (1973). The process of causal attribution. *American Psychologist, 28,* 107–128.

Klinnert, M. D., Campos, J. J., Sorce, J. F., Emde, R. N., & Svejda, M. (1983). Emotions as behavior regulators: Social referencing in infancy. In R. Plutchik & H. Kellerman (Eds.), *Emotions in early development: Vol. 2. The emotions* (pp. 57–86). New York: Academic Press.

Largo, R. H., & Howard, J. (1979). Developmental progression in play behavior of children between nine and thirty months. I. Spontaneous play and imitation. *Developmental Medicine and Child Neurology, 21,* 299–310.

Lock, A. (1976). Acts not sentences. In W. von Raffler-Engle & Y. Lebrun (Eds.), *Baby talk and infant speech* (pp. 148–161). Amsterdam: Swets & Zeitlinger.

Lowe, M. (1975). Trends in the development of representational play in infants from one to three years: An observational study. *Journal of Child Psychology and Psychiatry, 16*, 33–47.

Martin, G., & Clarke, R. (1982). Distress crying in neonates: Species and peer specificity. *Developmental Psychology, 18*, 3–10.

Meiland, J. W. (1970). *The nature of intention.* London: Methuen.

Miller, G. A., Galanter, E., & Pribram, K. H. (1960). *Plans and the structure of behavior.* New York: Holt, Rinehart & Winston.

Pea, R. (1982). What is planning development the development of? In D. Forbes & M. T. Greenberg (Eds.), *Children's planning strategies* (pp. 5–27). San Francisco: Jossey-Bass.

Piaget, J. (1954). *The construction of reality in the child* (M. Cook, Trans.). New York: Basic. (Originally published in French, 1937).

Poulin-Dubois, D., & Shultz, T. R. (1987). *The infant's concept of agency: The distinction between animate and inanimate objects.* Manuscript submitted for publication.

Robertson, S. S., & Suci, G. J. (1980). Event perception by children in the early stages of language production. *Child Development, 51*, 89–96.

Sackett, G. P. (1978). *Observing behavior.* Baltimore, MD: University Park Press.

Scaife, M., & Bruner, J. (1975). The capacity for joint visual attention in the infant. *Nature, 253*, 265–266.

Scoville, R. (1984). Development of the intention to communicate: The eye of the beholder. In L. Feagans, C. Garvey, & R. Golinkoff (Eds.), *The origin and growth of communication* (pp. 109–122). Norwood, NJ: Ablex.

Sexton, M. (1983). The development of the understanding of causality in infancy. *Infant Behavior and Development, 6*, 201–210.

Shantz, C. V. (1983). Social cognition. In J. H. Flavell & E. M. Markman (Eds.), *Handbook of child psychology: Cognitive development* (Vol. 3, P. H. Mussen, General Ed., pp. 495–555). New York: Wiley.

Shatz, M., Wellman, H. M., & Silber, S. (1983). The acquisition of mental verbs: A systematic investigation of the first reference to mental state. *Cognition, 14*, 301–321.

Shultz, T. R. (1980). Development of the concept of intention. In W. A. Collins (Ed.), *Development of cognition, affect, and social relations: The Minnesota symposia on child psychology* (Vol. 13, pp. 131–164). Hillsdale, NJ: Erlbaum.

Shultz, T. R., & Wells, D. (1985). Judging the intentionality of action-outcomes. *Developmental Psychology, 21*, 83–89.

Shultz, T. R., Wells, D., & Sarda, M. (1980). Development of the ability to distinguish intended actions from mistakes, reflexes, and passive movements. *British Journal of Social and Clinical Psychology, 19*, 301–310.

Smith, M. C. (1978). Cognizing the behavior stream: The recognition of intentional action. *Child Development, 49*, 736–743.

Snow, C. (1977). The development of conversation between mothers and babies. *Journal of Child Language, 4*, 1–22.

Stern, D. (1974). Mother and infant at play: The dyadic interaction involving facial, vocal and gaze behaviors. In M. Lewis & L. Rosenblum (Eds.), *The effect of the infant on its caregiver* (pp. 187–214). New York: Wiley.

Stern, D. (1977). *The first relationship*. Cambridge, MA: Harvard University Press.

Sugarman, S. (1978). Some organizational aspects of preverbal communication. In I. Markova (Ed.), *The social context of language* (pp. 49–66). New York: Wiley.

Taylor, C. (1964). *The explanation of behavior*. London: Routledge & Kegan Paul.

Taylor, R. (1966). *Action and purpose*. Englewood Cliffs, NJ: Prentice-Hall.

Trevarthen, C. (1977). Descriptive analyses of infant communicative behavior. In H. Schaffer (Ed.), *Studies in mother–infant interaction* (pp. 227–270). London: Wiley.

Trevarthen, C. (1979). Instincts for human understanding and for cultural comprehension: Their development in infancy. In M. von Cranach, K. Foppa, W. Lepenies, & D. Ploog (Eds.), *Human ethology: Claims and limits of a new discipline* (pp. 530–571). Cambridge University Press.

Tronick, E. (1981). Infant communicative intent. In R. E. Stark (Ed.), *Language behavior in infancy and early childhood* (pp. 5–16). New York: Elsevier.

Tronick, E., Als, H., & Adamson, I. (1979). Structure of early face-to-face communicative interactions. In M. Bullowa (Ed.), *Before speech* (pp. 349–370). Cambridge University Press.

Watson, M. W., & Fischer, K. W. (1977). A developmental sequence of agent use in late infancy. *Child Development, 48*, 828–836.

Wolf, D. (1982). Understanding others: A longitudinal case study of the concept of independent agency. In G. Forman (Ed.), *Action and thought* (pp. 297–328). New York: Academic Press.

Wolf, D., Rygh, J., & Altshuler, J. (1984). Agency and experience: Actions and states in play narratives. In I. Bretherton (Ed.), *Symbolic play* (pp. 195–217). New York: Academic Press.

Zahn-Waxler, C., Radke-Yarrow, M., & King, R. (1979). Child-rearing and children's prosocial initiations toward victims of distress. *Child Development, 50*, 319–330.

Zaslow, M. (1978, March). *The infant's appraisal of behavioral components in the encounter with a stranger*. Paper presented at the International Conference on Infant Studies, Providence, RI.

7

Early forms of thought about thoughts: Some simple linguistic expressions of mental state

CAROL FLEISHER FELDMAN

What is needed for a theory of mind is the insight that the universe that may be taken as given consists not just of things but also of abstract or mental stipulations, abstract or mental objects of thought. For to have a theory of mind is to be able to think about such abstract stipulations as thoughts, as if they, like physical objects, could be taken as objects of thought.

Abstract objects are surely very difficult to learn about. In the world of things it is obvious that the mother, as the agent of the culture, can identify for the child's benefit what counts as object and background, what counts as another version of essentially the same object, what counts as another instance of essentially the same *kind* of object, what counts as an attribute of an object. The child's natural disposition to adopt a joint focus of attention is unique to our language-using species. It gives enormous effectiveness to the procedures of mothers who identify and describe objects for their children, procedures that Bruner (1983) has vividly illustrated in his book *Child's Talk*. But for mental objects, these particular procedures will not do. How, then, does the child acquire them?

Nelson Goodman (1984) says that we make our worlds, rather than find them, and that we make them largely with words:

Just as we make constellations by picking out certain stars rather than others, so we make stars by drawing certain boundaries rather than others. Nothing dictates whether the skies shall be marked off into constellations or other objects. We have to make what we find, be it the Great Dipper, Sirius, food, fuel or a stereo system. (p. 36).

Of more abstract "objects" – pain, dreams, God, square roots, beliefs – it is perhaps evident on the face of it that our conceptions of them cannot be mere copies of someone else's conception. Goodman's claim extends to "mere" concrete objects: Even they, or, to be more precise, our ideas of them, have to be made out of the raw materials we find in perception and in the culture. The culture is essential, for it provides earlier versions from which new ones can be constructed – through such processes as composition and decomposition, weighting and emphasis, imposing order and reordering. Goodman says that there is no raw aboriginal reality to make them from, but only earlier versions from which the new versions are made. Whether or not one accepts his metaphysical argument, it is plain that the "objects" we think about are mental representations that are symbolic rather than physical; that if symbolic, then not found but made; and if made, then made with language – "not with hands but with minds, or rather with languages or other symbol systems" (p. 42).

If Goodman is right that the universe has to be constructed by each individual – not, so to speak, from scratch, to be sure, for individuals in a culture are exposed to others' versions, versions embodied in the structure of language and in the ways in which it can be used – then we ought to be able to see signs of active efforts at world building in children. But when and how?

If worlds are made with words, the constructed or "construed" objects in those worlds will, when talked about, appear as topics of discourse. I don't propose here to try to untangle the difficult and interacting patterns of word building and world building; rather, I want to assume that in some complex way they amount to much the same thing – that if we want to know what objects a person has constructed, then we can look at the topics he has created, and if we want to know how the new world version was created from a previous one, then we can look at how a new topic was made and from what.

Making mental objects

From a Goodmanian point of view, the development of a theory of mind will hinge on the construction of mental objects that can be thought about. At first, the child does not have such abstract objects as mental states. I am going to assume that in the early years, mental states do not exist as *ding an sich*, but that they do have an existence of a kind as attitudes toward events in the child's world. They appear in speech not as things talked about, but rather as markers of how those things are construed. One way to describe this is to say that mental language appears exclusively in the form of markers of the young speaker's stance, or expressions of mental attitude.

As Olson and Astington (1986) have shown, between 2 and 3 years of age the child acquires a great variety of means for marking mental attitude or stance. They include the mental state verbs *hope, suppose, believe* and *doubt, think,* and *know,* and epistemic adverbs such as *maybe, actually, probably;* and the modal verbs *would, should, could, might,* and *may.*

If mental expressions first appear in the speech of young children as mental attitudes toward events and things outside them, and if children are eventually to be able to express mental attitudes about mental attitudes themselves, they will need a mechanism for reconstructing those mental attitudes as objects. For, if our child is to have a theory of mind, we want her or him to be able not just to express mental attitudes toward the things of the world but also to reflect on his or her own former mental attitudes. This is the particular construal given here to the problem of acquiring a theory of mind – acquiring a procedure for reflecting on one's own prior mental attitudes. One way children might do this, if they have mental attitudes but no mental entities as I have supposed, would be to ·move mental attitudes from an initial occurrence as comments about real-world events into a stipulative given where they themselves could be talked about. To do this, children could make use of a general recursion rule – that is, a procedure for standing back from a process (in this case a construal) in order to turn it into a product (a constructed mental object). If they could do this, they would be expressing a mental attitude about a mental attitude.

When the problem of acquiring a theory of mind is viewed this way, as a matter of reflecting on one's own former mental attitudes, a developmental program with two parts seems to be indicated. The first requirement would be to learn how to express mental attitudes; the second, to learn a mechanism for reflecting on prior processes, a general mechanism of recursion. These are, I conjecture, constituents of the acquisition of a theory of mind in the young child, because together they would make possible the construction of such abstract objects of thought as mental states from prior mental attitudes.

Recursion

The mechanism of taking the new as given is crucial both in adult cognition, where it makes reflection possible, and in adult discourse, where it permits the expression of thoughts about thoughts. I propose that this is accomplished by means of general procedures for taking the new and stipulating it as a given about which something new can be said. Recursion is a progressive procedure in which one "goes meta" on what was formerly new, and "pushes it down" into the given. This is the procedure of choice for creating abstract objects, for it makes use of the basic topic-comment organization of language to take whatever one can think about something as itself a thing that can be thought about.

The irreducible units of both language and cognition are two-term expressions. They are composed on the first hand of topics, of that which is known, taken for granted, or stipulated as given, and on the other hand, of comments, of the new, of that which can be predicated or thought of the given – that is, of patterns of construal of whatever is already before us. Topic and comment have been described by linguists, beginning with the linguists of the "Prague school" (Steiner, 1982), as the basic functional organization of the sentence or, more latterly, the utterance. At an intuitive level, the topic is what the speaker announces he will talk about, the comment is what he says about it. Or, the topic has the status of a stipulation, the comment is a specification or elaboration of what is stipulated. Or, in this sense of being stipulated or taken as given, the topic is "old" whereas the comment is "new."

Obviously, topic and comment bear some relationship to the structural sentence constituents subject and predicate. In many circumstances the structural and functional dichotomies are perfectly aligned: The subject is the topic and the predicate is the comment. But there is a large variety of circumstances in which that alignment can break down. So, let us stick with topic and comment, the functional units, accepting, for present purposes, both the ambiguity of their mappings to linguistic structure and the dependency of their correct identification on how a speaker's communicative intentions are construed in a context.

The process of recursion in which we reflect on a former pattern of construal is crucial in concept formation and is spontaneously produced by adults when they are exposed to new material. After sufficient exposure, they start reasoning about the pattern of construal itself.

Let me give an example from a data set that I have been collecting with David Kalmar. Our first subject was a psychology graduate student at Yale, and no aficionado of poetry. We presented him with a series of eight poems, with these instructions: "Pretend you are the editor of a poetry magazine. You can publish as many of these poems as you like, but you must pick some. What we want you to do with each poem is read it and describe it. Then tell us on what basis you have decided to include or exclude it." The description of the poems constitutes an initial stipulative given, the criteria of inclusion an initial comment on it.

As we went through the series of eight poems the first time, our subject gave increasingly interesting descriptions of the poems themselves, and as he did so, his criteria of inclusion grew in interesting ways. First, they grew more numerous. As to numerosity, from the first to the fourth poem he went from an initial list of four rules to a list of eight. Next, he organized the rules categorically, and finally, as our subject read the set through for a second time, he created a metarule about the rules themselves.

As to categorical structure, it developed in a small subset of the eight rules. This is what happened: On the third poem he introduced a partial categorical rule: no *story* poems without a *moral*. But this was, for him, a special case and it was on the fifth poem that he introduced his first real category – *descriptive* poems, with a criterion or rule of *parsimony*. On the sixth poem, he introduced the residual category – *narrative* poems, and a rule of *having insight*. He continued with this same pattern for nine more trials.

On the last trial, he reconsidered, and said: "Because I can't think of a way to discriminate descriptive from narrative [poems], I am going to do away with the distinction entirely. Parsimony and insight are each additively weighted criteria that apply to all poems." A new rule has appeared – a rule of weighting – to replace the rules of parsimony and insight. It applies to parsimony and insight, which are now being taken as given. The former given – categories called "descriptive" and "narrative" – has to be, and is, rejected in order to empty the level of the given and make room in this two-term system for the new given of parsimony and insight. We might say that the two former rules – parsimony and insight – have been *pushed down* from the new to the given. Or we might say that they have been *dumped* from the epistemic, where they were a way of thinking about the categories, into the ontic, where they are stipulative things in themselves that can now be thought about with a new epistemic procedure of "weighting."[1]

As it is in cognition, so it is in language. In interviews with adults, when we see conversation progress in a natural way, we find our subjects pushing down comments into topics. In the interview that follows, the first topic is graduate school. The first comments are *positive aspects* and *negative aspects*.

E: Like I told you before, I want you to tell me your thoughts concerning graduate school and graduate education.
S: Well – that's quite a complex question, and I was thinking how differently I can answer that question depending on what aspect I focus on. Immediately so many negative aspects flood to mind, but there must be some positive aspects that keep me here.

Now the subject pushes down positive aspects from comment to topic and comments on it with *a degree at the end* and *knowledge I can pursue*.

S: Well, right off the bat – I can think of two positive things about graduate school, what you get at the end of it and what you get during it. Along pragmatic lines, hopefully you will receive a degree at the end of graduate school that will allow you to pursue your career goals. Along more academic lines, while I'm in graduate school, there's a great potential of knowledge that I can pursue.

Next, the subject pushes down negative aspects and comments on it with *long process* and *obstacles*.

S: It's a long process and at each crossroad it seems as if you run into another obstacle or task to overcome...

So for both language and thought we find comments turning into topics that can be taken as given, a move from an epistemic function to an ontological one. Can this process be used to explain the development of a theory of mind?

Emmy at 2 to 3 years: From topicalization to recursion

I turn now to the speech of one child, Emmy, who was tape-recorded in her crib before sleep over a one-year period. The transcribed data consist of bedtime dialogues with parents, and monologues that begin after they leave the room.[2] In Emmy's speech one sees events that are plainly recursive mainly in the heavily scaffolded context of dialogue with a parent who frames and keeps clear the topic–comment structure of the utterances. Emmy learns a great deal about recursion from her second to her third year, for at 2 she does not do it but as she approaches 3 years, examples begin to appear in her dialogues. At 2, however, she is busily occupied in learning the topic–comment structure of utterances, and we may speculate that mastery of that pattern precedes mastery of the more difficult task of conversion of comments into topics that characterizes recursion.

To learn the topic–comment structure of the language is to learn how to produce comments appropriate to ongoing topics and how to introduce into discourse topics that the interlocutor will comment on. In her conversations with her parents, from just before 2 years of age, Emmy both produces appropriate comments and introduces topics. Her efforts at topic introduction are sometimes hotly contested, for to introduce a topic into discourse successfully is to control the discourse, to frame her parent's comments.

Both commenting and topic introduction may be conventional or creative in that they may introduce material that occurred earlier in the conversation (or in similar conversations), or they may be original. Because we do not have a complete record of all of Emmy's conversations, we cannot be sure whether a seemingly new topic is one that Emmy actually invented herself or whether it is borrowed from an earlier conversation we don't have on tape. All we can say with certainty is that some of her topics and comments are borrowed from earlier in the same conversation, while others are new to that particular conversation.

Here are some examples of comment production and topic introduction. The following dialogue is a good example of comment production. Emmy's father's topic is *crying*. He wants to talk about who does it. Emmy supplies *babies* at line 2 and *the one at house* at line 4. *Babies* is a borrowed comment. *The one at house* is original. This dialogue also contains an example of topic introduction at line 6, when Emmy asks *who cries*? This is plainly not an original topic. She was 1 year, 11 months and 14 days old.

(1) Fa: Claire, who's a little, bit of a baby, and Stephen, they cry. . . . *They* cry, but *big* kids, like Danny and Leif, and Carl and Emily, and Dick, they don't cry cause they're big kids . . .

(2) Em: Babies cry at Tanta's when baby.

(3) Fa: Yeah, the *big* kids don't.

(4) Em: The one at house don't cry.
(5) Fa: The babies cry, huh, but not the big kids.
(6) Em: Um, who cries at, who cries?
(7) Fa: Libby and Angie and Stephen.
(8) Em: And Lise.
(9) Fa: No Lise's a big kid. Claire, the little girl who was here tonight, she cries sometimes.
(10) Em: Oh, baby.

The next two examples are from about the same age. In them, Emmy introduces topics that are new to the conversation on the night when they occur. In the first example her topic is *alligators*.

(1) Mo: I asked Tanta today, honey, and Tanta said Carl goes to bed at seven-thirty just like Emily.
(2) Em: Alligators.
(3) Mo: *No* alligators. . . . You're just silly about that now.
(4) Em: Silly.
(5) Mo: Okay, sweetie. . . . Good night.

In the second example Emmy introduces a seemingly new topic (*Mommy*) and comment (*doing* at line (2)) and gets her father to produce comments of the kind she has specified.

(1) Fa: Well, you stand up, then I can't put a blanket on you, and then I'll just have to go out, hunh?
(2) Em: What Mommy doing?
(3) Fa: Mommy's going to get ready to go to bed, too.
(4) Em: Mommy in *bath*tub.
(5) Fa: Mommy's going to go in the bath, take a *bath* in the bathtub and then go to bed, too. That's *right*!
(6) Em: Mommy, mommy taking *bath*.
(7) Fa: Mommy's going to take a bath in the bathtub and then go to sleep.
(8) Em: I want – , I want, I w – *see* Mommy.

Emmy's presleep dialogues at this age offer many examples of both commenting and the offering of topics. Her father tends to offer standard topics familiar to her for her to comment on: who cries, what color is this, what kind of animal is this, what will we do tomorrow, and so on. Not only are the topics familiar, but there is a conventional set of acceptable comments that she is also learning. At times, she breaks out of his patterns by offering new comments or by offering topics herself. Sometimes these are his topics – for example, *she* asks *him* the colors. In these cases it seems that the novelty she is after is not a matter of content but rather a novelty of dialogic role. At other times, when she introduces new topics, she seems to be in search of novel matter as well.

The highly patterned nature of these dialogues is probably a result of their taking place at bedtime when her father is trying to calm her with familiarity and order into sleep. But it also has the effect of making the topic–comment patterns of the utterances very distinct. Topics are recurrent across bedtimes and they have a large number of known comments. In these patterns, the categories of topic and comment are made very distinct from each other, and it is always very clear what the topic is. This is the sense in which these bedtime dialogues seem to be a format for the acquisition of topic–comment structure.

It is one thing to acquire control of the topic–comment structure of dialogue and another to be able to transform or convert it. Control of the structure precedes conversion, perhaps because it is necessary to it. At 2 years, although Emmy successfully produces comments and introduces topics, there are no clear examples of comments being converted into topics. But as Emmy approaches 3, examples of comments being turned into topics begin to appear. They are still very uncommon. In the one that follows, from age 2-8-26, her mother starts it first and then Emmy follows. The relevant portion begins like this:

(1) Em: I got a *hug* for Mommy, too.
(2) Fa: A hug, too ... Big hug, huh?
(3) Em: [over Fa] And Mommy, too.
(4) Mo: Okay.
(5) Em: On my back.

So far, all of this has been about a *hug* that is the topic. The comments are *for Mommy, too* and *on my back*. Her mother now makes the last comment (*on my back*) the topic through recursion and comments on it ("Why do I only get to hug your back?"):

(6) Mo: Well, why does? and I only get to hug your back ... I love your back, and your [dress], and your nose, and every other part of you. Good night.

Emmy's response is also recursive, for she comments on her mother's entire prior utterance:

(7) Em: No, you're teasing.
(8) Mo: No, I'm not teasing, honey. I'm telling you true.

Now Emmy introduces a new topic (*Stephen*) and comment:

(9) Em: No, just ... [take] and I won't – , and Stephen come and sleep in there.

Again, her mother produces a recursive response, a comment on the prior proposition (Stephen sleeps in here):

(10) Mo: Yeah, that would be ridiculous.

In the example above, it seems that her mother has pointed out the way to do recursions. In the next example, from two weeks later at age 2-9-12, it seems that Emmy is creating recursions on her own.

Em: Where's Nick and Claire?
Fa: Well, they're ... they're back in their home in Boston.

This has begun with Emmy introducing Nick and Claire as the topic and their whereabouts as the comment. Her father responds with the requested detail (*Boston*) in his comment. But now Emmy is recursive. She assumes that they are in Boston, and wants to know *about* that, is it where they live? *Live* is her new comment, Boston her new topic.

Em: They live in Boston?
Fa: Yeah.
Mo: Mm, hmm.

And now she does another recursion, this one is on their living there. Given that they live there, do her parents visit them?:

Em: But ... but do *you* go in Boston, sometimes?
Fa: Sometimes, yeah.
Em: And visit Nick?
Fa: Well, we haven't for a while. We did a little bit.

From recursion to thoughts about thoughts

We would like to see Emmy show a recursion on a comment that expresses a mental attitude, for that would constitute a reflection on a reflection, and that is what we're after. But Emmy has not produced an example of just this kind when we stop following her at age 3.

The problem is twofold. First, she is just beginning to acquire procedures of recursion, and there are very few cases of them. Second, the dialogues have very little mental state talk in them altogether, even mental states as comments. Hence, whatever recursions take place are not likely to find mental state comments to be recursive about. This is a rather surprising state of affairs, for we know that children of this age do have some mental state talk in their dialogues. For example, Dunn and Kendrick (1982) report children's talk about *others'* mental states, specifically those of younger siblings. Moreover, on other grounds, we know that Emmy is able to put mental states into the comment position of her talk.

I have mentioned that Emmy was also tape-recorded in monologue. In these soliloquies there is a good deal of talk about what she knows and doesn't know, what she thinks and supposes (Feldman, 1987). Let me give one typical example from 2 yrs, 4 days:

1 The bed falling down. *Actually*, the bed broken. Hunh. *That's funny*.
   ...
2 Maybe the baby and the Mommy buy different crib. Maybe do that 'cause the other one broken.
3 What be the tree fell down. Could be. I don't know which. Maybe

tree fell down and broke that crib. I don't know what thing fell down.

But mental state comments occur very infrequently in her bedtime dialogues. This may be precisely because they are *bedtime* dialogues, or it may have more generally to do with the constraints imposed by dialogic patterns. Or it may be because mental state comments are musings that have their proper place in the private talk of soliloquy even in children of this age. For it is evident in adults that the natural setting for musings is talk to the self, as in Hamlet's famous soliloquy and in diary writing. There may be something about the narrative patterns found in soliloquy, perhaps the fact that they always tell a story from some perspective, that invites or facilitates the inclusion of such other perspectival information as mental attitudes.

This suggests that there are two possible routes to expressing thoughts about thoughts. The first route would be through dialogue and would require insertions of mental comments into dialogue. One way this could happen would be for the child to bring into her dialogues the storylike patterns of soliloquy, with their extensive marking of perspective. There are hints in the Emmy transcripts that she is beginning to do this. At just the age we leave Emmy here (2-9-15), she brings one of her stories into a dialogue with her mother for the first time: She begins, "You know what the bear do today?" Her mother asks, "What?" and Emmy says: "He paint." A story unfolds. The narrative markers in this story, told in dialogue, are very minimal when compared with her productions when she is alone; but what we may be seeing here is a beginning. Has she begun to import the rich mental life she has in monologue into dialogic structure that will give her the rules for how to be recursive about it?

The other route would be through monologue: Thought about thought could be achieved if the recursive patterns developed in dialogue were imported into the musings of monologue. In Emmy's monologues, we see hints that she may be on the verge of doing this, too: At times she seems to "go meta" on some process. The best example is when she goes meta on story making itself and gives a rule for how to make stories. This is from age 2-9-1.

So they can be anything they wanna be ... bisons ... or anything. Bunny rabbits. Bunny rabbits they could be, or anything. They could – but there's no bunny rabbit.

Conclusion

I have discussed two acquisitions that, once put together, would seem to be sufficient for the acquisition of a theory of mind in the sense of reflections on one's own prior reflections. They are stance marking as a way of expressing mental attitudes and the conversion of comments to topics as a mechanism of recursion. Each – stance marking and recursion – seems to be tied to a patterned framework of language use that facilitates its acquisition at the developmental start. The narrative patterns found in monologue seem to invite the expression of mental attitudes, while the careful patterning of topic and comment found in highly ritualized bedtime dialogues seems to invite the mastery of topicalization procedures required for the later recursive ability to turn a comment into a topic. This 3-year-old child seems to have a variety of patterns of language use, and the different patterns appear to invite the discovery of different aspects of language function as well as different cognitive procedures. The cognitive procedures of giving a perspectival frame and of recursion both look like good candidates for world making. But to make a world of mental objects out of prior mental processes, they would have to be put together somehow.

There may be other ways to construct the abstract mental objects that we began this discussion with than by pushing them down recursively from comments into topics. Perhaps we make them out of the versions of others – for example, versions we read in literature. And perhaps this is as far as some of us get: that we have a way of talking about mind, ours as well as others', but that we cannot go a step farther and reflect on it. It could be that this recursive step is not a universal acquisition and requires special linguistic contexts to invite it to develop, just as the simpler steps did, but that in this case, the special language context is far from universal. Perhaps the dialogue of psychoanalysis is one scaffolding form of language use that invites reflection on reflection; perhaps certain kinds of academic talk or writing are another.

I leave Emmy in particular, however, with the strong feeling that at least her particular contexts of language use, along with her particular habits of mind, will lead her to reflect on reflections before too long, and that she may do it by putting the two systems of stance marking and recursion together. Whether her reflections on reflections should properly be considered a *theory* of mind before they acquire more systemlike organization is another matter. True theories, as organized systems, will have to await other, much later, developments.

NOTES

1 I discuss this model in more detail in Feldman (1987).
2 This data set was collected by Katherine Nelson and was collectively analyzed for different aspects by a group of us consisting of Katherine Nelson, Jerome Bruner, John Dore, Julie Gerheart, Joan Lucariello, Dan Stern, and Rita Watson. These analyses are to appear in a volume edited by Katherine Nelson called *Narratives from the crib*.

REFERENCES

Bruner, J. (1983). *Child's talk*. New York: Norton.

Dunn, J., & Kendrick, C. (1982). *Siblings*. Cambridge, MA: Harvard University Press.

Feldman, C. (in press). Problem solving monologues. In K. Nelson (Ed.), *Narratives from the crib*. Cambridge, MA: Harvard University Press.

Feldman, C. (1987). Thought from language: The linguistic construction of cognitive representations. In J. Bruner & H. Weinreich-Haste (Eds.), *Making sense*. London: Methuen.

Goodman, N. (1984). *Of mind and other matters*. Cambridge; MA: Harvard University Press.

Olson, D. & Astington, J. (1986). Children's acquisition of metalinguistic and metacognitive verbs. In W. Demopoulos & A. Marras (Eds.), *Language learning and concept acquisition*. Norwood, NJ: Ablex.

Steiner, P. (Ed.) (1982). *The Prague school:Selected writings, 1929-1946*. Austin: University of Texas Press.

PART II

Coordinating representational states
with the world:
Understanding the relationships
among perception, knowledge, and
reality

8

Developing semantics for theories of mind: From propositional attitudes to mental representation

JOSEF PERNER

This chapter describes children's acquisition of a "theory of mind" in terms of their growing ability to understand the *semantics* of mental states. *Semantics*, a term commonly used in linguistics, denotes the relationship between linguistic expressions and their meaning in the world. In treating the mind as a symbolic, representational domain (Fodor, 1975) similar semantic problems arise as in linguistics. By borrowing some concepts from linguistic semantics I hope to gain some useful tools for our investigation into children's understanding of the representational relationship between mental states and the world.

Under the heading of *semantics and models* I start with Brentano's (1924) thesis leading into the idea that mental states are representational states and use the semantic concept of a *model* to explicate what it means to be a representational state. This exposition of models is then used to characterize children's intellectual progress in terms of *three levels of semantic awareness*. They proceed from the level of (1) *presentation*, where the child merely *has a mental model* of the perceived reality, to the level of (2) *re-presentation*, where they can construct and *use mental models* to think about hypothetical situations. The final level of (3) *meta-representation*, is reached when the child becomes capable of not just using but *modeling mental models*.

To give this theoretical exposition a concrete focus I use my analysis to explain why children find it easier to understand pretense than false belief. This developmental fact posed a problem for our (Wimmer & Perner, 1983) original theoretical outlook, and the problem is discussed by several other contributors to this volume. To demonstrate children's gain in theoretical power by the postulated increase in semantic awareness I have to consider the relationship between *mental states and behavior*, which makes clear that proper understanding of belief must include its relationship with intention. This relationship is discussed in three subsections: *intention and reality, intention and counterfactuals*, and, finally, *intention and belief as models*. In this section the critical difference between belief and pretense is analyzed. The conclusion is that pretense can be adequately understood by associating oneself or another person with a particular alternative situation, while understanding false belief requires the meta-representational skill of modeling the representational relationship between a model and the world. I end the chapter with a *comparison to other work* in this volume, which focuses on *opacity and meta-representation* and on the relation between *perception and knowledge*.

Semantics and models

Franz von Brentano (1924) stipulated that the mark of the mental is its intentionality. According to this view mental processes are internal processes that *aim* at external objects or events in the world (their intentional content). This point of view seems clearly supported by our language about the mind. In contrast to nonintentional internal states, for example, "Mary is *hungry*," our descriptions of mental states make reference to external situations, as in "Mary *believes* that *the ice-cream van is in the park*." This statement describes Mary's mental state of believing by reference to the external situation of the ice-cream van's being in the park.

This example was inspired by a situation used in one of our experiments (Perner & Wimmer, 1985), which I will adopt with some changes as a worked example for the present theoretical exposition. One way Mary develops the belief that the ice-cream van (ICV) is in the park (PK), could be that John has misinformed her, telling her it is in the park when in fact it is at the church (CH). Figure 8.1 captures the moment in the story when Mary is sitting at home over her lunch and thinking of the ice-cream van's location.

In cognitive science it is common to capture the intentionality of Mary's mental state by assigning a representational structure to her mind. I have chosen a simple version of a semantic net for Figure 8.1. To make precise in which way that structure is representational, I like to think about it as a *model* of the external situation. To get an immediate intuitive understanding of what a model is, one may think of the sandbox in army headquarters with miniature tanks and soldiers, which the generals use as a model of the real battlefield with its real tanks and soldiers. Because I do not want to stretch this analogy to suggest that miniature soldiers are marching in our minds, a slightly more abstract notion of a model, as in model-theoretic semantics (Dowty, Wall, & Peters, 1981), needs to be considered.

To get the necessary conceptual grip on the world, it has to be decomposed into elements, which are objects – park (PK), church (CH), and ice-cream van (ICV) – and various predicates, such as the spatial relations 'left of' – (LEFT) and 'being at' (AT), which are the only

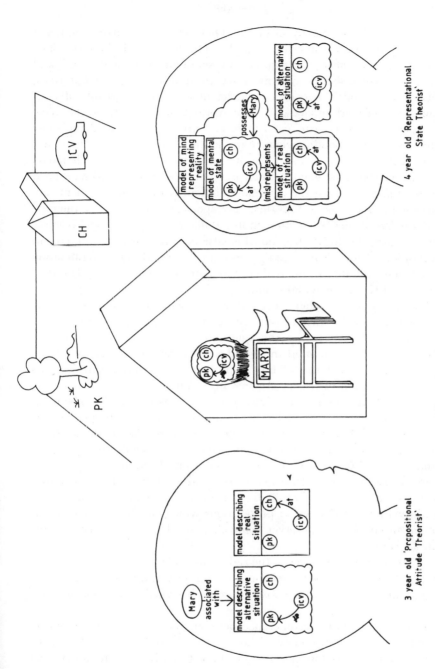

Figure 8.1. Two children concerned about Mary's belief about the ice-cream van's location. The younger child on the left-hand side conceives of her mistaken belief by associating Mary with a counterfactual situation, while the older child conceives of her belief as a mental representation of the actual situation.

ones explicitly used in my example. These elements can be combined according to certain rules, for example, 'The ICV is AT the CH'.[1] The model in Mary's head also consists of a set of elements: nodes "O" and arcs "→", which can be combined according to certain syntactic rules. This mental model[2] becomes a model of the external reality if each element is assigned an element in the world as its *interpretation*. To make this correspondence clear, each node and arc is labeled with the same letters as its corresponding element in the world, for example: "(icv)" has 'ICV' and "—at→" has 'AT' as its interpretation. Once each model element has been assigned its interpretation, the model in Mary's head can be *evaluated* against the external situation. If the model elements are combined in the same way as their corresponding real elements, then the model is *true*; if they are combined in a different way, the model is *false*.[3] Unfortunately for Mary, her model is false because one of its component propositions "(icv) —at→ (pk)" does not correspond to the combination of real elements, that is, the real elements are not combined as 'The ICV is AT the PK' in the actual situation.

Not every philosopher of mind agrees with Brentano about the intentionality of the mental, but even if one goes along with Brentano's thesis, there still remains the question of how the relationship of intentionality between mind and world is best construed. Figure 8.1 shows two possibilities in terms of how two observers construe Mary's belief about the location of the ice-cream van in different ways.

The left-hand observer in Figure 8.1 entertains two models about the external situation. The model closer to the eyes is a true model describing the external situation as it is. The other model is false. It describes an alternative, counterfactual situation, which corresponds to what John wrongly told Mary about the ice-cream van's location. The observer expresses Mary's mistaken belief by associating Mary with that counterfactual situation. One could say the belief is conceptualized as an attitude of Mary's toward that set of propositions which constitute the counterfactual situation. The observer could therefore be dubbed a *propositional attitude theorist*.[4]

In contrast, the observer in the right-hand side of Figure 8.1 construes Mary's belief as Mary possessing a (mis)representation or false model of the real situation, and the observer could be called a *representational state theorist*.[5]

I will argue that the difference between these two observers corresponds to the difference between how a typical child before and after the age of about 4 years conceptualizes mental states. In order to understand the nature and consequences of this proposed developmental transition, it is advisable to describe first the very young infant's representational abilities.

Three levels of semantic awareness

1. Presentation: Having a mental model

Even the very young infant knows something about the surrounding world. This knowledge may be encoded as a mental model of the world. If the infant looks at the scene in Figure 8.1, he or she may build a mental model of one object (the ice-cream van) being next to another object (the church), and so on. However, this model is entirely determined by the perceptual input. Although we, as external observers, may consider this mental structure a model of the external world and hence call it a representation ("primary representation": Leslie, Chapter 2) or an expression in a language of thought (Fodor, 1975), it is not much of a model for the child because he or she has no notion at all that or how it is related to reality. That the model does relate to reality is entirely due to the causal makeup of the child's perceptual apparatus (Fodor, 1987). The child has no command over the structure of this model. It is reality that presents itself to the child in the model, which *constitutes* but does not represent reality for the child. For this reason Piaget (Furth, 1969) prefers to talk about "knowledge" rather than "mental representation," and other people prefer "presentation" to separate this level of mental activity from "*re*-presentation."[6] I will refer to this causally determined mental structure as "knowledge base."

Notice that direct causal determination (Fodor, 1987) of the knowledge base is viable only if the knowledge base is linked to the usually highly reliable perceptual input (Gibson, 1979), but would be disastrous if it were linked in that way to symbolic input, like language. Because linguistic statements can be unreliable (mistakes, lies) and are subject to frequent errors of interpretation, the child's knowledge base would become alarmingly unstable.

If children are equipped with only a knowledge base, a major limitation is that they cannot build a model of reality they can manipulate to think about and explore the hypothetical and counterfactual. The only model children have is a straight reflection of reality.

2. Re-presentation: Using mental models

After the first year of life things begin to change. The infant begins to appreciate symbolic information (language and pictures), starts to pretend (Piaget, 1945/1951), develops an understanding of alternative hiding locations (Piaget, 1936/1953; Gopnik & Meltzoff, 1984; Somerville & Wellman, in press; Forguson & Gopnik, Chapter 12). There are clear indications that the infant's mind begins to transcend the constraints of reality and branch into the hypothetical and counterfactual. As Leslie (1987; Chapter 2) has argued, if this is to be possible without utter confusion about reality an adequate mechanism of mental representation has to be available. My suggestion is that this mechanism consists in manipulable models. The infant transports the mental elements of his knowledge base into another model where he can rearrange these elements in different ways. Figure 8.2 gives a graphic illustration of these possibilities.

Like the younger infant the child in Figure 8.2 looks at the scene with the ice-cream van, park, and church, and sees that the ice-cream van is at the church. This reliable perceptual information is encoded in the square box of the child's knowledge base. Unlike the young infant, however, this child can also create new models (shown inside the cloud-shaped frames) by copying elements from the knowledge base and rearranging them. Figure 8.2 shows two such models. One (right-hand cloud) remains a faithful copy of the knowledge base, but in the other (left-hand cloud) the elements are combined in a different way, therefore describing a different situation than the external situation reflected in the knowledge base.

Figure 8.2 also illustrates an important use of such a model. A model can be used to interpret incoming linguistic information, providing a buffer between that kind of unreliable information and the knowledge base. The model created on the basis of linguistic information can be evaluated against the knowledge base and if it does not correspond to the knowledge base, it is rejected as false. Research in progress by Wimmer indicates that children may be able to do this almost as soon as they become able to name things. This is interesting because having a model as a buffer is crucial to safeguard the knowledge base from containing too much inconsistent information. The model enables the child to check that the linguistic information is compatible with the known facts before using any new information contained in the message to update the knowledge base.[7]

This use of a mental model for evaluating information demonstrates that the model can clearly be *used as a model*. When evaluating the linguistic information the child has to compare the model to the external situation. Obviously this comparison cannot be carried out on the real situation directly but only on its mental representative, that is, the knowledge base. This comparison process is indicated in Figure 8.2 by the double-lined arrows labeled "semantic procedures," which link the models with the knowledge base. The term *semantic procedure* comprises those actions necessary (.1) to realize when the model is meant to *refer* to the external situation (when the model is not intended to refer to any situation the question of truth does not arise); (2) to realize which elements in the model correspond to which elements in the external

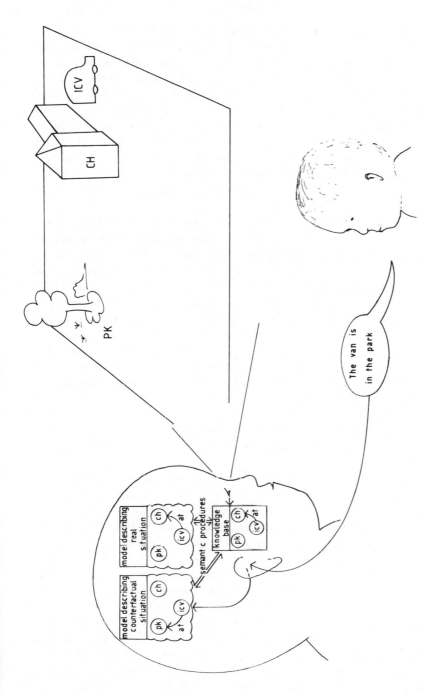

Figure 8.2. Illustration of the use of mental models. Perceptual contact with a scene creates a mental model (knowledge base), which presents perceived reality to the mind. Through the application of semantic procedures alternative models can be created and used to interpret linguistic information about the perceived situation or to think about alternative situations.

situation, that is, in the knowledge base (*interpretation*); and (3) to determine the truth of the model by checking whether the structure of the model corresponds to the structure of the external situation (*evaluation*).

It is also the ability to *use* counterfactual models that accounts for the emergence of pretend play and for the understanding of other people's pretend activity. Dunn and Dale (1984) give an impressive example of 2-year-old Richard joining into a railway pretend scene initiated by his older sister. When she formed a tunnel of cushions, Richard happily pushed a tractor into it pretending the tractor was a train. When the train got stuck, Richard proclaimed that its engine had broken down. On his sister's suggestion Richard then pretended to fill up the train with gasoline by imitating the sound of filling.

From this protocol it seems clear that 2-year-old Richard was able to entertain a model describing the pretend situation, relate action instructions to that model, determine which objects are referred to and then relate back to the real objects in the external situation. When his sister asked him to put gasoline into the *train* he understood immediately that "train" was a descriptor used for an object in the pretend model, the counterpart of which in the external situation is described as a tractor. Similarly, the reference to 'gasoline' is understood as an instruction to create an entity with that property in the pretend model, for which there is no corresponding entity in the external situation. This analysis of Richard's reasoning in response to his sister's instructions demonstrates nicely his ability to interpret her instructions within the pretend model, and his ability to *treat* that model as a model of the external situation, that is, he has the necessary semantic procedures to find the elements in the external situation that correspond to the referenced elements in the pretend model.

In view of this sophisticated *use* of mental models one has to carefully analyze what these models *denote*. It is tempting, as I will argue later that Leslie (Chapter 2) does, to consider these models as *meta-representations*. This is an important issue, since my claim is that at this developmental level children can use models only to represent situations, but not to meta-represent, that is, represent other models and how they represent situations. The implications of this claim are illustrated in an example used in a discussion with Heinz Wimmer about these matters. Let us assume the child observer in Figure 8.2 who is told that the ice-cream van is in the park, answers: "That's wrong." It is very compelling to admit that the word *That* in this reply refers to a representation, namely, the sentence "The van is in the park" and the word *wrong* points out that this representation does not match reality. So, apparently 2- and 3-year-old children, who are able to make such a comment, have meta-representational awareness of a sentence (mis)representing a situation.

However, the same comment, "That's wrong," can be made in a situation where no representational relationship is at stake. For instance, when a friend tries to put her left shoe on her right foot, a 2- or 3-year-old may correct her by saying: "That's wrong." Obviously, in this case the trying on of the shoe on the wrong foot is not a representation of putting it onto the right foot. Consequently, the *That* is not used meta-representationally to refer to a representation, but is used rather to refer to a particular situation and the *wrong* comments on the mismatch between this situation and the usual situation where the shoe is put on the right foot.

My claim is that young children treat the case of a false statement in the same way as the case of the shoe on the wrong foot. They do not comment on the mismatch between a representation (sentence) and the represented situation, but on the mismatch between two situations: the situation described by the false sentence and the actually perceived situation.[8]

This example illustrated an important distinction between the use of two models to describe two situations, which allows the young child to talk about a comparison of these two situations, and the meta-representational use of two models, where one is used to refer to a situation and the other, to refer to a model representing that situation. With this distinction it should be clearer what was meant by saying that the young child in Figure 8.1 interprets mental expressions like "think" as a relation between a person and a described situation (propositional attitude). According to this view, talk about a person's 'thinking' and 'pretense' are understood in essentially the same way, namely as an instruction to interpret and predict that person's actions within a particular hypothetical world.

As the work by Wellman and his collaborators (Chapter 4) has shown, children's understanding of alternative models has become quite sophisticated by the age of 3 years. They understand that thoughts and images are not tangible but allow you to do things impossible in the real world. I maintain that this sophistication is possible because of a sophistication in constructing alternative models, interpreting and evaluating these models against the real situation, and associating people selectively with the situations described by these models.

Again, in view of such sophistication with even mental terminology at such a young age, one has to remind oneself of the limitations at this developmental level. As we have seen, the ability to construct models of the real situation gave the young infant the freedom to think about alternatives to reality. Without the active construction and manipulation of models the child would have stayed tied to reality. The same consideration about flexibility can be brought to bear on the semantic procedures (Figure 8.2) that link models with the knowledge base. These procedures are just used but not yet modeled. Their use establishes the representational nature of models. Without the semantic link these models would not be models but uninterpreted physiological states.

The child's limitations arise from the fact that at this level the semantic procedure, albeit used for modeling, is not yet modeled itself. The resulting rigidity can be illustrated when a semantic procedure is used to evaluate a particular model. The evaluation process compares the model to the knowledge base and yields a standard result: "true" in the case of a match and "false" in the case of mismatch. No alternative result can be contemplated. As we have argued (Perner, Leekam, & Wimmer, 1987), assignment of standard truth values to models is sufficient for understanding the counterfactual nature of pretense (pretense is not for real, and no confusion about that fact has to be considered). In contrast, for understanding false belief assignment of standard truth value is not sufficient, since a false belief is characterized not only by its being *false* but also by the holder of the belief deeming it *true*. To gain the necessary flexibility to contemplate that somebody else may attach a different truth value to a model (evaluate it differently) than the value it objectively deserves, requires that alternatives to the standard truth-value assignment must be considered. This flexibility is achieved by constructing a model of the semantic procedure (with principal elements: 'model,' 'semantic procedure,' and 'real situation') and by rearranging its elements. This meta-representational achievement constitutes the next level of semantic awareness.

3. Meta-representation: Modeling mental models

At this level the child acquires the meta-representational ability to model the semantic relationship between a model and what it models. The origin of this ability may lie in a process of making knowledge explicit which exists only implicitly in the use of existing procedures (Karmiloff-Smith, 1986). By reflecting on the semantic procedures which they have used already at the previous level for interpreting representations, children form an explicit concept of these procedures by modeling their use.

Although my claim is that mental states are not seen as representational states before about the age of 4 years, in the case of external means of representation children may develop an explicit theory of representation as early as 3 years of age. This possibility is indicated in a study by DeLoache (in press). In her study children had to find an object which was hidden under some furniture in a room. They were shown in a three-dimensional model of the room where a model of the object was hidden. Children younger than 3 years seemed incapable of taking advantage of this information. In contrast, children 3 years and older had no problem with the task, which suggests that they had the concept that the model room represented the real room, that is, that a one-to-one relationship between elements in the model and elements in the real room can be established, and that this correspondence between elements can be used so that information about the model object's location in the model room can give information about the real object's location in the real room.

It is important to point out that the younger children had no problem extracting knowledge about the object's location from a picture of the room. This is not all that surprising because even very young children have learned to extract information from symbolic media. If children had been told where to look in the real room, they surely would have been able to follow these linguistic instructions as well as use a picture of the room. Pictures and language differ from the three-dimensional model used by DeLoache in that children had long experience in how to interpret pictures and words, whereas the use of the model as a representational medium is new. Children cannot rely on learned strategies for using a familiar medium. To see the relevance of the model immediately, they need an abstract concept of representation. As Dennett (1978) has emphasized for the case of deception, it is this flexibility in application that characterizes the possession of an abstract concept as opposed to competence through training. For this reason I interpret the ease with which 3-year-olds are able to adopt a new means of representation as evidence that they possess an explicit concept of representation.

Although children may develop an explicit theory of representation at the age of 3 years, it is not until about 4 years that they use their concept of representation in their theory of mind. A similar delay between developing a concept and applying it to the mind may occur at the previous developmental level, where after 1 year children can talk about and pretend to be in alternative situations but do not start talking about the mind until after 2 years (Bretherton, McNew, & Beeghly-Smith, 1981; Shatz, Wellman, & Silber, 1983).

By conceptualizing the mind as a representational medium the child gains a theoretical understanding of how the mind relates to the external world, in particular of the role of mental states in acquiring information and in guiding behavior. For full understanding of knowledge acquisition the child needs meta-representational abilities. For he has to understand how contact with the world (a certain situation) sets the mental model (internal representation) into a corresponding state (same structural combination of elements). Conceptual understanding of this process means the child has to model the process of informational contact. He has to build a model of the external situation and another, meta-representational model of the mental state, which is itself a model of the external situation. Note that it would not do to interpret the mental state of knowledge as a description of another situation beside the external situation, since the point of a state of knowledge is that it *represents* the external situation. I will return to the topic of knowledge acquisition when discussing the relation between my approach and that of Wimmer, Hogrefe, and Sodian (Chapter 9).

My emphasis for this chapter is on the role of mental states in guiding behavior. Pretense and false belief are particularly interesting in this respect because they involve aberrant or strange behavior. At the level of propositional attitudes the child can make sense of these behaviors by seeing people as acting in aberrant or strange situations, that is, pretense consists in acting as if the actual situation were a different situation. This level of understanding, however, leads to a paradox in the case of false belief: Why should people act inappropriately in the real situation even though they decidedly want to act in a for-that-situation appropriate way. This paradox can be resolved by understanding that people act not according to situations (as assumed at the previous level) but according to mental representations of situations. By understanding mental states as representations they can be understood as "stand-ins" for reality, and the occurrence of strange and inappropriate behavior can be explained by the meta-representational insight that the semantic relationship between reality and stand-in goes awry.

I want to discuss this point in some detail for concrete experimental problems. For this I need to digress and explain how mental states and behavior are related.

Mental states and behavior

In their explication of what it means to have a theory of mind, Premack and Woodruff (1978, p. 515) suggest the following:

In saying that an individual has a theory of mind, we mean that the individual imputes mental states to himself and to others . . . . A system of inferences of this kind is properly viewed as a theory, first, because such states are not directly observable, and second, because the system can be used to make predictions, specifically, about the behavior of other organisms . . . . Purpose or intention is the state we impute most widely.

The link between mental states and behavior has long ago been emphasized by Aristotle in his "Practical Syllogism." Such a "syllogism" can be loosely formulated for our ice-cream story:

Mary wants to go to the ice-cream van (intention premise)
Mary knows the van is at the church (epistemic premise)
Therefore:
Mary will go to the church (behavioral conclusion)

In principle both premises are equally necessary for drawing the behavioral inference. Neither premise alone would lead to a definite prediction. Knowing just Mary's intention but not knowing whether she knows where the van is stationed does not allow an inference, since Mary might believe the van is in the park and go there. Similarly, merely knowing that Mary knows where the van is does not warrant the inference either, because she might not want ice cream but want to go play in the park. These considerations suggest that both premises are *logically* of *equal* importance for predicting behavior.

For practical everyday use, however, there exists a marked asymmetry. Knowing Mary's intention gives one a good idea of what she will do, whereas just knowing what she knows helps little. Consider the following two scenarios.

  1 After lunch Mary proclaims that she intends to go to the ice-cream van and leaves the house.

When asked where Mary has gone, I would feel quite justified in answering that she had gone to the church. Of course, I might be wrong, but it is a reasonable bet that will be right in most cases. The reason why I can justify such a guess in the absence of any explicit knowledge about Mary's epistemic state is that knowledge about the relevant aspects of our surroundings is *usually* shared. On those grounds I can infer where she has gone on the basis of her stated intention and *my own knowledge* about the ice-cream van's location. In other words, under normal circumstances the epistemic premise ("Mary knows the van is at the church") can be replaced by a factual premise ("The ice-cream van is at the church").

In contrast, the intention premise cannot be easily replaced. Consider the second scenario:

  2 Mary comes home from the church and tells me that the ice-cream van is stationed there and that a circus is in town, and so on. After lunch Mary gets up and leaves the house without stating any intention.

In this case I feel unable to predict where Mary might have gone, even though I know that she knows where the ice-cream van is. This knowledge is useless unless I also know about Mary's desire for ice cream.

The reason for this asymmetry is that knowledge tends to be shared whereas intentions are not but are highly correlated with the different actions people engage in, for example, Mary wants ice cream, I want to play football, Mother wants to watch the news and Father wants to do the dishes, but we all know where the football field is, where the television set is, and so on.

Because it is essential for a "theory of mind" to understand the link between mental states and behavior, and because beliefs have no predictive value in themselves but only in connection with intentions, we have to analyze further children's ability to reason about intention and belief.

Intention and reality

Before analyzing how an observer can use belief and intention to predict behavior, I will look first at how the child herself might plan her own behavior, for example, how a child like Mary in Figure 8.1 figures out where to go when she intends to go to the ice-cream van. There would be less of a problem for the child if she intended to go to the park, because she could draw on her well-established expertise of going from the home to the park: out the door, right, down the alley, and so on. However, the child's destination is the ice-cream van, which is not a fixed location but a mobile object, and so the child cannot have a ready planned route. In order to find a route she has to do some reasoning, which consists in consulting her knowledge base to find the location where the ice-cream van is stationed. The relevant parts of the child's mind at this point can be given as:

> *Goal specification*:   "(icv)—at→(?)"
> *Knowledge base*:   "(icv)—at→(ch)"

The problem for the child is to find a match for the incomplete expression "(icv)—at→(?)" of the goal specification in the knowledge base. There the obvious match is: "(icv)—at→(ch)," and so the child can specify her desired location more adequately as the permanent location "church." This solves the child's little problem because there is a known way of getting to the church from home.

Children are probably able to carry out such reasoning at a very early age. Parental reports show that even at 1 year infants seem able to search for objects in known locations (Ashmead & Perlmutter, 1980; Huttenlocher, 1974). I do not know of any direct investigation into infants' understanding of other people's goals. Some evidence from Kagan (1981) suggests that around 20 months children become acutely aware of an adult's expectation of what they should be able to achieve that does not match what they themselves think they will achieve. This competence can be accommodated in my proposal because children at that age can construct multiple models that designate alternative situations. Goals are models that specify a desired situation, and reasoning consists in finding a way of transforming the present situation into the desired situation.

For analyzing children's understanding of pretense and false belief, the use of the knowledge base for planning actions is not sufficient. We have to go one step more complicated and consider reasoning with hypothetical, counterfactual situations.

Intention and counterfactuals

I want to discuss three cases: a typical pretend scenario; an adaptation of the not-own version of Wellman's (Chapter 4) belief–desire task; and a typical false belief task (Wimmer & Perner, 1983). The three cases will all be phrased as variants of the by now familiar situation of Mary and the ice-cream van. These cases, however, differ in terms of how difficult it is to find a match for Mary's goal specification. I will try to demonstrate that a correct answer to where Mary will go in search of the ice-cream van can be found on the basis of alternative situations for the first two scenarios, but not for the false belief story. An insightful solution to the false belief problem can be found only if the belief is conceptualized as a representation of the world, that is, by explicitly modeling the semantic relationship between belief and world.

> *Pretend scenario*: There is *no real* ice-cream van. Mary loves to pretend going shopping for ice cream. She pretends that there is an ice-cream van in the park. She leaves the house to go to the ice-cream van. Where is she going?

Three models have to be considered for this scenario. As in every other of the three scenarios there is one model with Mary's goal specification, and there is the subject's knowledge base, which in this case does not show any ice-cream van. The third model is necessary to capture Mary's pretense, showing an ice-cream van in the park. The relevant propositions in each model can be summarized as follows:

> *Goal specification*:   "(icv)—at→(?)"
> *Knowledge base*:   "(pk)—left→(ch)"
> *Mary's pretense*:   "(icv)—at→(pk)"

The problem for Mary is to fill in the "?" in her goal specification so that she knows where to go, by matching it to some model of the current situation. Since the subject's task is to predict where Mary will *actually* go, the most natural solution would be to match Mary's goal specification to the knowledge base, or reality itself. However, the knowledge base does not show any ice-cream van and the child will realize that a match has to be sought in some other model of the external situation. Because Mary is engaged in pretend play the obvious best choice is then the model that describes Mary's pretense. In that model the subject will find a satisfactory match for Mary's goal specification leading to the correct answer "Park."

Such reasoning with counterfactual models is acquired rather early. Piaget (1945/1951) reports an incidence at about 1 year, and Dunn and

Dale (1984) provide impressive protocols of elaborate pretend sequences at the age of 2 years.

As our next example let us consider a *belief* scenario, which is an adaptation of the not-own version of Wellman's (Chapter 4) belief–desire task.

> *Belief scenario*: There is a real ice-cream van, but we don't know where it is. The subject makes a guess that it is at the church but is told that Mary thinks it is in the park. Mary leaves the house to go to the ice-cream van. Where is she going?

For this scenario four models with the following relevant propositions have to be considered:

Goal specification:	"(icv)—at→(?)"
Knowledge base:	"(icv)"
Mary's belief:	"(icv)—at→(pk)"
Subject's guess:	"(icv)—at→(ch)"

Here, too, children's task is to predict where Mary will go in the actual world and so the most obvious search for Mary's destination would be the knowledge base, which reflects the external situation. However, in the knowledge base there is no record about the ice-cream van's location and no satisfactory match for Mary's goal specification is available. The next best strategy is to consult Mary's belief. In any case, it is a far better strategy than to look in somebody else's model (e.g., subject's own guess). The situation described by Mary's belief does provide a satisfactory match yielding the correct answer "Park." Wellman (Chapter 4, Fig. 4.5) found that 3- and 4-year-olds had no difficulty arriving at this solution, which attests again that at this age and probably much earlier children are very proficient in reasoning within hypothetical situations. Wellman's result contrasts quite sharply with 3-year-olds' difficulty in *false belief* tasks (Wimmer & Perner, 1983; Perner et al., 1987).

> *False belief scenario*: There is a real ice-cream van stationed at the church, but Mary was told it was in the park. Mary is leaving the house to go to the ice-cream van. Where is she going?

In this case the following three models have to be considered:

Goal specification:	"(icv)—at→ (?)"
Knowledge base:	"(icv)—at→(ch)"
Mary's belief:	"(icv)—at→(pk)"

Again, Mary wants to find the van in the real situation, so the obvious strategy would be to look where the van is in the real situation. The knowledge base gives a clear, but wrong answer: "Church." And that is the answer of the typical 3-year-old.

The correct answer, of course, is that Mary will go to the park, and this answer can be found by matching her goal specification to her belief model. The decision to make that match raises, however, what I would call the *puzzle of false belief*. The puzzle is: If it is Mary's goal to achieve an outcome in the *real world*, why should a match for her goal specification be sought in the *counterfactual situation* described by her belief. After all, one would not do that in the case of pretense. If Mary *really* wanted to find the van, one would not assume she would look for it in a location where she merely *pretends* it is. Now, of course, children could learn a rule that people who want to find something for real act according to a situation described by their belief but not according to a situation described by their pretense. This would certainly not be a theoretically elegant solution worthy of the epithet "theory of mind."

Intention and belief as models

The only insightful solution to this puzzle is to treat belief explicitly as a person's *model* (*representation*) of the real situation and not just as the description of a *counterfactual situation* with which the person is associated. This difference was graphically illustrated in Figure 8.1 (for simplicity's sake observers' knowledge bases were omitted, only what they explicitly model is shown). Figure 8.3 shows how the conceptualization of mental states as representations helps solve the false belief puzzle in an insightful way.

At the objective level of situations the puzzle of false belief exists because it is not clear why Mary's goal, which belongs in the real world, should be brought into contact with her belief, which describes a different world. The problem is solved at the level of representations. For as representations both the belief and the goal are *models* of the real world *in Mary's mind*, and for that reason will be connected by Mary's reasoning processes, which are carried out on her mental representations of situations and not on situations directly.

By interpreting belief as a representation of a situation and by having an explicit theory of the semantic relations that link the belief as a representation with the represented situation, the child can dissociate two aspects of representations that are usually merged: its content and its reference (Dretske, 1986; what Goodman, 1976, called "representing something *as* something" and "being a representation *of* something"). As Figure 8.3 illustrates, the child can see that the belief *refers* to the real situation, in which the van is at the church, even though the *content* (structure) of the belief describes a different situation, namely, one in

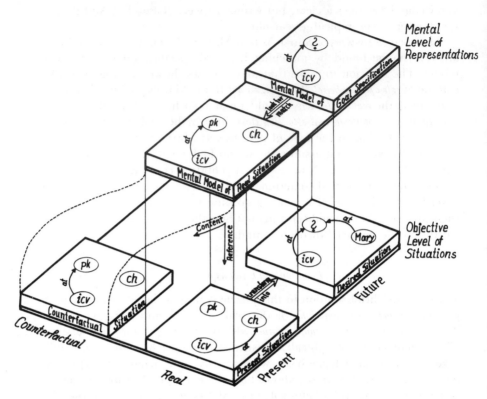

Figure 8.3. Three-dimensional explication of how a representational view of the mind solves the puzzle of false belief. The puzzle exists at the *objective level of situations* because the person intends to transform the real situation into the desired future situation, and so it remains mysterious why that person should act in a way appropriate for transforming a quite different, counterfactual situation into that desired situation. At the *mental level of representations* the puzzle can be solved by realizing that a false belief *refers* to the real situation but has a deviant *content* that describes the counterfactual situation in which the person's action would make sense.

which the van is in the park. It is the dissociation of these two aspects that allows understanding of *misrepresentation*, of which false belief is a typical instance. At the objective level of described situations this dissociation is not possible. There, the structure of the model defines the situation it describes. It is for this reason that the young propositional attitude theorist can understand actions within alternative situations but cannot solve the paradox of false belief.

Relation to other work in this volume

Opacity and meta-representation: Leslie; Forguson and Gopnik

Leslie (*Chapter 2*). The postulated transition from the initial level of presentation to the level of representation in the second year is an attempt to capture in my theoretical framework the changes that Leslie (1987) has identified as necessary for the occurrence of pretend play. My *knowledge base* corresponds to his "primary representation," and my *manipulable mental models* to his "secondary representations." They are, unlike the knowledge base, *detachable* from reality ("decoupled"), and because they are *separate models* from the knowledge base they are not confused with reality ("quarantined").

Leslie points out correctly that pretense raises the specter of so-called opacity, which is most frequently discussed in the logical literature in connection with belief reports. However, it seems rash to conclude from this commonality that there is a "deep isomorphism" between infant pretense and mental state reports. In fact, the three opacity phenomena mentioned by Leslie are also shared by many other areas of discourse, such as reference to time and possibility (Dowty et al., 1981; Fauconnier, 1983/1985). For instance, the problem of nonsubstitutability of identicals is discussed by Leslie for belief reports with the following example:

> *Ronald Reagan* is *the President of the United States.*
> John believes that *Ronald Reagan* is a movie star.
> It does not follow:
> John believes that *the President of the United States* is a movie star.
> (because John might not know that Ronald Reagan is the President of the United States).

Although Reagan and the President are the same person, one description cannot be substituted for the other within the "that" complement of the knowledge sentence without possibly affecting the truth value of the sentence. It is for this reason that the word *know* creates an *opaque* context for the sentence in its "that" complement. The same problem occurs in sentences that refer to different times:

> *Reagan* is *the President of the United States.*
> In 1978 *the President of the United States* was a peanut farmer.
> It does not follow:
> In 1978 *Reagan* was a peanut farmer.

Like "know that," "In 1978" can create an opaque context. These problems are solved in possible world semantics by stipulating that the meaning of expressions in opaque contexts is not what it is in the usual transparent context, namely, their meaning in the real world but their meaning across all possible worlds, which is the *intension* of the expression or, in the case of a sentence, the *proposition* expressed by the sentence. So, in an opaque context an expression can be substituted for another one only if it has the same intension. This solves the problem, because although Reagan and the President of the United States are identical in the real world, the intensions of these two descriptions are not identical, since there are plenty of possible worlds and different times where Reagan is and was not the President. Since the intension of "Reagan" and "President" are not the same, the two expressions cannot be substituted in opaque contexts without altering the meaning (truth) of the sentence.

My suggestion that the young child interprets pretense as a relation between the pretender and a situation (complex proposition) parallels the move by semanticists from meaning in the real world (denotation) to meaning in possible worlds (intension). Leslie's suggestion that the child interprets pretense according to the following representational schema:

Agent – informational relation – "expression"

also amounts to the same, provided the function of the inverted commas is only to "decouple" the enclosed expression from its usual meaning (denotation). Leslie, however, claims more. The inverted commas create a *meta-representation*. That is, the inverted commas do not widen the meaning of the expression from the real world to possible worlds but change its meaning altogether. Instead of referring to the meaning of the expression in the real (denotation) or in possible worlds (intension) the formula "expression" now refers to the expression as a symbolic entity.

Suggestions similar to Leslie's have been put forward by logicians in order to solve more pernicious opacity problems than the ones mentioned by him, which cannot be solved by possible world scmantics (Dowty et al., 1981, pp. 170–175; Konolige, 1985). These problems are closely related to mental state reports and concern, for instance, the substitutability of logically equivalent expressions, such as, "2 + 2" and "4." These two expressions are logically equivalent because "2 + 2" is "4" at all times in all possible worlds, and therefore their intensions are identical and so, according to possible world semantics, they can be replaced even in opaque contexts. For opaque contexts created by temporal references (e.g., "In 1978") or by possibility statements this provides no problem, since logically equivalent expressions are by definition equivalent (hence substitutable) at all times in all possible worlds. However, in belief contexts such a substitution can still change meaning:

2 times 38 is *76*.
Reagan believes that he is *76* years old.
It does not follow that:
Reagan believes that he is *2 times 38* years old.

If there is a deep isomorphism, as Leslie claims there is, between mental state reports and infant pretense, then it would be important to show that especially those types of opacity phenomena that are unique to mental state reports (e.g., nonsubstitutability of logical equivalents) also occur in early pretend play. If this could be demonstrated then there would also be a basis for claiming that infants capable of this type of pretense have meta-representational abilities. Unless this demonstration is possible I see no compelling reasons why the onset of pretend play, as described by Leslie, should mark the onset of meta-representation.

Now back to nearer home. There is, quite independently of considerations about opacity, a strong intuitive temptation to consider mental models that are detached from the knowledge base ("secondary representations") as meta-representational. Looking at the semantic link in Figure 8.2 between model and knowledge base, it is tempting to think that the model represents the knowledge base. Because the knowledge base is itself a representation of the external situation, the model representing it would then deserve the status of "meta-representation." However, this conclusion would be erroneous.

Although the knowledge base plays a special role as the origin of other models and as a representative of reality on which the truth of models is assessed, the models still are models of the external situation not of the knowledge base. Let me make this point absolutely clear by an analogy. I want to make a drawing of Alan Leslie, for which I do not use the original as a model but a photograph of Alan instead. To check whether the final product is a reasonable facsimile of Alan, I compare my drawing not with Alan himself but with the depiction of Alan on the photograph. Now, despite my heavy reliance on this photograph, my drawing of Alan is still a representation of Alan and not a representation of the photograph of Alan (that drawing would have to show a photograph with Alan on it). For the production and evaluation of my drawing, the photograph served the same role as the knowledge base for other mental models, and so mental models, too, are representations not of the knowledge base but of the external situation.

Forguson and Gopnik (*Chapter 12*). I am in almost complete agreement with Forguson and Gopnik's description of representational development. We agree on what happens in the second year of life. Around 18 months infants become able to " 'run through' possible courses of action and consequences in their heads without actually having to experience those actions or consequences," which suggests "that the child can contrast a possible state of affairs . . . with the actual state of affairs." We also agree that children do not develop an explicit understanding of mental representation before the age of about 4 years: Even when talking about representation "the contrast for the 3-year-old is between real and not real" whereas "4-year-old children are beginning to recognize representations as representations."

What I find puzzling is Forguson and Gopnik's use of the word *meta-representation*. They say that 4-year-olds begin to "recognize represen-tations as representations," but I would have thought that without such recognition the younger child could not be thought capable of meta-cognition. Yet even children as young as 2 years are deemed capable of meta-representation since they use "terms to refer to representations." I find this criterion too permissive. Let me defend my position by way of an analogy with the term *metalinguistic*.

On a night out with a visitor from Greece we get involved in an argument about the number of letters in the English word "*bar*". (My friend thought it was spelled "*mpar*"). To prove my case I point to the sign above the entrance to a bar and say: "Look, it has only three letters." With this comment I was making a *metalinguistic* statement because I was referring to the letters above the entrance *as* linguistic entities.

In contrast, let us assume that these letters above the entrance to that bar have been installed by two illiterate workers who had been told that each object to be mounted is called a "letter" and that these letters have to be mounted in the right sequence to form a "word." When in this context one worker said to the other, "This word was easy, because it has only three letters," then the speaker was *not* making a metalinguistic statement even though reference was made to the same (linguistic) entities as in the previous example. The difference is that the workman was referring to these entities not *as* linguistic entities but as a bunch of heavy objects.

Thus, for a statement to be called "metalinguistic" it has to make reference to linguistic entities *as* linguistic entities. By analogy, if Forguson and Gopnik state that only by 4 years can children "recognize represen-tations *as* representations," then the term *meta-representational* should not be applied to younger children's reference to representations unless the reference to them is *as* representations.

Apart from this terminological difference I agree with Forguson and Gopnik that the 3-year-olds in a study by Wellman and Estes (1986; Wellman, Chapter 4), who referred freely to such internal representations as images, dreams, and thoughts, did not yet understand these represen-tations as representations of reality.

Perception and knowledge: *Wimmer et al., Flavell, Chandler, Taylor*

Wimmer, Hogrefe, and Sodian (*Chapter 9*). Wimmer et al. argued on the basis of data by Sodian and Wimmer (1987) and by Wimmer, Hogrefe and Perner (1988) that children before the age of 4 years do not understand the importance of informational access for acquisition of knowledge. That the 3-year-olds would not have explicit understanding of knowledge acquisition fits my proposal. For the full story of knowledge acquisition is that through perceptual contact, information about the perceived situation is transmitted to the mind, where a model (knowledge base) is set up with a structure that corresponds to the structure of real elements in the perceived situation. Explicit understanding of this process requires that the child be able to *model* the process mentally. Within the model of that process a mental model of knowledge *as* a model of the perceived situation has to be constructed (Figure 8.1, right-hand observer). Such a meta-representational construction is exactly what I claim that the child younger than 4 years has difficulty with.

The problem, however, is why such explicit understanding of the process of knowledge acquisition should be required for giving correct answers in the typical test paradigm. For instance, in the study by Wimmer et al. (1988) subjects see whether a person has or does not have access to relevant information (e.g., whether the person looks or does not look into a box) and have to judge whether that person knows or does not know what is in the box. The problem for my account is why children of 3 years or younger could not make correct knowledge judgments by following the strategy of forming an association between the person and the perceived situation (propositional attitude). If the person has perceptual contact, a knowledge association is formed, and if no perceptual contact occurs, no such association is formed.

The solution to this problem is, I think, that young children in fact do use such a strategy – on occasion. Such occasional use explains why a higher percentage of 3-year-olds give correct responses under some conditions (e.g., Hogrefe, Wimmer, & Perner, 1986) than under slightly different conditions (Marvin, Greenberg, & Mossler, 1976; Mossler, Marvin, & Greenberg, 1976; Wimmer et al., 1988) and why most 3-year-olds seem able to adjust their responses to a question to the question asker's existing "knowledge," that is, his or her previous access to informational access. When asked in the test by Wimmer et al. (1988)

Young children's use of this strategy is unreliable because informational access, which we consider essential for the existence of knowledge, is not their only criterion for forming a knowledge association. They also use several other aspects that common language use associates with "to know" (Richards, 1982), for example, that knowledge tends to lead to correct action (as in "He knows how to do it"). So although the 3-year-old is able to take informational access into account in a knowledge judgment, other associations compete with the association based on informational access. When asked in the test by Wimmer et al. (1988) whether the other person knows what is in the box, the 3-year-old may answer in terms of how likely the person is to give a correct answer based on the person's performance on previous occasions, for example, an adult will get it probably right (hence to be judged as *knowing*), whereas another child might get it wrong (hence to be judged as *not knowing*).

In summary, the 3-year-old uses a series of reasonable heuristics for judging another person's knowledge. What the child lacks is an understanding of the relative importance of these heuristics. This changes at 4 years when knowledge can be conceptualized as a representational state created by informational access and enabling the knower to act correctly. Now the relative importance of various associated aspects becomes clear: Informational access is absolutely crucial for the acquisition of knowledge, whereas correct action is merely a likely consequence of knowing. In other words, by seeing a mental state as a representation that stands in for reality, children can understand the role of the mental state in the "causal fabric" (Leslie, Chapter 2) that reaches from perception to behavior. Unlike Leslie, I see children's understanding of the causal role as a consequence of their emerging concept of mental representation, and so it is interesting that 3-year-olds have difficulty understanding how internal states are caused specifically in the case of representational states like *knowledge*, but much less so in the case of nonrepresentational states like *hunger* (Perner & Ogden, in press).

Flavell (Chapter 13). Flavell and his collaborators have investigated children's understanding of visual perception. Masangkay et al. (1974) found that young children had little difficulty determining what another person can and cannot see. I explain this early competence by suggesting that these children take a "nonepistemic" interpretation of the word *see* (Dretske, 1969). They simply judge the external spatial relationship between a person's eyes and a target. If there is no object blocking the line between eyes and target, then the person sees it, otherwise the person cannot see it. In line with the argument by Wimmer et al. (Chapter 9), there is no understanding of the effect this perceptual contact has on the mind.

Masangkay et al. also showed that children younger than 4 years have difficulty with so-called Level 2 visual perspective problems. In these tasks two people are looking at a drawing of a turtle, but one looks at it from its feet, and therefore sees (in the epistemic sense: Dretske, 1969) it

Table 8.1. *Percent correct answers*

	Age	
Task/Study	3–4	4–5
Level 2 perspective tasks (Turtle)		
Masangkay et al. (1974)	53	96
Flavell, Abrahams, Croft, & Flavell (1981)	23–52	
Appearance–reality distinction		
Flavell, Flavell, & Green (1983, Experiments 1 & 3)	33–47	54–84
Flavell, Green, & Flavell (1986)	44–54	
False belief (real persons–deceptive content)		
Hogrefe, Wimmer, & Perner (1986, Experiments 2 & 3)	21–36	71
Perner, Leekam, & Wimmer (1987, Experiment 2)	45	

as standing on its feet, while the other person looks at the drawing from the other side and therefore sees the turtle as lying on its back.

Essentially the same problem is posed in the appearance–reality task by Flavell, Flavell, and Green (1983), except that different representations need be attributed not to different people but to different perceptual modalities in the same person. For instance, a piece of sponge with the appearance of a rock is perceived as a rock when being looked at, but perceived as a piece of sponge under tactile exploration.

These tasks are difficult for young children because they cannot be solved by associating viewers with different situations, since there is only a single situation being perceived. The difference between viewers or perceptual modalities can only be understood as a difference in content between two representations that, nevertheless, refer to the same situation. Because this representational problem is common to the Level 2 visual perspective task, the appearance–reality distinction, and the false belief task (Wimmer & Perner, 1983), it is remarkable that children's mastery of these tasks develops around the age of 4 years, as Table 8.1 shows. The developmental synchrony between understanding false belief and the appearance–reality distinction has been confirmed directly in the study by Astington and Gopnik (Chapter 10).

Chandler (Chapter 20) and Taylor (Chapter 11). Chandler (Chandler & Boyes, 1982) assumes that young children conceive of the mind as making a copy (which is a form of representation) of those parts of reality which are perceptually encountered. As Wimmer et al. (Chapter 9) point out, the findings on children's understanding of knowledge formation pose a problem for this position, because children younger than 4 years do not seem to have any consistent notion of how the mind relates to the world, not even as a copy of reality.

Chandler also claims that children adhere to their copy theory until they are 6 years or older (Chandler & Boyes, 1982). This claim seems contradicted by 4-year-olds' good performance on the false belief task (Perner et al., 1987) and the appearance–reality distinction (Flavell et al., 1983), because it suggests that at this young age children must have a more sophisticated conception of the mind than a mere copy theory. Chandler argued that this can be concluded not from false belief and appearance–reality tests but only from the more difficult, so-called role-taking tasks (e.g., the droodles task used by Chandler & Helm, 1984, and by Taylor, Chapter 11) where children cannot get by on a copy theory of mind but must conceive of the mind as an active interpreter of information (*constructivist theory of mind*). According to Chandler "role-taking" tasks index the acquisition of this more powerful theory of mind because they satisfy the following criterion: They demonstrate that children "appreciate that one and the same stimulus event can generate different interpretations as a function of the different histories of the onlookers involved."

Leekam and Perner (1987; and in ongoing research by G. Davies) adapted the false belief and appearance–reality paradigms so as to conform to Chandler's criterion. For instance, in two stories a listener received the same false information about an object's location (i.e., the same stimulus event), but listeners differed in their relevant background knowledge about the object's location (i.e., different histories). In one story the listener was under the impression that the object was indeed where she was wrongly told it was, while in the other story the listener had discovered the true location just before being given the false information. If Chandler is right and 4- to 6-year-olds entertain a copy theory of mind, then these children should assume that in both stories the false information will be copied into the listener's mind. The finding, however, was that 4- to 6-year-olds had little difficulty understanding that listeners will use their background knowledge to evaluate the received information critically, that is, they understood that the ignorant listener will be fooled by the wrong information while the knowledgeable listener will reject it as false. Clearly, children younger than 6 years conceive of the mind as a more active processor of information than the term *copy theory* suggests.

However, there remains the problem of explaining why "role-taking" tasks are so much more difficult than the false belief and appearance–reality tasks, because we have shown that Chandler's criterion cannot differentiate between the difficult and easy set of tasks. A possible explanation for children's difficulty with role-taking tasks emerges naturally from the "model theoretic" approach taken in this chapter, as discussed extensively in Leekam and Perner (1987). Here just briefly: I have argued that children come to understand false belief and the appearance–reality distinction by forming an explicit understanding of the semantic procedures that link a mental model to the external situation that the model represents. One of these is the *evaluation* procedure, which compares the structure of the model with the structure of the represented situation. Another, logically prior, one is the *interpretation* procedure, which assigns model elements to real elements. Since situations constantly change, children have great experience in how the structure of models has to be constantly updated and how a mismatch in structure can occur. In contrast, the interpretation of model elements does usually not change. It is fixed at the beginning and is meant to stay. For this reason it is plausible that children may learn that somebody does not know the correct evaluation of a model earlier than they are able to conceive of a person not knowing the interpretation of a model.

Leekam and Perner argued that under standard analysis of predication the models that have to be constructed to understand false belief and the appearance–reality distinction differ only structurally (difference in evaluation) from reality, while the model specified by a droodle (or an ambiguous reference, as the droodle's linguistic counterpart) suffers from lack of interpretation. Under the plausible assumption that mismatch in structure is understood earlier than lack of interpretation, this approach explains why false belief and appearance–reality is understood earlier than role-taking tasks.

On the basis of this analysis there is, then, some agreement with Chandler that role-taking tasks index the onset of understanding the mind as an active interpreter ("constructivistic theory of mind"), provided "interpreter" is understood as relating to the technical sense of "interpretation" in model theoretic semantics. Yet, agreement with Chandler's position is only partial since our analysis also suggests that the false belief and the appearance–reality tasks show that 4-year-olds understand the mind as a processor that actively evaluates information and that is not limited to merely copying information, as Chandler and Boyes (1982) have suggested.

Summary

I explain children's growing understanding of the mind by their increasing awareness of the semantics of representational states. For easy exposition, development was described in three steps: (1) The young infant *has a mental model* of the world (knowledge base) but no semantic awareness of how it relates to the world. (2) By the end of infancy the child develops a practical awareness of semantics by being able to *use semantic procedures* to construct and use alternative mental models detached from reality. With this the child can think of alternatives to reality and conceptualize pretense and belief by associating people with alternative situations (propositional attitude theorist). Finally, (3) at about 4 years the child becomes capable of meta-representation by explicitly *modeling* the *semantic relationship* between a mental model and the situation modeled (representational state theorist). This intellectual advance gives the child's theory of mind new coherence about the role that mental states play in the causal determination of behavior.

The child can understand that perceptual contact is necessary for knowledge acquisition, because it ensures that the content (structure) of the resulting mental model matches the external situation, and behavior, which is causally dependent on the content of the mind, will be successful. When this structural similarity is not guaranteed, as in the case of false belief, *content* and *reference* of the mental model diverge. Consequently, behavior intended for the real situation (reference) will be inappropriate for that situation because it is causally determined by a mental representation whose content describes a different situation.

The main difference between my approach and the approach taken by other authors in this volume hinges on the emergence of a *representational theory of mind*. My claim is that such a theory emerges at the age of 4 years and that this meta-representational achievement is responsible for the intellectual changes at this age documented in this volume. I see the theoretical achievements of the younger children as a result of their ability to think about alternatives to reality. Most other authors attribute these early achievements to meta-representational abilities. At first glance, intuition appears to be on their side. The reason is, I think, because we cannot conceive of and refer to hypothetical situations without a model that describes the situation, whereas we can refer to real situations by pointing to them. However, as I argued, using a model to describe a hypothetical situation does not require the meta-representational ability to conceptualize that model *as* a model. This ability, however, is required to understand how the mind's representational function relates to its causal role in determining behavior.

ACKNOWLEDGMENTS

I would like to thank Sue Leekam for helpful comments and her efforts with data collection, Heinz Wimmer and Alan Garnham for their constructive criticism, and Graham Davies for giving an artistic touch to my figures. The empirical research that made this paper possible was funded by the Economic and Social Research Council, Research Grants C00230076 and C00232199, and the constraints on my time for theoretical analysis were eased by a Social Science Research Fellowship from The Nuffield Foundation.

NOTES

1 Because I cannot bring reality itself onto paper, I chose to use symbols ICV, AT, and CH for real elements and some English words to express how these elements are combined in the external situation.

2 I borrow this term from Johnson-Laird (1983), but I am not sure that my use entirely agrees with his (p. 169).

3 Although I want to adhere to the main ideas of model-theoretic semantics, I would also like to keep my use of the word *model* in tune with its everyday meaning. In model theory the term designates the entire enterprise of assigning real elements to each symbolic element, that is, words (Dowty et al., 1981, p. 11). In ordinary language, *model* refers only to the symbolic domain (i.e., only the sandbox, not the battlefield). I follow common usage. Furthermore, by combining model elements in a certain way, the model is put into a particular state (or, in the case of language, an expression is formed). It is these states of the model (expressions) that can be compared to situations (states of the world) and be assigned a truth value. To avoid the cumbersome expression *state of the model* I simply use *model* instead. It is only in this application of the word *model* that models can be said to be true or false.

4 I use the term *propositional attitude* with some hesitation. It is useful because it is a familiar expression and because it makes clear that the attitude links a person not to a representation but to a proposition. Propositions are not representations but abstract entities expressed by sentences or mental representations. For instance, in possible world semantics (Dowty et al., 1981) a proposition is defined as the set of possible worlds in which a sentence holds true (under a certain interpretation). To avoid well-known problems of interpreting mental states as propositional attitudes in this sense, it would probably be better to use a term like *situational attitudes*, but since this term is not familiar I decided to stay with *propositional attitudes*.

5 The difference in how these two observers construe Mary's belief corresponds to two approaches to attitude reports by Barwise and Perry (1983). In their chapter 9 they consider attitudes as *relations to situations* (the younger observer in Figure 8.1), while in chapter 10 they take the more powerful approach of *representing mental states* (the older observer in Figure 8.1).

6 My distinction between presentation and re-presentation differs from that of Piaget (1936/1953), who considered persistence beyond the duration of the eliciting stimulus as criterial for re-presentation (Huttenlocher & Higgins, 1978; Meltzoff, 1981). From my point of view this is not important. There is no reason why the knowledge base could not endure over time, thereby encoding and preserving information about past events.

7 There is an interesting parallel to language acquisition described by Clark (1983). Children initially accept only one name for each kind of object: For example, if an object is already known as "dog" then it cannot also be an "animal."

8 The child's lack of distinction between these two types of situation can be made concise in a play on words. The relation between a situation and an ideal (e.g., on which foot to put the shoe) is one of *correctness*, while the relation between a

representation and the represented situation is one of *truth*. The child at this
level, therefore, fails to distinguish between correctness and truth.

REFERENCES

Ashmead, D. H., & Perlmutter, J. (1980). Infant memory in everyday life. In M.
    Perlmutter (Ed.), *New directions for child development: Children's memory* (Vol.
    10). San Francisco: Jossey-Bass.
Barwise, J., & Perry, J. (1983). *Situations and attitudes*. Cambridge, MA: MIT
    Press.
Brentano, F. von (1924). *Psychologie vom empirischen Standpunkt* (Vol 1.). Leipzig.
Bretherton, I., McNew, S., & Beeghly-Smith, M. (1981). Early person knowledge
    as expressed in gestural and verbal communication: When do infants
    acquire a "theory of mind"? In M. E. Lamb & L. R. Sherrod (Eds.), *Infant
    social cognition*. Hillsdale, NJ: Erlbaum.
Chandler, M. J., & Boyes, M. (1982). Social-cognitive development. In B. B.
    Wolman (Ed.), *Handbook of developmental psychology*. Englewood Cliffs, NJ:
    Prentice-Hall.
Chandler, M. J., & Helm, D. (1984). Developmental changes in the contribution
    of shared experience to social role-taking competence. *International Journal of
    Behavioral Development*, 7, 145–156.
Clark, E. V. (1983). Meanings and concepts. In P. H. Mussen (Ed.), *Handbook of
    child psychology* (4th ed., Vol. 3). New York: Wiley.
DeLoache, J. S. (in press). The development of representation in young children.
    In H. W. Reese (Ed.), *Advances in child development and behavior*. New York:
    Academic Press.
Dennett, D. C. (1978). *Brainstorms*. Montgomery, VT: Bradford Books.
Dowty, D. R., Wall, R. E., & Peters, S. (1981). *Introduction to Montague semantics*.
    Dordrecht: Reidel.
Dretske, F. (1969). *Seeing and knowing*. Chicago: University of Chicago Press.
Dretske, F. (1986). Aspects of cognitive representation. In M. Brand & R. M.
    Harnish (Eds.), *The representation of knowledge and belief*. Tucson: University of
    Arizona Press.
Dunn, J., & Dale, N. (1984). I a daddy: 2-year-olds' collaboration in joint pretend
    with sibling and with mother. In I. Bretherton (Ed.), *Symbolic play*. New
    York: Academic Press.
Fauconnier, G. (1983/1985). *Mental spaces: Aspects of meaning construction in natural
    language*. Cambridge, MA: MIT Press.
Flavell, J. H., Abrahams, B., Croft, K., & Flavell, E. R. (1981). Young children's
    knowledge about visual perception: Further evidence for the Level 1 – Level
    2 distinction. *Developmental Psychology*, 17, 99–103.
Flavell, J. H., Flavell, E., & Green, F. L. (1983). Development of the appearance–
    reality distinction. *Cognitive Psychology*, 15, 95–120.
Flavell, J. H., Green, F. L., & Flavell, E. R. (1986). Development of knowledge
    about the appearance–reality distinction. *Monographs of the Society for Re-
    search in Child Development*, 51, (1).

Fodor, J. A. (1975). *The language of thought.* Cambridge, MA: Harvard University Press.

Fodor, J. A. (1987). *Psychosemantics: The problem of meaning in the philosophy of mind.* Cambridge, MA: MIT Press.

Furth, H. G. (1969). *Piaget and knowledge.* Chicago: University of Chicago Press.

Gibson, J. J. (1979). *The ecological approach to visual perception.* Boston: Houghton Mifflin.

Goodman, N. (1976). *Languages of art.* Indianapolis: Hackett.

Gopnik, A., & Meltzoff, A. N. (1984). Semantic and cognitive development in 15- to 21-month-old children. *Journal of Child Language, 11,* 495–513.

Hogrefe, G.-J., Wimmer, H., & Perner, J. (1986). Ignorance versus false belief: A developmental lag in attribution of epistemic states. *Child Development, 57,* 567–582.

Huttenlocher, J. (1974). The origins of language comprehension. In R. L. Solso (Ed.), *Theories in cognitive psychology: The Loyola symposium.* Hillsdale, NJ: Erlbaum.

Huttenlocher, J., & Higgins, E. T. (1978). Issues in the study of symbolic development. In W. A. Collins (Ed.), *Minnesota symposia on child psychology* (Vol. 11). Hillsdale, NJ: Erlbaum.

Johnson-Laird, P. N. (1983). *Mental models.* Cambridge University Press.

Kagan, J. (1981). *The second year.* Cambridge, MA: Harvard University Press.

Karmiloff-Smith, A. (1986). From meta-processes to conscious access: Evidence from children's metalinguistic and repair data. *Cognition, 23,* 95–147.

Konolige, K. (1985). Belief and incompleteness. In J. R. Hobbs & R. C. Moore (Eds.), *Formal theories of the commonsense world.* Norwood, NJ: Ablex.

Leekam, S. R., & Perner, J. (1987). *Belief and disbelief: Young children's conception of the mind as an active processor of information.* Manuscript submitted for publication.

Leslie, A. M. (1987). Pretense and representation: The origins of "theory of mind." *Psychological Review, 94,* 412–426.

Marvin, R. S., Greenberg, M. T., & Mossler, D. G. (1976). The early development of conceptual perspective taking: Distinguishing among multiple perspectives. *Child Development, 47,* 511–514.

Masangkay, Z. S., McCluskey, K. A., McIntyre, C. W., Sims-Knight, J., Vaughn, B. E., & Flavell, J. H. (1974). The early development of inferences about the visual percepts of others. *Child Development, 45,* 357–366.

Meltzoff, A. N. (1981). Imitation, intermodal co-ordination and representation in early infancy. In G. Butterworth (Ed.), *Infancy and epistemology.* Brighton: Harvester.

Menig-Peterson, C. L. (1975). The modification of communicative behavior in preschool-aged children as a function of the listener's perspective. *Child Development, 46,* 1015–1018.

Mossler, D. G., Marvin, R. S., & Greenberg, M. T. (1976). Conceptual perspective taking in 2- to 6-year-old children. *Developmental Psychology, 12,* 85–86.

Perner, J., & Leekam, S. R. (1986). Belief and quantity: Three-year olds' adaptation to listener's knowledge. *Journal of Child Language, 13,* 305–315.

Perner, J., Leekam, S. R., & Wimmer, H. (1987). Three-year-olds' difficulty with false belief: The case for a conceptual deficit. *British Journal of Developmental Psychology*, 5, 125–137.

Perner, J., & Ogden, J. (in press). Knowledge for hunger: Children's problem with representation in imputing mental states. *Cognition*.

Perner, J., & Wimmer, H. (1985). "John thinks that Mary thinks that ... ": Attribution of second-order beliefs by 5- to 10-year-old children. *Journal of Experimental Child Psychology*, 39, 437–471.

Piaget, J. (1951). *Play, dreams and imitation in childhood*. New York: Norton. (Originally published in French, 1945).

Piaget, J. (1953). *The origins of intelligence in children*. London: Routledge & Kegan Paul. (Originally published in French, 1936.)

Premack, D., & Woodruff, G. (1978). Does the chimpanzee have a theory of mind? *The Behavioral and Brain Sciences*, 1, 516–526.

Richards, M. M. (1982). Empiricism and learning to mean. In S. A. Kuczaj (Ed.), *Language development*: Vol. 1. *Syntax and semantics*. Hillsdale, NJ: Erlbaum.

Shatz, M., Wellman, H. M., & Silber, S. (1983). The acquisition of mental verbs: A systematic investigation of the first reference to mental state. *Cognition*, 14, 301–321.

Sodian, B., & Wimmer, H. (1987). Children's understanding of inference as a source of knowledge. *Child Development*, 58, 424–433.

Somerville, S. C., & Wellman, H. M. (in press). Where it is and where it isn't: Children's use of possibilities and probabilities to guide search. In N. Eisenberg (Ed.), *Contemporary topics in developmental psychology*. New York: Wiley.

Wellman, H. M., & Estes, D. (1986). Early understanding of mental entities: A reexamination of childhood realism. *Child Development*, 57, 910–923.

Wimmer, H., Hogrefe, G.-J., & Perner, J. (1988). Children's understanding of informational access as source of knowledge. *Child Development*, 59, 386–396.

Wimmer, H., & Perner, J. (1983). Beliefs about beliefs: Representation and constraining function of wrong beliefs in young children's understanding of deception. *Cognition*, 13, 103–128.

9

A second stage in children's conception of mental life: Understanding informational accesses as origins of knowledge and belief

HEINZ WIMMER, JÜRGEN HOGREFE, and
BEATE SODIAN

We propose that in the development of children's conception of mental life two broad stages should be distinguished. The first stage begins in the second year of life. Children at this age gain a first awareness of thoughts and wants as mental states. They start to insist on their wants, deny the truth of assertions, and even create alternatives to reality in pretend play. In the words of Pylyshyn (1978) these achievements show an underlying capability for meta-representation. This means that children are not just guided by implicit representations of the world that are experienced simply as "the world." The capability for meta-representation implies an understanding that representations can be true or false and an explicit conceptualization of at least some of the relationships a person can take toward representations (e.g., pretending that x or wanting that x). After this fundamental conceptual accomplishment in the second year of life (see Leslie, Chapter 2), children start to talk about mental states in the third year (Bretherton & Beeghly, 1982; Shatz, Wellman, & Silber, 1983), and in the fourth year their conception of the mental domain seems to be quite rich and coherent (Wellman, Chapter 4).

Our claim is that despite this early emergence of an ability for meta-representation, children's conception of the mental is still far from complete. The most serious failure is that children up to the age of 4 years have not yet conceptualized the most basic informational conditions, such as perception and communication, as origins of knowledge and belief in human minds. In other words, children up to this age have no idea of where knowledge or belief come from. Because of this basic conceptual failure children below this age do not understand why and how they themselves know something or why they were trapped into a false belief. In the same way that they do not understand the origins of their own knowledge, they do not understand what another person knows or believes when only the informational sources of the other person are available to them. They have no "theory" that specifies the epistemic effects of sources of information. Thus, we claim the existence of a second stage in children's conception of the mental domain that begins in the fourth and fifth years. In this second stage children relate such informational conditions as seeing or hearing in an explicit way to their already existing conceptions of knowledge and belief, and thus they become aware of these informational conditions as causal origins of knowledge and belief.

It is important to rule out possible misunderstandings of the claim that children up to the age of 4 years have no understanding of informational conditions as origins of knowledge and belief. This claim does *not* imply that perception or communication are not functioning as sources of knowledge and belief from early on. We do not deny the obvious fact that very young children acquire knowledge and beliefs by perception and, somewhat later, by verbal communication. It is only claimed that they do not understand from where and how they got their beliefs. Furthermore, our claim does not imply that young children have no concepts at all of seeing, hearing, touching, and so on. They may have concepts for these activities, for example, they may understand "seeing something" as "having direct eye contact with something." Such an understanding is limited to the physical aspect of seeing and does not entail an epistemic (knowledge or belief) result of seeing. This is a nonepistemic concept of seeing, which allows for statements like "I saw *x* without seeing that it was *x*."

In the following two sections we will substantiate our claim with two sets of studies on children's attribution of knowledge to self and other. The first set of studies shows that young children do not understand informational conditions as sources of knowledge, although these conditions function as sources of knowledge for themselves. In the second set of studies children's understanding of informational conditions is shown to proceed from a conceptualization of simple informational conditions, such as seeing, to an understanding of more intricate informational conditions, such as inferring.

In the subsequent section it is argued that the attribution of a false belief to another person can be interpreted as another manifestation of children's understanding of informational conditions. The same argument is put forward for children's understanding of the distinction between appearance and reality. Finally, some speculations are presented about *how* an understanding of informational origins might be acquired.

Understanding perception and communication as origins of knowledge

Children's understanding of visual access and verbal information as origins of knowledge was studied in a paradigm where children had to assess their own and another person's knowledge when they themselves or the other person saw a critical fact or were verbally informed about it (Wimmer, Hogrefe, & Perner, 1988).

The setup of the task in these experiments was rather simple. Two children were placed facing each other on opposite sides of a table. In each trial one child served as subject and had to assess the other child's knowledge and his or her own knowledge of the content of a closed box. The box was placed in the middle of the table between the two children. The outside of it was neutral and not suggestive of its content. In each box was a familiar object like a pencil, a comb, a piece of chocolate, and so on. The specific questions were: "Does (name of other child) know what is in the box or does she not know that?" and "Do you know what is in the box or don't you know that?" These questions were asked in German and employed the verb *wissen* for the English *know*. Unlike *to know*, *wissen* allows only the intended reading "Does she know which object is in the box?" and not the reading "Is she familiar with the kind of object that is in the box?" Thus, the German form of the knowledge-question excludes affirmative responses that might result from a familiarity interpretation of the English version of the knowledge-question. In German, the word *kennen* is used for *to know* in the sense of "to be familiar with."

Before the knowledge-questions were asked, either the other or the subject had access to the content of the box. One kind of access was visual perception. In this case either the other child or the subject had a chance to look into the box. The other kind of access was verbal information. Here the experimenter looked into the box and then informed one of the children by whispering the name of the content object into the child's ear. Because the two children were facing each other the subject was fully aware of the informational conditions the other child was exposed to, that is, of whether the other child did or did not look into the box and of whether the other was or was not informed.

Table 9.1 shows how children 3, 4, and 5 years of age assessed the other's knowledge and their own knowledge. Because knowledge assessments in the two access conditions were similar the data from the two conditions were collapsed.

From Table 9.1 it is evident that 3- and 4-year-olds' assessment of the other child's knowledge differed from the assessment of their own knowledge both in amount and kind of error. The most frequent error was denial of the other child's knowledge ("no" bias pattern in Table 9.1), when the other had looked into the box or was informed by the experimenter.

Most 3-year-olds and some 4-year-olds said that the other did not know what was in the box. This kind of error was nearly absent in children's assessment of their own knowledge. When subjects themselves had looked into the box or were informed, then they claimed to know and they could,

Table 9.1. *Frequency of answer patterns in assessing the knowledge of self and other for perceptual or communicative access*

			Person and age					
	Access		Other			Self		
Answer pattern	+	−	3	4	5	3	4	5
Correct	*y*	*n*	9	9	16	8	15	16
"No" bias	*n*	*n*	3	5	0	0	0	0
"Yes" bias	*y*	*y*	2	0	0	7	1	0
Inverse (egocentric)	*n*	*y*	2	2	0	1	0	0

Note: The plus sign (+) indicates the condition *with* informational access, the minus sign (−) no access; *y* indicates that subjects attributed knowledge, *n* indicates that they denied knowledge.

of course, tell what was in the box. The errors made by some 3-year-olds in the assessment of their own knowledge were quite the opposite of the errors they committed in the assessment of the other. In their self-assessments they claimed to know even without having had any informational access ("yes" bias pattern in Table 9.1). The opposite of the correct answer pattern ("inverse" in Table 9.1) occurred quite infrequently. This is interesting because the inverse pattern in the assessment of the *other* person could result from egocentric responding.

Two further experiments replicated and extended this pattern of results. In the second experiment the same task was used but with perceptual access only. All four combinations resulting from variation of the other's perceptual access (present vs. absent) and of subject's perceptual access (present vs. absent) were realized. The important finding was that 4-year-olds again tended to neglect the other's perceptual access even when both subject *and* other had looked into the box. Again they themselves had no problem in using perceptual access for knowledge acquisition. In the third experiment 3- and 4-year-olds were asked either whether the other child had looked into the box or whether the other child knew what was in the box. Children consistently responded affirmatively to the look-question but again quite frequently responded negatively to the knowledge-question. The finding that children of this age have no difficulty in assessing whether the other person had visual contact with something, is in agreement with Flavell's well-known claim (Chapter 13) that 3-year-olds have mastered Level 1 of visual perspective-taking. The important point, however, is that the ability to assess another person's visual contact with something might be present in the child without being used in the assessment of another person's knowledge.

We take the remarkable difference between the assessment of the child's own knowledge and the assessment of the other's knowledge as indication that quite different mental processes occurred in the assessment of the other than occurred in the assessment of the self. In short: The correct assessment of the child's own knowledge indicates the mere *functioning* of perception and communication as origins of knowledge, while the correct assessment of the other's knowledge indicates an *understanding* of these origins.

First the mental process that may underly the child's answers to the questions about his or her *own* knowledge, should be sketched out. It is assumed that these questions are answered without any consideration of informational conditions. In response to the question "Do you know what is in the box?" the child simply checks whether she or he has an answer to the embedded question "What is in the box?" If a proposition about the content is in the child's knowledge base, then an answer to the embedded question is available and the knowledge-question is answered affirmatively. If no answer to the embedded question is available, the knowledge-question is answered negatively. The important feature of this *answer check procedure* is that it leads to a correct assessment of the child's own knowledge without any consideration of informational origins of mental representations.

The correct assessment of the *other* child's knowledge in the present experiments is a completely different story. It should be remembered that the other person did not express his or her knowledge of the box's content. The only procedure that provides correct assessment of the other's knowledge consists in a check whether the other person had informational access to the content of the box. So for a positive assessment it has to be ascertained either that the other had a chance to look into the box or that the other was informed. If neither source of information was present, then the assessment should be negative. Obviously, such a procedure incorporates an understanding that the other person's knowledge is dependent on his or her informational access to the critical fact. This *direct access check procedure* was used by a substantial number of 4-year-olds and by all 5-year-olds in the present experiments. However, this procedure was not used by 3-year-olds. This youngest age group quite consistently attributed ignorance even when the other had perceptual or communicative access. These attributions might have resulted from the application of the *answer check procedure* that was used in the assessment of the child's own knowledge. In applying this procedure, 3-year-olds, in response to the question whether the other knows what is in the box, simply checked whether the other had uttered a correct statement about the box's content. Recognition that this was not the case resulted in a negative assessment of the other child's knowledge.

The central finding of the present group of experiments is that 3-year-olds and even some 4-year-olds do not understand the importance of simple informational conditions when questioned about another person's knowledge. This finding raises two questions: First, how does this finding relate to the development of visual perspective-taking? Flavell and collaborators have convincingly shown that 3-year-olds and even some 2-year-olds are quite able to determine whether another person does or does not see a critical object when they are directly questioned about that (see Flavell, Chapter 13, for review). Yaniv and Shatz (Chapter 5) present similar findings. In the third experiment mentioned in preceding paragraphs, we also have shown that our children were quite able to assess correctly whether the other child had looked into the box when directly questioned about that. One should note, however, that the ability to assess correctly the other person's visual contact with the critical fact is only a necessary precondition for the correct assessment of the other person's knowledge. As specified in the direct access check procedure, the correct assessment of the other person's visual access is indeed an integral part in the correct assessment of the other person's knowledge. The point, however, is that in assembling such a procedure the child has first to understand that seeing the critical fact is the causal origin for knowing the critical fact. It is exactly this insight into the causal origin of knowledge that, according to the present analysis, distinguishes visual perspective-taking from the assessment of the other person's knowledge.

The second question is whether the present finding of 3-year-olds' and some 4-year-olds' difficulty in assessing another person's knowledge are in agreement with other research on this problem. This is definitely the case. A detailed discussion of this issue is provided in Wimmer et al. (1988). Here just two studies by Marvin and collaborators should be mentioned (Marvin, Greenberg, & Mossler, 1976; Mossler, Marvin, & Greenberg, 1976). The procedures used in these studies were quite similar to the procedure of the present study. As in the present study, children had to assess the knowledge of another person (the child's mother or the experimenter) who was physically present but whose informational accesses differed from that of the child. The developmental trends reported in these studies correspond closely to the developmental trend found here. Marvin et al. found that only 10% of their 3-year-olds but 88% of the 4-year-olds and 95% of 5-year-olds considered the other person's informational access in the assessment of the other person's knowledge. The percentages correct reported by Mossler et al. were 5%, 60%, and 85%. It must be mentioned, however, that the majority of errors found in 3-year-olds' assessment of the other person's knowledge in these studies were of the "yes" bias type and thus just the opposite from what was found here. The most plausible explanation for this difference is that Marvin et al. and Mossler et al. used "omniscient" adults (the child's mother and the experimenter) as other persons, whereas in the present study a child served as other person.

Understanding inference as origin of knowledge

The pattern of knowledge attribution to self and other shown by 3-year-olds for perception and communication was again found for inference, although in somewhat older children (Sodian & Wimmer, 1987). Four- and 5-year-olds relied on inference in their own acquisition of knowledge but denied that the other person might know via inference.

Inferential access was realized in these experiments in a very simple and concrete way. In a first step the child and the other person together inspected the content of a container and agreed that only sweets of a certain kind, for example, black chocolate nuts, were in the container. In a second step the other person or the subject was prevented from seeing how one choconut was transferred from the container into an opaque bag. However, this person was explicitly informed by the experimenter about this transfer, for example, "I've just taken one of the things out of this box and put it in the bag."

The condition where knowledge could be acquired via simple inference was contrasted with a condition where knowledge depended on actually seeing the critical object's transfer. In this latter condition two kinds of sweets were in the original container, and thus one could only know what the content of the critical bag was by having seen the transfer from container to bag. All four combinations of presence and absence of inferential and perceptual access were realized with subjects assessing both the other's knowledge and their own knowledge.

Table 9.2 shows the results of the first experiment of this series where, in addition, the assessment of an adult other person was contrasted with the assessment of a child-doll other person. Because this variation was not effective, Table 9.2 shows the combined results.

Table 9.2 shows that most 4-year-olds but few 6-year-olds showed the response pattern "inference neglect," that is, they denied that the other person knew, when in fact the other person knew via inference in the absence of visual access (task $P - I +$ in Table 9.2). However, when these children had to assess their own knowledge when supplied with inferential access only, they claimed to know and could specify the content of the bag. The response pattern "inference neglect" means that the other person was assessed according to perceptual access: When the other person saw the object's transfer to the bag, 4-year-olds attributed knowledge; when the other did not see this transfer, ignorance was attributed even when the other person in fact knew via inference.

Neglect of the other person's inferential access proved to be a stable

Table 9.2. *Frequency of response patterns in the assessment of the knowledge of self and other for inferential access*

		Person and age			
	Task	Other		Self	
Response pattern	P + − + −	4	6	4	6
	I + + − −				
Correct	y y y n	4	24	19	27
Inference neglect	y n y n	23	8	1	1
Yes bias	y y y y	4	0	11	4

Note: P = perceptual access; I = inferential access; +/− = access present/absent; y/n = affirmative/negative answer to knowledge question.

phenomenon. It was also found when the other was not in the opposite perspective but shared the subject's perspective and thereby at every moment received the very same information as the subject (Sodian & Wimmer, 1987, Experiment 2). Even when the other person gave evidence of his or her inferential knowledge by explicitly stating the conclusion, 4-year-olds disregarded the other's inferential access and judged the conclusion to be a guess (Experiment 3).

The interpretation of the self–other discrepancy shown by 4- and 5-year-olds in the case of inferential access is the same as the interpretation of this discrepancy in the case of perceptual and communicative access. Correct self-assessment shows the mere functioning of inference. Such a functioning means that automatically and without conscious awareness of its origin a proposition about the critical fact is built up, for example, "a chocolate nut is in the bag." This proposition in the subject's knowledge base supplies an answer to the question "What is in the bag?" which is embedded in the question "Do you know what is in the bag?" The presence or absence of such an answer determines the affirmative or negative response to the question about the child's own knowledge. This is the *answer check procedure* already postulated for children's self-assessment in the case of perceptual access.

For the correct assessment of the other person's knowledge children must have relied on a procedure that incorporates an understanding of inference. This procedure might consist of the following steps and will be called *extended access check*.

1 Did other (O) have perceptual access to bag's content?
2 If yes, then O knows content. If no, then (3).

3 Did O have access to information that allows O to figure out the content?

4 If yes, then O knows content. If no, then O does not know content.

This *extended access check procedure* starts with an assessment of whether the other had direct access. Here only perceptual access is specified as direct access, although communicative access might be included as well. The important feature of this procedure is that a negative assessment of direct access does not lead to an ignorance attribution but leads to a further check whether the other person might have acquired knowledge indirectly. Four-year-olds' problem in ignoring the other person's inferential access can be located at this step 2. They just performed a *direct access check* and attributed ignorance when the other had inferential access but no perceptual access. Interestingly, they adhered to this procedure rather strictly (Sodian & Wimmer, 1987, Experiment 3). Thus, when the other person stated the inferentially gained conclusion, these children did not fall back to an *answer check procedure* that would have resulted in positive knowledge assessment. Instead, the application of the *direct access check procedure* made them discount the other's conclusion as a guess.

Two aspects of this group of experiments on the understanding of inference should be noticed. The difference between the assessment of subject's own knowledge and the assessment of another person's knowledge supports the theoretically important distinction between the simple functioning of an informational condition and the understanding of this very informational condition. Correct responding to questions about subject's own knowledge required only access to the products of automatically performed inferences, while correct responding to questions about other's knowledge required an explicit understanding of inferential access, that is, of the causal connection between knowledge of the critical premises on the one hand and knowledge of the conclusion on the other. The important findings were (a) that this explicit understanding of inferential access was acquired rather late, and (b) that the younger children were systematically mistaken in their assessment of the other person's knowledge in the inferential access situation. Their assessments reflected a first level in the understanding of sources of knowledge. In contrast to the 3-year-olds discussed in the previous section, the 4- and 5-year-olds in the present experiments understood quite well that one has to consider the other person's informational conditions when one is questioned about the other person's knowledge. Their only problem was their limited understanding of informational conditions. They understood only direct visual access as source of knowledge and this led them to mistaken but systematic ignorance attributions in the case of inferential access.

It should be noted that exactly this limited understanding of sources of knowledge might also explain why in other situations 4- to 6-year-old children were found to exhibit mistaken positive knowledge attributions to other persons. Studies by Chandler and Helm (1984), Olson and Astington (1987) and Taylor (Chapter 11) have shown that children up to age 6 or even older mistakenly attribute knowledge of a hidden object to another person when this person has visual access to an uninformative part of this object, for example, when the other person sees only a gray spot of a hidden elephant. Similarly, Sodian (1988) found that 4-year-olds but not 6-year-olds attribute knowledge to another person when this person has received an ambiguous referential message. However, Sodian's 4-year-olds admitted their own ignorance when they themselves received the ambiguous message. The explanation of these mistaken knowledge attributions is basically the same as the explanation of the mistaken ignorance attributions in the case of inferential access. Children of this age just check the presence or absence of visual or communicative access when questioned about the other person's knowledge. They do not yet consider informativeness of informational sources and they do not yet consider inferential access.

The discussion of findings concerned with children's assessment of another person's knowledge can be summarized by positing three developmental stages in children's understanding of informational accesses as origins of knowledge (see Table 9.3).

False beliefs: Understanding informational origins or a problem of representational complexity

The informational origins account of belief understanding

The stages posited for children's understanding of informational accesses as origins of knowledge suggest that children's understanding of another person's false belief is just a particular manifestation of their general understanding of the epistemic effects of informational accesses on human minds.

To show how an understanding of informational origins is required in understanding another person's false belief, a particular belief attribution task will be described. This task was introduced in a recent study by Hogrefe, Wimmer, and Perner (1986) and used also in studies by Perner, Leekam, and Wimmer (1987) and Astington and Gopnik (Chapter 10).

In a first episode of this task, subjects themselves experienced informational conditions that led them to a false belief. Thus, for instance, subjects were presented with a matchbox and were asked, "Look what I've got: What is in there?" By just having a look at the outside of the box

Table 9.3. *Three stages in children's understanding of informational accesses as origins of knowledge*

Stage	Evidence
Stage 0 (age: 3 years) Informational accesses function as origins but are not understood as such.	The assessment of knowledge is dependent not on informational access but on the proven or assumed ability to give a correct answer.
Stage 1 (age: 4 and 5 years) Understanding of perceptual and verbal access.	Other's knowledge is no longer assessed by the other's ability to give a correct answer but by the presence of perceptual or verbal access.
Stage 2 (age: 6 years and older) Indirect origins and quality of sources are understood.	Besides direct access, the presence of inferential access as well as the quality of sources are checked in assessing the other's knowledge.

all subjects were led into a false belief and responded, for example, with "matches." This belief was proven wrong by showing something else, for instance, a piece of chocolate, as the content of the box. In a second episode, subjects had to imagine a friend, who actually waited outside the room, experiencing the same informational conditions they themselves had experienced. Thus, the experimenter might proceed by saying, "Now we will call Peter in and I will ask him: 'Peter, look what I've got, what is in this box?' What will Peter say is in this box?"

Our claim now is that for an understanding of the other person's false belief, subjects have to understand the effects of informational conditions on the other's mind. Such an understanding manifests itself in a procedure by which the other person's access to informational sources is checked and inferentially used. This *access check procedure* is similar to the one postulated for the correct attribution of knowledge when the other had gained knowledge by inference. In response to the above-mentioned test question "What will other say is in the box?" the following *extended access check procedure* might be performed:

1 Will other have a chance to look into box?
2 If yes, then other knows what is in box and will respond with "chocolate." If no, then other does not know what is in box and then proceed to (3).
3 What will other see or hear about box? Answer: Looks at outside of matchbox only.

4 If other looks at matchbox outside only, then other will think "matches are in the box."

In Hogrefe et al.'s Experiment 2 where the present task was used, it was found that of twenty-four children at each age level only five 3-year-olds but seventeen 4-year-olds and nineteen 5-year-olds correctly predicted that the other would respond according to the appearance of the box, for example, with "matches." All the other children predicted that the other would respond with the actual content, for example, with "chocolate."

In our present task, one could argue that the correct answers to the *belief question*, that is, to "What will other say is in the box?" show nothing more than a repetition of subjects' own answers to the same question. This interpretation is not plausible because the age trend found with the task described was also found with tasks where subjects never experienced a false belief themselves (Hogrefe el al., 1986, Experiments 4 & 5; Perner et al., 1987, Experiments 1 & 2; Wimmer & Perner, 1983). So one can safely assume that children's correct attributions of false belief are based on an assessment of the other's informational access, or in other words, that the children responding correctly inferred the other's belief from a check of the relevant informational conditions the other person was exposed to.

The representational complexity account of belief understanding

The informational origins account of belief understanding was developed in the present chapter to provide a coherent explanatory framework that accounts both for young children's difficulty in understanding another person's knowledge and for their difficulty in understanding another person's false belief. However, it is not the only account of young children's problem with another person's false belief.

The main alternative account explains young children's problem with the representational complexity involved in false beliefs. This account was proposed by Josef Perner and the first author of the present chapter, in previous publications. The first interpretation (Wimmer & Perner, 1983) of young children's difficulty with false beliefs located the problem in the contradiction between the other's belief (e.g., the chocolate is in the green cupboard) and the actual state of affairs (e.g., the chocolate is in the red cupboard). A profound analysis of representational requirements posed by pretend play (Leslie, 1987, and Chapter 2) convinced us that this first account couldn't be correct. The problem is that according to our first account, pretense poses the same representational problem as false belief.

However, pretense is acquired in the child's second year of life, while false belief attribution is mastered in the fifth year.

A more refined version of the representational complexity account of false belief attribution that circumvented the problem posed by the early emergence of pretend play was therefore developed (see General Discussion section in Hogrefe et al., 1986). There we argued that the representational problem posed by false beliefs is not simply the contradiction between the actual and something false. The difficulty was seen as arising because it has to be represented that the other believes a certain proposition to be a *true representation* of a state of affairs. This very same proposition, however, has to be also marked as false to avoid confusion for the subject, who is aware of the actual state of affairs. The essence of this account is that the mental "truth" of the other person that is actually false has to be represented in contrast to subject's own truth. Perner (Chapter 8) provides an elaborate exposition of this version of the representational complexity account of false belief understanding.

Evaluation of the two accounts

For a decision on whether young children's difficulty with false beliefs is caused by a failure to understand informational origins or by representational complexity, it is useful to consider the relationship between the two accounts in information-processing terms. In this perspective the informational origins account is more basic because it locates children's difficulty at an earlier processing stage than the representational complexity account. In understanding another person's mind, two broad stages can be distinguished. In a first stage the other person's informational access has to be checked and inferentially used before, in a second stage, the resulting epistemic state of the other can be set up and maintained. From this sequence it follows that any failure in the first processing stage is a sufficient condition for children's failure to understand the other person's epistemic state independently of whether this epistemic state is easy (knowledge) or difficult (false belief) to represent. Of course, a failure in the first processing stage is not a necessary condition for a failure to understand the other person's epistemic state. It could well be that no failure occurs in the assessment of the other person's informational access but that a failure occurs in the second stage, when the resulting epistemic state requires a complex representation that is difficult to set up and to maintain. The question now is whether children's failure to understand another person's false belief results from a failure in the first processing stage or whether it results from a failure at the second processing stage.

A tentative answer to this question is possible by comparing the assessment of another person's knowledge when the other gained this knowledge via inference with the assessment of another person's false belief. Why is this comparison relevant? It is relevant because the two assessments pose quite similar requirements in the first processing stage but the representational complexity involved in the second processing stage differs. In the first processing stage, both assessments demand an extended check of the other person's informational access. With inferentially acquired knowledge, it has to be ascertained that the other person has no direct access but that she has access to other information that allows her to infer the critical fact. Similarly with false belief, it has to be ascertained that the other person has no direct access to the actual state but that the other has access to relevant, but misleading, information. In the former case the "other information" results in knowledge, while in the latter case the "other information" leads to a false belief. If understanding of another person's false belief is a manifestation of understanding informational origins, then there should be no developmental difference between the attribution of inferentially gained knowledge and the attribution of false belief. If, however, false belief attribution poses an additional problem because of the representational complexity involved, then false belief attribution should be more difficult than the attribution of inferentially gained knowledge.

The different predictions following from the two accounts can be evaluated by comparing the findings of Sodian and Wimmer (1987) on children's attribution of inferentially gained knowledge with the findings on children's attribution of false beliefs (Hogrefe et al., 1986; Perner et al., 1987; Wimmer & Perner, 1983). This comparison contradicts the prediction following from the representational complexity account of false belief attribution, because false belief attribution (high representational complexity) was in fact easier and acquired earlier than the attribution of inferentially acquired knowledge (low representational complexity). The mean percentage correct of 4- and 5-year-olds' attribution of inferentially gained knowledge found by Sodian and Wimmer in 3 experiments (110 subjects) was 17%. The corresponding mean percentage correct for 4-year-olds' (not 5-year-olds') false belief attribution derived from a total of 10 experiments was 67%, as compiled in Table 5 in Perner et al. (1987). (See also for illustration Table 8.1 in Perner, Chapter 8.) It should be noted that the salience of the other person's access to premise information in the Sodian and Wimmer study seems to be even higher than the salience of the other person's access to misleading information in the false belief studies. So we are quite certain that there is a real difference between the attribution of inferentially acquired knowledge and the attribution of false belief, despite the obvious problem resulting from a comparison between experiments. That the attribution of inferentially acquired knowledge is more difficult than the attribution of false belief is damaging for the representational complexity account. However, this difference also poses a problem for the informational origins account because the procedures by which the informational accesses of the other person are checked are quite similar in the case of inferentially gained knowledge and in the case of false belief. A plausible explanation exists, however, for this unexpected difference, and for it one has to consider in more detail the relationship between test questions and the first steps in the proposed *access check procedures* (see previous section). In the case of inferentially gained knowledge, the test question (e.g., "Does other know what is in the bag?") has already an appropriate but false answer ("no") when in the first step of the proposed *access check procedure* the other person's direct perceptual access is checked. So further checks are not encouraged for indirect access that would give an alternative answer ("yes") to the test question. In the case of false belief, the situation is quite different. Here the first step in the proposed *access check procedure* is helpful. The test question is, for instance, "What will other say is in the box?" and the first step in the *access check procedure* again consists in a test whether the other has informational access to the actual content. The negative result of this first check is helpful because it rules out the possible but false answer that the other will respond with the actual content to the test question. Thus, left with no answer after this first check, further checks of relevant access are encouraged.

There is additional circumstantial evidence that assessment of the other person's informational access is the important factor in children's understanding of another person's false belief. Over the last years our research group "detected" an ever increasing number of 4-year-olds and, to a minor extent, of 3-year-olds with correct false belief attribution. When the story tasks for false belief attribution were first applied with Austrian children (Wimmer & Perner, 1983; Wimmer, Gruber, & Perner, 1984), not even half of the 4-year-olds showed false belief attribution. In the most recent study using the same story task (Perner et al., 1987, Experiment 1) more than 80% of 4-year-old English children showed false belief understanding. In our opinion, this difference has nothing to do with an acceleration of children's conception of mind or with a basic difference between English children and Austrian children. This increase in percentage correct seems to be because in the Perner et al. (1987) study the other person's informational accesses – that is, what she did see and what she did not see – were made very salient by prompt questions and repetitions. This was not the case in the earlier studies. That high salience of the other person's informational conditions leads to increased performance of false belief attribution was in fact shown experimentally for second-order false belief attribution (Perner & Wimmer, 1985, Experiment 4).

The appearance – reality distinction: Understanding informational origins or a problem of representational complexity?

In a series of studies by Flavell and collaborators on the development of understanding of the appearance–reality distinction, 3-year-olds were found to be quite incompetent in making this distinction (Flavell, Flavell, & Green, 1983; Taylor & Flavell, 1984). From the present perspective 3-year-olds' failure to distinguish between how something looks and what it really is, is just another symptom of their general failure to understand informational origins. The important point of the appearance–reality distinction is that mental representations are marked according to where they come from, that is, according to their informational origins. For example, one representation of an object's categorical identity (e.g., "This is a rock") has to be marked as false and as resulting from simply looking at the critical object, while an alternative representation (e.g., "This is a sponge") of the same object has to be marked as true and as resulting from the more reliable touching of the object. If there is no understanding of these origins, it is impossible to represent that one belief resulted from one's looking at the object and that the other belief resulted, for instance, from touching the object. It is, however, still remarkable that the quite explicit reference to the "looking" origin in the appearance questions ("How does this look to your eyes right now?") did not make 3-year-olds aware that one of their beliefs was caused by just looking at the object. Their failure to understand the origins of their own representations must be truly profound.

Flavell's (Chapter 13) analysis of children's difficulty with the appearance–reality distinction is quite different from the present perspective. According to his analysis the difficulty arises because the appearance–reality distinction requires that for one and the same object two contradictory representations are set up and maintained. So, in essence, he proposes a representational complexity account ("dual coding" theory) for children's difficulty with the appearance–reality distinction. In fact, this account is quite similar to Wimmer and Perner's (1983) original representational complexity explanation of children's difficulty with false belief understanding.

As pointed out, this version of the representational complexity account is at odds with the very early emergence of pretense, where also two contradictory representations of one and the same fact are set up and maintained (Leslie, Chapter 2). Furthermore, as argued above, even a sophisticated version of the representational complexity account (Perner, Chapter 8) is inconsistent with findings showing that knowledge attribution to other persons (with inferential access or with uninformative or ambiguous sources) is more difficult than false belief attribution.

According to the present perspective it is not a trivial coincidence that the appearance–reality distinction emerges at age 4 when children begin to consider systematically the other person's informational accesses in the assessment of the other person's knowledge (see Table 9.3). This correspondence in age of acquisition is, according to the present analysis, due to the common conceptual competence that underlies both knowledge assessment and appearance–reality distinction and that emerges around age 4. According to the present hypothesis this competence is the child's insight into simple informational causation of mental representations.

Why is understanding of informational accesses as origins of mental representations a late acquisition?

Possibly, the late acquisition of an explicit understanding of informational origins of knowledge and belief may be because these origins function without being experienced as origins. For example, seeing *x* supplies the child with knowledge of *x*. This happens quite efficiently without an explicit awareness and encoding that knowledge of *x* resulted from seeing *x*. Even in adult mental life, one does not have the impression that there is a permanent monitoring and encoding of the particular informational origins of particular pieces of knowledge and belief. In very young children, monitoring and encoding of informational origins seems to be a quite uneconomical burden. It seems to be far more important for the young child to understand relations between mental representations and the represented facts, particularly, whether a representation is true or false. This true–false marking of representations is important for effective action; the origins of particular representations seem to be of lesser importance.

Johnson (Chapter 3) argues that (a) even the very young child has the phenomenal experience of basic psychological modes, for example, of seeing, hearing, wanting or fearing an object; and that (b) development consists in conceptualization of these experiential givens. Our perspective is quite similar to Johnson's general view. We would only claim that a general experiential awareness of seeing is one thing and quite different from the experiential awareness of a particular seeing episode as causal origin of a particular piece of knowledge. This latter awareness is obviously informed by conceptual insight into mental functioning, but the former awareness might well be the precondition for the latter.

What are circumstances in the social and cultural environment of the child that might be helpful in the conceptualization of informational accesses as origins of knowledge and belief? The most obvious factor is the talk of adult persons about origins of knowledge and belief. For instance, the child may be asked questions like "How do you know . . .?" or "Why do you think . . .?" The informational accesses that actually gave rise to the knowledge or belief in question constitute the appropriate answers. It would be interesting to know the age of children when parents begin to ask such questions and when children become able to answer such questions in terms of informational conditions. One of the authors (H. W.) recently had first-hand experience with this parental function. On a walk his son (age 3.2) provoked a quite inadvertent "How do you know that?" question when he surprisingly claimed (because of previous walks in this area with his mother) that there was a campground beyond the next forest. In response to the "How do you know that?" question, Theo did not refer to his prior exploration but simply stressed the truth of his claim by answering "because it is so." Preliminary experimental evidence supports this expected inability of 3-year-olds to answer "How do you know?" questions in terms of informational accesses (Wimmer, Hogrefe, & Perner, 1988).

Another opportunity for the young child to gain insight into the causal connection between informational access and mental representation may be the participation in hide-and-seek games. Hide-and-seek games are apparently played by children in most cultures. Obviously the essential element in these games is to prevent the other person from gaining informational access to the location of the self or of a critical object. Participation in these games constitutes an optimal opportunity to acquire insight into the causal chain between presence or absence of informational access, knowledge or ignorance as resulting epistemic states, and success or failure in hiding or seeking. Studies by Gratch (1964), DeVries (1970), and Shultz and Cloghesy (1981) have shown that not before the age of 4 or 5 years are children able to participate in hide-and-seek games.

In essence, the explicit understanding of informational conditions as origins of knowledge and belief seems to be a quite difficult achievement for the child because of the "silent" functioning of the mental apparatus. What exactly the role of adult epistemic talk may be in the child's explicit conceptualization of the "silent" mental functioning has to be analyzed more carefully. The same must be said for the role of the child's participation in particularly revealing social interactions, such as hiding and lying. In this analysis of environmental factors it has to be taken into account that the child's emerging insight into the informational causation of mental representations is closely bound to age.

Such speculations about general conditions for acquiring the mentioned insight should not detract from the two main arguments of the present paper. One was that a definite sequence exists in children's understanding of informational accesses as origins of mental representations. Simple informational accesses, such as visual perception and verbal information, are understood at around age 4, while inferential access and the epistemic effect of poor quality of informational sources are understood around age 6. The second argument was that several superficially different abilities that appear around age 4 – specifically, understanding of another person's knowledge, understanding of another person's false belief, and the appearance–reality distinction – are just particular manifestations of the child's emerging understanding of informational accesses as origins of mental representations.

REFERENCES

Bretherton, I., & Beeghly, M. (1982). Talking about internal states: The acquisition of an explicit theory of mind. *Developmental Psychology, 18*, 906–921.

Chandler, M. J., & Helm, D. (1984). Developmental changes in the contribution of shared experience to social role taking competence. *International Journal of Behavioral Development, 7*, 145–156.

DeVries, R. (1970). The development of role-taking as reflected by the behavior of bright, average, and retarded children in a social guessing game. *Child Development, 41*, 759–770.

Flavell, J., Flavell, E., & Green, F. (1983). Development of the appearance–reality distinction. *Cognitive Psychology, 15*, 95–120.

Gratch, G. (1964). Response alternation in children: A developmental study of orientations to uncertainty. *Vita Humana, 7*, 49–60.

Hogrefe, G. J., Wimmer, H., & Perner, J. (1986). Ignorance versus false belief: A developmental lag in attribution of epistemic states. *Child Development, 57*, 567–582.

Leslie, A. L. (1987). Pretense and representation in infancy: The origins of "theory of mind." *Psychological Review, 94*, 412–426.

Marvin, R. S., Greenberg, M. T., & Mossler, D. G. (1976). The early development of conceptual perspective taking: Distinguishing among multiple perspectives. *Child Development, 47*, 511–514.

Mossler, D. G., Marvin, R. S., & Greenberg, M. T. (1976). Conceptual perspective taking in 2- to 6-year-old children. *Developmental Psychology, 12*, 85–86.

Olson, D. R., & Astington, J. W. (1987). Seeing and knowing: On the ascription of mental states to young children. *Canadian Journal of Psychology, 41*, 399–411.

Perner, J., Leekam, S. R., & Wimmer, H. (1987). Three-year-olds' difficulty with false belief: The case for a conceptual deficit. *British Journal of Developmental Psychology, 5*, 125–137.

Perner, J., & Wimmer, H. (1985). "John thinks that Mary thinks that ...": Attribution of second-order beliefs by 5- to 10-year-old children. *Journal of Experimental Child Psychology, 39*, 437–471.

Pylyshyn, Z. W. (1978). When is attribution of beliefs justified? *The Behavioral and Brain Sciences, 1,* 592–593.

Shatz, M., Wellman, H., & Silber, S. (1983). The acquisition of mental verbs: A systematic investigation of the first reference to mental state. *Cognition, 14,* 301–321.

Shultz, T. R., & Cloghesy, K. (1981). Development of recursive awareness of intention. *Developmental Psychology, 17,* 465–471.

Sodian, B. (1988). Children's attributions of knowledge to the listener in a referential communication task. *Child Development, 59,* 378–385.

Sodian, B., & Wimmer, H. (1987). Children's understanding of inference as source of knowledge. *Child Development, 58,* 424–433.

Taylor, M., & Flavell, J. (1984). Seeing and believing: Children's understanding of the distinction between appearance and reality. *Child Development, 55,* 1710–1720.

Wimmer, H., Gruber, S., & Perner, J. (1984). Young children's conception of lying: Lexical realism–moral subjectivism. *Journal of Experimental Child Psychology, 37,* 1–30.

Wimmer, H., Hogrefe, G. J., & Perner, J. (1988). Children's understanding of informational access as source of knowledge. *Child Development, 59,* 386–396.

Wimmer, H., & Perner, J. (1983). Beliefs about beliefs: Representation and constraining function of wrong beliefs in young children's understanding of deception. *Cognition, 13,* 103–128.

10

Knowing you've changed your mind: Children's understanding of representational change

JANET W. ASTINGTON and ALISON GOPNIK

Imagine what it would be like never to know that you had been mistaken, that you had held a false belief. This is not to say that all of your beliefs are true; you might be mistaken, but when you realize that your belief is false, you change the belief, and keep no record of your earlier belief. In this chapter we present evidence suggesting that is what it is like, if you are 3 years old. Three-year-olds have beliefs, that is, representations of the world, and they change those representations, but they have no understanding of representational change. That is to say, they do not know that their beliefs have changed.

This ability – to understand that one's representation of an object or a phenomenon has changed and to remember the previous representation – seems to resemble other metacognitive abilities discussed in this volume, for example, the ability to attribute false beliefs to others and the ability to recognize the distinction between reality and appearance. These other remarkable developments in children's metacognitive abilities have been well documented. At about 4 years of age, but not earlier, children are able to ascribe false beliefs, that is, beliefs different from their own, to another person and to anticipate that the behavior of the other may be premised on that false belief (Wimmer & Perner, 1983). Also at this age, but not earlier, children can appreciate that one and the same object may have the appearance of one thing but in reality be another (Flavell, Flavell, & Green, 1983). The three abilities are obviously related, at least in terms of surface expression: Representational change could be expressed "I used to think x but now I know y"; similarly, false belief could be expressed "He thinks x but I know y"; and the appearance–reality distinction could be expressed "It looks like x but really it's y."

But is there a deeper relation? Is understanding that one's own beliefs are subject to change needed to understand that others may hold beliefs different from one's own? Or is the reverse the case? And does understanding false belief, whether another's or one's own, help one appreciate the distinction between appearance and reality? Or do all three abilities appear at the same time, reflecting some more general change? Before we can answer any of these questions we need to show that there is, in fact, development in children's understanding of representational change, that young children don't know that their beliefs have changed and don't remember their previous beliefs.

Children's understanding of representational change

Casual observation suggests that very young children don't remember their previous mental states. There are also hints in the experimental literature that this phenomenon exists. Perner, Leekam, and Wimmer (1987, Experiment 2), trying to help 3-year-olds attribute false beliefs to others by having them actually experience a false belief themselves in a real situation, used a technique developed by Hogrefe, Wimmer, and Perner (1986). The procedure was this: A 3-year-old and her friend were taken to a room, the friend waited outside, and the experimenters showed the child a Smarties box and asked her what she thought was in the box, to which she said "Smarties." (Smarties is a well-known brand of candy that comes in brightly colored and easily recognizable boxes.) Then they showed her that the box actually contained a pencil. They put the pencil back, closed the box, and asked the child three questions: what was in the box, what had she thought was in the box, and what would her friend think was in the box. They found that although almost three quarters of the children remembered their own false belief ("I thought there were Smarties in there"), fewer than half of them attributed this false belief to the other person. About a third of the sample remembered their own false belief but did not ascribe it to the other, and only one child made the reverse error.

This result suggests that understanding representational change (change in one's own beliefs) precedes understanding that others' beliefs may differ from one's own. However, the way in which the child was asked about her previous false belief may have helped her respond correctly. First there was a control question, "Can you remember what's inside here?" to which children had to respond correctly with "Pencil" for the data to be included. Then they were asked, "But what did you think was in here?" The *but* there may be a clue that the required answer is not "Pencil." However, even with that clue, 8 of the 29 children said they had thought there was a pencil in the box. This was the hint that the phenomenon we were looking for did exist. Parenthetically, it might have occurred to you that the child who answers correctly "Smarties" is not remembering what she thought, but what she said in answer to the first question she was asked: "What do you think is in this box?" This suggestion is discussed later in the chapter.

Experiment 1

This, then, was the inspiration for our first experiment (Gopnik & Asting-ton, 1988). A typical protocol follows, this from a child 3 years and 8 months old:

Experimenter: Look. Here's a box.

Subject: Smarties!

E: Let's look inside.

S: Okay.

E: Let's open it and look inside.

S: Oh ... holy moly ... pencils!

E: Now I'm going to put them back and close it up again. [does so]

E: Now ... when you first saw the box, before we opened it, what did you think was inside it?

S: Pencils.

E: Nicky [friend of the subject] hasn't seen inside this box. When Nicky comes in and sees it ... When Nicky sees the box, what will he think is inside it?

S: Pencils.

The child's first comment ("Smarties!") and her evident surprise when the pencils were revealed ("... holy moly ... pencils!") indicate that she had expected the box to contain Smarties. However, when questioned a few moments later she asserted that she had thought there were pencils in the box when she first saw it.

As one does with any investigation of this type, we took care to ensure that children who failed the test were failing for the reason we claimed, that is, they could not recall their earlier belief. For example, a child might appear not to remember her earlier belief if she could not interpret the syntax of the question, or if she did not appeciate the distinction between past and present events. Thus, the children were given a control task, to ensure that they understood the form of the test question and its relation to past and present. They were shown a toy house and told to open it, and when they did so, they found an apple inside the house. We had them take the apple out, put a toy man inside the house, and close it up again. The apple was removed from view. Children were then asked what had been in the house when they first looked inside it. Only the data from children who passed this control task were used in the analyses – that is, the children understood and remembered change in a *physical* state of affairs, and the question they answered concerning this change had the same form as the questions used to test their understanding of change in their belief.

In addition, each question was followed with a forced choice, for example, "When you first saw the box, before we opened it, what did you think was inside it? Did you think there were pencils inside it or did you think there were Smarties inside it?" There were a lot of clues in the question that we were talking about a past event: "when you *first* saw the box, *before* we opened it, what *did* you think ..." In addition, the forced choice ("Did you think there were pencils or did you think there were Smarties ...") gave children a clue that it was reasonable to have thought of Smarties. Also, before the test questions were asked, the box was closed to hide the pencils again, so that children would not be tempted to respond incorrectly with "pencils" simply because that was what they could see in front of them.

In the first experiment the children were given similar questions about two sets of materials: the Smarties box with pencils inside, and a sponge rock like that used in Flavell et al.'s (1983) appearance–reality experiments. This is a piece of sponge painted to look like a rock, about which the children were asked: "When you first saw this, before you touched it or squeezed it, what did you think it was? Did you think it was a rock or did you think it was a sponge?" and "Nicky hasn't touched this, he hasn't squeezed it. If Nicky just sees it over here like this, what will he think it is? Will he think it's a rock or will he think it's a sponge?" We also asked questions about appearance and reality: "What does this look like? Does it look like a rock or does it look like a sponge?" and "What is this really? Is it really a rock or is it really a sponge?" The order of the forced choices, the order of questions (concerning the subject's own belief, the belief of the other, and appearance–reality), and the order of task materials (Smarties or rock) were balanced across subjects.

In this experiment 43 children were tested; 5 children failed the control test and their data were excluded from the analysis. The remaining sample consisted of ten 3-year-olds, twelve 4-year-olds, and sixteen 5-year-olds. The questions about their own previous belief and the belief of the other child were scored correct if children reported their initial wrong impression (Smarties or rock) and incorrect if they responded with what was later revealed (pencils or sponge). For appearance–reality, children had to get both the "looks like" question and the "really is" question correct; if they got only one of these correct (of a pair) they were scored as incorrect. Figure 10.1 shows the mean scores on each of the three test questions for each of the three age groups. There was a significant effect of age for all three types of question: concerning the subject's own belief, the belief of the other, and appearance–reality.

Thus we had clear evidence of development of understanding of representational change between 3 and 5 years of age; a majority of 3-year-olds reported that when they had first seen the deceptive objects they had thought they were what they were later revealed to be (pencils or sponge), whereas a majority of 5-year-olds remembered and reported their initial wrong impression (Smarties or rock). And the data for the false belief and appearance–reality tasks showed age effects similar to those reported by Perner et al. (1987) and Flavell et al. (1983).

However, unlike the data reported by Perner et al., we found that understanding representational change, that is, change in one's own beliefs, was more difficult than attributing a false belief to another, that is, recognizing that another's belief may differ from one's own. The question concerning the other's belief was significantly easier than the question

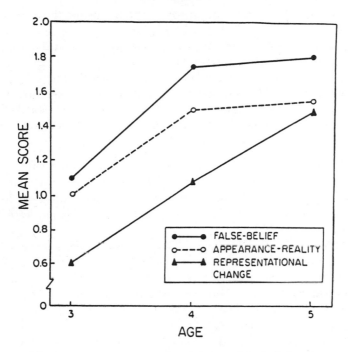

Figure 10.1. Mean scores on representational change, false belief, and appearance–reality questions for three age groups in Experiment 1 (from Gopnik & Astington, 1988).

concerning the subject's own belief; more children correctly ascribed a false belief to the other person than remembered their own previously held false belief. However, the questions that were asked concerning their own and the other's belief were not identical in form, and so we devised a subsequent experiment (Gopnik & Astington, 1988) in which the control question, the question for their own belief, and the question for the other's belief were exactly matched.

Experiment 2

There were two new forms of the test questions; for example:

Form A   *Control*: What was in the house before we took the roof off?

Subject's belief: What did you think was inside the box before we opened it?

Other's belief: X [another child, not yet tested] hasn't

seen inside this box. What will she think is inside it
before she opens it?

Form B   *Control*: When you first saw the house at the beginning,
what was inside it?

Subject's belief: When you first saw the box, all closed up
like this, what did you think was inside it?

Other's belief: X hasn't seen inside this box. When he
first sees the box, all closed up like this, what will he
think is inside it?

This time each question was not immediately followed with a forced
choice. In the first experiment many children answered as we were giving
the forced choice (as in the protocol quoted), and so in this experiment a
forced choice was not given unless the child did not respond to the open
question.

In addition, in this experiment three new sets of materials were used, as
well as the Smarties box containing pencils and the sponge rock, in order
to see whether the results could be replicated over a variety of materials,
involving changed beliefs about property and number as well as content
and identity. The first new task involved a changed belief about a pictured
identity, rather than an actual identity as in the case of the sponge rock.
The materials were inspired by Chandler and Helm's (1984) experiment.
Children were shown the front of a book that had animal pictures on it,
and then the first page of the book, which was quite blank except for a
circle cut out, through which dog's ears could be seen. We turned the page
and showed the child the dog, and then turned to the next page, also blank
with a circle cut out, through which rabbit ears were seen (most children
said "bunny") and then we showed them the bunny. The next peephole
showed what looked like ears, many children said "cat" or "pig," then we
turned the page and showed them that the "ears" were actually the petals
of a flower. The page was turned back so just the petals ("ears") could be
seen through the peephole again and the children were asked what they
had thought it was when they first saw it, and what another child would
think.

The second new task involved a changed belief about a perceptual property, that is, a color, and was inspired by materials used by Flavell et al.
(1983). At first children saw an apparently black cat, which turned out to
be green when a transparent pink cover was removed from over it. The
pink cover was put back and they were asked what color they had thought
the cat was, and what color another child would think it was.

The third new task involved a changed belief about an abstract property: number. Children were shown a rag doll, and then the doll's dress
was removed, revealing two dolls – the apparent first doll was actually the

head and arms of one and the legs of the other – then we dressed it again and asked children how many dolls they had thought there were when they had first seen it, and how many dolls another child would think there were.

In this experiment, appearance–reality questions were asked for only two sets of materials, those most like Flavell et al.'s, that is, the sponge rock and the colored cat. The order of questions (concerning the subject's own belief, the belief of the other, and appearance–reality), and the order of the five tasks were randomized across subjects. Children received questions all of Form A, or all of Form B, or questions like those used in the first experiment. Fifty-eight children were tested; twenty 3-year-olds, twenty-one 4-year-olds, and seventeen 5-year-olds. Five 3-year-olds failed the control task and their data were not included in the analysis. Again there was a significant effect of age for all three types of question, concerning the subject's own belief, the belief of the other, and appearance–reality. The syntactic form of the questions had no effect.

Thus again, and this time over a variety of different tasks, we had evidence that the understanding of representational change develops between 3 and 5 years of age. For each of the five tasks a majority of 3-year-olds reported that when they first saw the task materials they thought they were what they were later shown to be, whereas for all tasks except the doll, a majority of 5-year-olds said they had thought the materials were what they had at first appeared to be. Perhaps the doll task was harder for them because the mistaken belief here concerns the abstract property of number.

Once again it was easier for children to anticipate another's false belief than to remember and report their own previous wrong belief. That is, there was a significant difference between representational change and false belief scores. For every task, the representational change question was harder than the corresponding false belief question.

Explanation of the findings

These results are rather different from those reported by Perner et al. (1987), mentioned in the previous section. In their experiment 72% of the 3-year-olds correctly reported their own previous false belief, whereas in the experiments reported here correct responses for 3-year-olds ranged from 20% to 47%, depending on the task materials. Even the easiest task was failed by more than half the 3-year-olds. We have already suggested, at the beginning of this chapter, that Perner et al.'s subjects may have been helped by the sequence of questions they were asked, and by the contrastive use of *but* at the beginning of the crucial question. Our subjects, however, had no such help. Of course, it must be stressed that Perner et al. were not investigating the phenomenon we're interested in here, and the procedure they used was purposely designed to give children the experience of having a false belief, and to recognize that experience, in order to see if it helped them predict false belief in another. In fact, it is interesting to note that even though these children were given a lot of help to notice their own previous false belief, more than a quarter of them failed to report it.

It could perhaps be argued that the reason for the difference between the data we have reported and that of Perner et al. is that the children we tested never entertained the false belief we expected them to have; for example, they never thought that there was candy in the box, and so obviously they would not report it when we asked them about it later. On the other hand, Perner et al. were certain that their subjects entertained the false belief because the children were first asked what they thought was in the box, and they all said "Smarties." We deliberately did not ask that question because we did not want the children simply to remember and report what they had *said*.

However, in our experiments some of the children spontaneously expressed the false belief we expected them to hold, as in the example protocol given earlier in the chapter, even though we didn't ask them about it. Such expressions occurred for all the task materials, except that children did not name the color of the cat, and for the doll they represented number implicitly, saying "a doll." However, there were no differences in the data of subjects who did, or who did not, verbally represent the false belief; that is, children who expressed the false belief were no more likely subsequently to remember and report it than children who did not do so. Furthermore, to investigate the possibility that children simply remember and report what they say, we conducted a third experiment; twenty 3-year-olds were tested with the Smarties box containing pencils, using exactly the same procedure as in the other experiments, except that before we opened the box to reveal the pencils, the children were asked "What's inside the box?" and they all said "Smarties" (or "candy"). Even so, only 45% of them later remembered and reported correctly this false belief, which is comparable to the results from the first two experiments.

It might also be argued that our data could be explained by assuming that children lie to the experimenter, and don't report their previous false belief even though they remember it, because they are ashamed to admit they were wrong. This seems to us an unlikely explanation, because it would require that the younger children would be more likely to lie than the older ones, whereas the complexity of remembering the false belief and then deliberately concealing it is probably beyond the competence of 3-year-olds. Indeed, LaFrenière (in press) has demonstrated that children of this age are incapable of practicing deception. In his experiment 3- to 6-year-olds hid a toy and then were told to "try to fool" an adult who came in after the toy was hidden and asked the child about its location; the 3-year-olds were completely unable to conceal information. Similarly, Shultz and Cloghesy (1981) showed that 3-year-olds were unable to use deceptive strategies in a card-playing game, but 5-year-olds could use such strategies. Moreover, in our second experiment there were differences between the task materials; thus, children were consistently more likely to make the representational change error, that is, not to report their earlier wrong belief, on tasks that used some materials, such as the doll task, than on others. And so the explanation of the data that assumes children lie would require that they chose to lie to the experimenter about some task materials and not about others, and all children happened to choose the same materials to lie about.

It seems to us that a more plausible explanation is that understanding that one's own beliefs have changed is, in fact, more difficult than appreciating that others entertain beliefs different from one's own. Nor is this an unreasonable explanation. What is important about one's own beliefs is that they represent the way the world is. Information about one's earlier mistaken representations does not have much immediate practical utility. However, recognizing that another has a different representation of the world than one's own is useful in explaining and predicting his or her behavior, and indeed may be unavoidable where the other's beliefs conflict with one's own and argument ensues. This is a nicely Vygotskyan explanation: The child first arrives at a concept of false belief from social interaction, and is then able to apply the concept to the self, to understand the process of representational change. Vygotsky (1978, p. 57) argues that concepts originate in human interaction on the social level, and are later transformed into intrapersonal ones.

Another example of this phenomenon comes from a quite different task, which was given to some of the same children who were tested on the tasks reported here (see also Olson & Astington, 1987). In this other experiment the children were shown familiar colored figures (*Sesame Street* characters), which were then hidden in a house so that no features identifying the characters, only their colors, were visible through the windows. Two figures were uniquely colored and so could be identified just by their color, and two of the figures were the same color and so could not be identified when they were hidden behind the windows. Children were asked what they saw through the windows, and if they knew who it was. They were also asked what their friend would see, and whether the friend would know who it was in the window. The correct response for the uniquely colored figures is to identify the character, whereas the correct response for the figures that are the same color is to say that one does not know which character it is, and that one's friend would not know. Twice as many children answered this question correctly for the other than they did for the self. That is, they found it easier to recognize that the other would not know which character it was when the only information available was ambiguous between two alternatives, than they did to recognize that they themselves would not know. Once again the concept is first understood interpersonally, in terms of what another would not know, and then it is understood for the self.

Relation to other metacognitive abilities

Although children seem to understand false belief before they understand representational change, overall there is a striking similarity in the age of emergence of these two abilities and of the ability to distinguish appearance and reality. The data that we have reported, showing the development of children's understanding of representational change, support Perner's (Chapter 8) suggestion that there is an important general change in children's metacognitive abilities between 3 and 5 years of age. In Table 8.1 he shows that false belief tasks, appearance–reality tasks, and Level 2 perspective tasks are failed by a majority of 3- to 4-year-olds and passed by a majority of 4- to 5-year-olds. Our data from the representational change task fit right into this table: 35% of the 3-year-olds, and 67% of the 4- and 5-year-olds were correct, averaged over all task materials except the doll, which was difficult even for the oldest children. The range of correct answers is 20% to 47% for 3-year-olds, and 55% to 81% for 4- and 5-year-olds.

In addition, we have more compelling evidence than this that understanding false belief, understanding the appearance–reality distinction, and understanding representational change are closely related. In the first experiment reported, controlling for age, there were significant correlations between appearance–reality scores and both representational change scores ($r = .46$, $p < .01$), and false belief scores ($r = .49$, $p < .01$). In the second experiment, again controlling for age, there were significant correlations between scores on all three tasks: appearance–reality and representational change ($r = .49$, $p < .01$); appearance–reality and false belief ($r = .44$, $p < .01$); and representational change and false belief ($r = .62$, $p < .001$). We suggest that these correlations indicate that the three abilities are different expressions of some underlying new ability.

Theoretical implications of these findings

What is this underlying new ability? What is there about 3-year-old children's minds that makes it so difficult for them to understand representational change, false belief, and appearance–reality? Two general types of explanation for the shift in the child's abilities between 3 and 5 have been advanced in this volume. One group of explanations proposes that the child lacks important information about the causal relation between the world and the mind. Wellman (Chapter 4) suggests that 3-year-olds fail to appreciate that the mind is an active processor of information; Wimmer, Hogrefe, and Sodian (Chapter 9) suggest that 3-year-olds fail to appreciate the origins of their representations; while Leslie (Chapter 2) argues that 3-year-olds fail to treat mental representations as the effects of perceptual exposure and as the causes of behavior.

Another group of explanations proposes that the problem is a deeper one and has to do with the child's basic representational capacities. For example, Perner (Chapter 8) suggests that although 3-year-olds can form representations, even counterfactual ones, they cannot model the process of representation, whereas 4-year-olds can model this process; Forguson and Gopnik (Chapter 12) argue that before 4 years of age the child is unable to consider a representation both as an indicator of how things are in the world and as a mental entity; while Flavell's (Chapter 13) differentiation between cognitive connections and mental representations captures a similar distinction. These more conceptual explanations make stronger claims than the first type of explanation. In particular, the first type of claim follows from the second. If Flavell, Perner, or Forguson and Gopnik are right, it would follow that the child would be unable to appreciate the causal chain between the world and the mind; the representational deficit implies the causal one. However, the reverse is not true, because children might have the more general representational capacities and still lack specific information about the relation between world and mind.

As Wimmer et al. point out, the false belief and appearance–reality results could be explained in either way. Both these deficits might be the result of either a deeper representational problem or a more superficial inability to understand the details of the causal link between objects and beliefs. In these cases it might be prudent to accept the weaker explanation.

However, this does not seem to be true in the representational change case. This task does not require that children have any knowledge at all about the causal relation between the world and their beliefs. It is true that to predict another's false belief they have to understand the informational conditions leading to the other's belief; for example, that seeing a box with candy pictured on it would lead a person to believe that the box contained candy. However, to report their own previous belief no such understanding is required. Children simply have to remember that they thought there was candy in the box. Even if they simply think that the belief popped into their head out of the blue, they should still be able to remember and report that belief. In fact, Leslie (Chapter 2) uses the example of representational change, citing Perner et al.'s (1987) data, discussed earlier in this chapter, to support his claim that although 3-year-old children can correctly *report* their own false belief, they fail to *understand* the causal sequence leading to that false belief, and so they fail to predict their friend's false belief in exactly the same situation. However, as we have shown, in an experiment where this comparison is explicitly assessed, children who fail to predict the friend's false belief cannot report their own false belief, and so Leslie's argument does not go through.

On the other hand, the more abstract representational explanations do seem to account for this phenomenon. For example, Perner's proposal would suggest that the child must understand that his past belief was in fact his representation of reality at that time, even if the belief was later found to be false, that is, even if his model *mis*represented the real situation. In other words success on the task requires the ability to model the representational process. Similarly, on Flavell's view both representational change and false belief, like the appearance–reality task, involve the ability to make what he previously called "Level 2" distinctions, that is, the ability to understand that people form mental representations of the real world and that representations of the same object may differ from one another in contradictory ways. Finally, the ability to understand representational change is one of the key abilities that underlie the development of "commonsense realism" in Forguson and Gopnik's account; appreciating representational change requires that children be able to consider their past representation both as something that refers to the world and as a mental entity subject to change independently of the world.

We would argue, then, that the representational change results are particularly important ones because they allow us to adjudicate between the two principal types of explanation of 3-year-olds' inability to understand false belief and the appearance–reality distinction. The additional inability of 3-year-olds to understand representational change suggests that these deficits reflect a deep-seated and profound conceptual difference between 3- and 5-year-olds, and do not simply involve the demands of these specific tasks.

General implications of these findings

In addition to their implications for general accounts of the 3- to 5-year-old conceptual shift, these findings are also interesting in their own right. In particular, they may have implications for accounts of children's learning and memory capacities.

First, the representational change task may be thought of as a kind of memory task. The child has to remember and report his or her own past belief. That children are so bad at doing this may have implications for accounts of children's memory. One important aspect of the sort of full-fledged, episodic, autobiographical memory we have as adults is that it includes psychological information about our own past thoughts, beliefs, and perceptions of the world, as well as information simply garnered from past events, or even information about past events. In fact, William James suggested that this was a distinguishing feature of memory as opposed to simple learning: It "is the knowledge of an event, or fact . . . with the additional consciousness that we have thought or experienced it before" (James, 1892, p. 287, cited by Lockhart, 1984). It is clear from naturalistic investigations of early memory that young children can remember and report specific past episodes, they can tell you something about what happened yesterday. However, it is not clear when children can begin to report their own past psychological states, particularly their own past beliefs. It seems plausible that very young children simply update their beliefs as they receive new information, writing over their past beliefs. This would make their memory rather different from the memory of adults, who continue to retain information about their past beliefs even when those beliefs turn out to be false.

The inability to appreciate representational change also has implications for theories of children's learning. Much learning and, in particular, many conscious learning strategies depend on an ability to recall and reflect on past false beliefs and to retrace the steps that led to those beliefs. In machine learning programs, (e.g., Newell & Simon, 1963) much of the work of the system consists of "pruning" branches of an inference tree that led to mistakes. Similarly, many of our learning strategies depend on recognizing that our past beliefs were false, making generalizations about the conditions that led to those false beliefs, and avoiding those conditions in future. Any number of epistemological platitudes, from "first impressions can be deceptive" to "don't leap to conclusions," as well as more substantive claims like "don't believe everything you read in the papers" or "gnocchi never taste as good as you think they will" reflect this.

Our results suggest that very young children are unable to use these techniques, although 5-year-olds may be beginning to. An anecdote from our data suggests this: One of the 5-year-olds in the second experiment got every one of the first four tasks right; in each case, he was deceived and then correctly identified his own false belief. By the time we showed him the dressed doll in the last task, he said suspiciously, "I bet it turns out to be a rabbit"! This protective skepticism did not seem to be possible for the younger children.

In summary, then, the results we have reported here suggest that 3-year-old children are unable to appreciate that their own representations have changed, and that they develop this ability by the time they are 5 years old. This development has important implications for accounts of the young child's theory of mind as well as for accounts of the young child's learning and memory.

ACKNOWLEDGMENTS

This research was supported by a Connaught Foundation grant to the McLuhan Program in Culture and Technology, University of Toronto.

REFERENCES

Chandler, M. J., & Helm, D. (1984). Developmental changes in the contribution of shared experience to social role-taking competence. *International Journal of Behavioral Development*, 7, 145–156.

Flavell, J. H., Flavell, E. R. & Green, F. L. (1983). Development of the appearance–reality distinction. *Cognitive Psychology*, 15, 95–120.

Gopnik, A., & Astington, J. W. (1988). Children's understanding of representational change and its relation to the understanding of false belief and the appearance–reality distinction. *Child Development*, 59, 26–37.

Hogrefe, G.-J., Wimmer, H., & Perner, J. (1986). Ignorance versus false belief: A developmental lag in attribution of epistemic states. *Child Development*, 57, 567–582.

James, W. (1982). *Psychology*. London: Macmillan.

LaFrenière, P. J. (in press). The ontogeny of tactical deception in humans. In R. W. Byrne & A. Whiten (Eds.), *Social expertise and the evolution of intellect: Evidence from monkeys, apes and humans*. Oxford University Press.

Lockhart, R. S. (1984). What do infants remember? In M. Moscovitch (Ed.), *Infant memory* (pp. 131–143). New York: Plenum.

Newell, A., & Simon, H. A. (1963). GPS, a program that simulates human thought. In E. Feigenbaum & J. Feldman (Eds.), *Computers and thought* (pp. 279–293). New York: McGraw-Hill.

Olson, D. R., & Astington, J. W. (1987). Seeing and knowing: On the ascription of mental states to young children. *Canadian Journal of Psychology*, 41, 399–411.

Perner, J., Leekam, S., & Wimmer, H. (1987). Three-year-olds' difficulty with false belief: The case for a conceptual deficit. *British Journal of Developmental Psychology*, 5, 125–137.

Shultz, T. R., & Cloghesy, K. (1981). Development of recursive awareness of intention. *Developmental Psychology*, 17, 465–471.

Vygotsky, L. S. (1978). *Mind in society*. Cambridge, MA: Harvard University Press.

Wimmer, H., & Perner, J. (1983). Beliefs about beliefs: Representation and constraining function of wrong beliefs in young children's understanding of deception. *Cognition*, 13, 103–128.

11

The development of children's understanding of the seeing–knowing distinction

MARJORIE TAYLOR

In 1929, Piaget made the claim that young children do not clearly differentiate their internal mental life from the events of the external world. There are major consequences for failing to make this kind of distinction. Children who do not differentiate mentality from reality might not understand that their own thoughts are private, would not appreciate that people can differ in their interpretations of the same event, and would not recognize the subjectivity and perhaps uniqueness of their own thoughts and feelings. In these and other ways, the differentiation of mental life from external reality is important in coming to understand other people and in developing an accurate perception of oneself.

There is a long history of research on egocentrism and perspective-taking that addresses or is related to this claim of Piaget's. Recently, however, many new aspects and ideas about the mentality–reality distinction have been investigated, including children's comprehension and production of mental verbs (Miscione, Marvin, O'Brien, & Greenberg, 1978; Wellman & Johnson, 1979); children's ability to appreciate the differences between real and imagined objects (Wellman & Estes, 1986); their understanding of the distinction between appearance (the way something looks) and reality (what it actually is) (Flavell, Flavell, & Green, 1983; Taylor & Flavell, 1984); children's conception of beliefs (Olson & Astington, 1987); their ability to monitor reality (Johnson, Raye, Hasher, & Chromiak, 1979); and their understanding of false belief (Wimmer & Perner, 1983). In general, the findings of research on these topics indicate that children develop a conception of mental life as distinct from external reality much earlier than Piaget supposed. In particular, Wellman (Chapter 4) asserts that a rudimentary theory of mind in which mentality and reality are differentiated is in place by 2½ to 3 years of age.

Wellman is careful to temper his claims about the child's early competence in making mentality–reality distinctions with a description of what is missing in the young child's theory of mind. In this chapter, I will describe research that investigates a component of any mature theory of mind that Wellman suggests is perhaps the major limitation in the theory possessed by the typical 3-year-old child, namely, the notion that the

mind is not just a registry but instead "perceives, construes, and interprets information about the world." According to Wellman, this type of
understanding is a relatively late acquisition. Preschoolers may be able to
distinguish between imagined and real objects, but they tend to assume
there is a very close correspondence between objects and events in the
world and mental representations of them. Thus, instead of conceptualizing the mind as an interpreter of ongoing reality, they may believe there
is an objective reality that is similarly apprehended by all. Chandler and
Boyes (1982) can be credited with perhaps the strongest statement of this
hypothesis. They claim that young children initially tend to equate seeing
with knowing, not allowing for the possibility of multiple interpretations.
In other words, children assume that someone who sees an object or event
automatically shares the children's own knowledge of it, equating their
own subjective interpretation of an event with an objective reality that is
external to the self and is shared with other people.

It is important to be clear that the seeing = knowing hypothesis does
not require that the child believe knowing to be equivalent to seeing
(knowing = seeing). There could well be an asymmetry such that seeing
is equated with knowing, but knowing is not equated with seeing. For
example, the child might appreciate that it is possible for someone to
share the child's knowledge about something without seeing it (e.g.,
someone told the person about it), but assume that if someone sees an
object or event, that person necessarily shares the child's knowledge of it.
Also, the seeing = knowing hypothesis does not necessarily imply that
background information stored in memory and information from the
present perceptual display are mutually exclusive. There might often be
considerable overlap, but when information in memory is not available in
the perceptual display, taking the perspective of another person involves
being able to distinguish the two sources of information.

The seeing = knowing hypothesis is consistent with Flavell's discussion
(Chapter 13) of developmental levels in children's thinking about the
mind. In the context of conceptual perspective-taking, Flavell's Level 1
could be described as a tendency to equate seeing with knowing. If the
other person sees the object or event, then that person shares the child's
knowledge about it. Children at this level would not clearly separate their
own knowledge or interpretation of what they see from the perceptual
information that is given in the environment and is available to all
observers. Note that Level 1 perspective-taking is not the same as just
assuming that someone knows what you know. According to the seeing =
knowing hypothesis, if the other person does not see the event, then the
child assumes that person does not share the child's knowledge of it.

Level 2 competence in conceptual perspective-taking would be reached
when children come to understand that seeing is not equivalent to

knowing. Thus, two people may differ in the knowledge that they have of a shared visual event. At Level 2, children would take into account differences in background knowledge when determining how someone else would interpret a perceptual display. Thus, only at Level 2 could a child be said to possess a "constructivistic" theory of mind (see Chandler, Chapter 20).

In this volume, Flavell describes the Level 1–Level 2 distinction as a general way of characterizing the child's developing understanding of the mind; however, the Level 1–Level 2 distinction was originally proposed in the context of *visual* perspective-taking, where it is well documented (Flavell, 1974; Masangkay et al., 1974). In addition to providing a theoretical model for thinking about the seeing = knowing hypothesis, Flavell's work on visual perspective-taking describes the skills young children bring to conceptual perspective-taking tasks. As suggested by Yaniv and Shatz (Chapter 5), children's ability to determine what another person does and does not know is in part dependent on children's knowledge about what is perceptible to that person. Thus, children's ability to determine what other people can see, that is, their Level 1 *visual* perspective-taking skill, may form the basis for their competence at Level 1 *conceptual* perspective-taking. If they use their assessment of what a person can see when making decisions about what that person knows, they will not assume the person shares their knowledge of an object if the person cannot see the object. However, the concept of interpretation is implicated in answering Level 2 conceptual perspective-taking questions correctly.

Empirical evidence supporting the seeing = knowing hypothesis

In recent research (Taylor, in press), I have found the Level 1–Level 2 distinction to be an accurate way to describe the development of conceptual perspective-taking. Children aged 3 to 8 years were given a series of perspective-taking tasks in which the children knew more than an observer about animals depicted in three pictures. (Figure 11.1 shows one of these pictures.) This research employed a modified version of a task used by Chandler and Helm (1984).

The experimenter began the test session by putting a hat on a puppet and explaining that the hat prevented the puppet from hearing what was being said about the pictures. Then the puppet was placed facedown on the experimenter's lap, and the child was shown the first of the three pictures. For each picture, the animals were identified and the child was given information about what one of the animals was doing (e.g., the giraffe was sitting down) and personal information about one of the animals (e.g., the giraffe's name was George). Then the experimenter

Figure 11.1. Picture of the giraffe sitting down beside an elephant. From Taylor
(in press).

explained that she was going to show the picture to the puppet, but first
she was going to cover the picture so that the puppet could see only a little
bit of it. When the cover was in place, the experimenter held the puppet
up to view the picture and said to the child, "(Puppet's name) has never
seen this picture before and this is what she can see." (The experimenter
pointed to the part of the picture that was still visible.) "Does (puppet's
name) know there is a (giraffe) in the picture? Does (puppet's name) know
there is an (elephant) in the picture?" The children were asked these
questions for five different restricted views of the pictures. The restricted
views for the giraffe–elephant picture are shown in Figure 11.2.

The rationale for including the five restricted views was as follows:

1 Empty (no part of the picture showing). This view was included
  because children who have Level 1 competence should claim that if
  no part is in view, then the observer does not know what is in the
  picture.
2 A tiny edge of one line. This view was included to see how far it was
  possible to push the seeing = knowing hypothesis. If Level 1 children
  make only a very crude distinction between seeing none of an object
  and seeing some of it, they might attribute knowledge of the object to
  an observer who sees only a tiny edge.
3 A small part of one of the objects. This view provides an adequate
  but less stringent test of the Level 1–Level 2 distinction. Children at
  Level 1 should claim that the puppet can identify the object that is
  partially in view, but not the object that is completely covered.
4 Small parts of both objects. Level 1 children should claim that the
  puppet knows about both objects. This view was included so that
  Level 1 responding will differ from always reporting that the puppet
  knows about only one of the two objects.

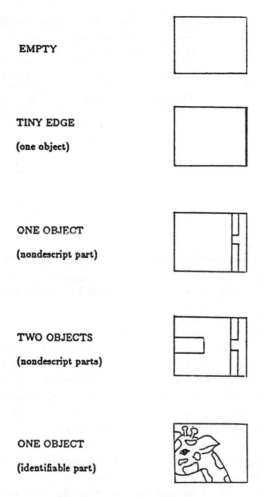

EMPTY

TINY EDGE
(one object)

ONE OBJECT
(nondescript part)

TWO OBJECTS
(nondescript parts)

ONE OBJECT
(identifiable part)

Figure 11.2. Restricted views for the giraffe–elephant picture. From Taylor (in press).

5 A part that was sufficient to allow identification of one of the objects. This view was included so that correct responding could be distinguished from a response bias always to say that the puppet did not know what was in the picture.

Table 11.1 shows Level 1 and Level 2 responses for the five views of the giraffe–elephant picture.

Children's answers to questions about the observer's ability to identify the objects from the restricted views were examined to determine if there were systematic patterns to their responses. Four response patterns were identified: (1) a "yes" bias – the child answered yes to all questions; (2) a

Table 11.1. *Level 1 and Level 2 responses for the elephant–giraffe picture*

| Type of restricted view | Does the puppet know there is a _____ in the picture? | | | |
| | Level 1 responses | | Level 2 responses | |
	Elephant	Giraffe	Elephant	Giraffe
Empty	no	no	no	no
Tiny edge (one object)	no	yes/no*	no	no
One object (nondescript part)	no	yes	no	no
Two objects (nondescript parts)	yes	yes	no	no
One object (identifiable part)	no	yes	no	yes

*There is no prediction for the answer to this question. Both "yes" and "no" answers could be interpreted as consistent with Level 1 perspective-taking.

"no" bias – the child answered no to all questions; (3) Level 1 – the child reported that the observer could identify the objects whenever a part of that object was in view; and (4) Level 2 – the child reported that the observer could identify an object only when there was sufficient information. Table 11.2 shows the number of children at each age level who were categorized as having a consistent response pattern. The "No pattern" column includes children whose responses appeared to be random or were inconsistent.

Children categorized as having Level 1 perspective-taking included both children who believed the tiny-edge view was sufficient to allow identification and children who reported that the tiny edge was not sufficient, but the small, nondescript part was. Of the 18 children categorized as showing this pattern, 4 consistently thought that the nondescript parts, but not the tiny edges, were sufficient to allow identification; 5 consistently thought that even the tiny edges were sufficient to allow identification; and 9 thought the tiny edges were sufficient to allow identification for one or two of the three stimuli. The number of 3-, 4-, 5-, 6-, and 8-year-old children who reported at least once that the tiny edge was sufficient to allow identification of the object was 10, 6, 8, 2, and 1, respectively. Reporting that the tiny edge was sufficient to allow identification decreased as a function of age and almost never occurred with children over 5 years of age. Half of the children aged 3 to 5, however, reported at least once that the tiny edge was sufficient to allow identification.

Table 11.2. *Number of children at each age level showing consistent response patterns*

Age	Response pattern				
	Level 2	Level 1	"Yes" bias	"No" bias	No pattern
Three	0	0	5	3	8
Four	1	6	1	4	4
Five	5	6	0	1	4
Six	8	5	0	1	2
Eight	15	1	0	0	0

The frequency of the tiny-edge error was surprising because it is so obvious to an adult, or even to an 8-year-old child, that no one could ever identify an object on the basis of so little information. The tiny-edge view showed the minimum amount necessary to produce a view that was not completely empty. A child's claim that a naive observer could identify the object by looking at a tiny edge suggests that once that child determined that there was something to see in the view, no further analysis of the informativeness of the view was performed. This response would represent one end of a continuum of children's ability to assess the informativeness of a partial view of an object. The response that a small nondescript part, but not a tiny edge, is sufficient to allow identification of an object is less extreme but still indicates very little ability to assess the informativeness of a restricted view.

The results of the study provided support for the Level 1–Level 2 distinction and the seeing = knowing hypothesis. Three-year-old children were pre–Level 1 in that they did not base their answers to the questions on an analysis of the information given in the restricted views. Instead, they reported that the observer knew what the children themselves knew, or their responses were uninterpretable ("yes" bias, "no" bias, or random). These children did not understand that someone who could not see an object would not be able to identify it, and so they had not reached Level 1. This result is consistent with Wimmer, Hogrefe and Sodian's claim (Chapter 9) that 3-year-old children's assessment of another person's knowledge is not dependent on an assessment of informational access. However, in contrast to Wimmer et al.'s results, 3-year-olds in the present experiment were more likely to claim that the other person was knowledgeable rather than ignorant of the relevant information.

By about 4 years of age, children had acquired Level 1 competence. Their responses indicated that these children tended to equate seeing with knowing. When no part of an object was visible, they correctly reported that a naive observer would not know that the object was in the picture. However, when a small, nondescript part of an object was in view, they incorrectly reported that the observer would be able to identify the object. Level 2 developed between 6 and 8 years of age. Level 2 children recognized that a small piece of an object might not provide sufficient information to allow identification of the object. Thus, the interpretation of a person who did not see the entire picture might differ from the child's more informed interpretation.

In addition to testing for the developmental levels predicted by the seeing = knowing hypothesis, I also examined the generality of the claim that young children may be willing to attribute their own knowledge of an object or event to a naive observer who has less background knowledge about what is seen. The seeing = knowing hypothesis has been stated in a general way, but the data supporting it show only that children assume another person can identify what he or she sees (Chandler & Helm, 1984). The identity is only a fraction of the information that a child might know about what is seen. For example, a child looking at his or her pet dog can identify it as a dog, but also knows a host of information about the animal's habits, likes and dislikes, and past history. How far do we want to push the seeing = knowing hypothesis? It seems unlikely that a child would think a new friend would acquire all the child's knowledge of the pet as soon as she or he saw it for the first time. It is more likely that some kinds of information are more apt than others to be attributed to a naive observer who sees an object or event. Children may make distinctions among different kinds of information (e.g., semantic versus episodic) originating from diverse sources (e.g., being told versus personally experiencing), and varying in degrees of importance. The seeing = knowing hypothesis as stated is almost certainly too simplistic. The hypothesis that children confuse information stored in memory with perceptual information that is presently available could well be limited to very specific types of knowledge.

In a preliminary attempt to test the generality of the notion that children conflate seeing with knowing, the children in the study described above were asked if naive observers who saw small, nondescript parts of animals in a set of pictures knew what the animals were doing (e.g., the giraffe was sitting down) and if they knew the personal information about the animals (e.g., the giraffe's name was George), in addition to being asked if they knew the animals' identities. Information about what the animals were doing was given in the pictures (e.g., anyone who saw the picture could see that the giraffe was sitting down), but was not given in the restricted views of the pictures. The personal information given by the experimenter included details that could not be ascertained by visual inspection of the pictures. It was hypothesized that children might recognize that information that is not perceptual, such as an animal's name, is not known by someone whose only source of information is the restricted view of the animal.

The questions about the observer's knowledge of the action and personal information were asked for two of the restricted views: (1) the view with small, nondescript parts of both objects; and (2) the view with an identifiable part of one object. For each of these restricted views, the experimenter positioned the cover, and asked children questions like the following: "Does (puppet's name) know the giraffe is sitting down? Does (puppet's name) know the giraffe's name is George? Does (puppet's name) know what the elephant's name is?"

The results indicated that 3-year-olds did not use the information available in the restricted views as the basis for their answers about the action and personal information. On the other hand, 8-year-old children made almost no errors on these questions. For the analysis of the 4- , 5- , and 6-year-old data, each child was given six scores that indexed the number of times (out of three) that they attributed knowledge to the observer about the identity, action, or personal information on the basis of seeing the view of a nondescript part or the view of an identifiable part. A 3 × 2 ANOVA of these data yielded a significant type of view × type of information interaction, $F (2, 90) = 11.74, p < .001$. Children were more likely to attribute knowledge of the objects' identities to the observer than the two other types of information, and this difference was greater when the view showed an identifiable part. Children differentiated between the two views only for questions about identity.

One interpretation of this analysis is that children tend not to attribute information other than the identities of objects to observers who see restricted views. Clearly, the children in this experiment were more apt to claim that an observer could identify the giraffe, for example, than to claim the observer knew the giraffe was sitting down or that his name was George. Thus, children do not necessarily assume that a person who shares their visual perspective will share all the children's knowledge of the object. However, almost half of the children who appeared to base their decisions about what the observer knew on the information available to him or her, sometimes attributed action and/or personal knowledge of the animal to the observer who saw a nondescript part. Perhaps children might be more likely to attribute action and personal information to a naive observer in other kinds of tasks. Overattribution of knowledge about identity may have been particularly pronounced in this study because the child and the observer were both exposed to part of the relevant information for learning the animal's identity, that is, the stimulus drawing. By contrast, the relevant information for acquiring the personal and action information were not shared in any part with the observer (e.g., the observer did not hear part of what was said to the children to inform them of the giraffe's name or see the part of the giraffe that was involved in sitting). The results of the present study are preliminary, but suggest that more specific hypotheses about the kinds of information children may conflate with perceptual input and the circumstances that give rise to such confusions need to be explored.

In sum, the results of this research indicate that until about 6 years of age, children have difficulty differentiating their own knowledge about an object in a picture from the perceptual information available to a less informed observer. In particular, preschool children tended to report that an observer could identify small, nondescript parts in pictures, even though the observer did not share the children's background knowledge of the pictures. The ambiguity of the nondescript parts, that is, the fact that they could have turned out to be a variety of things, seemed to have been lost on these children.

The bias against multiple interpretations of the same information

What accounts for the tendency of young children to attribute knowledge about the identity of what is seen to anyone who sees even a small bit of it? According to Flavell's analysis (Chapter 13), the Level 2 understanding that people may differ in the way they interpret the same information requires children to code information in more than one way. In his chapter, Flavell discusses research findings in such areas as visual perspective-taking, communication development, and the appearance–reality distinction that are consistent with the claim that dual coding is problematic for young children. In addition, the idea of a bias in young children against multiple representations of the same information has emerged in recent theorizing about language learning. Markman (1987) suggests that this bias has considerable utility in the context of figuring out the meanings of new words. The problem of determining which words refer to what objects is reduced if children can rule out all the objects that they can already name as possible referents for a new word. Markman calls this strategy for interpreting new words "the assumption of mutual exclusivity." Children assume that names for objects are mutually exclusive, and so a new word must name an object that the child has no word for already.

A bias against dual coding might originate in language learning because it is an advantage to a young child faced with the task of learning the meanings of words, but the research reported here indicates that the same bias could adversely affect children's performance on other kinds of tasks. Perhaps an early cognitive bias against dual coding contributes to children's tendency not to search for alternative perspectives to their own, or not to consider the possible interpretations that an ambiguous surface structure might engender. In the restricted-view task, children did not seem to speculate on what the part might have been, or how it might be interpreted by someone who had never seen the picture. It did not seem to occur to them to assess the informativeness of the part in view.

In a training study, I tested the possibility that children might benefit from a demonstration of how the possibility of multiple interpretations of a stimulus was relevant in the context of perspective-taking (Taylor, in press). Children were given training that focused on making them notice the ambiguity of a stimulus. The subjects were 32 children in each of two age groups: 4 and 6 years. The experimenter told the children that they were going to play a guessing game with a puppet. In the game, the children were shown a series of pictures of a house, boot, ship, cow, and pig. For each picture, the children were asked to identify the object, the picture was covered so that only a small part was showing, and the puppet tried to guess the identity of the depicted object after looking at the restricted view. In both training and control conditions, the puppet correctly guessed the identities of the house and cow, but made incorrect guesses for the other three target stimuli. In the training condition, the three restricted views of these stimuli looked identical, although the pictures were of different objects. In the control condition, the same pictures were used, but the restricted views looked different. Figure 11.3 shows the pictures as they appeared when covered and uncovered for the training and control conditions.

In the training condition, the puppet guessed that the boot was a box, the ship was a boot, and the pig was a boot or a ship. When the puppet made a mistake, the cover was removed to show the puppet its mistake, the cover was repositioned, and the covered picture was placed near the child. With the second and third mistakes, the experimenter pointed out that the restricted views were identical. When the guessing was finished, the experimenter picked one of the three pictures, showed the full picture to the child, repositioned the cover, and held the puppet up to face the covered picture. The child was asked if the puppet knew what the picture was. After the child answered, the puppet guessed incorrectly, and the procedure was repeated with another picture. This part of the procedure was meant to make the child realize that the three restricted views were identical. In the control condition, the parts of the boot, ship, and pig that were visible in the restricted views had different appearances. The puppet guessed that the boot was a ball, the ship was a shark, and the pig was a hand.

For the test trials, children in both conditions decided if an observer would be able to identify the objects in a series of pictures from restricted

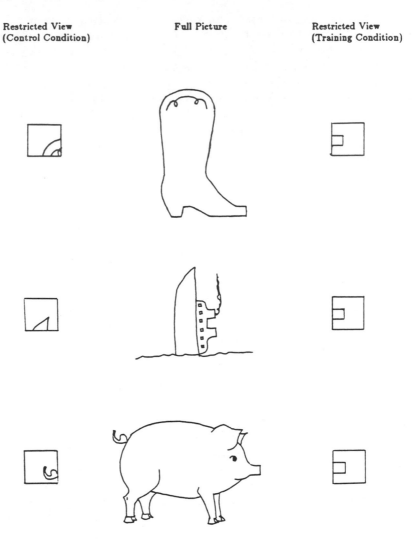

Figure 11.3. Restricted views used for the boot, ship, and pig stimuli in the training and control conditions. From Taylor (in press).

views. Six of the pictures had restricted views that did not provide sufficient information for identification. The three remaining stimuli had restricted views that were sufficient for identification of the objects. These items were included so that correct responding could be distinguished from a bias always to say that the observer does not know what is in the picture.

Each child was given two scores that indexed (1) the number of correct

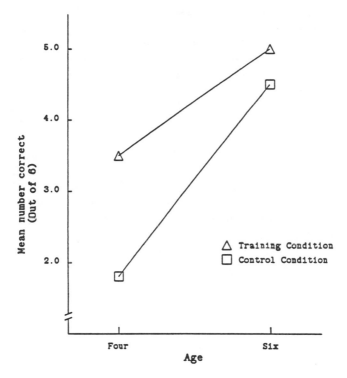

Figure 11.4. Mean number correct on perspective-taking trials as a function of age and condition (training or control). From Taylor (in press).

responses on trials in which there was not sufficient information for a naive observer to identify the objects (the six unidentifiable test trials); and (2) the number of correct responses on trials in which there was sufficient information to allow identification (the three identifiable test trials). A 2 × 2 ANOVA on the number of correct responses for unidentifiable test trials, with age and condition (trained or control) as between groups factors, yielded significant main effects for condition, F (1, 60) = 5.56, $p < .025$, and age, F (1, 60) = 20.39, $p < .001$. Figure 11.4 is a plot of the mean number of correct responses on the test trials (out of six) as a function of age and condition. The performance of 4-year-old children in the training condition was significantly better than in the control condition, t (60) = 2.6, $p < .025$. However, the performance of 6-year-old children in the training and control conditions was not significantly different, t (60) = .77, $p > .05$. The performance of 4-year-old children in the training condition and 6-year-old children in the control condition was not significantly different, t (60) = 1.54, $p > .05$.

These results show that training had a significant effect on the ability of 4-year-old children to recognize ambiguity. Trained 4-year-old children did better than untrained 4-year-old children. The training brought their scores up to the level of children 2 years older who had not received the training. Training did not have much effect on the performance of 6-year-old children, probably because there was not much room for improvement in their scores. Even 6-year-old children in the control condition did quite well on the perspective-taking trials. These children did somewhat better than might be expected from the results of other studies, but it is possible that the control procedure in this experiment had some effect on their performance. Although the demonstration that the same information can have multiple interpretations was much more dramatic in the training condition, children in the control condition heard alternative interpretations (the puppet's incorrect guesses) for the boot, ship, and pig restricted views.

In general, the children were always correct when asked if a naive observer would be able to identify an object when there was, in fact, enough information to allow identification. This result is important because it indicates that the children in the study did not have a bias always to say no. Children who reported that the observer could not identify the objects on the test trials probably did so because they believed the information to be insufficient for identification, not because of a response bias.

It was hypothesized that one effect of the training condition might be to make children realize that the observer made mistakes because the task was difficult, rather than because the observer was not very good at guessing. To test this hypothesis, children in the two conditions were asked why the puppet made so many mistakes. Their answers were categorized as attributing the observer's failure to the difficulty of the task or the ability of the observer. Ten of the sixteen 4-year-old children in the training condition compared with five of the children in the control condition attributed failure to the difficulty of the task, $\chi^2_{(1)} = 3.14$, $p <$ .05 (one-tailed test). The 4-year-old control condition was the only group in which the majority of the children (11 out of 16) believed the failure of the observer to identify the objects in the pictures was due to the observer's lack of ability.

In this study, the control and training conditions differed in that the restricted views in the training condition looked identical while those in the control condition looked different. This relatively subtle difference between the conditions affected the subsequent performance of 4-year-old children. Children in the control condition claimed that an observer could identify an object on the basis of a small, nondescript part significantly more often than children in the training condition. This result suggests

that once children are made aware that the same information can be interpreted in different ways, they are better equipped to take the perspective
of someone who knows less than themselves.

A difference in the spontaneous comments of 6- and 4-year-old children
as they performed the task, is consistent with the hypothesis that the
ability to speculate on possible interpretations of the restricted views helps
children appreciate that someone may not necessarily arrive at the correct
interpretation. Over half of the 6-year-old children in both the training
and the control conditions spontaneously speculated on alternative hypotheses for the identities of the parts in the restricted views. For example,
children observed that someone might think the rabbit was a boomerang,
submarine, airplane, or plant. None of the 4-year-old children in the
control condition, and only three of the 4-year-old children in the training
condition, made this type of comment. Their spontaneous comments
suggest that older children used their assessment of whether there were
alternative possibilities for what the restricted view might be when decid
ing if the observer would be able to guess the correct identity. Perhaps the
procedure in the training condition led some 4-year-old children to
approach the task in this way.

Conclusion

The research discussed in this chapter investigated children's tendency to
confuse seeing and knowing, that is, to conflate information that is known
about an object or event with present perceptual information available to
all observers. It was found that between about 4 and 6 years of age,
children greatly overestimated what an observer could be expected to
know on the basis of seeing a small, nondescript part of an object. The
tendency to behave as if seeing an object were a sufficient condition for
someone to share the children's knowledge about the object was called
"Level 1 conceptual perspective taking." The Level 1 performance by the
preschoolers in this research is consistent with the idea that they lack a
theory of mind which would allow for the possibility that the same
information can be mentally represented or interpreted in different ways
by different observers. Between 6 and 8 years of age, children were
described as having Level 2 competence because they realized that a
small, nondescript part might be mentally represented in different ways
and hence may not provide sufficient information to allow identification of
an object.

The results of the research reported here also indicated that some types
of information are more likely than others to be attributed inappropriately
to a naive observer. In particular, preschool children are more likely to
claim that an observer can identify an animal by looking at a small,

nondescript part than to claim that the observer knows what the animal is doing, or knows the animal's name, its likes, or about its family. Perhaps children have had more experience identifying objects than acquiring personal and action information about them on the basis of partial views. It is important to note that although the restricted views used in these experiments were much more impoverished than typical views of objects, identification of three-dimensional objects is usually based on partial views. No single view of a giraffe, for example, would include all its parts (left side, right side, front, and back), and other objects might partially occlude one's view of the giraffe. Children are used to seeing partial views and being able to identify what they see. Identity information might also be special to children because it is particularly important and long-lasting (i.e., identities usually do not change). In any case, the results of this research suggest that young children's theories about knowledge must incorporate distinctions among various kinds of information.

By 8 years of age, children have no problem with Level 2 conceptual perspective-taking tasks as instantiated in these experiments. However, Level 2 abilities in other domains have been described as present much earlier. For example, in visual perspective-taking, 4-year-old children typically do well on Level 2 kinds of tasks. As Flavell (Chapter 13) discusses, there are probably many determinants of difficulty in a Level 2 task, and accordingly, the age that children show Level 2 competence will vary. In addition, it may be that some of the tasks described as Level 2 actually require only Level 1 competence (see Chandler, Chapter 20). In any case, it would probably be wrong to think that the ability to determine how another person will interpret an event is ever complete. The task of taking the conceptual perspective of someone who knows less or thinks differently than oneself remains difficult, even for adults (Flavell, 1985; Piaget, 1928). The literature on adult social cognition provides many examples of adults making mistakes that are reminiscent of the error that children make on the restricted-view task. For example, Fischhoff (1975) has demonstrated that adults tend to overestimate the inevitability of an outcome once they know it to have occurred. The perceived inevitability of outcomes after the fact is accompanied by the tendency for adults to believe that the outcome could have been more easily predicted than was actually the case. In other words, adults tend to believe that they would have known all along what they could only have known with outcome knowledge. This tendency is not unlike children's belief that a naive observer will be able to identify an object by looking at a nondescript part.

According to Fischhoff (1975), outcome knowledge is integrated with other information about an event in a way that adjusts the relative importance assigned to previous knowledge. Information that is consistent with the actual outcome becomes more salient, while inconsistent or contradictory information is forgotten or reinterpreted. Thus, the way new information is integrated in memory seems to work against perspective-taking capabilities. In addition, the "availability" of information, that is, how readily information is perceived or retrieved from memory, also may contribute to the difficulty of the conceptual perspective-taking. Tversky and Kahneman (1973) have described availability as a measure that people use when making inferences about how frequent an object or event is, or how probable the event is to occur. In many cases, availability works well as a heuristic for assessing frequency or probability, but it also causes systematic error. The information consistent with the outcome of an event is disproportionately available to people who are trying to estimate how likely the actual outcome appeared to be before it occurred. According to Flavell (1985), "our own perspectives produce clear signals that are much louder to us than the other's, and they usually continue to ring in our ears while we try to decode the other's. It may take considerable skill and effort to represent another's point accurately through this kind of noise, and the possibility of egocentric distortion is ever present" (p. 125).

Although presumably most adults view the mind as an interpreter of reality rather than a passive registry of information, we may often overestimate how much others share our own point of view. In fact, the findings of research on adult social cognition (Fischhoff, 1975; Ross, Lepper, & Hubbard, 1975; Tversky & Kahneman, 1973) suggest that some of the difficulties underlying children's poor performance on the restricted view task may be due to cognitive biases that do not change appreciably with age. However, there are developmental differences to account for, and changes in one's theory of mind are important to consider in this context. The preschool children in the studies described here showed very little understanding that information can be *interpreted*. They did not consider or search for alternative representations to their own. In the training study, however, children who were made aware that multiple interpretations of a picture were possible, were less likely to assume that a naive observer shared their own interpretation of an ambiguous stimulus. This result is consistent with the idea that changes in one's insights about the mind and about mentality—reality distinctions affect perspective-taking ability, but it is likely that learning how to determine just what another person's interpretation might be like remains a lifelong developmental task.

ACKNOWLEDGMENTS

Support for this research was provided by NICHD grant HD 09814 awarded to John Flavell and a Social Sciences and Humanities Research Council of Canada fellowship awarded to the author. The research reported here was presented at the International Conference on Developing Theories of Mind, Toronto, May 1986.

REFERENCES

Chandler, M., & Boyes, M. (1982). Social cognitive development. In B. B. Wolman (Ed.), *Handbook of developmental psychology* (pp. 387–402). Englewood Cliffs, NJ: Prentice-Hall.

Chandler, M. J., & Helm, D. (1984). Developmental changes in the contribution of shared experience to social role-taking competence. *International Journal of Behavioral Development, 7*, 145–156.

Fischhoff, B. (1975). Hindsight = foresight: The effect of outcome knowledge on judgment under uncertainty. *Journal of Experimental Psychology: Human Perception and Performance, 1*, 288–299.

Flavell, J. H. (1974). The development of inferences about others. In T. Mischel (Ed.), *Understanding other persons* (pp. 66–116). Oxford: Blackwell Publisher.

Flavell, J. H. (1985). *Cognitive development* (2nd ed.). Englewood Cliffs, NJ: Prentice-Hall.

Flavell, J. H., Flavell, E. R., & Green, F. L. (1983). Development of the appearance–reality distinction. *Cognitive Psychology, 15*, 95–120.

Johnson, M. K., Raye, C. L., Hasher, L., & Chromiak, W. (1979). Are there developmental differences in reality-monitoring? *Journal of Experimental Child Psychology, 27*, 120–128.

Markman, E. M. (1987). How children constrain the possible meanings of words. In U. Neisser (Ed.), *Concepts and conceptual development*. Cambridge University Press.

Masangkay, Z. S., McCluskey, K. A., McIntyre, C. W., Sims-Knight, J., Vaughn, B. E., & Flavell, J. H. (1974). The early development of inferences about the visual percepts of others. *Child Development, 45*, 357–366.

Miscione, J. L., Marvin, R. S., O'Brien, R. G., & Greenberg, M. T. (1978). A developmental study of preschool children's understanding of the words "know" and "guess." *Child Development, 48*, 1107–1113.

Olson, D. R., & Astington, J. W. (1987). Seeing and knowing: On the ascription of mental states to young children. *Canadian Journal of Psychology, 41*, 399–411.

Piaget, J. (1928). *Judgment and reasoning in the child*. New York: Harcourt Brace.

Piaget, J. (1929). *The child's conception of the world*. London: Routledge & Kegan Paul.

Ross, L., Lepper, M. R., & Hubbard, M. (1975). Perseverance in self-perception and social perception: Biased attributional processes in the debriefing paradigm. *Journal of Personality and Social Psychology, 32*, 880–892.

Taylor, M. (in press). The development of children's ability to distinguish what they know from what they see. *Child Development*.

Taylor, M., & Flavell, J. H. (1984). Seeing and believing: Children's understanding of the distinction between appearance and reality. *Child Development, 55*, 1710–1720.

Tversky, A., & Kahneman, D. (1973). Availability: A heuristic for judging frequency and probability. *Cognitive Psychology, 5*, 207–232.

Wellman, H. M., & Estes, D. (1986). Understanding reality: Children's ability to distinguish reality from mentality. *Child Development*, *57*, 910–923.

Wellman, H. M., & Johnson, C. N. (1979). Understanding mental processes: A developmental study of remember and forget. *Child Development*, *50*, 79–88.

Wimmer, H., & Perner, J. (1983). Beliefs about beliefs: Representation and constraining function of wrong beliefs in young children's understanding of deception. *Cognition*, *13*, 103–128.

12

The ontogeny of common sense

LYND FORGUSON and ALISON GOPNIK

The commonsense view of the world

The commonsense view of the world (CS) is the interconnected network of implicit beliefs about the world and our relation to it that informs our everyday thought and behavior as adults, and to which we appeal in defending our everyday claims and explaining our own and others' actions. CS is the common background we implicitly presuppose whenever we interpret others as rational beings inhabiting a common world with ourselves. As Davidson (1974, 1986) has argued, if we could not presuppose that we share with others an enormous number of basic beliefs, most of which are true, we could not begin to interpret their behavior as human actions. They would be unintelligible to us. The commonsense view of the world, then, is that shared web of beliefs, whatever their specific content may be, which we as adult rational humans individually hold true, which we mutually attribute to one another, and which we presuppose as a condition of interpreting one another's behavior.

There are two components to CS, one psychological and the other metaphysical. CS psychology is the view that human actions are causally dependent on the agent's epistemic state (i.e., on knowledge and beliefs concerning what is or was the case, and concerning what will or would be the case if . . .) and on the agent's desires (i.e., on what states of affairs the agent wants to obtain, on balance). When we attempt to explain someone's actions, we do so by attributing relevant epistemic states and desires to them and claiming that the action was performed because they were in the posited mental condition. Also, our rejection of someone else's proffered explanation of our own actions will typically take the form of explicitly denying that we had either the epistemic state or the desire (or both) they attributed to us. It is difficult to overestimate the extent to which our commitment to CS psychology is implicated in our everyday lives as adults. Our ability to make cooperative plans; our deeply ingrained practice of praising, blaming, excusing, and justifying behavior; our ability

Both authors contributed equally to the chapter and are listed alphabetically.

to predict what others will do under various conditions; our ability to influence others' behavior (e.g., to cajole, entreat, persuade, bribe, motivate, etc.), all depend on attributing beliefs, expectations, knowledge, wants, fears, wishes, motives, strategies, and the like to others and using these attributions in "practical reasoning."

CS metaphysics is the view that there is a single world of objects, events, states of affairs, people, and other sentient beings that I (and others) experience perceptually and think about, and that this world is independent of the thoughts and experiences I and others have of it. In short, it is the view that the world is *external* to and *independent* of my (or anyone else's) mind, whereas imagined, dreamed-of, or pretend objects, events, and situations are internal (i.e., subjective) and mind-dependent. Furthermore, CS metaphysics holds that people have *differential informational relationships* to the mind-independent world: that so-and-so is a fact does not mean I know it; what I know, others may not know; what others know, I may not know.

This view, often called "commonsense realism," is deeply implicated in all our speech and behavior. It is not simply that our behavior (including our speech behavior) is consistent with CS realism; much of what we do and say would be inexplicable or absurd on the hypothesis that we hold any other view or, indeed, on the hypothesis that we hold no metaphysical view at all. For what we do and say presupposes the view that different people can (and frequently do) experience and think about the same objects and events, that the same objects are experienced and thought about by the same person on different occasions, that objects continue to exist when unperceived by oneself or by anyone else, that one can alter the world by physical action but not simply by thinking, wishing, wanting, and so on.

It is not merely that these features of realism form the *background* to things we explicitly and consciously believe, as Searle (1983) says; on the contrary, propositions expressing central tenets of realism are often the focus of our conscious and explicit beliefs and utterances. No doubt, much that is implied by CS realism is part of the background, in the sense that our behavior conforms to propositions we never explicitly formulate to ourselves and espouse *as* beliefs. In any case, the distinction between propositions expressing one's beliefs and those expressing the background of one's beliefs is both relative and labile; anything may move from the background into the foreground under the appropriate circumstances.

The commonsense view of the world seems to be a universally held, albeit implicit, view among adults of our species. Even professional philosophers, who during business hours may argue against the adequacy of "folk psychology" and "naive realism" as explanatory theories, during their nonprofessional lives constantly offer explanations of people's behavior and of facts and events, which are intelligible only if they are interpreted as particular applications of CS psychology or CS metaphysics construed as explanatory theories.

There is, however, ample evidence that important elements of CS are absent in very young children. There are certain underlying *cognitive abilities* required for CS that are acquired gradually over the period extending from about 18 months to about 5 years of age. In the next section we identify and briefly discuss the central characteristics of these abilities; in the following section we survey a growing literature devoted to tracing the ontogeny of these abilities. Finally, we focus on a crucial threshold in the development of CS that occurs at about age 4, and we make a suggestion as to the nature of the cognitive development that enables children to pass this threshold and thus become more or less adult practitioners of CS psychology and of CS metaphysics.

Cognitive abilities underlying common sense

To characterize the cognitive abilities underlying the commonsense view of the world it will be convenient to make use of the technical concept of *mental representation*. Such a concept is needed in order to refer conveniently to a common feature of such familiar phenomena as the following: Objects perceptually appear differently to us from different points of view or under different conditions of observation (i.e., we represent them differently); we have beliefs about the world that may or may not be true (i.e., we represent the world as containing situations that it may or may not really contain); we have wishes, hopes, fears, wants about the future (i.e., we represent the future as containing this, that, or the other situation); our actions are a function not of the way the world is but of the way we think it is and want it to be (i.e., our actions are a function of representations).

Because the ontology of mental representation is a much debated topic in philosophy (for a survey, see Fodor, 1985), and because it is not the objective of the present chapter to contribute to that debate, we will need a minimalist concept of mental representation: one that commits us to as little ontological baggage as possible. Accordingly, we will understand by the term *mental representation* a mental state consisting of (a) a *representational attitude* (e.g. believing, wanting, wishing, regretting, fearing), and (b) a *symbolic content* (which can be expressed propositionally, either by the person whose mental representation it is, or by whoever attributes the mental representation to the person) that differentiates one belief from another, one desire from another, and so on. Examples of mental representations of a person S are: S's *belief* that the peasants have no bread to eat; S's *fear* that the peasants have no bread to eat; S's *regretting* that the peasants have no bread to eat; S's *desiring* the peasants to have no bread to eat.

Mental representations are defined over their *satisfaction conditions*: namely situations that, if they are (or were to be) realized in the world, do (or will or would) satisfy the intentional attitude. For example, if you are driving on a long, straight highway on a hot day and the road in the distance visually appears to be wet, then you are mentally representing a wet road ahead, which representation is satisfied if, and only if, there actually is a wet road ahead. Similarly, if you want to inherit your Aunt Matilda's fortune, your intentional attitude will be satisfied just in case you do inherit the fortune. In these respects, our characterization of mental representations follows Searle's (1983) account of what he calls "intentional states."

We typically attribute mental representations not only to adult language using humans but also to prelinguistic human infants and to some animals, as part of our attempt to explain and predict their behavior. In these explanations, we typically do not allege that those to whom we ascribe mental representations consciously experience the representations we attribute to them. Indeed, even we language-using adults typically do not consciously experience our own mental representations as such; they are psychologically transparent, not noticed (or perhaps better, beneath notice).

The cognitive ability to become aware of one's own mental representations, or to ascribe mental representations to others, is the ability to engage in *second-order* representations (or meta-representations). One does not merely fear that the United States will invade Nicaragua; one is aware of oneself as fearing this, and one may attribute the same fear to others. The *representational content* of a second-order representation is thus a first-order mental representation: one mentally represents oneself (or someone else) as mentally representing some situation. To believe that whales are fish is to have a first-order mental representation; to imagine oneself believing that whales are fish, or to believe that someone else believes that whales are fish, is to have a second-order mental representation.

It is evident that the ability to form second-order representations is a prerequisite for the development of the commonsense view of the world. If children cannot represent themselves and others as having beliefs and desires, they obviously cannot explain their own and others' actions as intentional: that is, as resulting from or expressing beliefs and desires. If they cannot represent themselves and others as merely thinking about (e.g., imagining, remembering) situations and contrast that with perceiving situations with one's senses, or if they cannot represent someone else as perceiving a situation that they themselves do not or cannot perceive, then they obviously cannot construe things in the world as being independent of people's thoughts and experiences.

In order to be a commonsense realist, however, it is not enough merely to be able to form second-order mental representations; one must also have the ability to make at least three kinds of comparative distinctions among the variety of mental representations we recognize. The first of these is the *ability to distinguish between appearance and reality* (ARD). Tree-covered mountains appear to be purple when viewed from a distance. Straight sticks partially immersed in water appear to be bent. Green objects viewed through red transparent film appear to be black. The Doppler effect causes the sound of the siren to appear to change pitch as the ambulance passes by. A hunter shoots what appears (in that light, in the dense woods) to be a deer; but it is really another hunter.

If naive realism is the view that everything is as it appears to be, then commonsense realism is not naive realism. For although we occasionally mistake appearance for reality (and vice versa), for the most part we make the distinction quite well. More important for the present context, not only does our ability to distinguish between the way things appear and the way things are independently of experience underlie much of our everyday behavior, we mark it in our language. We could not give a verbal account of this distinction, however, if we did not recognize that for something to appear a certain way is for it to be mentally represented in that way, and if we could not reflect on our first-order representations and somehow compare them with our memory representations of how things have appeared under various conditions of observation.

Closely related to the ability to mark the distinction between appearance and reality is the *ability to recognize representational diversity* (RD). This has two aspects. Not only must I be able to realize that other people (and other sentient beings, such as dogs and cats) have mental representations that I do not have; I must also be able to recognize that others often represent the same objects, situations, and events in a different way than I do. They can see what I can't see (because of our different relative spatial positions), and they see differently what both of us see. They not only know things I don't know (and therefore have representations that I can't have); they also have knowledge that I don't have about some of the same situations, objects, and events about which we both have some knowledge (and therefore represent these differently than I do).

To recognize representational diversity is not merely to recognize that others represent things differently; it is also to recognize that their representations of reality are sometimes better, more adequate than my own, in the sense of being more truly indicative of how things stand, and also in the sense of being more appropriate to how things stand (e.g., in the case of desires). But it is also, of course, often to recognize that my own representations are better, more adequate than theirs. The ability to recognize representational diversity clearly, underlies the theoretical conviction, central to commonsense realism, that there is a single reality common to all sentient beings, the features of which are independent of the representations that any of those beings may have of it. It also underlies our ability to explain the actions of others by attributing to them beliefs and desires that we do not share. The recognition of representational diversity is especially important in explaining those unsuccessful actions of others which require us to attribute a false belief to the other.

The *ability to recognize representational change* (RC) is the third ability to make comparative distinctions among mental representations that underlies the commonsense view of the world. One's first-order representations change all the time, of course. Not only do sensory representations change as I change the location of my body, the orientation of my eyes and of my head, and so on; I represent things differently as I acquire new knowledge. I continually "update" my overall representation of the world in the light of every new belief I acquire. But to say that my representations change is not to say I recognize that they change. To do that I must not only meta-represent my present representation; I must also simultaneously represent my earlier representations and recognize that they are different. I not only recognize representational change in myself; I also acknowledge it in others. In the case of myself and of others, I also frequently acknowledge that the change constitutes progress: For example, that what I (or they) believe now is more adequate than what I (or they) used to believe. But sometimes I recognize that representational change constitutes deterioration, as when I come to realize that I can no longer see as well as I could when I was younger, or that as a result of an addiction or an obsession I now desire (with inappropriate intensity or with inappropriate frequency) that to which I formerly had a more appropriate representational attitude.

The origins of common sense

There is beginning to be some evidence about the origins and development of CS in children that suggests that although the view is widespread among adults, and may even be universal, it was not always held. In particular, the crucial prerequisites for this view appear to be developed between the ages of about 18 months and 5 years. This period has been rather a mysterious one in developmental psychology, partly because of the practical difficulties of testing children this age, and partly because Piagetian theory had little to say about it. Nevertheless, some recent work suggests that the central components of commonsense psychology and commonsense metaphysics are developed between 2 and 5. This may, indeed, be the central cognitive achievement of this period.

Although there is much controversy over the exact nature of infant cognition, it seems reasonably clear that infants have little capacity for the kind of meta-representational skills that we have argued underlie the commonsense view, although they may have some other components of common sense. First, in terms of commonsense psychology, infants do clearly distinguish between people and objects, and differentially respond to the two. Moreover, some of this responding suggests that infants have primitive notions of such distinctions as the distinction between agency and causality (Leslie, Chapter 2; Poulin-Dubois & Shultz, Chapter 6). Similarly, on the metaphysical side, infants can predict the behavior of objects, and even construct generalizations about that behavior. It is clear that, contra Piaget (1954), their representations of the world are not strictly limited to their actions on the world in this period. Nevertheless, although these representations may be more abstract than Piaget supposed, infants still seem to base their representations of the world on their immediate experience of it. They show little capacity to invent or imagine possible states of affairs radically different from those they have experienced in the past. Equally, they show little capacity to meta-represent their representations, to consider and reflect on those representations and their relation to the world. Infants don't seem to distinguish between immediate experience, representations, and mind-independent reality.

At around 18 months there appears to be a radical change in the child's cognitive abilities. The most striking and well-investigated manifestation of this change is the emergence of the ability to invent or deduce solutions to difficult problems. If you give 18-month-olds a toy rake and place a toy out of reach, they will immediately use the rake to get the toy, even if they have never previously experienced this use of the rake. Similarly, 18-month-olds will often invent intelligent solutions to even very complex "object-permanence" problems. If you hide an object in a complicated way, infants can deduce the likely location of the object even if they have never seen it at that location before.

One plausible explanation of the development of these abilities is that infants become able to reflect on their own intellectual processes, at least to some extent. When infants invent new solutions to problems they seem to "run through" possible courses of action and consequences in their heads without actually having to experience those actions or consequences (see Gopnik, 1982). Similarly, solving the complex object-permanence problems may also require some ability to make generalizations about the relationship between the child's perceptual system and the world. (Gopnik, 1984a).

Similar and more direct manifestations of the ability to meta-represent appear in the child's language and symbolic play in this period. Some of the very earliest words encode aspects of the relationship between the child's representations and the world. In particular, children comment on contrasts between (a) merely represented states of affairs, such as the object of a desire or goal, or a possibility that is entertained or imagined, and (b) the actual state of affairs.

For example, children typically use words like *there* and *uh-oh* in the one-word stage to comment on the fact that their plans succeed or fail. To use these words in this way, children must be able to compare a merely represented state of affairs (the one they intend to bring about) and the actual state of affairs. Moreover, they must see that this relationship is similar to the one between represented goals and compliant or resisting reality in other cases of success and failure (Gopnik, 1982). Similarly, children use words like *allgone* to comment on the fact that they do not see an object. Again, *allgone* encodes a contrast between the child's immediate perceptual representation, in which the object is not present, and the child's belief in the continued existence of the object (Gopnik, 1984a). Slightly later in their development children begin to use *no* to negate propositions. A child may say "no hat on" pointing to a doll without a hat, again suggesting that the child can contrast an imaginary state of affairs, a state of affairs that is represented by the proposition "hat on," with the actual state of affairs. It is interesting that this use of *no* seems to develop out of earlier uses of *no* to encode the failure of plans (Gopnik & Meltzoff, 1985). It seems plausible that the contrast between merely represented worlds and the actual world is first understood in the context of plans and intentions.

The ability to contrast represented and actual states of affairs is perhaps most dramatically manifested in the emergence of symbolic play in this period (Leslie, Chapter 2). In these contexts 18-month-olds appear to be deliberately manipulating the contrast between represented, possible states of affairs and actual states of affairs. The pretend banana, like the desired banana, is a possible represented state of the world that contrasts with the actual state. All these examples involve cases in which children generate alternative, hypothetical representations, ones that are not directly given by the child's experience. The ability to generate these hypothetical representations, to imagine all the different ways the world could be, as well as the way the world actually is, is a dramatic advance over the cognitive abilities of infancy. Generating hypothetical representations is particularly useful because sometimes we can actually change the world and make it the way we want it to be, instead of the way it is. Empirically and theoretically this ability to generate representations of hypothetical states of affairs seems to be bound up with the ability to meta-represent, although the exact relationship between the two abilities is still unclear.

These changes in commonsense metaphysics are accompanied by changes in commonsense psychology. The most dramatic changes involve a contrast between the child's mental states, particularly the child's desires, and the mental states of other people. Typically, it is at around this point that children begin to willfully differentiate their own desires and intentions from the desires and intentions of others. This is connected with changes in the child's self-concept and is perhaps most dramatically mani-

fested in the emergence of the "terrible twos." Two-year-olds are notori-
ously countersuggestive: They will do something simply because they are
told not to or vice versa. This bloody-mindedness suggests that children
are exercising their newfound ability to represent their own intentions and
desires and to contrast them with the intentions and desires of others.

Some other evidence, coming from slightly later in development, also
suggests that toddlers have some of the beginnings of commonsense psychology and metaphysics and, in particular, have some meta-representational abilities. Explicitly psychological terms, such as terms for desires or
emotions, as well as epistemological and metaphysical terms, such as
think, know, real, and *pretend,* begin to appear in the child's language sometime during the second year (Bretherton, McNew, & Beeghly-Smith, 1981;
Shatz, Wellman, & Silber, 1983). It is, of course, difficult to know for
sure whether children use these terms in the same ways that adults do,
but at least some examples from this period suggest that they do, in
fact, use them to refer to representations rather than, or in contrast to,
mind-independent realities (see Wellman, 1985).

A second indicator that children at this age may have some ability to
meta-represent comes from studies of visual perspective-taking. These
tasks involve the ability to see that another person may have a different
view of the world than they do. By the time children are 2 years old they
seem to be able to recognize that another person could fail to see an object
they themselves see. However, only at about age 4 do they realize that
another person might represent an object differently than they do: that,
for example, a person who sees an object from a different angle will
perceive the object differently (Flavell, Everett, Croft, & Flavell, 1981).

Perhaps the most convincing example of meta-representation in this
early period comes in a recent study by Wellman and Estes (1986). In this
study children were asked to contrast dreams, images, and thoughts with
real objects. Even the 3-year-old children in this study were able to make
the distinction. Moreover, they could intelligently justify it. These data
form a particularly convincing demonstration of the fact that even very
young children can form second-order representations and can contrast
"mere" representations and "actual" reality.

However, as in the earlier period children seem to make this contrast in
terms of a distinction between mental states that are mere representations
on the one hand, and an independent reality, on the other. Just as the
younger children can implicitly distinguish mental states such as desires
or imaginings from real objects, so the older children can explicitly make
these distinctions. However, these children do not seem to be able to distinguish between the different informational relationships that may hold
between representations and reality. As we will see, they show little understanding of the principles of representational change, representational
diversity, or the appearance–reality distinction.

All these abilities require that the child simultaneously consider a particular representation as a representation *and* as an indicator of how the world really stands. Three findings in particular point to such limitations in the child's conceptual abilities. First, children seem to be unable to make the appearance–reality distinction in this period. When presented with a sponge painted to look like a rock, they are likely to say either that it looks like a rock and really is a rock, or that it looks like a sponge and really is a sponge (Flavell, 1986). Second, they appear to be unable to appreciate representational diversity. This is demonstrated in the "false belief" paradigm that has been extensively explored by Perner and Wimmer and their colleagues (Wimmer & Perner, 1983; Perner, Leekam, & Wimmer, 1987). If a 3-year-old is shown a candy box full of pencils, for example, he is likely to say that another child will immediately know there are pencils in the box even before opening it. Similarly, children of this age appear to be unable to appreciate representational change. If children are shown a closed candy box full of pencils and the box is then opened, they are likely to say that they knew there were pencils in the box all along (Gopnik & Astington, 1988; Astington & Gopnik, Chapter 10). All three of these abilities develop in the period from 3 to 5, and recent research suggests that all three of these abilities are correlated with one another.

The development of the representational model of the mind

How are we to account for the appearance of the ability to recognize the appearance–reality distinction (ARD), the ability to recognize representational diversity (RD), and the ability to recognize representational change (RC) at about the same time in a child's development?

As we have seen, all three abilities presuppose the underlying ability to form second-order representations of first-order mental representations. The mere ability to form second-order representations, however, cannot by itself account for the appearance of these abilities at about age 4. For, as we have seen, there is ample evidence that children are able to meta-represent first-order mental representations as early as age 2.

In our view, the explanation is that ARD, RD, and RC, unlike the meta-representational achievements of 3-year-olds, require the child to recognize that *real* objects, events and states of affairs *are mentally represented*, as well as "unreal" objects (e.g., winged pencils), events (e.g., dreams), and states of affairs (e.g., the desire to have a puppy of one's own, just like the boy next door). As we have seen, the 3-year-olds' achievements require them to contrast real objects or states of affairs with *merely* represented objects or states of affairs. So these children seem to be able to differentiate between real things and desires, dreams, imaginings, thoughts and the like. To make these contrasts, however, 3-year-olds do not have to take cognizance of the fact that they are also mentally representing the real objects and states of affairs. The contrast for 3-year-olds is between the real and the not real, with the recognition that "unrealities" can be "present" to one only as mental representations. In the ARD, RD, and RC cases, on the other hand, the child must be able to make distinctions between *representations* of real things and states of affairs (i.e., realities *as represented*) and the real things and states of affairs themselves.

The conflicting representations involved in representational diversity, representational change, and the appearance–reality distinction are not simply objects of desire, goals, or possibilities that are imagined or entertained. They are full-fledged, serious beliefs. They are representations that are supposed to correspond with the way the world really is, rather than representations that point to how it could be. We suggest that 3-year-olds are unable to appreciate that these representations, too, are like the representations involved in desire or imagination. This ability begins to emerge in the period from 3 to 5.

We do not wish to imply, of course, that 5-year-olds always or even usually treat serious beliefs as mere representations. Even adults don't do that. As mentioned, most of the time we treat our beliefs as if they were transparent, as if they were the objects and events they represent. But as adults we *can* consider these representations as mental entities if we have to, when, for example, we run across representational change and diversity and instances when appearance and reality diverge. Five-year-olds, like adults, seem to be able to treat beliefs as representations when they need to, whereas for the 3-year-old, all beliefs are transparent.

The difference between the 3-year-olds and the 4-year-olds might be summarized as follows: The 4-year-olds have developed a *representational model of the mind*. This model construes the relation between the mind and external reality as mediated by mental representations: mental states with contents that have satisfaction conditions in the external world. Some of these states are satisfied (roughly: the world is as it is represented as being); some of them are not. The world is independent of our thought and experience; but it is *represented in* thought and experience. To think about or experience is always to represent mentally, whether or not it is always the case that the content of one's experience or thought constitutes accurate (or adequate) information about how things stand in the world.

Four-year-old children, then, are beginning to recognize representations as representations, and they are beginning to adopt a metacognitive policy about them: namely, that some of these representations are one's own personal viewpoint on a reality independent of this or any other private, personal viewpoint; that they are effects in oneself caused by the action of that independent reality on one's senses; that representations provide information about the way reality stands; that different people have a different informational relation to reality than oneself; that one's own informational relation to reality changes constantly. By the time children are about 6 years old, the development of the realist viewpoint is virtually complete. They have become adept at verbally distinguishing between appearance and reality, and they have no difficulty recognizing representational diversity and representational change.

We believe this general metacognitive ability underlies some of the more specific abilities advanced in other chapters in this volume to explain this 3- to 6-year-old shift. A number of contributors (Wellman, Chapter 4; Wimmer, Hogrefe, & Sodian, Chapter 9; Leslie, Chapter 2), particularly those impressed by the early meta-representational abilities, have suggested that 3-year-olds lack specific information about the relation between the world and the mind. For example, Wellman suggests that 3-year-olds do not think of the mind as an active information processor, and Wimmer, Hogrefe, and Sodian suggest that children are unable to understand the origins of their representations. These specific abilities require that the child be able to distinguish representations of real objects from the real objects themselves. Information processing requires precisely an understanding of how "real" (or true or accurate) representations are related to the real world. This contrasts with the more passive view in which children might simply see minds as the receptacles for representations of the unreal ("that's where thoughts, dreams, wishes, images, etc., live"), in contrast to the real things that live in the world. Similarly, understanding the origins of representations requires an ability to distinguish between representations, even "real" representations, and the informational relationship between those representations and the world. We agree that children do come to understand during this period that the mind is an information processor, and that representations have sources (see Gopnik & Graf, in press); but this is a consequence of a more general change in their view of the relationship between representation and reality. In particular, the inability to understand representational change suggests that 3-year-olds have a more profound representational deficit (Astington & Gopnik, Chapter 10).

In this respect our view is closer to the views advanced by Perner (Chapter 8) and Flavell (Chapter 13). They also see the 3- to 6-year-old shift as a profound change in the child's representational capacity or world view rather than as a more superficial (though still serious) matter of acquiring detailed information about the relationship between the world and the mind. On our view 3-year-olds don't have detailed information about the relation between the world and the mind because they haven't made the necessary distinctions between the world and the mind that are a prerequisite for understanding this relation, although they may have made other distinctions between the world and the mind.

We think that this important and profound difference between the minds of 3- and 5-year-olds is best understood as a qualitative difference, almost a "paradigm shift," in the child's theory of mind; in this respect our view *is* similar to Wellman's (Chapter 4). This view is in contrast to the view that 5-year-olds simply have a more computationally complex representation of the mind, as advanced here by Leslie (Chapter 2) and Shultz (Chapter 18). It is not simply that the 5-year-olds have extra concepts or processing capacities that are not available to the 3-year-olds. Instead, we would say that the 5-year-old has a better theory of the mind than the 3-year-old in the same way that the 5-year-old has a better theory of the physical world than the 3-year-old or, to choose a more contentious example, the way that cognitivism is a better theory of the mind than behaviorism. The difference between these theories isn't just a difference of complexity; in fact, the more advanced theories are often computationally simpler than the less advanced ones. Instead it's a difference in how well a theory explains the relevant data and allows one to interact effectively with the world.

We would argue, then, that between ages 5 and 6 most of the fundamental elements of commonsense realism are in place. Children at this age appreciate not only that representations may differ from reality but also that there may be alternative representations of reality, as in the cases of representational change and diversity and in the appearance–reality distinction. Five-year-olds have substantially acquired the commonsense beliefs that allow us to understand each other.

However, there are aspects of the commonsense view of the world that still may not be apparent to young children. For example, although children may be able to appreciate that people's perceptions or representations may differ, they may still be unable to understand that other people might draw different inferences than they do. For example, Chandler and Helm (1984) and Olson and Astington (1987) found that 5-year-olds who were presented with a restricted view of an object, and were then allowed to see the whole object, assumed that other people who saw the restricted view would immediately infer that the restricted view was part of a larger object. In other words, although these children presumably knew that other people might have different representations than they did if they were given substantially different kinds of information, they still thought that with similar information other people would draw the same inferences they did.

This finding points up another aspect of children's understanding of these matters that may continue to develop. There is some evidence that children's ability to deal with change and diversity may differ depending on the kinds of subject matter they are dealing with. For example, we have noted that an ability to appreciate representational diversity apparently appears first in a perceptual context (Flavell, Flavell, & Green, 1983);

then, in a context in which the participants have different information (Wimmer & Perner, 1983); and finally, in a context in which participants draw different inferences from similar information. Similarly, in our experiments even 5-year-old children had difficulty understanding representational change in an abstract context in which their representation of number changed, although they had no such difficulties in dealing with a more perceptually based representation (Gopnik & Astington, 1988).

Finally, it is perhaps worth noting here that the system of commonsense realism that children build up so painstakingly in the preschool years is subject to revision and criticism by adults later on. Philosophers are, of course, the worst culprits in this regard. However, Chandler (in press) has made the interesting suggestion that adolescents may typically discover, and may even advocate, the alternative metaphysical positions of solipsism and idealism, a cognitive fact that might help to explain typical adolescent malaise.

General implications of this view for child development

We suggested earlier that the development of at least the basic elements of commonsense psychology and metaphysics may be the most significant development of the preschool years. Certainly it seems to us that many of the significant and striking differences between preschool and school-age children may be explained in terms of the differences in these beliefs.

For example, it has commonly been noted that preschoolers are cognitively labile, and strongly context-dependent. That is, their representations of objects may vary widely depending on contextual factors. Children may, for example, respond very differently on a task that involves familiar rather than strange objects (Donaldson, 1978). This aspect of preschool cognition may be the result of the fact that preschoolers do not feel it is imperative to relate alternative representations to a single real world. Preschoolers seem to accept the idea that there might be different "realities" at different times or for different people, or that their present reality need not be compared with past representations or with the representations of others. If preschoolers, as we have suggested, don't compare their present representation of an object with past representations, it may not be surprising that they are willing to answer a cognitive question one way at one moment and another way at the next, without apparent conflict.

At around 5 children typically lose this characteristic cognitive flexibility. In fact, if anything, children at this period become hyperrealists. The discovery of commonsense realism involves the discovery that there is only one world against which alternative representations must be assessed. But 5-year-olds will extend this discovery to areas in which it is inappropriate. For example, there is no single real world in the realm of social conventions such as table manners or games, or in the realm of pictorial representation or language. Manners, games, pictures, and words gain their meaning from conventions not from some intrinsic relationship to an external world. Five-year-olds, however, typically treat these areas as if the tenets of commonsense realism also applied here: That is, that words, rules, and pictures are unalterable "real" things. For example, 6-year-olds are unwilling to admit that people could agree to change the rules of a game, that there could be alternative pictorial representations, or that a word could have several meanings (Piaget, 1929).

Although this overextension of realism may lead to mistakes in certain areas, in general, realism underpins many of the most impressive achievements of childhood. For example, the achievement of conservation abilities depends crucially on the view that there is a single world that may give rise to different appearances. The same is true of the notion of "natural kinds" (Keil, 1986). Both these cognitive achievements appear in this period.

Moreover, in addition to these cognitive differences the development of the commonsense view leads to a variety of social and temperamental differences. We have noted that our sharing of commonsense beliefs underlies much of our ability to interpret the actions and behavior of others. It seems to us that 6-year-olds typically share the essential features of this background, while younger children do not. This may explain at least in part our common impression that preschoolers, especially younger preschoolers (3- and 4-year-olds) are flaky, fey, and unfettered, that they are more different from us than (say) 6-year-olds are. This impression is reflected in our institutional practices, such as the start of formal schooling or even such religious practices as confirmation. Indeed, it would be difficult to see how we could formally instruct children in the beliefs of adult life if they did not share the basic tenets of common sense. It is also reflected in common psychological characterizations of the preschooler as a creature without logic or reason (see, for example, Piaget's description of the preoperational child). More recent investigations have demonstrated that there is considerable method in the 3-year-old's madness, but since the method is so different from our own, our normal interpretive assumptions tend to break down.

Finally, the cognitive differences reflected in the development of common sense are also reflected in personality and temperament differences. The classical psychoanalytic notion of "latency" captures an interesting temperamental difference between preschool and school-age children. Preschoolers typically give the impression of being more imaginative and uninhibited, more likely to fantasize and confabulate than their more literal-minded, serious, and restrained elders. The two groups of children conform to a common caricature of the artist and the scientist respectively.

But that caricature may capture a genuine cognitive difference in artists and scientists, and in preschoolers and schoolchildren. The cognitive agenda (as it were) of 3-year-olds seems to be to generate and create alternative representations of the world and, in particular, to move beyond the experience-driven representations of infancy. The 5-year-old, on the other hand, seems to be more concerned with evaluating alternative representations of the world, and measuring them against a single "real" external world.

In addition to telling us something about the difference between younger and older children, studying the ontogeny of common sense tells us something about the process of conceptual change itself. A striking consequence of this work is that even fundamental assumptions about the way we work and the way the world works are neither directly given by our experience nor innately specified. Rather, these cognitive structures are constructed by children as they interact with the world and learn more about it and about themselves. This may sound, and should sound, like a Piagetian conclusion; but where Piaget linked constructivism with biological principles we would prefer to link it to principles of theory construction. Commonsense metaphysics and psychology are constructed in the same way that scientific and philosophical theories are constructed. That is, children and adults posit theoretical entities (including psychological entities such as beliefs and desires, and metaphysical entities such as those involved in the distinction between appearance and reality) to help explain the regularities in the world and in their own behavior and that of others. This theory-construction process is implicit rather than explicit, of course, as are commonsense theories themselves; but in other respects it is similar to the more conscious processes that adult psychologists and metaphysicians engage in. This view of conceptual change as theory construction is beginning to emerge in a number of areas of developmental psychology (see Gopnik, 1984b; Carey, 1986; Wellman, Chapter 4). Interestingly, the particular view that commonsense psychology and metaphysics are theories (sometimes called the "theory theory") has also been advanced by a number of philosophers (Lewis, 1972; Churchland, 1984; Stich, 1983). We suggest that children not only adopt the commonsense view in psychology and metaphysics; they do so because they are psychologists and metaphysicians themselves.

REFERENCES

Bretherton, I., McNew, S., & Beeghly-Smith, M. (1981). Early person knowledge as expressed in gestural and verbal communication: When do infants acquire a "theory of mind"? In M. E. Lamb & L. R. Sherrod (Eds.), *Infant social cognition*. Hillsdale, NJ: Erlbaum.

Carey, S. (1986). *Conceptual change in childhood.* Cambridge, MA: MIT Press.

Chandler, M. (in press). The Othello effect: An essay on the emergence and eclipse of skeptical doubt. *Human Development.*

Chandler, M. J., & Helm, D. (1984). Developmental changes in the contribution of shared experience to role-taking competence. *International Journal of Behavioral Development, 7,* 145–156.

Churchland, P. M. (1984). *Matter and consciousness.* Cambridge, MA: Bradford Books/MIT Press.

Davidson, D. (1974). The very idea of a conceptual scheme. *Proceedings and addresses of the American Philosophical Association, 47.*

Davidson, D. (1986). A coherence theory of truth and knowledge. In E. LePore (Ed.) *Truth and interpretation.* Oxford: Blackwell.

Donaldson, M. (1978). *Children's minds.* New York: Norton.

Flavell, J. H. (1986). The development of children's knowledge about the appearance–reality distinction. *American Psychologist, 41,* 418–425.

Flavell, J. H., Everett, B. A., Croft, K., & Flavell, E. R. (1981). Young children's knowledge about visual perception: Further evidence for the Level 1–Level 2 distinction. *Developmental Psychology, 17,* 99–103.

Flavell, J. H., Flavell, E., & Green, F. L. (1983). Development of the appearance–reality distinction. *Cognitive Psychology, 15,* 95–120.

Fodor, J. A. (1985). Fodor's guide to mental representations: The intelligent auntie's vade mecum. *Mind, 94,* 76–100.

Gopnik, A. (1982). Words and plans: Early language and the development of intelligent action. *Journal of Child Language, 9,* 303–318.

Gopnik, A. (1984a). The acquisition of gone and the development of the object concept. *Journal of Child Language, 11,* 273–292.

Gopnik, A. (1984b). Conceptual and semantic change in scientists and children. *Linguistics, 20,* 163–179.

Gopnik, A. & Meltzoff, A. N. (1985). From people to plans to objects. *Journal of Pragmatics, 9,* 495–512.

Gopnik, A., & Astington, J. W. (1988). Children's understanding of representational change and its relation to the understanding of false belief and the appearance–reality distinction. *Child Development, 59,* 26–37.

Gopnik, A., & Graf, P. (in press). Knowing how you know: Young children's ability to identify and remember the sources of their beliefs. *Child Development.*

Keil, F. (1986). The acquisition of natural kinds and artifact terms. In W. Demopoulos & A. Marras (Eds.), *Language learning and concept acquisition.* Norwood, NJ: Ablex.

Lewis, D. (1972). Psychophysical and theoretical identifications. In N. Block (Ed.), *Readings in the philosophy of psychology* (Vol. 1). Cambridge, MA: Harvard University Press.

Olson D. R. & Astington, J. W. (1987). Seeing and knowing: On the ascription of mental states to young children. *Canadian Journal of Psychology, 41,* 399–411.

Perner, J., Leekam, S. R., & Wimmer, H. (1987). Three-year-olds' difficulty with false belief: The case for a conceptual deficit. *British Journal of Developmental Psychology, 5,* 125–137.

Piaget, J. (1929). *The child's conception of the world*. London: Routledge & Kegan Paul.

Piaget, J. (1954). *The construction of reality in the child*. New York: Basic.

Searle, J. (1983). *Intentionality*. Cambridge University Press.

Shatz, M., Wellman, H. M., & Silber, S. (1983). The acquisition of mental verbs: A systematic investigation of the first reference to mental state. *Cognition, 14,* 301–321.

Stich, S. (1983). *From folk psychology to cognitive science: The case against belief*. Cambridge MA: Bradford Books/MIT Press.

Wellman, H. M. (1985). The origins of metacognition. In D. Forrest-Pressley, C. MacKinnon, & T. Waller (Eds.), *Metacognition, cognition and human performance*. New York: Academic Press.

Wellman, H., & Estes, D. (1986). Early understanding of mental entities: A reexamination of childhood realism. *Child Development, 57,* 910–923.

Wimmer, H., & Perner, J. (1983). Beliefs about beliefs: Representation and constraining function of wrong beliefs in young children's understanding of deception. *Cognition, 13,* 103–128.

13

The development of children's knowledge about the mind: From cognitive connections to mental representations

JOHN H. FLAVELL

The development of children's knowledge about the mind is becoming a very exciting area of research. Researchers are investigating such interesting topics as children's understanding of false belief; their perceptual, conceptual, and affective perspective-taking skills; and their knowledge about various distinctions: distinctions between real and mental, real and pretend, real and apparent, what is said and what is meant, and what is seen and what is known. In addition, there seems to be a growing sense that many of these acquisitions are developmentally related, despite their apparent diversity and heterogeneity (e.g., Perner, Leekam, & Wimmer, 1987). A number of them seem to develop around the same age and may be mediated by the same insights into the nature of mind. In short, there is a lot of interesting research activity in this area, and it seems to be producing converging results.

What is the nature of this convergence? How can we tie these findings together theoretically? I am currently trying to do it by elaborating and generalizing my distinction between Level 1 and Level 2 knowledge about visual perception (Flavell, 1978; Flavell, Everett, Croft, & Flavell, 1981). My current theory also owes much to the developmental ideas of Chandler and Boyes (1982); Forguson and Gopnik (Chapter 12); Pillow (in press a); Taylor (Chapter 11; in press); and Wellman (Chapter 4; 1987).

The theory

Cognitive connections

According to this theory, by 2 to 3 years of age children have learned that they and other people can be epistemically related or "cognitively connected" to things in the external world in a variety of different ways. An example of a cognitive connection is seeing something. Young children know that they can become cognitively connected to something by seeing it; they also understand that they may not see it - that they may not be connected to it in this way at a given moment. They further understand that they may be cognitively connected, or not connected, to things in many other ways as well. That is, they understand at least roughly what it is to hear or not hear something, to taste it, smell it, feel it by touching it, know it, think of or about it, remember it, dream of or about it, image or imagine it, pretend with it, want it, intend to do something with it, and have specific feelings and emotions regarding it – like it, fear it, be angry at it, and so on.

They also have some understanding that: (a) these cognitive connections can change over time; (b) they are largely independent of one another; (c) their own connections are independent of those of other people; (d) connections entail inner, subjective experiences. As examples of (a), they realize that they dreamed of x last night but are not dreaming of it now, and that they see y now but did not see it a minute ago. Thus, there are developmentally early analogues of Gopnik and Astington's *representational change* (1988; Chapter 10). As examples of (b), they understand that they can hear something either with or without also seeing it, know or think about it with or without simultaneously perceiving it, and the like. To illustrate (c), they are capable of recognizing that another person may perceive, know, want, dislike, and so on, something that they do not or vice versa. This recognition is a developmentally early analogue of Forguson and Gopnik's (Chapter 12) *representational diversity*; it is also a clear early instance of nonegocentric social cognition. As to (d), recent research by Wellman, Bretherton, and others (Dunn, Bretherton, & Munn, 1987; Wellman, Chapter 4; Wellman & Estes, 1986) suggests that young children can distinguish to some extent between such subjective acts and experiences as seeing and feeling something and that objective something itself. That is, it seems likely that they tend to interpret perceptions, feelings and the like as mental events that go on inside themselves and others. When they see another child cry, for instance, they are likely to assume that the child is experiencing unpleasant inner feelings. Similarly, when they see a person look at something or behave purposefully, they are likely to represent that person as having the internal experience of seeing or intending something (see Johnson, Chapter 3). This recent evidence suggests, therefore, that children possess "a rudimentary but coherent mentalistic theory of human action" (Wellman, Chapter 4) even at age 3.

Children of this age also believe, as we generally do, that each object or event in the world has only one nature – one "way that it is" – at any given point in time. It cannot be two or more very different, mutually contradictory, and incompatible things at the same time; rather, it can only be one thing. Consequently, it makes no sense to them to hear something described as being radically different than the single way it "is" (with "is" not differentiated from "seems to them at that moment").

Mental representations

However, young children tend not to understand that forming cognitive connections to things entails mentally representing those things in various ways. They tend to be largely ignorant of the fact that it is possible to represent a single thing with its single nature in several different ways – ways that would be mutually contradictory if they described the object itself rather than mental representations of it. Thus, they do not clearly understand that even though something may be only one way out there in the world, it can be more than one way up here in our heads, in our mental representations of it.

This view of the young child's metacognitive limitations is very similar to the views of other theorists in this area. Chandler and Boyes proposed that there is "a shift from an object-centered or copy theory of knowledge to a subject-oriented or constructivistic epistemology within which it becomes possible to make sharp category distinctions between material events and their psychological representations" (1982, p. 393; see also Chandler, Chapter 20). Forguson and Gopnik suggest that young children need to develop "a representational model of the mind" (Chapter 12). Wellman claims that young preschoolers "have yet to achieve an understanding of the mind as an interpretive, executive, mediating entity" (Chapter 4). Wellman (Chapter 4) and Pillow (in press a) suggest that young children tacitly conceive of the mind as a passive receptacle that takes in contents as is, without interpretation, selective encoding, or any other kind of mental modification. As a consequence, they are likely to assume that whatever content is presented to a person is automatically attended to, perceived, recognized, understood, and retained in memory by that person, because they have little conception as yet of mental processes that act on content received. In Chandler and Boyes's words again, they have a "copy theory of knowledge" rather than a "constructivistic epistemology" (1982, p. 393). Similarly, in my earlier Level 1–2 formulation I claimed that the young child "thinks about viewing objects . . . but not yet about views of objects" (Flavell, 1977, p. 126), that is, about *whether* something is seen (cognitive connections) but not yet about *how* it appears to the viewer (mental representations).

I am suggesting, then, that young children are cognizant of cognitive connections to things but are relatively ignorant of the mental representations of the things these connections engender. How might such children respond to tasks or situations that require cognizance of representations? The tasks we have used to assess children's understanding of the appearance–reality (AR) distinction will serve to illustrate how they might respond (e.g., Flavell, 1986; Flavell, Flavell, & Green, 1983; Flavell, Green,

& Flavell, 1986). Following brief pretraining on the meaning of the AR distinction and the words used to express it (*looks like* vs. *really and truly*), we present the children with, say, a sponge that looks like a rock. After they have manipulated the object, we ask the A and R questions. The A question is: "When you look at this with your eyes right now, does it *look like* a rock or does it *look like* a sponge?" The R question is: "What is this really and truly – is it *really* and *truly* a sponge or is it *really* and *truly* a rock?" Order of questions and of options within questions are counter-balanced or randomized.

Let us suppose that after manipulating it but just before the A and R question, the children decide the object is a sponge, not a rock. For them, therefore, it "is" just one thing – a sponge. We then ask them our A and R questions. We interpret these questions as questions about the two very different, incompatible-seeming ways this one object can be mentally represented, namely, as a rock in its visual appearance and as a sponge in its enduring reality (texture, function, etc.). We mentally tag each representation for the cognitive perspective or stance that gave rise to it, for its epistemic credentials, so to speak. In this case, we tag one as "what it looks like it is" and the other as "what it really is." However, because they lack adequate understanding of mental representations they should tend to interpret them simply as two differently worded requests for the object's single-identity-in-the-world and should therefore give the same answer to both questions: "sponge." If they had decided instead that the object was a rock, they should, of course, answer "rock" to both questions. Our studies show that 3-year-olds tend to perform poorly on simple AR tasks such as the one utilizing the sponge–rock. Moreover, consistent with the process analysis just given, by far their most common error pattern is to give the same answer to both questions.

In summary, the theory claims that children begin their discovery of the mental world by learning that they and other people have internal experiences that are cognitively connected to external objects and events, experiences such as seeing objects, wanting them, and so on. Later, they gradually realize that these cognitive connections engender inner, mental representations of their external objects, and that the same object can be represented in different, seemingly contradictory ways.

Evidence for the theory

The theory predicts that young children should perform well on tasks calling for knowledge about cognitive connections but poorly on those calling for knowledge about mental representations. The available evidence tends to support these predictions.

Cognitive connections

Evidence that young children possess some understanding of cognitive connections is most abundant in the case of seeing (Churcher & Scaife, 1982; Cox, 1980; Flavell, 1978; Flavell et al., 1981; Flavell, Shipstead, & Croft, 1978, 1980; Hobson, 1980; Hughes, 1975; Hughes & Donaldson, 1979; Lempers, Flavell, & Flavell, 1977; Masangkay et al., 1974; Yaniv & Shatz, Chapter 5; for a brief review of this evidence, see Flavell, 1985, pp. 136–138). Let S = the child, O = another person, x = the visual target (a real or depicted object), and a = any large object interposed between O and x such as to block O's vision of x. By the age of $2\frac{1}{2}$–3 years, children act as if they know implicitly that the following four conditions must hold if O is to see x (Flavell, 1978; Lempers et al., 1977): (a) At least one of O's eyes must be open; (b) O's eyes must be aimed in the general direction of x; (c) there must be no vision-blocking a on the line of sight between O and x; (d) what S sees and does not see with regard to O, x, or, a has no bearing on what O sees; that is, the child's cognition is fundamentally nonegocentric when dealing with "what is seen" type problems.

Tacit knowledge of these four facts permits children of this age to *produce*, *prevent*, and *diagnose* object seeing by the other person. They can produce or engender the seeing of x by O by pointing to or verbally designating x, by getting O to open his or her eyes and face x, by moving or reorienting x so that it is in O's line of sight, and by repositioning either a or x so that a no longer blocks O's seeing of x. They can prevent O's seeing of x by moving x behind a, or a in front of x, and by getting O to close his or her eyes or turn away from x. Finally, they can diagnose or assess whether or not O currently sees x by noting whether or not conditions (a)–(c) obtain. Thus, the research evidence indicates that children of this age are nonegocentric showers (e.g., they will orient a picture so that O, but not they, can see it), nonegocentric hiders (e.g., they will place an object where they, but not O, can still see it), and nonegocentric percept assessors (e.g., they know that their bodies are still visible to O when their eyes, but not O's, are closed).

Children of this age can also understand that a person may be cognitively connected to an object in one way but not in another. For example, they understand that they (Flavell, Green, & Flavell, 1987) or another individual (Yaniv & Shatz, Chapter 5) can hear something but not see it, see and hear it but not smell or touch it, and the like. They also possess a kind of low-level analogue of the appearance–reality distinction that undoubtedly originates in their discovery of object permanence during infancy. That is, they can recognize that a hidden object is not presently perceptible to them (a kind of "appearance") but is nonetheless physically present, behind the screen ("reality") (Flavell, Green, & Flavell, 1987).

Some studies suggest that 3-year-olds are aware that people who have had no perceptual access to information do not know that information (Hogrefe, Wimmer, & Perner, 1986; Pillow, in press b); other studies suggest that they may lack this awareness (Wimmer, Hogrefe, & Perner, 1988; Wimmer, Hogrefe, & Sodian, Chapter 9). To my knowledge, however, no one doubts that they have at least some grasp of what it is to know versus not know a piece of information, and are aware that one person may know something that another person does not.

Finally, for evidence that young children possess some understanding of memories, dreams, images, desires, intentions, feelings and emotions, see Bretherton, Fritz, Zahn-Waxler, and Ridgeway (1986); Dunn et al. (1987); Estes, Wellman, and Woolley (in press); Wellman, (Chapter 4); Wellman and Estes (1986), and Yuill (1984). In the case of feelings and desires, for example, we have some pilot data indicating that 3-year-olds easily understand that, say, a cat may like cat food even though they themselves do not like it.

Mental representations

Appearance–reality. As mentioned previously, young children tend to give a single answer to both A and R questions in AR tasks, as would be expected if their understanding of mental representations were limited. They tend to have such problems with the distinction between an object's real and apparent identity, as in the sponge–rock example described previously. In addition, they have been shown to have similar problems with the distinction between real and apparent color, size, shape, number, object presence, actions, emotions, and gender identity (Flavell, 1986; Flavell et al., 1986, in press; Harris and Gross, Chapter 15; Trautner, 1985). The same is true when the discrepant-from-reality appearance is auditory or olfactory rather than visual (Flavell et al., 1986).

Three lines of evidence indicate that young children's difficulties with the AR distinction are nontrivial, deep-seated, genuinely intellectual ones.

1. Young children of the same age from different countries perform similarly poorly on the same AR tasks: children from the United States and People's Republic of China in the case of real versus apparent color, size, and object identity (Flavell, Zhang, Zou, Dong, & Qi, 1983); children from Great Britain, the United States, and Japan in the case of real versus apparent emotions (Harris and Gross, Chapter 15). These results suggest that their difficulties with the distinction are robust and substantial enough to survive at least some major differences in language, culture, and child-rearing practices.

2. We have attempted to uncover any nascent, fragile AR competence

young children might have by using seemingly easier, less demanding tests of this competence (Flavell et al., 1986; Flavell, Green, Wahl, & Flavell, 1987). Most of these attempts have failed, however. For example, we tried to ask 3-year-olds for an object's real color in a color AR task without using a "really and truly" question, arguably too difficult a question for young children (Flavell, Green, Wahl, & Flavell, 1987). With the child watching all proceedings, the experimenter placed, say, a white card under a blue color filter so the card looked blue. Then, with the card still under the filter, he detached a precut piece from the card, put the piece into his closed hand, removed the closed hand from behind the filter, placed on the table that white piece and a blue piece of the same size and shape, and then simply asked the child, "Which is the piece I just took out of the card?" This question is similar to the standard reality question ("Is this card really and truly blue or really and truly white?"), but does not require understanding of the expression *really and truly* and does not require a verbal response. Nevertheless, our young subjects did not find it any easier than the standard question. That is, they frequently responded by pointing to the blue piece, the one that matched the card's present apparent color rather than its real color, just as they frequently responded to the standard R question by saying "blue."

   3. Flavell et al. (1986) and Marjorie Taylor (personal communication) tried to teach the distinction between real and apparent color to 3-year-olds who performed poorly on standard color AR tasks. Braine and Shanks (1965) attempted to do the same with the distinction between real and apparent size. None of these attempts was successful. Thus, all three lines of evidence suggest that young children's difficulties with the distinction between appearance and reality are very real indeed.

Visual perspective-taking. According to my Level 1–2 account of the development of children's knowledge about perception (Flavell, 1978; Flavell et al., 1981), at Level 1 (2–3 years) children understand that another person may or may not see something, whereas at Level 2 (4–5 years) they further understand that something seen may present different appearances or engender different visual experiences if the observer views it from different positions in space. Level 1 knowledge can therefore be conceptualized as part of knowledge about cognitive connections, and Level 2 knowledge about visual perspectives as part of knowledge about mental representations. In several studies Flavell et al. (1981) and Masangkay et al. (1974) administered both Level 1 and Level 2 tasks to groups of 3- and 4-year-olds. In one of the Level 2 tasks, for example, children had to infer that a horizontally displayed depicted turtle that looked upside down (or right side up) to them, looked right side up (or upside down) to an observer seated opposite; precautions were of course taken to ensure that the children knew what these expressions meant. The results of these studies supported the earlier Level 1–2 account and the present theory. That is, the 3-year-olds performed very well on the Level 1 tasks but poorly on the Level 2 tasks, whereas the 4-year-olds performed well on both sets of tasks. Furthermore, reminiscent of the AR studies just reviewed, an attempt to teach Level 2 thinking to children who did not already think that way proved largely unsuccessful. Another comparison of younger and older preschoolers' performance on a different sort of Level 2 task also yielded results consistent with the theory (Flavell, Flavell, Green, & Wilcox, 1980). Our impression was that it simply made no sense to the younger children to characterize the turtle as simultaneously both "upside down" for them and "right side up" for the other observer; to them the turtle simply "was" whichever single way it looked to them at the moment the questions were asked.

We recently compared young 3-year-olds' understanding of a visual "appearance," an auditory "appearance," and a "reality" at both the connections and representations levels (Flavell et al., 1987). In the connections task, the experimenter (Frances Green) held a bell out of sight behind a screen and asked the children if at that moment they saw it, if they heard it (the bell sounded), and if there was a bell there; thus they were questioned about the object's visibility and audibility (two different "appearances"), and about its physical presence ("reality"). For the representations version, after appropriate pretraining she put on a dog mask, stepped behind a screen so only the mask was visible, and asked the children if she presently looked like Francie, if she sounded like Francie (as she talked normally), and if she really was Francie; thus they were questioned about her visual appearance, auditory appearance, and real identity. They were also asked the same questions substituting "a dog" for "Francie." We predicted that the children would perform well on the connections task but poorly on the representations task, because only the latter required them to represent one object in two different ways: dog in visual appearance, Francie in auditory appearance and in reality. It also required them to differentiate between two different appearances, one visual and one auditory, and thereby constituted a kind of within-person rather than between-persons Level 2 perspective-taking task. As predicted, the children performed very well on the connections task but quite poorly on the representations task.

Of course an object does not change its real, objective size and shape when moved toward or away from an observer or when rotated. However, there is a certain sense in which it can be said to change its apparent size and shape for the observer under these transformations. That is, the observer can voluntarily focus on its retinal or projective size and shape, and experience these as changing, even while remaining aware (and perhaps still perceiving, via perceptual constancy mechanisms) that objective size and shape have not really changed. Representing them in these two different ways would seem to require an understanding of representations similar to that required for differentiating appearance and reality representations in AR tasks and for differentiating two perspectively given visual representations in Level 2 visual perspective-taking tasks. Accordingly, Pillow and Flavell (1986) predicted, and found, that 4-year-olds were considerably more able than 3-year-olds to attend to and reason about projective size and shape. For example, most 4-year-olds could predict, before actual experience, that objects moved away from them and toward the experimenter would appear smaller to them and larger to the experimenter, even though they recognized that the object's real size remained unchanged. Although we have not tested this yet, we suspect that the ability to think about the two visual representations that result from prolonged scrutiny of a perceptually ambiguous figure would show a similar developmental course.

Conceptual perspective-taking. The interesting recent evidence concerning the seeing–knowing distinction (Chandler & Helm, 1984; Olson & Astington, 1987; Taylor, Chapter 11; in press), representational diversity and change (Astington & Gopnik, Chapter 10; Gopnik & Astington, 1988), and false belief (Hogrefe et al., 1986; Perner, Chapter 8; Perner et al., 1987; Wimmer, Hogrefe, & Sodian, Chapter 9; Wimmer & Perner, 1983) is also consistent with the connections–representations theory.

In the seeing–knowing case, the theory predicts that young children with inadequate understanding of interpretation, belief, or other forms of mental representation would not readily understand that different observers may interpret the very same visual stimulus as being different things. Such children understand "seeing" (a visual cognitive connection) but not "seeing as" (a mental representation of that to which one has become visually connected). In the Chandler and Helm (1984) and Taylor (Chapter 11) task, a naive observer sees, through a hole in a cardboard cover, a small, uninformative segment of what the child now knows is an elephant's trunk. Even though the younger subjects themselves had interpreted the very same segment as a meaningless pair of lines, before discovering what it really was, they nevertheless assumed that the equally naive observer would correctly identify it as an elephant's trunk. For children insufficiently knowledgeable about mental representations, the task must seem a simple one: the segment *is* in fact part of an elephant's trunk; the naive observer *sees* it; consequently, the naive observer *knows* it is an elephant's trunk. For children who still tend to conceive of the mind as a passive, nonconstructive receptacle, when a person makes sensory contact with a content, that content automatically enters the person's mind just as is (cf. Chandler & Boyes, 1982; Wellman, Chapter 4; Wimmer et al., Chapter 9).

The theoretical argument with respect to the other closely related work on conceptual perspectives is essentially the same. For example, if young children know that there is a pencil rather than Smarties in a Smarties box, they will automatically assume that a naive other child will think so too (Perner et al., 1987). They may be able to understand that the other child does not *know* what is in the box, that is, may not be in possession of that fact or may not have mentally apprehended that content. Recall that knowing versus not knowing, like seeing versus not seeing, is assumed in the theory to be a distinction available to young children. However, children who only understand connections cannot imagine a *positive* mental characterization of the same situation that is different from and contradictory to what is actually the case – namely, a mental picture of the box in which the box contains Smarties rather than a pencil. To do this would be to think of the other child as an active interpreter or construer of content rather than as a passive receiver of content, and to understand that the same content can have two different, mutually contradictory mental representations. The fact is that the box now has a pencil in it, not Smarties; consequently, for children who have a poor grasp of representations, if the other child has a mental picture of something being in that box, that something will of course be a pencil, because a pencil is what is there. In a representational change task (Astington & Gopnik, Chapter 10; Gopnik & Astington, 1988) the false belief to be identified is the subject's previous belief rather than the other child's future one, but the theory applies in the same way.

Finally, Hogrefe et al. (1986) have made a direct test of the hypothesis that children understand that someone may not know something (ignorance) earlier in development than they understand that someone may hold a false belief about something. They argue that ignorance and false belief knowledge are similar to Level 1 and Level 2 knowledge, respectively, or to connections and representations knowledge, as I now prefer to conceptualize it. The hypothesis was confirmed: At 3–4 years of age children were able to attribute ignorance but largely failed to attribute false belief.

Language and communication. According to the theory, young children assume as we do that each thing in the world has only one nature or "way that it is" at any given moment but, unlike us, do not understand that each thing may nevertheless be mentally represented in more than one way. This assumption together with this ignorance of representations may lead them to believe that things and the way they are described must stand in one-to-one relationship to each other. That is, in many situations, at least, they may assume (a) that things can only be characterized in one way (because they have only one nature), and (b) that one characterization can only characterize one thing or type of thing.

Assumption (a) may influence children's early word-learning strategies. Markman (1984) has argued that when first acquiring category terms, young children seem to follow a learning strategy she calls "the assumption of mutual exclusivity"; for a recent discussion of this and related strategies in language acquisition, see Clark (1987). That is, they tend to assume that category terms are mutually exclusive and that consequently only one category term can be applied to any one object. Having learned that cats are called "kitty," for example, the mutual-exclusivity assumption may lead them to balk for a time at accepting *cat* or *animal* as a verbal characterization of the very same creature. I suspect that the mutual-exclusivity assumption may only be assumption (a) expressing itself in the domain of word learning. That is, the child may think that the word *kitty* describes or characterizes the single way that cats are, and consequently that calling them "cat" or "animal" amounts to claiming that they are some other way than that. It is possible, therefore, that young children are loath to accept two category names for the same thing, for much the same reason they are loath to accept two perspectives, or both the appearance and the reality, as two equally valid characterizations of the same thing: namely, because one thing has only one nature and should therefore be characterized in only one way.

Young children often exhibit what appears to be a similar difficulty in accepting hypothetical and counterfactual statements, as these examples illustrate (Reilly, 1983, pp. 5–6):

Adult: "What if you were a bird?"
Wynn (2, 8): "I'm not a bird, just a people."
Adult: "What if you were a snake?"
Three-year-old: "I'm not a snake. I'm Janine."

Assumption (b) may express itself in young children's difficulties in understanding that communicative messages and other bodies of information may be referentially ambiguous (Beal, Chapter 16; Beal & Flavell, 1984; Bonitatibus, Chapter 17; Bonitatibus & Flavell, 1985; Olson, in preparation; Robinson & Robinson, 1982; Robinson & Whittaker, 1986). They tend to think that one verbal message can only characterize or refer to one thing. Consequently, they tend to be insensitive to the possibility that it may be referentially ambiguous and can therefore refer equally well to two or more different things. As speakers they often fail to realize that their listener may interpret their message differently than they intended. Similarly, as listeners they often fail to realize that they may be interpreting the speaker's message differently than the speaker intended. The problem may again be that, insufficiently aware of mental representations, they are insufficiently aware that people may be able to interpret or represent the same thing (in this case, the message) in two or more quite different ways. Notice the parallel between the communicative message case and the Chandler and Helm (1984) and Taylor (Chapter 11; in press) seeing–knowing case. In the latter, the same visible "message" (a pair of lines showing through a hole in a piece of cardboard) is interpreted as a meaningless pair of lines by the naive "listener" and as an elephant's trunk by the informed "listener." In fact, Robinson and Robinson (1982) have shown that young children fail to recognize that perceptual information can be ambiguous in meaning and therefore interpretable in more than one way, just as they fail to recognize that verbal messages can be (see Olson, 1986).

Maps and scale models. There are other tasks and situations that may similarly require for their successful management the recognition that one thing can be mentally represented in more than one way. The understanding and correct use of maps and scale models are cases in point. Maps, and to an even greater extent scale models, have their own salient "ways that they are" as physical objects, which a person who uses them may find difficult to wholly ignore. In addition, however, the user must also represent them as something entirely different – that is, as symbols of larger spatial layouts in the world. The ability to interpret simple maps and scale models first emerges in the early preschool years and improves considerably during the preschool period (Blades & Spencer, 1987; Bluestein & Acredolo, 1979; DeLoache, 1987). The age trend observed by DeLoache (1987) was particularly dramatic: Children aged 36–39 months who saw an object hidden in a scale model of a room knew where to find an analogous object hidden in the corresponding location in the room; children of 30–32 months of age did not. DeLoache also argues that this task requires thinking of the model in two different ways at the same time.

Seriation and transitivity. Piaget long ago showed that preschool children have considerable difficulty in seriating objects by size and in understanding that such series are transitive (Flavell, 1963, p. 193). Subsequent research by Halford (1984) also suggested that children have trouble understanding serial order or transitivity until about 5 years of age. Piaget attributed the difficulty to their failure to conceive of each object in the series as simultaneously being both smaller than its neighbor on one side and larger than its neighbor on the other side. Perhaps part of their problem, then, is that conceiving of the same object as simultaneously both "smaller" and "bigger" violates the general one object–one characterization bias I am claiming they have.

Simultaneous contrasting social roles, emotions, and traits. Watson (1986) has argued that the development of children's understanding of social role relations parallels that of their understanding of appearance and reality. He and his co-workers found that 3- and 4-year-olds could not understand how one person could occupy two social roles. For instance, they could not grasp how a person could be both a doctor and a father, or both a father and a grandfather. It seems that, for them, a person "is" only one thing, not two different things. Between 4 and 6 years they understood that a person could occupy two such roles, but thought the person could only do it successively, not simultaneously. Beginning at about 6–7 years of age they could further imagine the simultaneous as well as successive occupancy of different social roles.

Harter (1986; Harter & Buddin, 1987) has found a similar developmental progression in children's understanding that a person can experience two conflicting emotions at the same time. Children of 4 or 5 years of age deny that one can experience two emotions simultaneously. "You'd have to be two different people to have two feelings at the very same time," said one of her young subjects (Harter, 1986, p. 122). However, as with social roles, appearances and realities, visual perspectives, and so on, young children do agree that a person can experience two emotions successively. An example: "I'd be scared in the haunted house but then happy when I was out of it" (Harter & Buddin, 1987, p. 392). Later, children accept the possibility of experiencing two emotions simultaneously, but only if the two are both positive or both negative (e.g., happy and proud, sad and mad). Later still, they accept the possibility of simultaneously experiencing two emotions of different valences. To illustrate, one child said: "I was happy that I got a present but mad that it wasn't what I wanted" (Harter, 1986, p. 128). Similarly, children only gradually come to understand that it is possible to represent the same person as possessing two opposite traits, for example, "smart" and "dumb" (Harter, 1986).

Other tasks and situations. We have seen that young children tend to assume that "presented" implies "correctly identified"; this is the lack of the seeing–knowing distinction described in the section on conceptual perspective-taking. It was argued that they do so because they conceive of the mind as a passive, nonconstructive, nonrepresenting receptacle that automatically comprehends whatever is presented to the senses. Recent evidence by Pillow (1988) shows that they also tend to assume that "presented" implies "understood," and probably for the same reason. He found that 3-year-olds believed that a listener who heard two tape-recorded messages that were presented simultaneously would understand everything the messages said. In contrast, 4-year-olds seemed to understand, even before having the experience, that hearing two messages at once would impede understanding, and showed a clear preference for listening to them one at a time. Pillow (in press a) suggests that young children may also and for the same reason assume that "presented" implies "remembered," and that this assumption may explain their observed tendency to attribute unrealistically high memory spans to people (Flavell, 1985, p. 231). Although this possibility has not yet been tested, they may similarly assume that "perceptible" automatically implies "perceived." For instance, they may assume that another person will immediately locate an embedded figure it just previously took them some time and effort to locate. Thus, it may be that for the young child who understands connections but not yet representations, a content presented to the senses automatically is assumed to be a content attended to, perceived, identified, understood, and remembered.

Two other sets of data might be regarded as evidence for the theory. In one, children of different ages are presented with photographs of wholes made out of parts that are unrelated to the whole; for example, a house (the whole) made out of crayons (the parts). Younger children tend to represent it either as "a house" or "crayons," whereas older children are more likely to represent it as both, that is, as "a house made of crayons" (Elkind, Koegler, & Go, 1964; Prather & Bacon, 1986). The other is recent evidence by Acredelo and Horobin (1987a, 1987b) suggesting that younger children are more prone than older ones to assume that all problems will have exactly one solution, not more and not less. That is, they assume that problems with more than one possible solution have one solution (cf. Somerville & Wellman, in press), and they assume that problems with no solution have one solution. In both sets of data young children may be showing what the theory describes as a tendency to assume that things should be characterized or represented in only one way.

Developmental synchronies and asynchronies

How much developmental synchrony is there within each of the two metacognitive domains described by the theory – that is, within that of cognitive connections and within that of mental representations? In the former domain, what evidence we have suggests that much of the child's basic understanding of these connections is acquired between the ages of 1 and 3 years. However, there undoubtedly are developmental asynchronies within this age period, with knowledge of one kind of connection beginning to be acquired earlier than knowledge of another kind. For example, I suspect that children understand something about seeing and hearing earlier than they understand anything about, say, imaging, dreaming, or remembering. However, exactly how much acquisitional synchrony there is in the case of connections must be a question for future research; we simply do not know at present.

In the case of mental representations, it is apparent from this chapter and others in this volume that a great deal of developmental movement takes place between the ages of 2 or 3 and 5 or 6 (see also Perner et al., 1987). Two sets of correlational studies provide particularly compelling evidence of developmental synchrony in this domain. In two separate studies we (Flavell et al., 1986) administered a set of appearance–reality tasks and a set of Level 2 visual perspective-taking tasks to the same groups of 3-year-olds. The correlations between these two types of tasks proved to be both positive and high (.67 to .87) – about as high, in fact, as the between-task correlations within each type of task. Although, of course, these results do not constitute proof than an understanding of mental representations helps mediate solution of both kinds of tasks, as the theory suggests, it is certainly consistent with this possibility. In two studies also, Gopnik and Astington (1988; Astington & Gopnik, Chapter 10) obtained positive correlations (with age controlled) among representational change, false belief, and appearance–reality tasks ranging from .24 to .62. Their results suggest that understanding of these three domains also develops more or less synchronously during the preschool period.

However, there is also evidence for systematic asynchronies or *décalages* in this metacognitive domain. It appears that young children find it easier in some task situations than in others to understand that it is mental representations of objects rather than objects per se that are at issue, and consequently that the same object can be represented in more than one way. In particular, they seem to find it easier to understand that pretend representations are merely representations, and that they can pretend that one thing, which they know to be an *a* in reality, is a *b*, a *c*, or most anything else they want it to be (see Leslie, Chapter 2). There are at least two reasons to believe that pretense may constitute children's earliest window on mental representations (Flavell, Flavell, & Green, 1987). First, children begin to pretend at 12 to 18 months of age, about the same age they start to acquire some understanding of cognitive connections. Second, we have recently shown in three studies (Flavell, Flavell, & Green, 1987) that 3-year-olds can reflect on the pretend–real distinction significantly better than they can reflect on the apparent–real distinction. Thus, whereas appearance–appearance (Level 2 perspective-taking) and appearance–reality tasks are about equally difficult for 3-year-olds, as noted in the previous paragraph, pretense–reality tasks are easier than both. It is possible that young children may construe pretending as something they *do* with objects, akin to seeing or thinking about them, more than as a *description of* them, even a nonserious one. If this is true, it might help explain why knowledge about pretense seems to develop as early as knowledge about cognitive connections.

Similarly, young children may also find it easier to countenance two different mental representations of something when that something is not yet known or has not yet happened (cf. Somerville & Wellman, in press). Examples are two different guesses, hopes, wishes, or expectations about an unknown or future event. Like pretend representations, these "iffy," not-yet-real representations may seem to young children more like descriptions of people's thoughts than descriptions of the world. Louis Moses of our research group at Stanford is currently exploring this possibility.

Young children may likewise find it easier to accept contrasting representations when they are representations of different personal opinions or tastes rather than representations of different states of the world; for example, whether the candy in the box tastes good (a subjective opinion) as contrasted with whether the box contains candy at all (an objective fact). The reason is, again, that young children may more easily construe expressions of opinion and taste as originating in the person rather than in the world. Consequently, they may see nothing wrong with there being a multiplicity of such clearly subjective representations of a single object. Consistent with this possibility, we have recently found in pilot work that 3-year-olds readily understand that a cat thinks cat food is good-tasting or "yummy" even though they themselves think it is "yukky." It appears they can understand diversity of belief in matters of taste more easily than in matters of fact (cf. Mansfield & Clinchy, 1985).

An analysis of the phenomenology of tactile as compared to visual perceptual experiences (Flavell, Green, & Flavell, in press) suggested the hypothesis that young children would find tactile appearance—reality and perspective-taking tasks easier than visual ones. We argued that it is easier for the child to recognize that tactile feelings are subjective happenings than to recognize that visual experiences are. The data from three recent studies confirmed this hypothesis (Flavell et al., in press). For example, we found that 3-year-olds who had difficulty with visual AR tasks (real vs. apparent object identity, color, and number) could easily say that an ice cube they were feeling with a heavily gloved finger did not feel cold to that finger (tactile appearance for self), did feel cold to the experimenter's ungloved or thinly gloved finger (tactile appearance for other), and was a cold ice cube, really and truly (reality).

Other easier tasks might be those in which differences between representations, representers, or representers' epistemic circumstances are made very salient for the subject. For instance, the experimenter re-

peatedly calls the subject's attention to the distinction between appearance and reality, or to the different viewing positions of subject and other,
or to the difference between what the subject knows and what the other
knows in a false belief task. Similarly, one would expect even quite young
children to be able to imagine that others whose knowledge and abilities
are very conspicuously different from their own (e.g., infants, animals)
might represent or experience a content differently than they do. Imagining
different representations of a single content should be easier and earlier
developing in situations that strongly suggest the possibility of such differences. Although these suggestions seem obvious almost to the point
of tautology, they still might be wrong, or at least not quite right, and
therefore should be tested experimentally.

There are also situations in which it is either harder to entertain the
possibility of different representations, harder to infer what these different
representations might consist of if the possibility is entertained, or both.
There are probably numerous determinants of difficulty here; more
thorough discussions of some of them appear in Chandler & Boyes (1982)
and Higgins (1981). Entertaining the possibility of different representations may become more difficult, and hence be later developing, when the
bases of such differences are less salient and more subtle. In the elephant
task (Chandler & Helm, 1984; Taylor, Chapter 11; in press), for example,
two very similar cognitive creatures (subject and naive other) view the
very same segment of the elephant from the very same viewing position;
the only difference is the relatively nonsalient fact that the naive other
viewer has only that segment on which to base an identification. Likewise,
when similar-looking people confront identical content it is difficult to
suspect possible differences in representation based on differences in their
perceptual or intellectual abilities; in their relevant knowledge, experiences, attitudes, biases, and attentional preferences; in the cognitive
strategies they use to try to understand and remember the content; and
the like. The disposition and ability to detect such differences are undoubtedly late developing, depending as they must on the acquisition of
a great deal of other knowledge about the mind. In fact, research by Ross
(1987) and others (e.g., see Fiske & Taylor, 1984) clearly shows that
adults are less skilled at it than we might assume. Although obviously
aware of the existence of representations and perspectives, adults tend not
to take adequate account of their own and others' construals of situations
in their everyday judgments:

Our construal interpretation, it should be emphasized, depends on more than the
simple assumption that subjects engage in variable construals of situation and
context. It depends on the additional assumption that in doing so they fail to
recognize, and/or fail to make *adequate inferential allowance* for the fact that many if
not most of their peers may construe the "same" situation quite differently. In a

sense, our contention is that subjects fail to recognize the degree to which their interpretation of the situation is just that – a set of constructions and inferences rather than a direct perception of some objective and invariant reality. (Ross, 1987, p. 127)

In short, we are "at risk" for unconscious egocentrism all of our lives (Flavell, 1985, p. 125).

What develops in the domain of children's knowledge about mental representations after the age of 5 or 6? I have just suggested that with increasing age children become increasingly attuned to the possibility of multiple representations in situations where this possibility is hard to notice or credit, and also increasingly able to determine exactly what these different representations might be.

In addition, they probably arrive at some important new insights concerning mental representations. One likely candidate is the awareness that mental representations are potentially *recursive* – for example, the recognition that I can think about your thoughts about my thoughts, and so on (Feldman, Chapter 7; Flavell, 1985, pp. 145–146; Perner & Wimmer, 1985). There are two reasons why this insight could be regarded as a particularly important metacognitive acquisition:

First, as we have seen, potential recursiveness is a distinctive property of mental representation; it helps set mental representation apart from other human activities. One could hardly be said to have acquired a mature, adult level of knowledge about thinking if one did not know that thoughts can recursively take other thoughts as cognitive objects. Second, a surprising amount of the ordinary, everyday social thought and communication of adolescents and adults seems to presuppose this knowledge. Consider, for example, the sorts of things two people often say to each other when analyzing and clearing up a previous misunderstanding between them: "Oh, you thought I meant X," "I thought you already knew about Y," and even "I didn't realize you thought I really meant it when I said that." Although statements like these are fairly commonplace in adult conversations, they surely reflect a tacit assumption on the speaker's part that thoughts can recursively include other thoughts. In fact, that assumption seems to be in the background of a lot of everyday speaker and listener behavior among mature communicators. (Flavell, 1985, p. 146)

Another key insight may be the one described by Chandler (Chapter 20). He suggests that during middle childhood children discover that different people may represent things differently because of differences in their biases, relevant knowledge, and the like. Nevertheless, children of this age still assume that there must always be some single, potentially knowable fact of the matter, some "correct" representation that can be agreed on once we know all the facts. As they become adolescents, however, they may come to believe that there is not always a single, ascertainable truth in any given case, and that knowledge may be inherently subjective and relative. In a sense, these adolescents have gone from believing that there are mental representations to believing that mental representations may be all that there is. This insight obviously constitutes a new and radically different theory of mind and mental representation.

There are undoubtedly other important, fundamental acquisitions that occur during the middle childhood and adolescent years. For example, I suspect that there may be some having to do with the notion that people's representations of situations are systematically influenced by their personal characteristics, for example, their biases, prejudices, cognitive styles, emotional hang-ups, and so on. Identifying and investigating these acquisitions will clearly be a major task for future research in this area. Our theory of the child's theory of mind, like the child's theory itself, still has considerable developing to do.

Explaining the transition from connections to representations

In this as in other areas of cognitive growth, development is easier to describe than to explain. One possible mediator of the transition is an increase with age in information-processing capacity (e.g., Case, 1985; Halford, 1982). Children may find it easier to entertain the possibility of different representations of the same thing as age-dependent increases in short-term-memory capacity make it easier for them to hold more than one representation in mind at the same time. This possibility is supported by the recent finding (Flavell, Green, Wahl, Flavell, 1987) that 3-year-olds perform better on color appearance–reality tasks if visual evidence, suggesting what the object's real color is, remains available during questioning. For example, they find it easier to say that a white object held behind a green filter is really and truly white if the white handles used to hold the object extend out laterally beyond the edges of the filter, and therefore continue to look white instead of green. The handles may help by reminding the children of what the object's real color is.

Such capacity increases could hardly be the sole developmental mediator, however. For instance, young children who maintain that, say, a white object behind a blue filter both looks blue and really is blue are usually well aware that the object will look white again when the filter is removed (Flavell el al., 1986; Flavell, Green, Wahl, & Flavell, 1987). Thus, even when both real and apparent color are highly available to them cognitively, young children will refuse to attribute both to the object at any one point in time. This chapter also cites many other examples where inability to keep two representations in mind at once could not be the child's root problem; Watson's (1986) evidence concerning simultaneous social roles is a case in point.

Young children also have experiences that might help mediate the transition. In their pretend play they have repeated experiences representing things in multiple ways and seeing their playmates do the same. Perhaps these experiences help sensitize children to the possibility of multiple representations in other situations (Flavell, Flavell, & Green, 1987). In addition, people must frequently make salient to the child differences between the child's representations of reality (e.g., beliefs) and their own or those of others. The child says a toy is hers; her playmate strenuously objects, saying that it belongs to him. Parents explicitly call young children's false beliefs to their attention, point out differences between different people's beliefs or feelings, and otherwise help the child become aware that the same thing can be mentally represented in more than one way. It is clear that young children hear a lot of talk about mental events from their parents and older siblings (Dunn el al., 1987). Finding out whether and how and to what extent such experiences are developmentally formative is going to be a difficult scientific task. It is clearly a very important task, however.

ACKNOWLEDGMENT

I am very grateful to Eleanor Flavell, Frances Green, Paul Harris, Carl Johnson, Ellen Markman, and David Olson for their helpful criticisms of various drafts of this chapter.

REFERENCES

Acredelo, C., & Horobin, K. (1987a). *Children's reasoning when confronted with problems having more than one solution.* Paper presented at the meeting of the Society for Research in Child Development, Baltimore, MD.

Acredelo, C., & Horobin, K. (1987b). Development of relational reasoning and avoidance of premature closure. *Developmental Psychology, 23,* 13–21.

Beal, C. R., & Flavell, J. H. (1984). Development of the ability to distinguish communicative intention and literal message meaning. *Child Development, 55,* 920–928.

Blades, M., & Spencer, C. (1987). The use of maps by 4–6-year-old children in large-scale mazes. *British Journal of Developmental Psychology, 5,* 19–24.

Bluestein, N., & Acredelo, L. (1979). Developmental changes in map-reading skills. *Child Development, 50,* 691–697.

Bonitatibus, G. J., & Flavell, J. H. (1985). The effect of presenting a message in written form on young children's ability to evaluate its communicative adequacy. *Developmental Psychology, 21,* 455–461.

Braine, M. D. S., & Shanks, B. L. (1965). The development of conservation of size. *Journal of Verbal Learning and Verbal Behavior, 4,* 227–242.

Bretherton, I., Fritz, J., Zahn-Waxler, C., & Ridgeway, D. (1986). Learning to talk about emotions: A functionalist perspective. *Child Development, 57,* 529–548.

Case, R. (1985). *Intellectual development: Birth to adulthood.* New York: Academic Press.

Chandler, M., & Boyes, M. (1982). Social-cognitive development. In B. B. Wolman (Ed.), *Handbook of developmental psychology* (pp. 387–402). Englewood Cliffs, NJ: Prentice-Hall.

Chandler, M., & Helm, D. (1984). Developmental changes in the contributions of shared experience to social role-taking competence. *International Journal of Behavioral Development, 7,* 145–156.

Churcher, J., & Scaife, M. (1982). How infants see the point. In G. Butterworth & P. Light (Eds.), *Social cognition: Studies of the development of understanding* (pp. 110–136). Chicago: University of Chicago Press.

Clark, E. V. (1987). The principle of contrast: A constraint on language acquisition. In B. MacWhinney (Ed.), *Mechanisms of language acquisition: Proceedings of the 20th Annual Carnegie Symposium on Cognition 1985* (pp. 1–33). Hillsdale, NJ: Erlbaum.

Cox, M. V. (1980). Visual perspective-taking in children. In M. V. Cox (Ed.), *Are young children egocentric?* (pp. 61–79). New York: St. Martiñs.

DeLoache, J. S. (1987). *Rapid change in the symbolic functioning of very young children.* Unpublished manuscript, University of Illinois, Urbana.

Dunn, J., Bretherton, I., & Munn, P. (1987). Conversations about feeling states between mothers and their young children. *Developmental Psychology, 23,* 132–139.

Elkind, D., Koegler, R. R., & Go, E. (1964). Studies in perceptual development: II. Part-whole perception. *Child Development, 35,* 81–90.

Estes, D., Wellman, H. M., & Woolley, J. D. (in press). Children's understanding of mental phenomena. In H. Reese (Ed.), *Advances in child development and behavior.* New York: Academic Press.

Fiske, S. T., & Taylor, S. E. (1984). *Social cognition.* Reading, MA: Addison-Wesley.

Flavell, J. H. (1963). *The developmental psychology of Jean Piaget.* Princeton, NJ: Van Nostrand.

Flavell, J. H. (1977). *Cognitive development* (1st ed.). Englewood Cliffs, NJ: Prentice-Hall.

Flavell, J. H. (1978). The development of knowledge about visual perception. In C. B. Keasey (Ed.), *Nebraska symposium on motivation* (Vol. 25, pp. 43–76). Lincoln: University of Nebraska Press.

Flavell, J. H. (1985). *Cognitive development* (rev. ed.). Englewood Cliffs, NJ: Prentice-Hall.

Flavell, J. H. (1986). The development of children's knowledge about the appearance–reality distinction. *American Psychologist, 41,* 418–425.

Flavell, J. H., Everett, B. A., Croft, K., & Flavell, E. R. (1981). Young children's knowledge about visual perception: Further evidence for the Level 1–Level 2 distinction. *Developmental Psychology, 17,* 99–103.

Flavell, J. H., Flavell, E. R., & Green, F. L. (1983). Development of the appearance–reality distinction. *Cognitive Psychology, 15,* 95–120.

Flavell, J. H., Flavell, E. R., & Green, F. L. (1987). Young children's knowledge about the apparent–real and pretend–real distinctions. *Developmental Psychology, 23,* 816–822.

Flavell, J. H., Flavell, E. R., Green, F. L., & Wilcox, S. A. (1980). Young children's knowledge about visual perception: Effect of observer's distance from target on perceptual clarity of target. *Developmental Psychology, 16,* 10–12.

Flavell, J. H., Green, F. L., & Flavell, E. R. (1986). Development of knowledge about the appearance–reality distinction. *Monographs of the Society for Research in Child Development 51* (1, Serial No. 212).

Flavell, J. H., Green, F. L., & Flavell, E. R. (1987). Unpublished study.

Flavell, J. H., Green, F. L., & Flavell, E. R. (in press). Young children's ability to differentiate appearance–reality and Level 2 perspectives in the tactile modality. *Child Development.*

Flavell, J. H., Green, F. L., Wahl, K. E., & Flavell, E. R. (1987). The effects of question clarification and memory aids on young children's performance on appearance–reality tasks. *Cognitive Development, 2,* 127–144.

Flavell, J. H., Shipstead, S. G., & Croft, K. (1978). Young children's knowledge about visual perception: Hiding objects from others. *Child Development, 49,* 1208–1211.

Flavell, J. H., Shipstead, S. G., & Croft, K. (1980). What young children think you see when their eyes are closed. *Cognition, 8,* 369–387.

Flavell, J. H., Zhang, X-D, Zou, H., Dong, Q., & Qi, S. (1983). A comparison between the development of the appearance–reality distinction in the People's Republic of China and the United States. *Cognitive Psychology, 15,* 459–466.

Gopnik, A., & Astington, J. (1988). Children's understanding of representational change and its relation to the understanding of false belief and the appearance–reality distinction. *Child Development, 59,* 26–37.

Halford, G. S. (1982). *The development of thought.* Hillsdale, NJ: Erlbaum.

Halford, G. S. (1984). Can young children integrate premises in transitivity and serial order tasks? *Cognitive Psychology, 16,* 65–93.

Harter, S. (1986). Cognitive-developmental processes in the integration of concepts about emotions and the self. *Social Cognition, 4,* 119–151.

Harter, S., & Buddin, B. J. (1987). Children's understanding of the simultaneity of two emotions: A five-stage developmental acquisition sequence. *Developmental Psychology, 23,* 388–399.

Higgins, E. T. (1981). Role taking and social judgment: Alternative developmental perspectives and processes. In J. H. Flavell & L. Ross (Eds.), *Social cognitive development: Frontiers and possible futures* (pp. 119–153). Cambridge University Press.

Hobson, R. P. (1980). The question of egocentrism: The young child's competence in the co-ordination of perspectives. *Journal of Child Psychology and Psychiatry, 21,* 325–331.

Hogrefe, G.-J., Wimmer, H., & Perner, J. (1986). Ignorance versus false belief: A developmental lag in attribution of epistemic states. *Child Development, 57,* 567–582.

Hughes, M. (1975). *Egocentrism in preschool children.* Unpublished doctoral dissertation, University of Edinburgh.

Hughes, M., & Donaldson, M. (1979). The use of hiding games for studying the coordination of perspectives. *Educational Review, 31,* 133–140.

Lempers, J. D., Flavell, E. R., & Flavell, J. H. (1977). The development in very young children of tacit knowledge concerning visual perception. *Genetic Psychology Monographs, 95,* 3–53.

Mansfield, A., & Clinchy, B. (1985). *The early growth of multiplism in the child.* Paper presented at the Fifteenth Annual Symposium of the Jean Piaget Society, Philadelphia, PA.

Markman, E. M. (1984). The acquisition and hierarchical organization of categories by children. In C. Sophian (Ed.), *Origins of cognitive skills* (pp. 371–406). Hillsdale, NJ: Erlbaum.

Masangkay, Z. S., McCluskey, K. A., McIntyre, C. W., Sims-Knight, J., Vaughn, B. E., & Flavell, J. H. (1974). The early development of inferences about the visual percepts of others. *Child Development, 45,* 357–366.

Olson, D. R. (1986). The cognitive consequences of literacy. *Canadian Psychology, 27,* 109–121.

Olson, D. R. (in preparation). *The world on paper.*

Olson, D. R., & Astington, J. W. (1987). Seeing and knowing: On the ascription of mental states to young children. *Canadian Journal of Psychology, 41,* 399–411.

Perner, J., Leekam, S. R., & Wimmer, H. (1987). Three-year-olds' difficulty with false belief: The case for a conceptual deficit. *British Journal of Developmental Psychology, 5,* 125–137.

Perner, J., & Wimmer, H. (1985). "John *thinks* that Mary *thinks* that ..." Attribution of second-order beliefs by 5- to 10-year-old children. *Journal of Experimental Child Psychology, 39,* 437–471.

Pillow, B. H. (1988). Young children's understanding of attentional limits. *Child Development, 59,* 38–46.

Pillow, B. H. (in press a). The development of children's beliefs about the mental world. *Merrill-Palmer Quarterly.*

Pillow, B. H. (in press b). Early understanding of perception as a source of knowledge. *Journal of Experimental Child Psychology.*

Pillow, B. H., & Flavell, J. H. (1986). Young children's knowledge about visual perception: Projective size and shape. *Child Development, 57,* 125–135.

Prather, P. A., & Bacon, J. (1986). Developmental differences in part–whole identification. *Child Development, 57,* 549–558.

Reilly, J. S. (1983). What are conditionals for? *Papers and Reports on Child Language Development, 22,* 1–9.

Robinson, E. J., & Robinson, W. P. (1982). Knowing when you don't know enough: Children's judgments about ambiguous information. *Cognition, 12,* 267–280.

Robinson, E. J., & Whittaker, S. J. (1986). Children's conceptions of meaning–message relationships. *Cognition, 22,* 41–60.

Ross, L. (1987). The problem of construal in social inference and social psychology. In N. Grunberg, R. Nisbett, J. Rodin, & J. Singer (Eds.), *A distinctive approach* to psychological research: The influence of Stanley Schachter (pp. 118–150). Hillsdale, NJ: Erlbaum.

Somerville, S. C., & Wellman, H. M. (in press). Where it is and where it isn't: Children's use of possibilities and probabilities to guide search. In N. Eisenberg (Ed.), *Contemporary issues in developmental psychology*. New York: Wiley.

Taylor, M. (in press). Conceptual perspective taking: Children's ability to distinguish what they know from what they see. *Child Development*.

Trautner, H. M. (1985). *The significance of the appearance–reality distinction for the development of gender constancy*. Paper presented at the meeting of the Society for Research in Child Development, Toronto, Canada.

Watson, M. W. (1986). The breadth of the appearance–reality distinction. Commentary on Flavell, Green, and Flavell's Development of knowledge about the appearance–reality distinction. *Monographs of the Society for Research in Child Development, 51*, (1, Serial No. 212).

Wellman, H. M. (April, 1987). *The young child's theory of mind*. Paper presented at the meetings of the Society for Research in Child Development, Baltimore, MD.

Wellman, H. M., & Estes, D. (1986). Early understanding of mental entities: A reexamination of childhood realism. *Child Development, 57*, 910–923.

Wimmer, H., Hogrefe, G.-J., & Perner, J. (1988). Children's understanding of informational access as source of knowledge. *Child Development, 59*, 386–396.

Wimmer, H., & Perner, J. (1983). Beliefs about beliefs: Representation and constraining function of wrong beliefs in young children's understanding of deception. *Cognition, 13*, 103–128.

Yuill, N. (1984). Young children's coordination of motive and outcome in judgements of satisfaction and morality. *British Journal of Developmental Psychology, 2*, 73–81.

PART III

Further development of a theory of mind: Understanding mental states in social interaction and communication

14

Higher-order beliefs and intentions in children's understanding of social interaction

JOSEF PERNER

This chapter is based on the idea that the social significance of human interaction depends on the mental states of the interacting parties, in particular their higher-order mental states. The same concepts that were used in previous chapters of this volume to analyze 3- to 5-year-old children's ability to attribute the basic mental states of belief and intention are here applied to study 6- to 9-year-olds' ability to combine these basic states recursively for attribution of second-order states, for example, beliefs about beliefs, intentions about beliefs, and the like. This recursive ability opens up understanding of a much richer variety of social interactions because it allows understanding not only of a particular person's perception of a social situation but also of different persons' concern about each other's mental states.

Let me illustrate the importance of higher-order mental states for social interaction with the statement "John is kicking Mary." Although it reports an interesting observation, it does not disclose the real nature of John and Mary's interaction. Further information is necessary: "Mary does not *notice* the teacher entering the classroom. John *realizes* that Mary is *not aware* of the teacher's arrival, but he *wants* her to *know* about it, so he gives her a kick." This background information is full of references to mental states and second-order mental states, for example: "John WANTS Mary to KNOW that the teacher is arriving." This state is second order because John's mental state of wanting is concerned with another mental state, Mary's state of knowing.

It is possible to attribute second- and higher-order mental states because of the special feature of mental states that they can be *recursively* applied. To explain this crucial feature in more detail, let me assume that a child who understands that John kicks Mary has formed a mental representation of a proposition that corresponds to the sentence "John kicks Mary." In such a proposition the verb *kicking* can be characterized as a relation between two individuals, John and Mary. Much of our knowledge about the present state of the physical environment can be expressed as a conjunction of such basic propositions:

(0) (John kicked Mary) and (Mary sat on the chair) and...

(To emphasize the conjunctive nature of this description, parentheses have been put around each basic proposition.) Although in some applications mental state verbs can be used like ordinary verbs as relations between individuals, for example, "John knows Mary," their important use is as *propositional attitudes* (Russell, 1919). For instance, in the sentence "John knows that (the teacher is arriving)," the mental verb *know* describes not a relation between individuals but between an individual and a proposition. It expresses that the individual John has an "attitude" of knowing toward the proposition that the teacher is arriving. Propositional attitude constructions pose a challenge to logicians and semanticists because they exhibit certain peculiar logical properties (e.g., Chisholm, 1967; Leslie, Chapter 2).

For present purposes I want to focus on the *recursive* property of these attitude constructions. Notice that the sentence

(1) John KNOWS that (the teacher is arriving)

expresses a proposition about John that contains an embedded proposition about the teacher. In other words, an attitude verb relates an individual to a proposition, thereby forming a new proposition. A propositional attitude construction, therefore, contains two propositions, one embedded within the other, which contrasts with the conjunctive formation of complex propositions in sentence (0) above. The fact that propositional attitude constructions form new propositions is important because it is a prerequisite for their recursive application, that is, that the new proposition can be embedded in a second attitude construction, for instance:

(2) John KNOWS (Mary doesn't KNOW [the teacher is arriving]).

By looking at sentences (1) and (2), we see that a child who can form an attitude construction containing an embedded proposition has the prerequisite for mentally representing and for attributing a *first-order mental state* as expressed in sentence (1). A child who realizes the recursive nature of this construction and can form doubly embedded propositions has the prerequisite for representing and attributing *second-order mental states* as expressed by sentence (2).[1]

This chapter focuses on children's understanding of social interaction based on second-order mental states. Second-order states are particularly interesting for two reasons. They are the first level at which social interaction can be understood as an interaction of minds where people are concerned about each other's mental states, which allows intentional social coordination to occur. Developmentally more important, second-order state attributions require understanding of the recursive nature of mental states (repeated embedding of propositions). It is plausible that this possibility for recursion is understood at a particular point in development and that, once understood, it is then widely applied for making social distinctions.

To explore this possibility further I will first discuss methods of assessing children's ability to attribute second-order mental states. I will then illustrate how these methods can be used for assessing children's ability to discriminate between different kinds of social interaction, using three examples from work by my colleagues at Sussex.

Experimental isolation of first- and second-order state representations

First-order states. To demonstrate that children are able to attribute mental states as part of a "theory of mind," one should ideally show that they can do two things (Premack & Woodruff, 1978, p. 515): (1) They can infer the mental state from observable events, and (2) they can use the inferred state to make predictions about behavior. The test we used to assess children's attribution of false belief (Wimmer & Perner, 1983) satisfies these two criteria. It requires children to infer a story protagonist's false belief about the location of an object from observing that the protagonist was absent when the object was unexpectedly transferred to a new location (1), and it requires subjects to predict where the protagonist would look for the object (2).[2]

Recent research suggests it is not the combination of both requirements that make the false belief task difficult but that each one of them in isolation has the same effect. Perner, Leekam, & Wimmer (1987) found that when children were asked a direct question about the protagonist's mental state, "Where does the protagonist *think* the object is?" which requires only inference of the belief, children did not perform better than when asked, "Where will the protagonist *look* for the object?" which required the additional step of making a behavioral prediction on the basis of the inferred belief. Harris, Johnson, and Harris (1987) reported the converse finding that children who were given a direct description of a person's false belief (no inference needed) still found it difficult to make a behavioral prediction on the basis of that belief.

Most investigations into children's understanding of mental states have relied on their ability to infer such states. Minimally such a test should establish that children know when a certain state is warranted and when not. Studies on children's ability to attribute first-order knowledge states have met this criterion (Johnson & Maratsos, 1977; Marvin, Greenberg, & Mossler, 1976; Mossler, Marvin, & Greenberg, 1976; Wimmer & Perner, 1983).

In contrast, observational studies where children are credited with a "theory of mind" on the basis of their use of mental verbs (Bretherton, McNew, & Beeghly-Smith, 1981; Shatz, Wellman, & Silber, 1983) have to contend with a serious problem of interpretation. For instance, most of the examples collected by Bretherton et al. (1981) of 2- to 3-year-olds' use of the verb *know* could be glossed as assertions of ability or inability (e.g., J's response "I don't know" to a question about where something was could be glossed as "I can't say" or "I can't get it for you"), and most uses of *think* can be glossed as expression of uncertainty (e.g., Ky: "I think it is a propeller airplane").

Shatz et al. (1983) were acutely aware of this problem of interpretation. In an attempt to obviate it, they selected examples where a mental state was explicitly contrasted with reality. Although this method ensures that the selected examples attest to the child's ability to understand the relationship between counterfactual statements and reality, it does not necessarily demonstrate that children are able to infer the verbally expressed mental state and realize its potential for behavioral prediction. For instance, Abe's (between 2½ and 4 years old) statement "The people thought Dracula was mean, but he was nice" shows that he understood the contrast between the counterfactual statement "Dracula was mean" and reality "Dracula is nice," but it does not make clear whether he understood under what conditions people would come to hold such a belief (inference) and the effect of this belief on the people (behavioral prediction). It is not implausible to assume that Abe just repeated what his father had told him to allay his fears about Count Dracula.

Another quite persuasive-looking example is "I thought there wasn't any socks, but when I looked I saw them." Because this is a report of Abe's own mistaken belief the question of inferring it from observable cues does not arise. However, it still remains to be established whether Abe understood the impact of his previous false belief, namely, how he would have acted on the basis of it (cf. Perner et al., 1987, discussion section).

To recapitulate, our false belief test (Wimmer & Perner, 1983) ensures that children understand the conditions under which a mental state comes about (inference) and that they understand the significance of the mental state for a person's actions (behavioral prediction). To infer the same abilities on the basis of linguistic observations is usually very difficult. I have discussed this problem at some length because the same problems of interpretation have to be faced by tests of children's ability to attribute higher-order mental states.

Second-order states. Perner and Wimmer (1985) extended their test for understanding first-order beliefs to assess children's ability to represent second-order beliefs. Children were told stories in which two characters (John and Mary) were *independently* informed about an object's (ice-cream van's) unexpected transfer to a new location. Hence, both John and Mary knew where the van was but there was a mistake in John's second-order belief about Mary's belief:

John THINKS (Mary THINKS [the van is at the old place]).

Children's understanding of this second-order belief was tested by asking where John thought Mary would go for ice cream. Correct answers could only be given if children had formed a mental representation of John's second-order belief, because all shortcut reasoning based on first-order beliefs or reality would have led to the wrong answer.

The important feature of this method is that the crucial second-order belief is isolated by experimental manipulation of the stimulus material (stories), so that systematically correct test responses can only be given if subjects detect and mentally represent the second-order state. This experimental approach helps overcome a problem of interpretation in previous, observational approaches to higher-order mental state attribution. The problem in these approaches is how to interpret what children's linguistic expressions of embedded attitude reports indicate about their understanding of higher-order mental states.

One type of experiment (Flavell, Botkin, Fry, Wright, & Jarvis, 1968; Selman, 1980; Shultz & Cloghesy, 1981) employed variants of Gratch's (1964) "hand-guessing game." This method is essentially observational in that children's introspective reports of their strategy are classified according to level of perspective-taking. Assignment of children's reports to level of linguistic embedding poses no serious difficulty, but there is a problem when these reports are interpreted as understanding of mental states. Let me explain this problem in more detail with an example from one of the earliest investigations into higher-order mental state attribution by Flavell et al. (1968).

Subjects played a game with a friend. While their opponent was not looking subjects had to take out either a dime from under one or a nickel from under the other of two cups. The opponent was then allowed to look under one of the two cups and keep his find. Subjects' objective was to empty the cup that they thought their opponent was going to pick. After having emptied one cup, subjects were asked for their reasons. For instance, a subject who took out the nickel explained his strategy as follows: "I thought he might think I will fool him and take the 10 cents out, so I had better take the 5 cents out" (Flavell et al., 1968, Experiment IB).

No doubt this answer contains a second-order sentence "I *thought* he might *think* I will fool him and ..." However, the crucial question is whether the second-order part of that sentence "I thought ..." reflects understanding that goes beyond the understanding already expressed by the embedded first-order proposition ". . . he might think I will fool him. . . ." This question remains unanswered by the observational approach. In our experimental approach (Perner & Wimmer, 1985), this question receives a clearly positive answer, since understanding the second-order aspect "John thinks Mary thinks ..." is necessary for giving correct test responses. Understanding of the embedded first-order expression "Mary thinks ..." alone would lead to wrong answers.

Also, experimental approaches can suffer from a problem of interpretation similar to the hand-guessing studies. Miller, Kessel, and Flavell (1970) investigated children's ability to verbally describe depictions of higher-order mental states (embedded think bubbles). Eliot, Lovell, Dayton, and McGrady (1979) gave children verbal descriptions and asked them to pick corresponding pictorial representations of higher-order mental states. Certainly these studies test children's syntactic ability in translating embedded bubbles into embedded sentences, but it is not clear what this tells us about children's *understanding* of higher-order mental states.

A particularly interesting problem of interpretation arises when children's ability to impute mental states is assessed on the basis of their remarks about emotions (Harris & Gross, Chapter 15; Landry & Lyons-Ruth, 1980). A problem arises because from an emotion report – for instance, "She is sad that she fell over" – even though the sentence contains an embedded clause, it is not clear whether the intended meaning is an embedded proposition:

(3)   She is sad that (she fell over),

which would indicate that the emotion is understood as a *propositional attitude* (intentional, mental state), or whether the intended meaning of the sentence is a *causal relationship*:

(4)   (She is sad) because (she fell over).

In this case the emotion is interpreted as a nonintentional internal state. A causal interpretation of the *that* complement in an emotion report is a serious possibility, whereas an analogous interpretation of a belief report (e.g., "She thinks that she fell over") would be plainly ridiculous:

(5)   (She thinks) because (she fell over).

There has been prolonged philosophical controversy (Calhoun & Solomon, 1984; Kenny, 1963) about the meaning of emotion reports and so it is not clear whether children, even when describing an emotion by means of an embedded *that* clause, are expressing a propositional attitude or a causal relationship.

This distinction becomes relevant when children's talk about emotions is taken as an indicator of their "theory of mind" (Bretherton et al., 1981) and their ability to understand higher-order mental states (Harris & Gross, Chapter 15; Landry & Lyons-Ruth, 1980). For instance, Harris and Gross (Chapter 15) describe an impressive example of a 6-year-old subject's explaining a person's motivation for hiding an emotion with a sentence containing a triply embedded clause, for example:

> She didn't want the other children to know that she's sad *that* she fell over.

This explanation would be indicative of "third-order mental state" attribution if the subject actually appreciated the full meaning of the *that* complement in distinction to:

> She didn't want the other children to know that she's sad *because* she fell over.

It would be extremely difficult to devise a test to demonstrate children's appreciation of such a subtle difference. Certainly, from the protocol it cannot be determined that one rather than the other meaning was intended, and so it is far from clear whether the subject in Harris's example was attributing a second- or third-order mental state.

In Perner and Wimmer's (1985) test of second-order belief understanding, these problems of interpretation were avoided by assuring that subjects could give a correct answer to test questions only if they attributed a second-order mental state. For this reason we adopted Perner & Wimmer's story method for studying children's ability to discriminate different types of social interaction in terms of participants' second-order mental states.

Social interaction and mental states

Various theorists of social cognition have recognized the importance of higher-order mental states for social interaction. For instance, game theorists emphasized their role in strategic interaction and social coordination (Goffman, 1970; Rapoport, 1967; Schelling, 1960); psychotherapists (Laing, Phillipson, & Lee, 1966), in the psychopathology of family dyads; communication theorists, in the formation of linguistic convention (Grice, 1957, 1975; Lewis, 1969) and taxonomy of speech acts (Searle, 1969, 1979).

If social interaction is based on higher-order mental states, then children's growing ability to understand social interaction should be related to their growing ability to attribute higher-order mental states. Selman (1980) has investigated this relationship for children's understanding of conflict resolution, leadership, friendship, and parent–child relations, by classifying children's ideas about these concepts in terms of level of perspective-taking.

Interviewing techniques, as used by Selman, have the advantage that they can constitute a rich source of new ideas about children's thinking. However, for establishing whether children do think in a certain way, these techniques suffer from the same interpretation problems as the observational method used in the hand-guessing games. In addition, in Selman's approach even the criteria for assigning levels of perspective-taking to children's verbal explanations are difficult to specify and have to be left to investigators' intuition. These problems of interpretation have been avoided in the studies reported in the following section by pursuing a strictly experimental approach.

The first of these studies explored children's ability to discriminate between different kinds of speech acts; the second explored children's ability to discriminate between nonverbal interactions in the case of a road accident. Both studies support a clear developmental picture. Second-order mental state attribution and the use of this attribution for discriminating differences in social interaction are mastered before the age of 10 years. The third study investigated children's understanding of social commitment. The results were unexpected and show that our experimental approach can serve the same creative purpose as interview studies in generating new theories about children's thinking.

Empirical investigations

Intention to deceive (Sue Leekam)

There are a variety of speech acts that involve false statements, for instance, a speaker may have been (1) mistaken, (2) lying, or (3) joking. The difference consists in the speaker's intentions. Hence, a child unable to make mental state attributions (zero order) should be unable to distinguish between these three cases as Piaget (1932/1965) suggested. A mistake can be distinguished from the other two cases by a first-order attribution. In the case of a mistake the speaker mistakenly *thinks* the false statement to be true, whereas a joking or lying speaker *knows* about the statement's falseness. In recent experimental work (Wimmer, Gruber, & Perner, 1984, 1985) most 4-year-old children, as soon as they were able to understand a speaker's mistaken belief, were also able to identify a mistake. Furthermore, they also understood that a mistakenly false statement is morally less reprehensible than an intended false statement.

The first-order distinction between intended and mistaken falsehood does not differentiate between lying and joking, because in both cases the speaker is aware of their falseness. The distinction can be made only on the basis of a second-order epistemic intention, what Coleman and Kay (1981) termed *intention to deceive*. This notion can be given a precise definition in terms of what the speaker *wants* the listener to *think*. A deceptive speaker wants the listener to think the false statement is true, whereas a joking speaker does not expect the listener to be misled by it.

Sue Leekam (in preparation) investigated children's ability to make this distinction by telling them stories of the following kind. A boy with his mother on the way out from school points to another child's beautiful painting and says, "Look, Mum, I painted that picture," and his mother is very pleased and praises him. In the *deceptive* story mother and son then go home. Next day the mother on her own initiative inspects the painting more closely. She then detects the name of the true artist and realizes that the painting was not her son's. In the *joking* story the boy, immediately after claiming to be the artist, directs his mother's attention to the true artist's name on the picture, so that his mother realizes that it isn't really his painting. Hence, in both stories the mother found out about the artist's real identity, but in one case the boy did *not want* her to *know* the truth and thought to the very end that his mother still believed that he was the artist, while in the other case he helped her to find out and obviously *wanted* her to *know* the truth.

Children were told both stories with the help of pictures and at the end of the second story were asked to compare the two stories:

Moral judgment: Which boy was naughtier for saying he did the picture?
Belief question: Mother doesn't think he did it anymore. But which boy still thinks she does believe him?

This procedure was repeated on another story pair and at the end a third question was added:

Joke question: "Which boy was just joking when he told his mum that he did the picture?"

Children's performance tended to improve from first to second story pair, but because the complete set of questions was asked only on the second pair, Table 14.1 shows the percentages of correct responses for the second pair.

The perfect performance on the belief question by 6-year-olds was surprisingly good in comparison to results by Perner & Wimmer (1985, Experiment 6: only 75% correct) but is probably a mere statistical fluke because performance by 7- and 8-year olds was not better than performance by similar age groups (Perner and Wimmer, 1985, Experiment 6: 87% and 96% correct). Yet despite good understanding of second-order belief, 6-year olds were not able to identify the joking boy or make a moral

Table 14.1. *Percentage subjects with correct answers on
second story pair in intention to deceive experiment*

Test question	Age			
	6	7	8	9
Belief	100	81	100	94
Moral	50	69	100	100
Joke	56	87	87	100

Note: n = 16 in each age group.

distinction between the two boys (50% = guessing level). By 7 years, however, these abilities emerge and are perfected by 8 and 9 years.

In summary, these studies suggest that children become able to distinguish between different speech acts and their moral implications fairly soon after becoming able to understand the necessary beliefs and intentions for making the distinction. At 4 years children learn to understand false belief and most of them can immediately use this understanding to distinguish between an intentionally false statement and a mistake (Wimmer et al., 1984, "Intention" question of Experiment 3) and make the correct moral distinction between these cases (Experiment 6). The study reported here shows that about 2 years later children are able to understand second-order beliefs and intentions and fairly soon thereafter, by about 7 and 8 years, are also able to draw the distinction between joke and deception and their moral implications.

Despite this good performance by children, there remains some puzzle about their understanding of the concept of "lying." Even though most 4-year-olds in the study by Wimmer et al. (1984, 1985) were perfectly able to tell a mistake from an intended falsehood, most 6-year-olds and even some 8- and 10-year-olds referred to both cases as "lies." Similarly, Sue Leekam found in a pilot study that some children who were perfectly able to decide which of the boys (in the stories just described) was joking, considered both boys to be lying.

Such judgment goes against adult intuition (at least mine). Mistakes and jokes are not lies. If this intuition is correct, then a statement would qualify as a lie only if it met all three of the following conditions:

1 It is false.
2 It is believed to be false by the speaker.
3 It is intended by the speaker to be believed by the listener (intention to deceive).

However, Coleman and Kay (1981) reported that even adults do not consider all three of these criteria as necessary. The three criteria define a prototypical lie, but even if a statement meets only one of them, it can be considered a lie. Children's judgment certainly conforms to this view.

Exceptions to trust (Nicola Yuill)

Belief and intention are important not only for speech acts; nonverbal interaction, too, depends on attribution of mental states. One such area is the judgment of responsibility for damage. When no beliefs and intentions are taken into account (zero order), then whoever caused the damage is to be blamed. However, this judgment may change if first-order attributions are made. Yuill (1984a) investigated children's understanding of responsibility for intended outcomes and accidents that were either foreseeable or unforeseeable.

By the age of 3 years children already have a very good grasp of the distinction between intended and accidental outcomes (Shultz, 1980; Yuill, 1984b), and by that age children can also use this distinction to attribute greater responsibility for an intended than for an accidentally caused outcome. By the age of 5 years children are also able to make the more subtle moral evaluation of foreseeable versus unforeseeable accidents. By the age of 7 years this moral distinction is understood by almost all children (Yuill, 1984a, Experiments 1 and 5).[3]

Recently, Nicola Yuill (Yuill & Perner, 1987) extended this line of research into children's ability to judge responsibility in terms of foreseeability based on second-order beliefs and knowledge states. This study was inspired by the Austrian Highway Code, which states a Principle of Trust: "Every road user may trust that other people will obey the relevant road traffic rules, except if there is evidence that it involves ... persons ... unable to recognize the danger of road traffic" (Oesterreichische Strassenverkehrsordnung, 1960, para. 3). For instance, if a cyclist rides by a parked car, she has a right to assume that the car occupant will abide by the rules and check whether anybody is coming before opening the door. Thus, should the driver not live up to his duty and cause an accident by opening the door in front of the cyclist, then the cyclist is not at all to blame for the accident. However, this verdict may change depending on the cyclist's second-order knowledge about the driver's knowledge. Let us assume the cyclist sees that the driver did not look back far enough and therefore knows that the driver did not see her come. In this case the cyclist *knows* that the driver *does not know* that she is coming, therefore she *has evidence that he is unable to recognize the danger*, consequently she loses her right to rely on the Principle of Trust and takes part of the blame for the accident. In contrast, she does not lose this right and stays blameless if she did not see that the driver had not looked, therefore *thinking* that he *knew* she was coming.

We re-created these two situations in two stories we told to 6- to 9-year-olds. We tested children's understanding of the cyclist's second-order knowledge by asking:

Belief question: "Did the cyclist *think* the driver *knew* she was coming?"

and children's ability to attribute responsibility was tested by asking:

Blame question: "How much is the cyclist to blame for what happened?"

After the second story, children were asked to remember both stories and to compare the two cyclists:

Direct comparison: "Which cyclist was more to blame?"

A child was scored as having made a correct responsibility attribution if the knowledgeable cyclist was given a higher individual blame rating and was judged as more to blame in direct comparison than the ignorant cyclist. A child was scored as understanding second-order belief if correct answers were given to belief questions in both stories. The percentages of children understanding second-order belief and making correct responsibility attributions are shown in the last row of Table 14.2.

As expected, there was a sharp increase from 6 to 9 years in children's ability to understand second-order beliefs and in their use of this ability for making correct responsibility attributions.

Table 14.2 provides a comparison of results of this experiment with Leekam's experiment on intention to deceive and with the original study by Perner and Wimmer (1985) on second-order beliefs. To make the data from these three studies as comparable as possible, Table 14.2 lists percentages of children who gave consistently correct responses on both stories used by Perner and Wimmer and on both story pairs used by Leekam (intention to deceive).

The comparison of these three experiments shows remarkable consistency. The data on second-order belief understanding (left half of Table 14.2) show that from 7 years onward a large majority of children gave consistently correct answers to relevant test questions. At age 6 performance varied across experiments. This is to be expected because the steepest improvement occurs between 5 and 7 years (Perner & Wimmer, 1985; Hogrefe, Wimmer, & Perner, 1986). Therefore, slight differences in sampling across experiments would lead to larger performance differences than at a later age where rate of improvement with age has flattened out.

Also, the data on moral judgment of speech acts agree nicely with the data on attribution of responsibility for accidents (right half of Table

Table 14.2. *Understanding second-order belief and moral or responsibility judgment: Comparison across three studies*

	Question and age								
	Second-order belief					Morality and responsibility			
Study	5	6	7	8	9	6	7	8	9
Second-order beliefs (Perner & Wimmer, 1985)	25	56	69	81	—				
Intention to deceive (Sue Leekam)	—	69	69	94	94	25	45	62	87
Exceptions to trust (Nicola Yuill)	—	25	62	70	75	6	33	42	69

14.2). At the age of 6 years there is no evidence that children can make any of these judgments. There is some evidence that by age 7, children are able to make correct responsibility attributions and correct moral distinctions between speech acts.[4] By the age of 8 a solid proportion of children can make both types of judgment, which by the age of 9 years has developed into a solid majority.

These data then do suggest that children under the age of 10 years not only understand second-order belief (Perner & Wimmer, 1985) but can also use this understanding to make relevant distinctions between speech acts and decide on responsibility for accidents. This conclusion contrasts with earlier claims that before their teens most children are not really able to understand second-order belief and its significance for interpersonal relations (Flavell et al., 1968; Selman, 1980; Shultz & Cloghesy, 1981).

Social commitment (Catherine Mant)

In a series of experiments Catherine Mant (Mant & Perner, in press) investigated children's understanding of when a person becomes socially committed to carrying out a planned action. These studies are most interesting, partly because they touch on the little-researched area of mutual intention (Power, 1984), and partly because results do not fit the clear picture presented in previous paragraphs. There is an interesting theoretical challenge. Our expectation was that children from 5 years onward should do very well in these experiments because (according to our initial analysis) only first-order attributions are required for making the necessary distinctions. To our surprise, children could not make the correct judgments until the age of 10 years.

As in previous experiments, children were asked to judge the moral responsibility of protagonists in two critical stories. In both stories the protagonist mentions to a friend his plan to go to the swimming pool after tea. In the *agreement story* the friend finds this a good idea and agrees with the protagonist to meet at the pool. In the *no-agreement story* the friend regrets that owing to other commitments, she cannot join in. Later at home, however, the friend discovers that her prior engagement has been canceled and decides to join the protagonist at the pool after tea. However, in both stories the protagonist changes his plan. He decides to cancel the trip to the pool and tidy up his bedroom instead. So in both stories his friend ends up alone at the pool, sad and longing for the protagonist's company. In both stories children are asked:

Moral judgment: "When the boy didn't go to the swimming pool, was that naughty not to go, or good, or in between?"

Belief question [first-order]: "Did the boy know the girl was going to the swimming pool?" [Correct answer: "Yes" in agreement story, "no" in no-agreement story.]

Children were scored as understanding the moral difference between the two stories if they rated the protagonist in the no-agreement story in a morally more favorable category than the protagonist in the agreement story. As Table 14.3 shows, only very few children younger than 9 years were able to do that, despite the fact that practically all of them answered the belief question correctly; in other words, they were aware of which boy knew and which one did not know that the girl would go to the swimming pool. Up to the age of 8 years children's typical error was to rate the boy in the no-agreement story as naughty. Around the age of 9, suddenly most children seemed to understand the relevant moral difference.

This late emergence of understanding is surprising because the relevant difference hinges only on the protagonist's first-order belief. In the *no-agreement* story the protagonist does *not know* that his friend will wait for him at the pool and hence could not foresee the consequence of his decision to stay home, whereas the protagonist in the *agreement* story did *know* that his friend would be waiting for him and hence was perfectly able to foresee the consequence. Yuill (1984a) reported that some 5-year-olds and practically all 7-year-olds understand that an actor is less to blame for a foreseeable than for an unforeseeable side effect of his action.

The late understanding of the no-agreement story seemed also surprising because that story is very reminiscent of an anecdote by Stern and Stern (1909/1931) about their 5-year-old son, who had told his aunt that he planned to become a surgeon and who then accused himself seriously of having lied to her when he changed his mind about his future a few days later. At first glance young Stern's unnecessary self-recrimination appears

Table 14.3. *Frequency of moral evaluation difference in*
agreement stories

Difference in moral evaluation	Age			
	6	7–8	8–9	9–10
Correct	7	6	6	20
None	40	17	14	8
Incorrect	1	1	0	2
Percentage correct	15	25	30	67

to be a case of moral realism (Piaget, 1932/1965). The boy considered himself morally bad because he had told his aunt something that has now become wrong. Such realism should also occur in the situation where something false is said by mistake. However, extensive investigation by Wimmer et al. (1984, 1985) showed little trace of such realism in children as young as 4 years old, who could judge accurately that only a message that was intended to be false is morally objectionable but not a false message that the speaker believed to be true.

Closer analysis shows that the purported similarity between falsity due to a later change of mind, as in Mant's no-agreement story (and the anecdote about young Stern), and a mistakenly false statement (Wimmer et al., 1984) holds only superficially. There is an important first-order difference between the two cases. A mistaken speaker does *not intend* his message to be false, whereas the protagonist in the no-agreement story changed his mind *intentionally* and therefore was responsible for making his earlier prediction false. So, if 4- to 6-year old children can discriminate between intentional and unintentional falsehood (as shown by Wimmer et al., 1984) but judge every intentional falsehood as morally reprehensible, then children in this age range (including young Stern) should hold the no-agreement story protagonist morally responsible for his friend's misfortune.

That this analysis reflects the way children perceive the no-agreement story receives some support from Mant's finding that children's wrong judgment of the no-agreement protagonist as naughty depended crucially on the fact that the protagonist's omission was intentional. This became clear in a condition where the protagonist stuck to his original intention but was physically prevented from going to the pool. Now only one of eighteen 6-year-olds considered him naughty. Similarly, if the protagonist never had the intention to go to the pool, but his friend just went there on the off chance of meeting him there, then only three of twenty-four 5-year-olds and no 6-year-old blamed the protagonist for his friend's disappointment. It seems clear that 5- and 6-year olds consider protagonists blameless when there was no intentional omission (new stories) but hold the protagonist responsible in the no-agreement story where the omission was intended. That children in this age range make a strict moral distinction between intended and unintended acts accords well with their competent moral distinction between intended and mistaken falsehood in the studies by Wimmer et al. (1984).

What is being proposed here is that the children in Mant's experiments did not base their moral judgment on the protagonist's first-order knowledge about the likely outcome of his omission (foreseeability), as we originally thought they would. Instead they seemed to focus on the falseness of the protagonist's prediction about his future action, which was the result of an intentional omission to act as predicted. The importance of the protagonist's original prediction became apparent in a "private intention" condition where the protagonist kept his intention to go to the swimming pool strictly to himself without telling his friend about it. His friend nevertheless went there in the off-chance hope of meeting him there. In this condition a majority of 6-year olds still blamed the protagonist for his friend's disappointment, but a solid majority of 79% of 7- to 8-year-olds (mean = 7 years 9 months) did not hold the protagonist responsible. Now that the misleading prediction has been eliminated, children's performance resembles what Yuill (1984a) found on her foreseeability stories where few 5-year-olds but a majority of 7-year-olds (mean age = 7 years 9 months in Experiment 9) showed clear understanding of foreseeability.

The results available so far indicate that children focus on the falseness of the protagonist's prediction. With that focus the contrast between agreement and no-agreement becomes a problem of higher-order mental states, similar to the contrast between deceptive lies and jokes studied by Sue Leekam. In all these stories speakers are responsible for the falseness of their statement. In Leekam's stories protagonists are responsible because they intend to say something false, while in Mant's stories they are responsible because they intentionally omit to act as predicted. The moral distinction can therefore not be drawn at the level of first-order intention by discriminating between intended and unintended falsehood, as in the studies by Wimmer et al. (1984). In Leekam's stories the moral distinction could be based on second-order epistemic intentions. The protagonist who *wanted* his mother to *believe* was more reprehensible than the one who did *not want* her to *believe* the falsehood. The question then is what kind of higher-order mental state would allow children to discriminate between protagonists in the agreement and no-agreement stories.

Obviously the difference lies in the fact that in the agreement story the protagonist knows that his friend *relies* on him to show up at the pool, whereas in the no-agreement story the protagonist has good reason to assume that his friend would not rely on him in that way, because his friend stated that she would not be able to go there. By rephrasing the word *rely*, one can see that the difference between stories involves a second-order belief. In the agreement story:

> the protagonist *knows* (that his friend will go to the pool because she *thinks* [that he will go there]);

while in the no-agreement story:

> the protagonist does *not know* (that his friend will go to the pool because she *thinks* [that he will go there]).

With this analysis children's unexpected problems in Mant's stories can be explained by their difficulty with higher-order mental states. However, further experiments are needed to establish that the proposed analysis in terms of reliance does, in fact, reflect the way children view responsibility in these stories. Yet even if empirical support were obtained, some difficult questions will remain; notably, why children understand the moral difference between agreement and no-agreement story only around the age of 10 years, when they understand other moral distinctions based on second-order belief somewhat earlier (e.g., Yuill's traffic accidents). The answer to this question may be linked to another troublesome question, namely, why the moral impact of foreseeability – which is presumably a first-order problem – is not really understood before the age of 7 (Yuill, 1984a; Mant's "private intention" story). A deeper understanding of this concept needs to be developed.

Yet despite (or because of) these problems, I find this line of research particularly interesting. It demonstrated how our method of manipulating story characters' beliefs and intentions helped gain new insights into how children view certain interpersonal situations and helped explain why children encounter serious difficulties that are not apparent to our intuitive judgment. In particular, it taught us that the anecdote about young Stern's self-recrimination should not be attributed to moral realism, that is, that any false statement constitutes a lie and is morally bad (Stern & Stern, 1909/1931; Wimmer et al., 1984). It also taught us that the easiest possible strategy to make correct discrimination (foreseeability) is not necessarily the one used by children. Instead of foreseeability we therefore came to think about other relevant social concepts, such as *reliance*. Most importantly, the experimental method could be adequately extended to isolate these highly relevant social concepts.

Summary

The results from these three empirical investigations support the view that understanding social interaction is based on understanding the mental states of the actors. This support rests on the fact that children were able to answer questions about second-order mental states earlier than they could draw the relevant moral distinctions or name the type of interaction (speech act). A not implausible alternative theoretical position would be that we are directly attuned to social situations as a whole. From this point of view one would expect the opposite results. Classification of a social situation and perception of its moral impact should be easier than abstraction of participants' intentions and beliefs.

The results also establish that children become proficient at understanding second-order mental states at around the age of 6–9 years, which is much earlier than previous research indicated (Flavell et al., 1968; Miller et al., 1970; Selman, 1980; Shultz & Cloghesy, 1981), where such proficiency would have been expected during the teens. Early competence for understanding second-order states was first found in the study by Perner and Wimmer (1985). The present results not only confirm this finding but also show that children can use this understanding to reason about some quite intricate social situations based on second-order mental states.

Discussion and conclusion

This chapter concludes by addressing an interesting point frequently raised in discussions of this topic. When the chapter was presented (as a paper) at Oxford, Colin McGinn remarked on the apparent discrepancy between my claim that second- and higher-order beliefs and intentions are not really understood before the age of 5 or 6 years and the fact that much younger children are effective intentional communicators. The discrepancy arises if one invokes Grice's (1957) view on intentional communication (rephrased by Levinson, 1983, p. 16): "communication consists of the 'sender' intending to cause the 'receiver' to think or do something, just by getting the 'receiver' to recognize that the 'sender' is trying to cause that thought or action." By this definition, if we admit that by saying, "Gimme cup," a 2-year-old intentionally communicates to his mother that she should give him his juice cup, we are then committed to the view that this 2-year-old attributes a second-order mental state to his mother. According to Grice's definition the communication is intentional only if "the child intends (his mother to *know* that [he *intends* (her to give him his cup)])."[5] Even worse, as Strawson (1964) has pointed out, normal communication achieves knowledge of the communicative intention at any level of recursive embedding (mutually known, according to Schiffer, 1972), for instance: The listener knows that the sender knows that ... the listener knows what the sender intends.

The suggestion that an intentional communicator has to represent mentally these complicated intentions contradicts the unreflective ease with which we use language to communicate (Clark & Marshall, 1981; Evans & McDowell, 1976). Evans and McDowell (1976, pp. xix–xxiii) likened our use of language to our use of money. The exchange of goods for money cannot constitute an exchange of goods of equal value since a piece of paper has no significant intrinsic value. Money has trading value based on a system of belief. A vendor is willing to give away valuable goods for money because he believes he will be able to get other goods for that money, and he believes that because he also believes that everybody else in the trading community believes that, and so on. This system of complex beliefs constitutes a necessary condition for a monetary economy, because if people started doubting other people's belief in the purchasing power of money, then their own belief would be eroded and with it the trading value of money. Notice, however, that what is necessary to save the economy is not so much people's belief in other people's belief, and so on, but that people do not doubt other people's belief. Smooth running of the economy seems to be based not on mental representation of complex beliefs but rather on the absence of mental representation expressing doubt in complex beliefs. To use money efficiently a simple view suffices: Money has its intrinsic value as stipulated by monetary convention. Only economists who are trying to establish a new means of payment or to troubleshoot an economic crisis need to concern themselves with complex beliefs in order to understand the root of the crisis.

The use of language has much in common with that of money. In regular usage we need not pay attention to mutual intentions but can rely on the "fossilized" meaning (Blackburn, 1984) of our linguistic conventions. Gricean considerations may be safely ignored. Only when trying to communicate by nonconventional means ("one-off predicament," Blackburn, 1984, chap. 4.1) does careful attention have to be paid to the intended receiver's ability to recognize the sender's communicative intention. Complex Gricean intentions also play a part in everyday communication when convention is transcended by indirect speech acts. Grice's (1957) definition of intentional communication is therefore not a description of conventional language use but serves as a basis for explaining how language can be used to communicate by violating the conventions (Grice's [1975] theory of implicature; cf. Levinson, 1983, p. 101).

Children do not have to develop their own communicative conventions but are socialized into an existing system. Thus there is no need for them to engage in sophisticated intentional analysis from the beginning. In fact, nonliteral use of language, for instance, irony, sarcasm, which does require complex analysis of communicative intention develops rather late (Winner et al., 1985). One reason for this late development may be that the prerequisite higher-order beliefs and intentions cannot be attributed before that age (Leekam, 1988).

This discussion shows that a Gricean (1975) view of communication is compatible with the course of development advocated in this chapter. Complex intentions and beliefs do not have to be considered for conventional language use. They are important for understanding the nature of such a system, its errors and exceptions. Infants can be competent communicators because normal communication is characterized by transparency ("openness," Blackburn, 1984) of intentions and beliefs (mutual knowledge). The infant operates with this openness by default, ignoring the underlying intentions and beliefs. As the young child starts to understand these intentions and beliefs the reasons for breakdown in social interaction become understood (mistakes, deception, accidents). When children develop an understanding of higher-order intentions and beliefs, they understand errors emerging from social coordination (breakdown in mutual trust and social commitment) and how apparent violations of social convention can be put to cooperative use (indirect speech acts).

ACKNOWLEDGMENTS

The author would like to thank Sue Leekam, Catherine Mant, and Nicola Yuill for their research efforts and helpful suggestions in writing this chapter. The research reported here has been financially supported by a research grant (C00232199) from the Economic and Social Research Council.

NOTES

1 This way of counting levels is natural if one talks about *understanding* mental representation or about *attribution* of mental states. If a child does not attribute or represent a mental state, we speak of zero-order attribution; if a child represents a mental state, of first-order attribution; and so on. However, an alternative way of counting levels is by considering the child's mental representation or attribution itself as a mental state (i.e., Dennett, 1978; Leslie, 1987; Leslie, Chapter 2). In this view a child thinking about a physical event *entertains* a first-order mental state or first-order thought. Thinking about a mental state (i.e., attribution of a first-order mental state), the child *entertains* a second-order mental state, and so on. In this chapter I strictly adhere to counting in terms of mental representation (understanding, attribution) of states, which can easily be translated into the other way of counting by the following formula:

Representing an *n*-order state = entertaining an $(n + 1)$-order state

2 This is not to say that our test establishes unequivocally that children make the correct prediction by attributing a false belief. As Premack and Woodruff (1978, p. 622) pointed out, correct prediction is still open to behavioristic interpretation (see also Chandler, Chapter 20). It is certainly possible that children solve the false belief task by applying rules about people's actions in certain situations bypassing any mental state attribution, for example, applying the rule "the pro-

tagonist will look for the object where he last put it." What speaks against this interpretation is the flexibility with which 4-year-olds can adjust their correct responses to changing situations in which this rule does not apply; for example, the protagonist is told that the object will be transferred from the location he put it in to a new location, but the transfer is never carried out (Perner, Leekam, & Wimmer, 1987, Experiment 1). In this situation the above-mentioned behavioristic rule would lead to the wrong response. Dennett (1978, pp. 274–277) has strongly emphasized flexibility and spontaneity as being characteristic of deception based on intentional concepts in contrast to mere instinctual display behavior of birds or conditioned responses of dogs, which achieve a desired effect by deceiving but which were not conceived as deception. For the same reason, I find reports of spontaneous deception in novel situations a more convincing indication that apes have a theory of mind (e.g., Waal, 1986) than deceptive acts that are the result of a history of laborious conditioning (Woodruff & Premack, 1979).

3 Nelson-LeGall (1985) reported that even 3-year-olds were able to make the moral distinction between foreseeable and unforeseeable events. Unfortunately, her test stories confounded foreseeability with intentionality. In her foreseeable-outcome stories the actor's intention to produce this outcome was explicitly stated, whereas in the unforeseeable-outcome stories no such intention was stated. Schleifer, Shultz, and Lefebvre-Pinard (1983) reported that 5-year-olds did not differentiate responsibility or morality according to foreseeability. Only 7-year-olds were able to do that. However, their manipulation of foreseeability in their stories was very indirect and children's interpretation of this difference was not independently assessed. The fact that 9-year-olds also failed to make the relevant moral and blame distinctions supports the suspicion that children simply did not understand the story cues as intended by experimenters.

4 The percentage of 7-year-olds giving consistently correct responses on the moral question in the intention to deceive experiment was not significantly different from guessing because the data were testable only on a nominal scale. The lower percentage of 7-year-olds in the exceptions to trust experiment were significantly different from guessing because the blame ratings allowed the use of an ordinal test.

5 It is interesting that Bretherton et al. (1981), who credit even 9-month-old infants with intentional communication use Bates's (1979) definition of the term, which remains ambiguous as to how much the infant, when "communicating intentionally," understands about the listener's mind: "Intentional communication is signaling behavior in which the sender is aware, *a priori*, of the effect that the signal will have on his listener, and he persists in that behavior until the effect is obtained or failure is clearly indicated" (p. 338). The ambiguity arises from the expression "effect on the listener" by which the infant judges the success of his communicative efforts. If this effect is a particular state of mind in the listener, then "intentional communication" clearly involves attribution of a mental state, but if the child is judging success on a purely behavioral basis, then an infant's "intentional communication" does not involve a "theory of mind." This ambiguity is also reflected in Bretherton et al.'s (1981) interpretation of Bates's definition: "Implicit in Bates' definition is the fact that the

infant recognizes a partner's capacity to *understand* a message. In other words, the infant attributes an internal state of *knowing* and *comprehending* to the mother as he or she communicates" (p. 339). However, these authors later explicitly deny that by crediting the 9-month-old with what they call a "theory of interfacible minds" would imply that infants can impute mental states: "When suggesting that infants as young as 9 months of age have something as outlandish as a theory of interfacible minds, we do not mean to suggest that they are *aware* of using such a theory, nor that they can impute *any* mental state" (p. 340).

REFERENCES

Bates, E. (1979). Intentions, conventions, and symbols. In E. Bates et al. (Eds.), *The emergence of symbols: Cognition and communication in infancy*. New York: Academic Press.

Bretherton, I., McNew, S., & Beeghly-Smith, M. (1981). Early person knowledge as expressed in gestural and verbal communication: When do infants acquire a "theory of mind"? In M. E. Lamb & L. R. Sherrod (Eds.), *Infant social cognition*. Hillsdale, NJ: Erlbaum.

Blackburn, S. (1984). *Spreading the word: Groundings in the philosophy of language*. Oxford University Press (Clarendon Press).

Calhoun, C., & Solomon, R. C. (Eds.). (1984). *What is an emotion? Classic readings in philosophical psychology*. Oxford University Press.

Chisholm, R. (1967). Intentionality. In P. Edwards (Ed.), *The encyclopedia of philosophy*. New York: Macmillan.

Clark, H. H., & Marshall, C. R. (1981). Definite reference and mutual knowledge. In A. K. Joshi, I. Sag, & B. Webber (Eds.), *Linguistic structure and discourse setting*. Cambridge University Press.

Coleman, L., & Kay, P. (1981). Prototype semantics: The English word *lie*. *Language, 57*, 26–44.

Dennett, D. C. (1978). *Brainstorms*. Montgomery, VT: Bradford Books.

Eliot, J., Lovell, K., Dayton, C. M., & McGrady, B. F. (1979). A further investigation of children's understanding of recursive thinking. *Journal of Experimental Child Psychology, 28*, 149–157.

Evans, G., & McDowell, J. (Eds.). (1976). *Truth and meaning*. Oxford University Press (Clarendon Press).

Flavell, J. H., Botkin, P., Fry, C., Wright, J., & Jarvis, D. (1968). *The development of role-taking and communication skills in children*. New York: Wiley.

Goffman, E. (1970). *Strategic interaction*. Oxford: Blackwell Publisher.

Gratch, G. (1964). Response alternation in children: A developmental study of orientations to uncertainty. *Vita Humana, 7*, 49–60.

Grice, H. P. (1957). Meaning. *Philosophical Review, 66*, 377–388.

Grice, H. P. (1975). Logic and conversation. In P. Cole & J. L. Morgan (Eds.), *Speech acts*. New York: Academic Press.

Harris, L., Johnson, C. N., & Harris, P. L. (1987). *Understanding false belief by young children*. Unpublished manuscript, University of Oxford.

Hogrefe, G.-J., Wimmer, H., & Perner, J. (1986). Ignorance versus false belief:

A developmental lag in attribution of epistemic states. *Child Development, 57,* 567–582.

Johnson, C. N., & Maratsos, M. (1977). Early comprehension of mental verbs: Think and know. *Child Development, 48,* 1743–1747.

Kenny, A. (1963). *Action, emotion and will.* London: Routledge & Kegan Paul.

Laing, R. D., Phillipson, H., & Lee, A. R. (1966). *Interpersonal perception: A theory and a method of research.* London: Tavistock.

Landry, M. O., & Lyons-Ruth, K. (1980). Recursive structure in cognitive perspective-taking. *Child Development, 51,* 386–394.

Leekam, S. R. (1988). *Children's understanding of intentional falsehood.* Doctoral dissertation, Experimental Psychology, University of Sussex.

Leslie, A. M. (1987). Pretense and representation: The origins of "theory of mind." *Psychological Review, 94,* 412–426.

Levinson, S. C. (1983). *Pragmatics.* Cambridge University Press.

Lewis, D. (1969). *Convention: A philosophical study.* Cambridge, MA: Harvard University Press.

Mant, C. M., & Perner, J. (in press). The child's understanding of commitment *Developmental Psychology.*

Marvin, R. S., Greenberg, M. T., & Mossler, D. G. (1976). The early development of conceptual perspective taking: Distinguishing among multiple perspectives. *Child Development, 47,* 511–514.

Miller, P., Kessel, F., & Flavell, J. (1970). Thinking about people thinking about people thinking about . . .: A study of social cognitive development. *Child Development, 41,* 613–623.

Mossler, D. G., Marvin, R. S., & Greenberg, M. T. (1976). Conceptual perspective taking in 2- to 6-year-old children. *Developmental Psychology, 12,* 85–86.

Nelson-LeGall, S. A. (1985). Motive-outcome matching and outcome foreseeability: Effects on attribution of intentionality and moral judgment. *Developmental Psychology, 21,* 332–337.

Perner, J., Leekam, S. R., & Wimmer, H. (1987). Three-year-olds' difficulty with false belief: The case for a conceptual deficit. *British Journal of Developmental Psychology, 5,* 125–137.

Perner, J., & Wimmer, H. (1985). "John thinks that Mary thinks that . . .": Attribution of second-order beliefs by 5- to 10-year-old children. *Journal of Experimental Child Psychology, 39,* 437–471.

Piaget, J. (1965). *The moral judgment of the child.* New York: Free Press. (Originally published 1932)

Power, R. (1984). Mutual intention. *Journal for the Theory of Social Behavior, 14,* 85–102.

Premack, D. C. & Woodruff, G. (1978). Does the chimpanzee have a theory of mind? *The Behavioral and Brain Sciences, 1,* 516–526.

Rapoport, A. (1967). Escape from paradox. *Scientific American, 217,* 50–56.

Russell, B. (1919). On propositions: What they are and what they mean. *Proceedings of the Aristotelian Society, 2,* 1–43.

Schelling, T. C. (1960). *The strategy of conflict.* Cambridge University Press.

Schiffer, S. (1972). *Meaning.* Oxford University Press.

Schleifer, M., Shultz, T. R., & Lefebvre-Pinard, M. (1983). Children's judgements of causality, responsibility and punishment in cases of harm due to omission. *British Journal of Developmental Psychology, 1*, 87–97.

Searle, J. R. (1969). *Speech acts*. Cambridge University Press.

Searle, J. R. (1979). A taxonomy of illocutionary acts. In J. R. Searle (Ed.), *Expression and meaning*. Cambridge University Press.

Selman, R. L. (1980). *The growth of interpersonal understanding: Developmental and clinical analyses*. New York: Academic Press.

Shatz, M., Wellman, H. M., & Silber, S. (1983). The acquisition of mental verbs: A systematic investigation of the first reference to mental state. *Cognition, 14*, 301–321.

Shultz, T. R. (1980). Development of the concept of intention. In W. A. Collins (Ed.), *The Minnesota symposium on child psychology* (Vol. 13). Hillsdale, NJ: Erlbaum.

Shultz, T. R., & Cloghesy, K. (1981). Development of recursive awareness of intention. *Developmental Psychology, 17*, 465–471.

Stern, C., & Stern, W. (1931). *Monographien über die seelische Entwicklung des Kindes*. 2. Band: *Erinnerung. Aussage und Lüge in der ersten Kindheit*. Leipzig: Barth. 4th edition. (Originally published 1909).

Strawson, P. F. (1964). Intention and convention in speech acts. *Philosophical Review, 73*, 439–460.

Waal, F. de. (1986). Deception in the natural communication of chimpanzees. In R. W. Mitchell & N. S. Thompson (Eds.), *Deception: Perspectives on human and nonhuman deceit*. Albany: State University of New York Press.

Wimmer, H., Gruber, S., & Perner, J. (1984). Young children's conception of lying: Conceptual realism – moral subjectivism. *Journal of Experimental Child Psychology, 37*, 1–30.

Wimmer, H., Gruber, S., & Perner, J. (1985). Young children's conception of lying: Moral intuition and the denotation and connotation of "to lie." *Developmental Psychology, 21*, 993–995.

Wimmer, H., & Perner, J. (1983). Beliefs about beliefs: Representation and constraining function of wrong beliefs in young children's understanding of deception. *Cognition, 13*, 103–128.

Winner, E., Windmueller, G., Rosenblatt, E., Bosco, L., Best, E., & Gardner, H. (1985). *Making sense of literal and nonliteral falsehood*. Unpublished manuscript, Project Zero, Harvard University, Cambridge, MA.

Woodruff, G., & Premack, D. (1979). Intentional communication in the chimpanzee: The development of deception. *Cognition, 7*, 333–362.

Yuill, N. M. (1984a). *Children's comprehension and judgements of human action: Motives, intentionality and foreseeability*. Unpublished doctoral dissertation, University of Sussex, Brighton.

Yuill, N. M. (1984b). Young children's coordination of motive and outcome in judgements of satisfaction and morality. *British Journal of Developmental Psychology, 2*, 73–81.

Yuill, N. M., & Perner, J. (1987). Exceptions to mutual trust: Children's use of second-order beliefs in responsibility attribution. *International Journal of Behavioral Development, 10*, 207–223.

15

Children's understanding of real and apparent emotion

PAUL L. HARRIS and DANA GROSS

A child trips over, gets up, and tries not to look too upset in order to avoid being teased. To truly understand this episode, children will need to understand several interrelated concepts: First, and most obviously, that the overt expression of emotion can be voluntarily controlled; second, that despite appearances, the child who has fallen over still really feels upset; and third, that if the deception is successful, then onlookers will falsely believe that the child is not upset. The experiments that we describe in this chapter concern children's understanding of such everyday episodes. Thus, they are most directly concerned with children's understanding of emotion. Nevertheless, they offer a further opportunity to study children's understanding of the appearance–reality distinction, and of false beliefs.

With respect to physical objects, there is now a good deal of evidence to show that an understanding of the distinction between appearance and reality emerges between 3 and 5 years of age across a wide variety of tasks (Flavell, 1986; Chapter 13). Given a sponge that looks like a rock, 5-year-olds can distinguish its real identity from its appearance. They claim that it is really a sponge but that it looks like a rock. If they are shown a white disk covered by a blue filter, they claim that it is really white but that it looks blue. When do children sort out this distinction for real and apparent emotions? Several experiments suggest that children find it hard to understand the distinction until quite late in the school years. Saarni (1979) asked 6- to 10-year-old children about the facial expression that story characters would display in situations where, to protect their own feelings or those of other people, it would be appropriate for them to hide their emotions. Ten-year-olds surpassed 6- and 8-year-olds, both in the number of display rules they offered and in the complexity of their reasoning, suggesting that the ability to distinguish real from apparent emotion is quite limited until about 10 years of age. Further support for this conclusion is provided by Gnepp (1983). She presented a wide age-range of children with a conflict between a story character's current situation and his or her pictured facial expression. Children aged 11 to 13 years were more likely than 3- to 7-year-olds to claim that the protagonist was attempting to mask his or her feelings. Finally, Gnepp and Hess (1986) in a study of display rules found that even 15-year-olds sometimes failed to realize when people might wish to conceal or control their facial expression. These various studies all lead to the conclusion that young children of 6 and even 8 years of age find it hard to make a distinction between what people really feel and what they actually express on their faces. If this conclusion is accepted, it is tempting to draw the further conclusion that young children find it much more difficult to distinguish between reality and appearance in connection with mental entities, such as emotional states, than in connection with the identity or properties of physical objects, such as a rock or colored piece of paper.

New findings

The tasks used in earlier studies require children to do two things: first, to work out that the story character might have some reason for hiding his or her feelings, and second, to appreciate, therefore, that reality and appearance might not coincide. We suspected that part of the difficulty in these earlier studies was in spontaneously appreciating that the person would actually want to hide his or her feelings. To rule out this problem, we told children stories in which such a motive was explicitly attributed to the protagonist (Harris, Donnelly, Guz, & Pitt-Watson, 1986, Experiment 2). Here is an example of one of the stories we used:

Diana wants to go outside, but she has a tummyache. She knows that if she tells her mom that she has a tummyache, her mom will say that she can't go out. She tries to hide the way she feels so that her mom will let her go outside.

In this story, two key elements are included: an event that produces an emotion – the tummyache – and also a reason for concealing the emotion. In the next example, an event that produces emotion and a reason for its concealment are again included, but this time the emotion to be concealed is positive rather than negative.

Diana is playing a game with a friend. At the end of the game Diana wins and her friend loses. Diana tries to hide how she feels because otherwise her friend won't play anymore.

Children were given eight such stories, four that involved hiding a negative emotion, and four that involved hiding a positive emotion. The children were 4 and 6 years of age. After listening to each story and being given an appropriate memory check, they were asked two questions: one about the story character's real emotion, and one about the story character's apparent emotion. In each case, they could choose between three alternative answers: "sad," "okay," and "happy." Notice that the answer to each of these questions had not been directly stated in the stories. To answer the

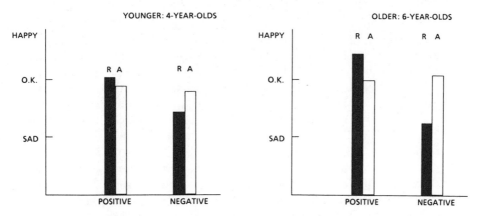

Figure 15.1 Mean emotion judgments by age, type of question (reality [R] vs. appearance [A]), and type of story (positive versus negative).

question about the story character's real emotion, children needed to work out the emotional impact of the precipitating event – the tummyache or winning the game – on the protagonist. To answer the question about the story character's apparent emotion, children needed to carry out a more complex analysis. They had to bear in mind that the protagonist did not *want* the other story character to *know* his or her real feelings, so that a misleading display had to be selected, one that did not correspond to an expression of the real emotion. Thus, a correct answer to the appearance question required an appreciation of second-order mental states (cf. Perner, Chapter 14), in which the desire of the protagonist is directed at the actual or possible beliefs of another person.

Figure 15.1 shows that 6-year-olds make different judgments for the real emotion (R) as compared to the apparent emotion (A). In each case, the story protagonist is judged really to feel an emotion that is more intense than the apparent emotion – more positive in the positive stories, more negative in the negative stories. The differentiation between real (R) and apparent (A) emotion is less obvious among the 4-year-olds. In fact, for the positive stories, the 4-year-olds do not make any significant differentiation between reality and appearance.

In our next study (Gardner, Harris, Ohmoto, & Hamazaki, in press) we looked at the possible impact of culture. Various anthropological (e.g., Hendry, 1986) and psychological studies (e.g., Ekman, 1982) suggest that the display of emotion is highly regulated in Japan. Japanese mothers expect their children to control or hide their feelings at an earlier age than do American mothers (Hess, Kashiwagi, Azuma, Price, & Dickson, 1980). Observational studies of Japanese children by Hendry (1986) suggest that even kindergarten children are encouraged to try to hide their feelings when they are upset, angry, or in physical pain. We wondered if an understanding of the distinction between real and apparent emotion would emerge earlier among Japanese children. Accordingly, we carried out a replication of our first study with 4- and 6-year-old Japanese children attending a kindergarten in Hiroshima. The stories were adapted slightly to make them more suitable for Japanese children; in particular, some of the stories were changed to include a reference to classmates rather than siblings, but in all other respects the study was an exact replication.

The simplest way to compare the results for the Japanese and British children is in terms of the proportion of children who scored above chance. (Our scoring system was such that children would be expected to be correct by chance on one third of the stories they listened to.) Table 15.1 gives the percentage of children scoring above chance. The table gives results for Oxford (study 1), for Hiroshima (study 2), and for Minneapolis, where study 3 – described in a later section – was carried out. In each location, there is a similar developmental trend. A minority of 4-year-olds but a majority of 6-year-olds scored better than chance. Thus, there is no clear indication of any accelerated understanding among the Japanese children, despite the strong pressure on them to conceal negative feelings.

Our third study (Gross & Harris, in press; Harris, Gardner, & Gross, 1987) was concerned with two issues. One was primarily methodological: Were children approaching the stories that we told them with a general set toward choosing different emotions for the reality question and the appearance question, or did they grasp that sometimes reality and appearance can coincide? To answer that question, we again told 4-year-olds and 6-year-olds eight stories. Four stories were discrepant ones similar to the negative stories used in the first two studies, where the protagonist should feel a negative emotion but display a more positive emotion. Four stories, however, were nondiscrepant stories, where the protagonist should feel a negative emotion but have no reason to hide it. An example of a nondiscrepant story is as follows:

Diana is eating dinner with her grandmother, but Diana doesn't like the food. Diana knows that if she shows her grandmother how she really feels, her grandmother will give her something else to eat. So Diana lets her grandmother see how she really feels.

The second issue focused on the other characters in the story. Conceivably, children might understand that the protagonist could express one emotion while really feeling a different emotion, without realizing that such a display is directed at the knowledge or beliefs of the other story

Table 15.1. *Percentage of children scoring above chance by age, location of study, and type of story*

	4-year-olds	6-year-olds
Oxford (positive stories)	46	67
Oxford (negative stories)	42	67
Hiroshima (positive stories)	39	65
Hiroshima (negative stories)	48	78
Minneapolis (negative stories)	33	79

characters. If, on the other hand, children appreciate that misleading displays are based on second-order mental states, they will understand not just that the protagonist wants to hide his or her feelings but also that the protagonist wants to mislead an onlooker. Specifically, children will understand that the protagonist wants to hide his or her feelings in order to create a false belief in an onlooker about the protagonist's real emotion. Note that such an understanding also implies that children appreciate how psychological entities such as emotional states can be the target of false beliefs just as easily as solid, physical objects. To assess children's understanding of these issues, we posed a third question about the on-looker's belief in addition to the reality and appearance questions. For example, in the case of the tummyache story, we asked: "How did Diana's mom think she felt?" Again, subjects made a choice between three options: happy, sad, and okay.

The results are shown in Figure 15.2. The 6-year-olds respond systematically and appropriately for both the nondiscrepant and the discrepant stories. In the nondiscrepant stories, they judge that reality (R), appearance (A), and the beliefs of the onlooker (O) will all coincide. In the discrepant stories, they judge that the story character will really be sad, but that he or she will appear more positive and that an onlooker will attribute positive rather than negative feelings. By contrast, the judgments made by the 4-year-olds are less systematic. Although they deal appropriately with the nondiscrepant stories where reality, appearance, and the beliefs of the onlooker all coincide, they do not differentiate among these questions for the discrepant stories as sharply as the 6-year-olds. Thus, they are likely to judge that the protagonist will look and feel the same way, thereby precluding any possibility for an onlooker to be misled.

After they had made their choice of emotion for the three questions (i.e., reality, appearance, onlooker's belief), children were asked to justify their answers. The focus of the justifications varied across the three questions. For example, asked to say why Diana was really sad, children would

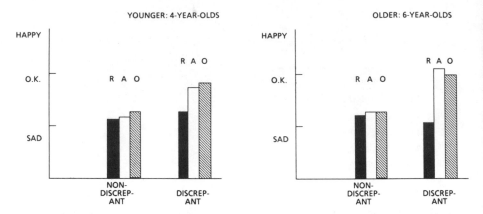

Figure 15.2. Mean emotion judgments by age, type of question (reality [R] vs. appearance [A] vs. other's belief [O]), and type of story (nondiscrepant vs. discrepant).

appropriately refer to the precipitating *Event* in the story: "She's sad 'cos she fell over." Asked to justify why she appeared happy, having just fallen over, they would appropriately refer to the protagonist's *Motive*: "She didn't want the other children to laugh at her." Asked to justify why the other children might judge her to be happy, they would appropriately refer to the expression on her *Face*: "'Cos she looked happy."

Table 15.2 shows the frequency with which children offered each type of justification when explaining their choices for the three questions in the discrepant condition. It is clear that 6-year-olds are quite selective in their responding. Thus, they justified their choice for the protagonist's real emotion by reference to the precipitating event in the story. They justified their choice for the protagonist's apparent emotion by reference to the protagonist's motive, and they justified their choice for the other's belief question by reference to the protagonist's facial expression.

By contrast, the 4-year-olds were much less selective. Although they appropriately referred to the precipitating event to explain the protagonist's real emotion, their justifications for the appearance and other's belief question were mostly inappropriate. In line with their incorrect judgment that the protagonist would appear sad, they persisted in referring to the precipitating event in explaining that appearance, and not to the protagonist's motive for concealment. Moreover, they referred less often to the protagonist's facial appearance in explaining what others would believe.

The syntactic structure of the children's justifications also proved informative. The replies were often quite complicated in the sense that they involved several embedded clauses. In response to the appearance question, one 6-year-old appropriately claimed that the protagonist would look

Table 15.2. *Mean number of references to event, motive, and face as a function of question type and age for the discrepant condition of study 3*

| | | Question type | | |
		Reality	Appearance	Other's belief
Younger	Event	2.79*	2.46	1.08
	Motive	0.13	*0.75*	0.13
	Face	0.00	0.00	*1.71*
	Residual	1.08	0.79	1.21
Older	Event	*3.42*	1.13	0.79
	Motive	0.50	*2.81*	0.21
	Face	0.00	0.04	*3.04*
	Residual	0.29	0.21	0.21

* Italicized scores correspond to correct category of justification. Some justifications included a reference to more than one category, so that column totals sometimes exceed 4.

happy, and in justification she said: "She didn't want the other children to know that she's sad that she fell over." If we take this sentence apart, we find that there are three embedding clauses in addition to the final embedded clause: "She didn't want," "the other children to know," and "that she's sad," yielding an overall total of four verb-containing clauses.

We examined the correct justifications that children produced in response to the reality and appearance questions of the Oxford study and counted the number of such verb-containing clauses. We arrived at the figures in Table 15.3, which give overall means and an indication of the overall maximum attained. (Note that we had to drop some subjects from this analysis, especially in the younger group because they failed to produce any correct justifications.)

Table 15.3 shows that justifications for the reality question were less complicated than justifications for the appearance question. This is scarcely surprising. Subjects could simply say "She fell over" or "She had a tummyache" to explain what the protagonist really felt. In contrast, appearance justifications needed to be more complicated. The 6-year-olds produced two clauses on average, and the minority of 4-year-olds who were included came close to that average. Thus, "Because she didn't want her Mummy to know" is a typical two-clause justification. But 11 of the 6-year-olds also produced at least one justification containing three clauses, for example: "She didn't want her sister to know that she hided her toy," and 3 of these 11 subjects produced a justification containing four clauses, such as the one mentioned earlier: "She didn't want other chil-

Table 15.3. *Mean number and maximum number of clauses in correct justifications as a function of age and question type*

Age	Mean		Maximum	
	Reality question	Appearance question	Reality question	Appearance question
Young ($n = 7^a$)	1.15	1.85	1.43	2.14
Older ($n = 17^a$)	1.21	2.04	1.65	2.77

[a] Only subjects who produced at least one correct justification were included.

dren to know that she's sad that she fell over." Note that these examples all contain references to second-order mental states. Children refer to the desires of the protagonist as being directed at the beliefs of the onlookers.

These results are intriguing because they suggest that children can take a proposition and make it the object of another proposition, particularly when the embedding proposition contains a mental verb. The embedding clauses usually involve a mental verb or predicate such as "wants", "knows" or "is sad." The possibility of taking one clause and embedding it within a second clause containing a mental verb seems to be fairly routine at 6 years, but is bettered on at least one occasion by about half the 6-year-olds who went still further and embedded those two clauses within a third.

Summarizing across the three studies, we may draw the following conclusions: First, between the ages of 4 and 6 years, children come to distinguish systematically between real and apparent emotion. Second, this age change occurs in diverse cultures. Admittedly it has not yet been shown to occur in a preliterate culture, but it does appear to take place at approximately the same age in cultures that have different expectations about when children should exert control over the display of emotion. Third, by the age of 6 years children understand the impact of a misleading display for onlookers. They appreciate that an onlooker will falsely attribute to the protagonist the emotion that he or she appears to be experiencing as opposed to the real emotion that they themselves attribute to the protagonist. Finally, again by 6 years of age, children are quite adept at putting into words the kind of recursive, second-order thinking that is required to understand deceptive ploys.

These results have a bearing on four interrelated issues: the discovery that beliefs about emotion can be false; the distinction between appearance and reality; the child's concept of emotion; and the understanding of deception.

Discovering that beliefs about emotion can be false

Previous demonstrations of children's understanding of false beliefs (Baron-Cohen, Leslie, & Frith, 1985; Perner, Leekam, & Wimmer, 1987) have been concerned with beliefs about the location of an object. The results from the final study reported here show that young children understand that one may also entertain a false belief about someone's mental state (i.e., their real emotion). It is worth stressing the special nature of such an insight. It seems likely that children will have many opportunities to discover that a belief about publicly observable facts, such as the location of a hidden object, may be false. As infants, they find that their expectations about the location of an object will prove incorrect when they engage in search (Harris, 1983a). By 2½–3 years children can spontaneously comment on such discrepancies between expectation and outcome (e.g., "I thought the socks were in the drawer 'cept they weren't" [Wellman, 1985]).

With respect to emotion, on the other hand, there will be fewer opportunities to discover that beliefs may be false. Consider, first, the child who is engaged in observing other people. If other people are successful at concealing their real emotions, then by definition the child who observes them will have no opportunity to detect the mismatch between real and apparent emotion, and hence no opportunity to discover that his or her belief based on apparent emotion may be false. Admittedly, other people may be unsuccessful in hiding their feelings from young children. Various nonverbal cues may leak their real feelings. However, it is likely that such cues will be quite subtle and difficult to detect. Even if young children are perceptive enough to distinguish between cues that result from nonverbal leakage of the person's real feelings, and those that are part of a deliberate display, they still face the further problem of deciding which set of cues to regard as veridical. Given these considerations, it is not surprising that young children perform poorly when given the task of distinguishing between genuine displays of emotion and deliberately deceptive displays (DePaulo & Jordan, 1982; DePaulo, Jordan, Irvine, & Laser, 1982). Thus, it seems reasonable to conclude that young children rarely discover, from a careful examination of the misleading display, that their belief about another person's emotion is mistaken.

So far we have considered the possibility that children might distinguish perceptually between genuine and false displays of emotion simply from their scrutiny of misleading displays. There is, however, another potential source of instruction. Consider a young child who sees another child trip over, and then get up, making a brave effort to smile. The observer has two potential clues that the smile is a fake: the nature of the smile itself – whether its composition corresponds to that of a genuine smile –

but also the context in which the smile is produced, because people do not usually smile when they trip over. However, observations of this latter type also seem unlikely to demonstrate that beliefs about emotion can be false. If the child observing the accident mistakenly concludes that the smile is genuine, then the incident will obviously fail to show that beliefs about emotion can be false. The observer will simply fail to be disabused of his or her false belief. If, on the other hand, the child observing the accident correctly concludes that the smile is no more than a brave face, the incident will again fail to show that beliefs about emotion can be false: The observer never entertains a false belief in the first place.

What about children's beliefs concerning their own emotions? Here, too, the distinction between real and apparent emotion is not obviously available. A discrepancy between real and apparent emotion will rarely arise: Children will be happy and know it, or sad and know it. We can imagine occasional circumstances in which children are initially misled by their own display rules, but eventually discover their real feelings. For example, a boy might persuade himself that he is not afraid by acting confidently, only to discover that his heart pounds as he approaches whatever it is that is the source of his fear. However, it seems unlikely that these opportunities for discovering the discrepancy between real and apparent emotion would often arise, because they depend both on children's power to persuade themselves temporarily that the emotion they are displaying overtly is what they actually feel, and on subsequent opportunities for discovering that they are wrong.

Overall, it appears difficult for children to discover that their own beliefs about emotion are incorrect whether the emotion is being experienced by someone else or by the children themselves. On the other hand, children will often have opportunities to discover that other people's beliefs about their own emotion are false. To avoid aggravation from their peers and disapproval from their parents, children will learn the instrumental value of inhibiting certain emotional displays. In such encounters, an observer will respond to the emotion that children display rather than to the emotion that they really feel. Under these circumstances, the mental processes that accompany the emotion, including thoughts about the situation that led to the emotion, will proceed normally. Only the facial expression will be changed. Such experiences will presumably teach the child that other people may be misled about what they really feel, depending on the facial expression they display. Thus, although children may be rarely confronted by the fact that their own beliefs about emotion are false, they may readily discover that other people's beliefs about their own emotions are false. This account predicts that children may learn to hide certain emotions before discovering the misleading impact that such displays have on other people. Strong support for this prediction is provided by Cole (1986). Adapting a paradigm developed by Saarni (1984), Cole filmed 3- to 4-year-old girls opening a disappointing gift either alone or in the presence of the person who had offered the gift. She found that the facial expressions exhibited in these two situations were different. When they opened the gift alone, the girls expressed their disappointment facially; when they opened the gift in front of the donor, the girls managed to conceal the expression of disappointment by means of a smile. Nevertheless, in a subsequent interview that focused on whether or not the donor knew how they felt about the disappointing gift, only one child explained that the donor would know her feelings by virtue of her facial expression, and none of the children spontaneously referred to the control of their facial expression.

Cole's results support the idea that children can learn to control their facial expression before they appreciate the misleading impact that such control will have on other people. If the above analysis is correct, however, the misleading impact will eventually be instructive. To the extent that other people make comments that indicate they have been misled, young children will be confronted by a conflict between two sources of information: their own knowledge of how they feel, and other people's inappropriate comments about how they feel. This conflict ought to teach children that other people do not necessarily know how they really feel, and eventually children may come to adopt display rules with the conscious intent of misleading other people.

This line of thinking illustrates an important feature of the child's understanding of mental life. It is tempting to assume that the child either adopts certain ideas about the mind on the basis of self-conscious introspection, or alternatively takes over a set of folk concepts from the community, concepts that do not necessarily pick out any irreducibly private mental state or sensation. These two models of the child's learning have been referred to elsewhere as the solipsistic and the sociocentric model respectively (Harris & Olthof, 1982). Some characteristics of mental life, however, can be appreciated only by a joint consideration of each source of information. This applies quite clearly to a key aspect of mental life: the potential privacy of various processes, including emotions, thoughts, and dreams. If children could not accurately monitor their subjective states, they would be forced to assume that those private states correspond to their public interpretation. Conversely, if the child did not monitor the public interpretation of those private states, it would be difficult to discover that the public interpretation may deviate from what the child knows from introspection. Thus, the mental world sometimes has a Janus-face; the child needs to see both faces to understand it fully.

Distinguishing reality from appearance

The argument in the preceding section implies that children can keep track of their real emotion, while they simultaneously notice other people responding to their apparent emotion. How do young children keep track of their real emotion? A long history of theorizing about emotion suggests that the experience of emotion is constituted by the expression that accompanies it. This claim is to be found in the James–Lange theory (James, 1894) and more recently in differential emotions theory (Izard, 1977). The implication of this line of theorizing is that if an emotion is displayed that is different from the emotion currently experienced, the feedback associated with that display will, at least in part, generate a different experience. Indeed, Laird, Wagener, Halal, and Szegda (1982) have shown that when subjects compose their faces into a particular expression, some subjects report experiencing the emotional state in question, and memory biases that would typically come into play during such an emotional state may be observed. However, such a setup is obviously unusual. Under normal circumstances, we encounter an emotionally charged situation, and this situation provokes appropriate thoughts and feelings. We are guided toward an understanding of what we feel by our appreciation of the situation we are in, and not by the facial expression we exhibit. Indeed, as adults, we readily distinguish between what we really feel and what we express facially. If the latter constituted the former, the distinction would be impossible. The fact that even 6-year-olds make the distinction strongly suggests that it is a deep-seated and inescapable fact of consciousness, notwithstanding the fact that the James–Lange theory and its descendants overlook it.

Even granting the distinction between the actual experience of emotion, and the facial display that may or may not express that emotion, we are still faced with a problem. When the child is asked how he or she really feels, or how someone else really feels, by what criterion does the child focus on the experience as opposed to the facial display? This is part of a much wider problem. Consider a child who is given a sponge that looks like a rock, or shown a white card behind a blue filter, how does the child decide on the real identity or property in such cases? Clearly, what counts as really being sad, or really being a sponge or really being white, depends on a heterogeneous set of criteria. In this respect, modifiers like *real* and *really* are like *good* – their production and comprehension depends on the invocation of local criteria pertinent to the domain under consideration. Still, there is a common thread running through these disparate criteria. In identifying the real identity or properties of an object we think of it as a causally coherent bundle. A rock has a causally coherent set of properties. It looks hard; it is solid to the touch; it does not bounce; it sounds solid when dropped. A fake rock made of sponge does not exhibit this coherence. It looks hard, perhaps, but it is not solid to the touch. Indeed, aside from its visible appearance we can easily discover that it has the coherent properties of a sponge: It yields to the touch; it does bounce; it makes no noise if dropped. Occasionally, of course, we are confronted by objects that have a dualistic coherence. The platypus has a bill and lays eggs; it has fur and four legs. Is it a bird or a mammal? We need to examine other properties to make a decision. Mostly, however, an apparent property is readily identified by two criteria: It lacks coherence in that other properties do not covary with it. Conversely, those other properties do cohere among themselves. Thus, the apparent hardness of the fake rock lacks coherence with its other properties: its touch, its sound on contact, its bounciness. Yet these latter properties cohere among themselves.

We arrive, then, at the conclusion that young children's facility with the appearance–reality distinction probably operates in the context of a powerful mechanism for what we can roughly describe as coherence analysis: an appreciation of properties that form a coherent bundle.

Further investigations of this coherence analysis are to be found in research on children's understanding of biological types. Keil (1986) has suggested that young children are quite slow to appreciate the coherence of certain biological properties. Thus, when shown a skunk that looks like a raccoon, young children say that the animal is in fact a raccoon. Apparently they are guided by the appearance of the animal, even if they know that it has various crucial properties associated with being a skunk (skunk bones, skunk blood, and skunk parents). However, Gelman, Collman, and Maccoby (1986) obtained good performance from preschoolers when they were tested on a task that tapped coherence analysis more directly. Specifically, the children were asked to infer the possession of a property rather than to assess class membership. For example, the children learned that a typical boy has androgen in his blood, whereas a typical girl has estrogen. They were then shown a picture of a boy who was named as a boy, but who, so far as clothes and hairstyle were concerned, looked like a girl. Despite this feminine appearance, children correctly inferred that he had androgen rather than estrogen in his blood. In terms of coherence analysis, therefore, they attributed that property which was associated with the coherent set of masculine properties that the boy possessed, not with the potentially more salient but incidental properties of clothes and hairstyle.

The category problems described so far have been drawn from the world of physical objects (rocks and sponges), or from the world of biology (species and gender). Can we apply the same type of analysis to emotion? In principle, we can. An emotion is part of a causally coherent train of events: A situation elicits various thoughts and feelings; these thoughts and feelings are in turn expressed facially; and the facial expression leads others to attribute emotion. Although this sequence normally runs off from beginning to end, certain components can be present without the others. For example, the facial expression can be simulated, in the absence of any emotionally charged situation, thoughts, or feelings.

The results of study 3 indicate that 6-year-olds grasp the normal causal sequence and deviations from it. In answering each of the three questions, they focus appropriately on an immediate antecedent that may or may not be part of the regular causal chain. Thus, asked to give a reason for the story character's real emotion, they focus on a regular cause, the preceding *Event*; asked to explain the protagonist's facial expression, they focus on a deviant cause, his or her *Motive*; and asked to explain the attributions of other people, they again focus on a regular antecedent, namely, the protagonist's *Face*, but an antecedent that is already part of a deviant causal chain. Based on their awareness of the normal causal sequence and departures from it, children can presumably conclude that the protagonist's experience constitutes the real emotion, whereas his or her display does not. The experience is part of a standard causal sequence, whereas the display is not. In summary, the above analysis suggests that both for physical objects and for mental entities children sort out what is apparent from what is real by looking for those properties that cohere in a causal fashion.

A mentalistic theory of emotion?

So far, we have argued for two conclusions. By the age of 6 years, children have come to notice that there can be a mismatch between how they really feel and the emotion that others attribute to them. Second, in deciding what they or another person really feel, 6-years-olds know that facial expression is a poor guide, whereas the immediately preceding situation is a relatively sure guide. These results strongly suggest that 6-year-olds do not have a behavioristic conception of emotion. In earlier studies (Harris, Olthof, & Meerum Terwogt, 1981; Harris & Olthof, 1982), we claimed that although 10-year-olds adopt a mentalistic conception of emotion, 6-year-olds tend to think of an emotion as a more or less overt behavioral response, coupled in a one-to-one fashion with the immediate situation. Thus, 6-year-olds but not 10-year-olds have difficulty in acknowledging that the same situation can be viewed from different perspectives, thereby eliciting two different and even conflicting emotions (Harris, 1983b; Harter, 1983). Similarly, 6-year-olds propose strategies for changing emotion that typically focus on changing the situation, whereas 10-year-olds often propose changing the thoughts or attitudes that the situation might elicit (Harris et al., 1981).

Central for the present discussion were the findings on children's understanding of display rules. Harris et al. (1981) interviewed children about strategies for hiding emotion from other people. The 6-year-olds acknowledged that one might display an emotion that was not appropriate to the situation, but only the two older groups aged 11 and 15 years spontaneously mentioned the conflict between the privately experienced emotion and the displayed emotion. These results are in agreement with other findings, mentioned at the beginning of the chapter (Gnepp, 1983; Gnepp & Hess, 1986; Saarni, 1979). These various studies all suggest that young children tend to think of emotion as a behavioral response rather than a mental experience. At the very least, they suggest that 6-year-olds have difficulty in separating these two aspects of emotion.

The three studies reported in this chapter indicate that this conclusion was premature. Although 6-year-olds even in the present studies do appear to tie an emotional response back to the precipitating situation or event in line with the account proposed earlier (Harris et al., 1981; Harris & Olthof, 1982), they do not appear to conceive of that response in purely overt, behavioral terms.

In all three studies, 6-year-olds distinguished between what someone really feels and the facial expression that is characteristic but not defining of that emotion. In addition, the 6-year-olds tested in the final study showed an appreciation of the potentially private nature of real emotion. They realized that other people may not know how the protagonist really felt, and would therefore mistakenly attribute the apparent emotion to the protagonist. These results strongly suggest that 6-year-olds can conceive of emotion as a private mental experience rather than as a public piece of behavior. More generally, the results indicate that 6-year-olds have at least some understanding that their mental lives may or may not be accessible to other people, and that they can exert some control over what is accessible.

Understanding deception

Why do 4-year-olds find it so difficult to distinguish apparent and real emotion? Memory checks indicated that although the 4-year-olds were slower to remember the entire story, still they almost always reached criterion. Reaching criterion required them to answer two questions about critical pieces of information in the story – the precipitating event and the consequences of revealing the emotion provoked by that event. Thus, difficulties in remembering the crucial parts of the story can be ruled out. The 4-year-olds also coped fairly well with other parts of the task. They were usually able to identify how the protagonist would really feel. Moreover, study 3 showed they could back up their choices by referring to the appropriate precipitating event. Where 4-year-olds had particular difficulty was in identifying the protagonist's apparent emotion. Again, study 3 was especially revealing in this respect. Instead of selecting an apparent emotion that was less negative than the real emotion, 4-year-olds tended to perseverate, claiming that the protagonist would look as he or she felt. They again referred back to the precipitating event when asked to justify their choice of apparent emotion.

To answer the appearance question correctly, 4-year-olds would need to know that various facial expressions can be deliberately simulated and that such simulations can mislead an onlooker. The production and understanding of pretense, including pretend emotion, seem to emerge in the second and third years of life (Bretherton, Fritz, Zahn-Waxler, & Ridgeway, 1986; Rubin & Wolf, 1979). It is unlikely, therefore, that 4-year-olds would fail to understand that an emotional expression can be deliberately simulated. The understanding of pretense, however, is in certain key respects simpler than the understanding of display rules. Pretense is not intended to mislead an onlooker (although, of course, it may happen to mislead). Display rules, by contrast, are intended to mislead.

It is interesting to note that 4-year-olds' difficulties with deceptive ploys have been found in other studies. Wimmer and Perner (1983) found that the ability to construct a misleading utterance about the location of a hidden object improved between 4 and 6 years. Similarly, Shultz and Cloghesy (1981) found that the ability to produce a misleading gesture about the color of a hidden object improved from 3 to 5 years. In both studies, as in our third study, the child's task is to translate an intention to deceive into a misleading message. Why should this be so hard? Data from Flavell (1986) have shown that 4-year-olds understand that appearance and reality need not coincide, so that the existence of a possible mismatch between apparent emotion and real emotion should not be a problem for 4-year-olds. Similarly, Perner et al. (1987) have shown that 4-year-olds readily appreciate how one person can have a true belief and another person a false belief about the same entity, so that the possible mismatch between protagonist and onlookers in their beliefs should also not be a problem for 4-year-olds.

Deception may be especially complex because it involves insight not just into the difference between the protagonist's mental state and the onlooker's mental state, but into the causal links between them. Specifically, the child must appreciate that the beliefs of the onlooker are not just different from those of the protagonist, rather they are a product of the deliberately misleading display produced by the protagonist, which is itself a product of the protagonist's beliefs and desires with respect to what the onlooker should know. In short, the child must appreciate the recursive relationship between the mental states of the onlooker and those of the protagonist. Such recursive thinking was, of course, quite explicit in the 6-year-olds' justification of the appearance question. A typical justification contained two verbs, a reference to the onlooker's mental state that was embedded within a reference to the protagonist's mental state – for example, "She doesn't want her mommy to know." The 4-year-olds, on the other hand, were particularly poor at providing appropriate justifications for the appearance question.

It is tempting to conclude that 6-year-olds have a better grasp of deception than 4-year-olds precisely because they are better at the kind of recursive thinking that deception involves. Indeed, the importance of developments in recursive thinking have been stressed elsewhere in this volume (Feldman, Chapter 7; Perner, Chapter 14). Beneath this consensus, however, lie several unresolved issues. First, it is important to note that a grasp of recursive embedding is not only needed for an understanding of mental states, and their accompanying linguistic expressions. It can also be needed for an understanding of social activities such as promising, dissuading, and inviting. Moreover, the linguistic expressions for these activities can be interrelated in an embedded sentence in much the same way as mental verbs (e.g., "I promised her to dissuade them from inviting him"). Indeed, such embedding can even be found in statements about entirely mechanical events: "A backup system prevented the loss of power from forcing the vehicle to crash." One important question for future research is whether there is a parallel development in recursive thinking across these different domains: the mental, the social, and the mechanical. Certainly, evidence from autistic children (Baron-Cohen, Leslie, & Frith, 1986) strongly suggests that an understanding of mental and mechanical causation need not develop in parallel.

A second issue concerns the equivalence of the various mental activities that can operate recursively. Although current analyses tend to focus simply on the level of embedding (e.g., first-order versus second-order embedding), it may be easier to conceptualize a given level of embedding with respect to particular mental activities. Thus, children may find it easier to conceptualize how another person may want them to believe something, than to conceptualize how another person may believe them to want something, even though these both involve second-order recursion.

Finally, recursive thinking was first analyzed in the context of linguistic embedding (Miller, Kessel, & Flavell, 1970). We do not yet know whether the child's skill at linguistic embedding keeps pace with, lags behind, or even promotes the recursive thinking that presumably operates at the nonverbal level as in games and practices that involve deception.

Conclusions

We have reached four tentative interpretations of the data that are currently available. First, a child probably discovers the existence of false beliefs about emotion by noticing that other people can be misled about the child's own emotion. This will occur when the child attenuates or changes his or her facial expression, and onlookers happen to be misled about what the child really feels. Second, in analyzing the causal sequence that is triggered by an emotionally charged event, children become sensitive to features that covary – that constitute a causally recurrent sequence – as opposed to features that are more incidental. Accordingly, children do not confuse the real emotion with its facial expression, a feature only weakly correlated with the regular causal sequence. Third, further research will be needed to establish exactly how 6-year-olds do conceive of emotion, but it is already clear that they do not treat it as being equivalent to its external expression. Finally, from their justifications, it is clear that 6-year-olds are adept at engaging in the kind of recursive thinking that underlies deception. They understand that the story protagonist may not want other people to know his or her feelings. The need for recursive thinking, or, more narrowly, the appreciation that one person's false belief can be another person's deliberate goal, may be a stumbling block for 4-year-olds.

ACKNOWLEDGMENTS

This chapter is based on a paper presented at the workshop on Children's Early Concept of Mind, Oxford, June 1986, and on a paper by P. L. Harris, D. Gardner, and D. Gross presented at the Society for Research in Child Development, Baltimore, April 1987. We thank Professor S. Sukemune and Dr. R. Matsuo, principal of Mimyo Nursery School, for help in carrying out the research in Hiroshima.

REFERENCES

Baron-Cohen, S., Leslie, A. M., & Frith, U. (1985). Does the autistic child have a "theory of mind"? *Cognition, 21,* 37–46.

Baron-Cohen, S., Leslie, A. M., & Frith, U. (1986). Mechanistic, behavioural and Intentional understanding of picture stories in autistic children. *British Journal of Developmental Psychology, 4,* 113–125.

Bretherton, I., Fritz, J., Zahn-Waxler, C., & Ridgeway, D. (1986). Learning to talk about emotions: A functionalist perspective. *Child Development, 57,* 529–548.

Cole, P. M. (1986). Children's spontaneous control of facial expression. *Child Development, 57,* 1309–1321.

DePaulo, B. M., & Jordan, A. (1982). Age changes in deceiving and detecting deceit. In R. S. Feldman (Ed.), *Development of nonverbal behavior in children.* New York: Springer-Verlag.

DePaulo, B. M., Jordan, A., Irvine, A., & Laser, P. S. (1982). Age changes in the detection of deception. *Child Development, 53,* 701–709.

Ekman, P. (1982). *Emotion in the human face.* Cambridge University Press.

Flavell, J. (1986). The development of children's knowledge about the appearance–reality distinction. *American Psychologist*, *41*, 418–425.

Gardner, D., Harris, P. L., Ohmoto, M., & Hamazaki, T. (in press). Understanding of the distinction between real and apparent emotion by Japanese children. *International Journal of Behavioral Development*.

Gelman, S. A., Collman, P., & Maccoby, E. E. (1986). Inferring properties from categories versus inferring categories from properties: The case of gender. *Child Development*, *57*, 396–404.

Gnepp, J. (1983). Inferring emotions from conflicting cues. *Developmental Psychology*, *19*, 805–814.

Gnepp, J., & Hess, D. L. R. (1986). Children's understanding of verbal and facial display rules. *Developmental Psychology*, *22*, 103–108.

Gross, D., & Harris, P. L. (in press). False beliefs about emotion: Children's understanding of misleading emotional displays. *International Journal of Behavioral Development*.

Harris, P. L. (1983a). Infant cognition. In M. M. Haith & J. J. Campos (Eds.), *Handbook of child development: Vol II. Infancy and developmental psychobiology*. New York: Wiley.

Harris, P. L. (1983b). Children's understanding of the link between situation and emotion. *Journal of Experimental Child Psychology*, *36*, 490–509.

Harris, P. L., Donnelly, K., Guz, G. R., & Pitt-Watson, R. (1986). Children's understanding of the distinction between real and apparent emotion. *Child Development*, *57*, 895–909.

Harris, P. L., Gardner, D., & Gross, D. (1987, April). *Children's understanding of real and apparent emotion*. Paper presented at the Society for Research in Child Development, Baltimore, MD.

Harris, P. L., & Olthof, T. (1982). The child's concept of emotion. In G. Butterworth & P. Light (Eds.), *Social cognition*. Brighton: Harvester Press.

Harris, P. L., Olthof, T., & Meerum Terwogt, M. (1981). Children's knowledge of emotion. *Journal of Child Psychology and Psychiatry*, *22*, 247–261.

Harter, S. (1983). Children's understanding of multiple emotions: A cognitive-developmental approach. In W. F. Overton (Ed.), *The relationship between social and cognitive development*. Hillsdale, NJ: Erlbaum.

Hendry, J. (1986). *Becoming Japanese: The world of the preschool child*. Manchester, U.K.: Manchester University Press.

Hess, R. D., Kashiwagi, K., Azuma, H., Price, G. G., & Dickson, W. P. (1980). Maternal expectations for mastery of developmental tasks in Japan and the United States. *International Journal of Psychology*, *15*, 259–271.

Izard, C. (1977). *Human emotions*. New York: Plenum.

James, W. (1894). The physical basis of emotion. *Psychological Review*, *1*, 516–529.

Keil, F. C. (1986). The acquisition of natural kinds and artifact terms. In W. Demopoulos & A. Marras (Eds.), *Language learning and concept acquisition*. Norwood, NJ: Ablex.

Laird, J. D., Wagener, J. J., Halal, M., & Szegda, M. (1982). Remembering what you feel: Effects of emotion on memory. *Journal of Personality and Social Psychology*, *42*, 646–657.

Miller, P., Kessel, F., & Flavell, J. H. (1970). Thinking about people thinking about people thinking about ... A study of social cognitive development. *Child Development, 41,* 613–623.

Perner, J., Leekam, S. R., & Wimmer, H. (1987). Three-year-olds' difficulty with false belief: The case for a conceptual deficit. *British Journal of Developmental Psychology, 5,* 125–137.

Saarni, C. (1979). Children's understanding of display rules for expressive behavior. *Developmental Psychology, 15,* 424–429.

Saarni, C. (1984). Observing children's use of display rules: Age and sex differences. *Child Development, 55,* 1504–1513.

Shultz, T. R., & Cloghesy, K. (1981). Development of recursive awareness of intention. *Developmental Psychology, 17,* 465–471.

Rubin, S., & Wolf, D. (1979). The development of "maybe": The evolution of social roles into narratives. In E. Winner (Ed.), *Fact, fiction, and fantasy in childhood.* San Francisco: Jossey-Bass.

Wellman, H. M. (1985), The child's theory of mind: The development of conceptions of cognition. In S. R. Yussen (Ed.), *The growth of reflection in children.* New York: Academic Press.

Wimmer, H., & Perner J. (1983). Beliefs about beliefs: Representations and constraining function of wrong beliefs in young children's understanding of deception. *Cognition, 13,* 103–128.

16

Children's knowledge about representations of intended meaning

CAROLE R. BEAL

A major theme of this volume is that young children must develop an understanding of the mental world and of how their own thoughts and beliefs depend on information provided through perception, inference, and other information sources. In addition, the child must also discover that other people have minds. Part of the child's developing theory of mind must therefore include the awareness that the knowledge, thoughts, and beliefs of others also depend on the information made available to them, and that their knowledge might at times be different from that possessed by the child. Because the child does not have direct access to the mental worlds of others, he or she must rely on the process of communication to discover what others know, believe, and desire and to convey information to them.

Communication involves the encoding of thoughts into messages that can be transmitted to others, as a bridge between the mental worlds of different people. The awareness that states of knowledge may differ between individuals is critical to the communication process, because a message will be effective only if it provides the information that the other person will need in order to understand. That is, the child must consider how the listener's mental state may differ from his or her own in order to produce a message that will provide the necessary information. The child must also consider his or her own state of knowledge when listening to a message and assess whether the message provided enough information for comprehension of the other person's intended meaning to be possible. Thus, an important component of the child's theory of mind is the understanding that the communicative quality of messages can determine the mental states of the self and of others.

Although young children learn relatively easily how to communicate their intended meanings, their understanding of the requirements for effective communication continues to develop into the early elementary school years (Dickson, 1981). Research on children's comprehension monitoring and message evaluation skills suggests that although children understand the purpose of communication, they do not understand the role of the message as a representation of intended meaning. That is, they do not understand that communication is limited by the quality of the message. Without this understanding, children often appear to assume that others will know what they mean and that they will understand what others mean. Children seem to have a "passive" theory of communication: Their default assumption is that individuals will understand one another as long as a message is produced and received (Pillow, in press). That is, hearing the message may be sufficient according to their view of communication. They generally do not consider the nature and quality of the information provided by the message itself and its relationship to the prior knowledge state of the listener.

Message evaluation

Many studies on the development of knowledge about communication have shown that preschool and elementary school children often overlook problems in messages and believe that they, or another person, somehow understood what the speaker meant even though the messages were actually uninformative (Dickson, 1981; Flavell, Speer, Green, & August, 1981; Markman, 1977, 1979; Robinson, 1981). The general method used in these studies is to prepare a message that is designed to be incomprehensible and then present it to the child, who is asked to report whether or not he or she understands what the speaker intended. The child may be confronted with a message that is incomplete, ambiguous, contains nonsense words, has pages missing, or is obscured by a loud sneeze. As a consequence, the child cannot know what the speaker really means, but before they are about 7–8 years of age many children do not recognize that fact. For example, Flavell et al. (1981) asked children to listen to a young speaker's tape-recorded instructions for making block buildings. Many of the instructions were so unclear that the children could not be sure how the speaker meant them to construct the buildings. The children were asked if the speaker had provided them with enough information, and whether they were sure they had made the buildings as she had intended them to. Kindergarten children were confident that she had told them exactly how to make the buildings, and that they had made the buildings just the same way that she had. Second graders were much more likely to recognize that her instructions were uninformative and that as a result they could not be sure they had carried out her intentions correctly. The results suggested that an understanding of the role of message quality in determining communication success or failure is gradually acquired in the early grades.

Much recent research has shown that several factors contribute to younger children's failure to evaluate messages accurately and to monitor their comprehension. For example, Speer (1984) has found that young children rely on their knowledge about conversations when they are in the more constrained referential communication task. They assume that the speaker will be cooperative and will provide enough information, but fail to consider that if the message is unclear, they may not understand even a willing and cooperative speaker. Another important factor is children's developing knowledge that mental representations of intended meaning can be encoded and communicated by linguistic messages or other types of symbols. Children must learn that a message may not capture one's intended meaning very clearly or accurately; that is, one can intend one thing and say something else. In addition, children must learn that the message has a "literal meaning" all its own, which is somewhat independent of what the speaker means by it (Olson & Hildyard, 1983). This is something they achieve only in the early school years. There is evidence that children at times fail to evaluate message quality accurately and thus overestimate their comprehension because they do not maintain a distinction between the literal meaning and intended meaning of the speaker. Bonitatibus (in press; Chapter 17) has found that children who can remember the exact words of the speaker are also more likely to evaluate the communicative quality of the message correctly than are their age-mates who do not have the concept of the "very words" of the message (see also Robinson, Goelman, & Olson, 1983).

In most studies of referential communication the child does not know what the speaker means, independently of the utterance. The child is presented with the message and is then asked whether he or she can know what the speaker meant, and whether the speaker's message provided enough information for understanding to be possible. When the child does have access to the speaker's intended meaning but must still evaluate whether the speaker's message literally expresses that meaning accurately, message evaluation may be particularly difficult. The child's knowledge about the speaker's intended meaning may encourage him or her to view the message with a less critical eye and to falsely "fill in" information that is actually not provided by the words of the message. There is some evidence that when children know what the speaker intends to communicate, they are less likely to detect that the message itself is uninformative. In a study by Beal and Flavell (1984), first and second graders were asked to evaluate the communicative quality of short written messages. The speaker prepared short written messages to tell the child which picture to select from a set of three pictures. Some of the messages were ambiguous. The children were warned that the messages did not always seem to be very clear, and were asked to help evaluate them. Half of the children in each grade were told in advance which picture the speaker had intended them to select, while the other children were uninformed about the speaker's intended meaning. The results showed that first graders who

knew what the speaker intended detected fewer of the message ambiguities than did their uninformed age-mates and both informed and uninformed second graders. Thus, when children have access to a speaker's
intended meaning, they find it particularly difficult to assess the communicative quality of the message. This hypothesis has implications for two
other communication tasks where children also know what the speaker intended but must still evaluate the quality of the message for communication to be effective: message revision, and evaluation of "messages to the
self" in prospective memory situations. In these tasks, recent research
suggests that access to the speaker's intended meaning also encourages
children to overestimate the message's quality.

Message revision

One communication task where the child has access to the speaker's
intended meaning but must still evaluate the message is in writing and
revising a message or text. As in referential communication tasks, the
writer must consider what knowledge the potential reader is likely to have
and what information should be provided in the message or text. When a
writer revises, he or she will work with the "very words" of the message to
try to express an intended meaning as clearly and accurately as possible.
However, when preparing and revising a message or text the author has
privileged access to his or her intended meaning, which may make it quite
easy to overlook the fact that the message will be uninformative to someone else who has different prior knowledge. For example, an expert computer programmer who prepares a user's manual for a new system may
review his or her text and decide that it is complete and comprehensible,
whereas a novice user may find the same text completely uninformative.

A simplified view of the revision process suggests that it involves three
steps: The child must first *evaluate* the message quality and ask whether
the message literally expresses his or her intended meaning (Scardamalia
& Bereiter, 1983). As already suggested, message evaluation in this context may be quite difficult because the child, as author of the message, has
direct access to the intended meaning. However, if the child does detect a
problem, the second step is to *locate* the problem in the words of the
message. That is, the child must identify exactly where the message is
unclear, given his or her assessment of the prior knowledge of the listener
or reader. The third step is to *repair* the inadequate message. This model of
the revision process suggests that correct evaluation of the message's literal meaning should be a prerequisite for subsequent revision, because if
children do not even notice that the message is not clear, they are unlikely
to revise it. However, it is not clear whether children will necessarily be
able to locate and repair a message problem once it has been detected. If a

child is unable to maintain a distinction between the literal and intended meanings, he or she may find it difficult or impossible to generate an alternative version of the message to express the intended meaning more clearly.

Children's ability to revise the "very words" of the message was addressed in two studies where children were asked to help the experimenter "fix up" (revise) uninformative referential communication messages (Beal, 1987). Children in first through third grade were asked either just to evaluate the quality of messages, or to evaluate and then also revise them. Half of the children in each grade were informed about the speaker's intended meaning before they were presented with the message. The hypothesis was that knowing the speaker's intended meaning should make it more difficult for children to notice the message problems and to revise them. In one of the tasks the children listened to simple instructions for driving a toy car along a road map to one of several houses on a game board (cf. Flavell, Green, & Flavell, 1985). The instructions were written on cards and read to the child by the experimenter, with the cards held so that the child could see the words. On different trials the instructions were either very clear, contained a conflict (the message described the road incorrectly), or were ambiguous (the message could have meant either of two roads). Children listened to the directions and then tried to follow them. Half the children were then asked if the instructions had told them exactly how to find the house that the message's author had intended, while the others were asked first to evaluate the instructions' quality and then to suggest changes to improve the message. The experimenter acted as a scribe for the child and wrote in the suggested changes on the card as the child directed.

The results showed that children in all grades who knew what the author of the messages had intended (that is, which house they were to drive to on the map) detected fewer of the message problems than those who did not know the intended meaning. Previous work (Beal & Flavell, 1984) had used only ambiguous messages, but in this study children overlooked even many of the relatively obvious conflict problems. Knowing the speaker's intended meaning reduced their ability to evaluate the communicative quality of short written messages. The effect is particularly striking because Bonitatibus and Flavell (1985; see also Bonitatibus, Chapter 17) have shown that children of this age find it easier to detect message problems when the messages are presented in written form.

Although children often initially overlooked the message problems, once they had detected that a message was not informative, they were quite frequently able to locate and revise the words of the message to express more clearly the speaker's intended meaning. Although the first step of the revision process (problem detection) was difficult for them, once a discrepancy between the intended meaning and the literal meaning of the message had been detected children were able to change the words to express the intended meaning more clearly. Research on children's writing in the classroom shows that they often fail to revise their work and that when they are encouraged to revise, they generally make superficial and cosmetic changes rather than changes that improve the communicative quality of their text for the reader. The results of the studies described above suggest that children may not revise in the classroom because they do not initially detect that their text will not be clear to the reader (rather than because they cannot think of appropriate revisions.) They may overlook the need to revise their work because they are continually reminded of their intended meaning as they reread their text. They may therefore find it particularly difficult to evaluate whether the text will be clear to another person who may not share the knowledge that they have about the topic.

"Messages to the self"

The production and evaluation of messages to convey information to others involves a consideration of their information needs and how their state of knowledge might be different from one's own. Research from referential communication and writing tasks suggests that in the early grades children do not have a clear conception of the message as a representation of their intended meaning, and that when the intended meaning is known they find it particularly difficult to evaluate the message's communicative quality. Although communication is generally thought to involve the transmission of messages between different people, part of the child's developing theory of mind must also involve the understanding that his or her own state of knowledge may be different at different times and under different conditions (see Astington & Gopnik, Chapter 10). The child may therefore also need to communicate with himself or herself in the future. This situation often arises in prospective memory tasks, where the goal is to remember something at a particular time in the future (Meacham & Leiman, 1982). For example, a child might want to remember to take a book to school the next day. The child could prepare a reminder, such as a note, or put the book by the door as a kind of "message to the self."

Referential communication and writing tasks require the child to consider what information the listener will need in order to understand. To accomplish this, the child must recognize that the listener's state of knowledge can differ from his or her own. Similarly, when preparing a message to the self in a prospective memory task the child must also consider what information he or she might require in the future, when the task goal may no longer be obvious or active in memory. That is, the child must predict what his or her state of knowledge might be like in the future and prepare a message that will provide the necessary information. However, as in the case of message revision, when we prepare a reminder, we know what it is we want to remember and our active knowledge of the intended meaning may lead us to overestimate the actual informativeness of the message. For example, a college student may take brief lecture notes that appear to be informative at the time because the information is still active in memory, but that are hopelessly uninformative at exam time six weeks later. One must take into account that a currently informative message can grow "cold" with time. Baddeley (1976) and Linton (1982) have pointed out that journal notes and other retrieval cues can become completely uninformative after very long delays. Thus, calibrating the amount of information in the message that will be necessary for successful communication after a delay may be quite difficult in certain tasks.

Studies of children's developing knowledge about prospective memory strategies show that 2- and 3-year-olds are able to use some simple strategies to help themselves find things, such as pointing to the location where an object has been hidden (DeLoache, Cassidy & Brown, 1985; Wellman, Ritter, & Flavell, 1975). However, research with preschoolers and children in the early grades suggests that they overestimate the prospective informativeness of reminders, much as they overestimate the informativeness of messages in referential communication tasks. For example, Ritter (1978) hid a piece of candy in a container surrounded by several identical containers. He encouraged the children to use a paper star to mark the baited container so that they could relocate the candy easily once he had shuffled the containers. He then asked them if adding more stars to other containers would also help them remember. Most of the children happily added more stars and even took away the original star, without realizing that after the containers had been moved they would probably search in the wrong one. In another study using the Ritter task (Beal, 1985), preschoolers saw where the object was hidden and were then asked whether markers of various types would help them find it later. That is, they were asked to evaluate the communicative quality of the markers. The results showed that many of the children thought that almost any type of marker would help them find the object. For example, about half of the preschoolers said that a marker placed on another unbaited cup, or even hidden inside the baited cup with the object, would tell them where to find the object. Almost all of the preschoolers failed to recognize the prospective communication problem posed by an "ambiguous" reminder: They thought that a correctly placed marker would be informative even though a second identical marker had been placed on another cup. It appeared that their knowledge about where the object was currently hidden made it difficult for them to reflect on the informativeness of the messages and to anticipate that they would not have enough information to find the object in the future.

Similar results have also been obtained with preschoolers in other more naturalistic prospective retrieval tasks. In a study I conducted with Wayne Fleisig, children were encouraged to choose an informative marker to help themselves find their own toothbrush after a week's delay. In the first session we met with each child to discuss dental care and then gave him or her a toothbrush to practise with. At the end of the session the child was prompted to put the toothbrush in a plastic bag and then to mark it with a cartoon sticker so that he or she could find it easily in the next session among the other children's identical yellow toothbrushes. Five different stickers were available, four of which had already been used by other children. The distractor set of five other toothbrushes was constructed so that four were marked and one was unmarked. This meant that the child could not choose to leave his or her toothbrush unmarked, and that only one sticker would be informative because the others had already been selected. Most of the children selected a sticker that another child had already used, failing to anticipate that the following week they might pick out the wrong toothbrush. Even when the problem was pointed out to them, some children insisted that they would just "know" which toothbrush was theirs. Their knowledge of its current location led them to overlook the problem presented by the duplicate "messages."

Similar results were also obtained in a study conducted with Julie Lenhard where the reminder was more complex and began to resemble a traditional referential communication message, although in a novel format. The child was asked to drive a car along a road map to a target house, and then to create a "message" to help him or her retrace that route after a delay. The messages consisted of five objects that corresponded to objects on the map and were arranged in sequence. For example, the child might drive past a tree on the first turn in the road, and then turn right at the next intersection and pass a cow, and so on. The message would consist of a tree, a cow, and the like. Distractor objects were placed at nonchoice points along the roads. The results showed that although preschoolers and kindergartners could "read" and follow the prepared messages easily, they did not select the most informative markers to help themselves retrace their steps. In addition, they were confident that their messages would help them re-create the route later, even though the messages would actually have left them stopped at the intersections, unable to determine which path to take. In contrast, 7- to 8-year-olds could both read the prepared messages and produce informative ones to communicate with themselves in the future.

Prospective memory tasks, like revision tasks, may be particularly difficult for children because they involve the preparation and evaluation of messages when the intended meaning is known. In several prospective memory tasks preschoolers have been shown to overestimate the informativeness of "messages to the self." They often believe that a hidden, uninformative or ambiguous reminder will help them relocate a target object. It seems that young children are influenced by their knowledge about an object's current location and do not estimate how informative they will find the reminder to be in the future when this information is no longer available.

Messages and the theory of mind

To communicate effectively, children must rely on their developing theory of mind. They must first recognize that thoughts exist, that their own knowledge, thoughts, and beliefs may not be shared by others, and that their own state of knowledge may change over time. Although much of the research described in the first two sections of this volume suggests that quite young children have some understanding of the existence of the mental world, research on children's communication skills suggests that it is not until the early grades that children understand how to represent their thoughts and knowledge in informative messages in order to communicate clearly with others. Because they do not clearly understand that the message is a representation of a speaker's intended meaning, they find it difficult to realize that the message may not represent the intended meaning accurately. In most research on comprehension monitoring children have not known what the speaker's meaning actually was. In tasks such as revision or prospective memory, where they do have access to the intended meaning, they appear to find it particularly difficult to evaluate the informativeness of the message, because it is hard to maintain the distinction between the speaker's thoughts and their expression in the message. Children tend to overestimate the quality of messages when they are asked to evaluate them in these tasks, but it also appears that once they realize there is a discrepancy between the intended meaning and the literal meaning of the message, they can revise the message to resolve the problem.

The understanding that one's intended meaning can be encoded into messages may need to be acquired in many symbolic domains, and we may find that children will also overestimate the informativeness of a wide variety of message types. There are many ways to communicate a message to another person or to yourself, using drawings, markers, semaphore flags, or novel symbol systems (Cohen, 1985). The same literal-intended meaning distinction can be made in these other domains as well. The similarity of children's performance on message evaluation, revision, and prospective memory tasks provides some supporting evidence for the notion that a fairly general understanding of the relation between messages and the mental world may be developing in the preschool and early elementary school years. A more provocative question is whether children's knowledge about internally originated representations, such as the experiences of visual perception (Taylor, Chapter 11) may also draw upon this understanding. That is, is distinguishing what you actually see from what you know, similar to distinguishing what your message actually says from what you know to be true? A related question is how knowledge about messages as representations of intended meaning is eventually acquired: How do children finally figure out that the message is not the thing it represents? The fact that performance in many of the different message-evaluation tasks improves in the early grades suggests that experience with written texts might contribute to the development of this skill, as Olson and his colleagues have suggested (Olson & Hildyard, 1983). However, the same pattern of results has been found with non-linguistic messages. Therefore, although it is possible and perhaps likely that learning to read and write helps children understand the literal–intended meaning distinction, this understanding does not seem to be limited to linguistic messages; it seems to be more generally applied to other kinds of representational systems as well.

ACKNOWLEDGMENTS

This chapter is based on a paper presented at the International Conference on Developing Theories of Mind, University of Toronto, May 1986. Preparation of the chapter was supported by NSF Grant No. IST-8413621.

REFERENCES

Baddeley, A. (1976). *The psychology of memory*. New York: Basic.

Beal, C. R. (1985). The development of knowledge about the use of cues to aid prospective retrieval. *Child Development, 56*, 631–642.

Beal, C. R. (1987). Repairing the message: Children's monitoring and revision skills. *Child Development 58*, 401–408.

Beal, C. R., & Flavell, J. H. (1984). Development of the ability to distinguish communicative intention and literal message meaning. *Child Development, 55*, 920–928.

Bonitatibus, G. J. (in press). Comprehension monitoring and the apprehension of literal meaning. *Child Development*.

Bonitatibus, G. J., & Flavell, J. H. (1985). Effect of presenting a message in written form on young children's ability to evaluate its communication adequacy. *Developmental Psychology. 21*, 455–461.

Cohen, S. (1985). The development of constraints on symbol-meaning structure in notation: Evidence from production, interpretation and forced-choice judgments. *Child Development, 56,* 177–195.

DeLoache, J. S., Cassidy, D. J., & Brown, A. L. (1985). Precursors of mnemonic strategies in very young children's memory. *Child Development, 56,* 125–137.

Dickson, W. P. (1981). *Children's oral communication skills.* New York: Academic Press.

Flavell, J. H., Green, F. L., & Flavell, E. R. (1985). The road not taken: Understanding the implications of initial uncertainty in evaluating spatial directions. *Developmental Psychology, 21,* 207–216.

Flavell, J. H., Speer, J. R., Green, F. L. & August, D. L. (1981). The development of comprehension monitoring and knowledge about communication. *Monographs of the Society for Research in Child Development, 46,* (5, Serial No. 192).

Linton, M. (1982). Transformations of memory in everyday life. In U. Neisser (Ed.), *Memory observed.* New York: Freeman.

Markman, E. M. (1977). Realizing you don't understand: A preliminary investigation. *Child Development, 48,* 986–992.

Markman, E. M. (1979). Realizing you don't understand: Elementary school children's awareness of inconsistencies. *Child Development, 50,* 643–655.

Meacham, J. A., & Leiman, B. (1982). Remembering to perform future actions. In U. Neisser (Ed.), *Memory observed.* New York: Freeman.

Olson, D. R., & Hildyard, A. (1983). Writing and literal meaning. In M. Martlew (Ed.), *Psychology of written language: A developmental and educational perspective.* New York: Wiley.

Pillow, B. H. (in press.) The development of children's beliefs about the mental world. *Merrill-Palmer Quarterly.*

Ritter, K. (1978). The development of knowledge of an external retrieval cue strategy. *Child Development, 49,* 1227–1230.

Robinson, E. J. (1981). The child's understanding of inadequate messages and communication failure: A problem of ignorance or egocentrism? In W. P. Dickson (Ed.), *Children's oral communication skills* (pp. 167–188). New York: Academic Press.

Robinson, E. J., Goelman, H., & Olson, D. R. (1983). Children's understanding of the relation between expressions (what was said) and intentions (what was meant.) *British Journal of Developmental Psychology, 1,* 75–86.

Scardamalia, M., & Bereiter, C. (1983). The development of evaluative, diagnostic, and remedial capabilities in children's composing. In M. Martlew (Ed.), *Psychology of written language: A developmental and educational perspective.* New York: Wiley.

Speer, J. R. (1984). Two practical strategies young children use to interpret vague instructions. *Child Development, 55,* 1811–1819.

Wellman, H. M., Ritter, K., & Flavell, J. H. (1975). Deliberate memory behavior in the delayed reactions of very young children. *Developmental Psychology, 11,* 780–787.

17

What is said and what is meant in referential communication

GARY BONITATIBUS

As children begin to mature cognitively, they begin to develop naive theories of mind. They come to be able to appreciate such things as the beliefs, motives, and intentions that underlie the behavior and language of themselves and others. These theories are powerful tools for making sense of the physical and social world. Although it is hard for an adult to imagine a world in which there is no distinction between seeing and knowing, knowing and believing, or action and intention, all of these distinctions seem to undergo development in the preschool or early school years.

An early understanding of the existence of mental states in themselves and others can be seen in the development of language comprehension. To understand an utterance, children must recover the mental state or intention of a speaker; a speaker has some idea in mind, and is attempting to communicate this idea. From a very early age, children are capable of knowing that speakers have a meaning or mental state behind their utterances, and that the apprehension of that meaning is the goal of comprehension (Bonitatibus, 1988).

However, the conception of the meaning of language as a veridical representation of the speaker's mental state is an inadequate one. Language is often an approximate process. The same sentence may be used by a speaker to express more than one intention, and one sentence may be taken by a listener as an expression of more than one intention. But the limitations of children's understanding of the relationship between utterances and intentions is revealed quite clearly in their inability to deal with misinterpretations. Young children appear to identify one utterance with one interpretation, and therefore they are incapable of dealing with ambiguous sentences in which one utterance may result in two or more interpretations. As a number of theorists have pointed out, although language is used to express a speaker's intention, that intention is often only partially present in the words themselves, and in some cases (e.g., indirect speech acts, irony) may be almost totally absent (Olson & Hildyard, 1983a, 1983b; Shatz, 1983; Winograd, 1980). In normal, everyday conversational settings, this does not pose much of a problem. People use conversational strategies such as implicature to understand each other more or less well in keeping with fairly loose communicative goals, and misunderstandings are either unimportant or quickly cleared up (Clark & Clark, 1977). However, there are a number of situations where it is important to recognize that a speaker's utterance is not an exact representation of his or her meaning, and that therefore, although one may have understood the utterance, the meaning behind it remains obscure. Such situations are generally not conversational in nature and usually involve a premium on precise communication of ideas (e.g., listening to directions to accomplish some task or solve a problem; didactic teaching situations in school). In such cases it is important for children to monitor their comprehension; that is, be aware that although they may have understood an utterance, that is, they understand the words and the grammar, they may not have understood exactly what the speaker meant by it.

A number of studies have examined the comprehension-monitoring abilities of children, usually through the use of the referential communication paradigm (Bonitatibus, 1988). In this paradigm children are typically given directions for building a block building or selecting one item from an array. Some of the directions are made referentially ambiguous; that is, they refer to more than one block or item. Children are then asked to assess the adequacy of the direction or the state of their understanding. Children younger than 5 or 6 years old often incorrectly state that the direction was adequate, or that their understanding of what the speaker meant is exact (Robinson, 1981).

A number of theorists have suggested that this is due to young children's inability to examine a message or direction in its own right; to examine what the words themselves mean as opposed to what the speaker may have meant (Donaldson, 1978; Flavell, Speer, Green, & August, 1981; Olson, 1977; Olson & Hildyard, 1983a, 1983b; Olson & Torrance, 1983; Robinson, Goelman, & Olson, 1983). In other words, being aware that the speaker intends to refer to only one of the referents, these children may inappropriately apply conversational strategies (such as implicature or guessing) to arrive at some unambiguous speaker's meaning and ignore the ambiguous meaning of the words themselves. Somewhat older children make the distinction between what is said and what is meant by it. They are aware that speakers' intentions are not always adequately expressed in their words, and that in some situations (e.g., referential communication) it is inappropriate to use the usual conversational strategies to resolve ambiguity. These children attend to and represent the literal meaning of a speaker's utterance and are therefore able to assess the exact state of their understanding more accurately. In essence, they are able to respond to an ambiguous direction by saying: "I know that *you* mean only one of these objects, but your *words* refer to more than one; therefore, I cannot be sure about which one you mean." Younger children who assume that people say what they mean and mean what they say are incapable of such an analysis.

A number of recent findings support the hypothesis that the cause of young children's inability to monitor their comprehension in the referential communication paradigm is a preoccupation with uncovering a speaker's intention and a corresponding inattention to the meaning of the words themselves. Several studies by Robinson and Robinson (1977a, 1977b; 1978) indicate a general insensitivity on the part of children who are poor comprehension monitors to the role of the message in producing success or failure in the referential communication paradigm. For example, the outcome of a communicative episode was found to influence these children's judgments of message quality. An ambiguous message that led to communication success by chance was judged to be of better quality than a similar message that led to failure. No such effect was found for children capable of monitoring their comprehension; for them, both types of messages were judged as equally ambiguous (Robinson & Robinson, 1977a, 1977b). Similarly, poor comprehension monitors have more difficulty producing good versus bad messages at will than their more capable counterparts (Robinson & Robinson, 1978). In addition to their insensitivity to the role of the message in communication, young children have been found to overemphasize the importance of the speaker's intention. For example, Beal and Flavell (1984) presented children with ambiguous referential communications under two conditions: They either knew which referent the speaker intended (informed) or did not (uninformed). First graders in the informed condition tended to respond that the ambiguous messages referred only to the referents that the speaker had meant. On the other hand, children in the uninformed condition realized that the message was ambiguous, that is, it referred to two potential referents. Taken together, these studies indicate that young children are primarily concerned with speaker's intentions (what is meant) rather than their expressions (what is said). Since in the referential communication paradigm, comprehension monitoring depends on an analysis of what was said, children who are interested only in what was meant should have difficulty performing well.

More direct evidence of the relationship between comprehension monitoring and the ability to differentiate and attend to the literal meaning of a speaker's message was provided by Robinson et al. (1983). A preliminary study indicated that when kindergarten children playing a referential communication game heard an ambiguous message ("Pick the red flower" with large and small red flowers present) and this led to communication failure, approximately 60% of the time they would wrongly accept a disambiguation of the original message "Pick the *big* red flower" as what had actually been said by the speaker. This was interpreted as an indication that these children were not discriminating the literal meaning of what had been said from what was meant. In a second study, this measure of attention to literal meaning was found to be highly associated with the ability to detect referential ambiguity. Children who in an initial trial were capable of detecting the inadequacy of an ambiguous message were more likely to reject a disambiguated version of a message on a subsequent trial than their counterparts who failed to detect the initial ambiguity. The authors concluded that the ability to detect referential ambiguity depends on the ability to discriminate and attend to the literal meaning of the speaker's words.

Bonitatibus (1988) has examined this relationship more closely. Although a general distinction between speaker's meaning and sentence or literal meaning is beyond the scope of this chapter, in the referential communication paradigm several operational distinctions can be made. The speaker's meaning is represented internally by the speaker and is therefore not directly accessible to a listener. However, the literal meaning is accessible to a listener; it is represented by the very words of the speaker in the context. Further, the instantiation of the speaker's meaning is some single object in the referent array (the speaker *intends* the listener to pick only one of the possible referents). The literal meaning is instantiated by the set of all possible referents in the array. Therefore, if children who are incapable of detecting referential ambiguity are interested only in the speaker's meaning, the only relevant information available to them is some single referent in the array. In other words, once they have mapped the speaker's words onto some referent, that referent should be the only communicatively relevant information for them. On the other hand, children capable of detecting referential ambiguity and attending to the literal meaning of the message should be attending to the very words of the message, as well as their multiple instantiations in the referent array.

Bonitatibus provided support for this hypothesis in a number of ways. He first classified 46 first-grade subjects as either capable or incapable of detecting referential ambiguity by having them explain the causes of two failed referential communications between two puppets. The children then observed two failed referential communications in which neither the speaker's meaning nor the literal meaning was available to the child (the speaker indicated that the listener's choice was incorrect without indicating his intention, and the message was either whispered between the puppets, or was too long and complex for the child to remember). Children were then presented with a forced choice as to which "clue" would help them diagnose the cause of the failure: the speaker's intention, or his words. Although knowledge of the speaker's intention is of little use in such a case (essentially redundant with the fact that the communication did fail, i.e., the listener chose a referent other than the one intended), children classified as incapable of detecting referential ambiguity (non-detectors) tended to request it as their clue. On the other hand, children capable of detecting ambiguity tended to request correctly what was said as their clue (in this case the essential information is whether or not the speaker adequately expressed his intention).

In the next part of the study children witnessed four referential communication failures; first, two in which they could not see the referent array, followed by two in which they could. Children were asked to (a) judge the adequacy of the message, (b) predict the outcome, and (c) recognize either the original message or a disambiguation as what had been said. It was found that children incapable of detecting referential ambiguity differed from those who could in several respects. First, nondetectors were overall less likely to recognize correctly what had been said, an indication of insensitivity to literal meaning(s) of that particular utterance. Second, the nondetectors' recognition of the original utterance declined significantly when the array was visible to them. That is, these children took as "what was said" any sentence so long as it referred to the "correct" referent, whether or not it was similar in wording to the original. In other words, because these children attend primarily to the speaker's intentions, this is what they base their answers to questions about the speaker's utterances on. Third, when the array was absent (and therefore it was impossible to determine the adequacy of the message) the nondetectors tended to predict clear messages and communicative success, whereas the detectors did not. This was interpreted as an indication of a false sense of security in a situation where communication failure was likely. Again this difficulty may be attributed to children's conflation of literal and speaker's meaning. If children feel that expressions are always adequate representations of a speaker's intention, then messages are assumed to be clear and the only possible cause for failure is the listener's intransigence. Fourth, there was no relationship between judgments of message quality and subsequent utterance recognition for nondetectors, while there was a significant correlation between judging a message inadequate and subsequent utterance recognition for children capable of ambiguity detection (i.e., they tend to judge messages as inadequate only when they can recall them). Fifth, when nondetectors did indicate that the message was inadequate, about a third of the time they would still go on and predict communicative success. This pattern was never seen in the group who did detect ambiguities. Finally, there was no difference between the groups in ability to free-recall the words of the message. The differences in recognition performance were due to differences in what the words were interpreted to mean, rather than simple memory differences. Taken together, these results indicate that children capable of detecting the ambiguity of an utterance do so by differentiating speakers' words from their intentions; those not recognizing ambiguity do not.

A subsequent study provided even stronger evidence of nondetectors' conflation of what was said with what was meant. In this study, instead of there being a forced-choice recognition between the original message and two disambiguated versions of that original message, children were allowed to accept more than one version as what had actually been said. In this situation, more than half the time the nondetectors accepted two or more versions of the message. This was taken as evidence that these children have little or no conception of the meaning of a sentence apart from its intended meaning. For them, two different sentences that convey the same speaker's intention are the same utterance. The results of these studies provide strong evidence for the idea that much of young children's difficulty with detecting referential ambiguity stems from an inability to distinguish and attend to what speaker's words or utterances mean, apart from what speakers themselves mean.

If this is the case, then children of this age should be better able to evaluate messages if it is made clear to them that speakers themselves, rather than simply their words, could refer to more than one referent.

To test this hypothesis, Bonitatibus and Carrier (1986) tested 36 first-grade and kindergarten children (mean age 6.10) in a referential communication paradigm. Their assumptions about the speaker's meaning were varied in two ways. First, subjects in one group were given typical referential communication task directions. They were told that the speaker would try to describe one of the referents, and their job was to decide if he or she "told enough to pick exactly the right one" (ambiguity assessment group). The second group was explicitly informed that the *speaker* (not just his or her words) might refer to two or more referents. Their directions stated "sometimes [the speaker] tells about one picture, and sometimes he/she tells about two. Your job is to decide if he/she is telling about one or two" (number of referents assessments group). Within each group, the type of item was also varied to mark more or less explicitly the possibility that the speaker was referring to more than one referent. Four items as in traditional referential communication paradigms marked the speaker's intention as unambiguous (e.g., "Pick *the* red square"). Five of the items explicitly marked the speaker's intention as ambiguous (e.g., "Pick *any* red square"), and four items left the speaker's intention unmarked (e.g., "Red square"). In addition, children's attention to actual wording was assessed by asking them to recognize any of three versions of the message (the original and two disambiguations).

The results indicated that the number of referents assessment group performed significantly better than the ambiguity assessment group ($F_{1,34}$

$= 12.02, p \leq .01$). Interestingly, there was no effect found for the type of item ($F_{2,34} = .36$, n.s.). This suggests that although general task directions served to increase children's ambiguity detection, the specific wording of items (*the* vs. *any*) was largely ignored by subjects. These findings are reminiscent of those of Ackerman (1981), who found that children were better able to evaluate messages from a potentially deceptive speaker than those from a potentially incompetent one. Although Ackerman (1981) did not assess attention to the particular wording, Bonitatibus and Carrier (1986) did, and the results proved informative. Although children in the number of referents assessment group outperformed children in the ambiguity assessment group in terms of message evaluation, the reverse was true for their attention to literal meaning as assessed by the sentence recognition measure. Overall, children in the ambiguity assessment group correctly recognized the original and rejected disambiguated versions significantly more often than did those in the number of referents assessment group ($T_{34} = 2.15 \, p \leq .05$). This indicates that although children can detect ambiguity when led to expect it by a speaker who sometimes refers to more than one referent, they do so by and large without attending to actual wording. They attend to the intended referents rather than to the utterance. It seems that these children exhaustively search the array for all the objects that would satisfy the speaker's intention, whereas young children faced with honest (if potentially incompetent) speakers terminate their search after finding a single object satisfying the speaker's intention. In such a case, the speaker is ostensibly referring to only one referent; the only way to detect the ambiguity in such a case is to realize that the speaker's words (rather than the speaker) could refer to more than one. Interestingly, in a recent replication of the Ackerman (1981) study that included an original sentence recognition measure it was found that children faced with potentially dishonest speakers detected more ambiguities, and correctly recognized more original sentences than their counterparts faced with potentially incompetent speakers (Bonitatibus, 1987). That is, when faced with a speaker who may be deliberately trying to mislead them, children pay closer attention to the exact wording of the utterance and therefore detect more of the utterances that refer to more than one referent. That a similar interpretation problem could be due to speakers' incompetence seems not to occur to them.

These results are in accord with the findings of investigators who have studied children's "comparison activities," that is, the ability to compare the differentiating characteristics of referents and nonreferents. In general, it has been found that children are capable of engaging in the appropriate comparisons, but often fail to do so spontaneously in the referential communication paradigm (Robinson, 1981; Whitehurst & Sonnenschein, 1978, 1981). The current results suggest that until children realize that although an honest, cooperative speaker intends to refer to only one referent, his or her words can refer to more than one (i.e., until children distinguish speaker's from the sentence's literal meaning), they consider exhaustive search and comparison unnecessary, and fail to detect referential ambiguity.

This raises the question of how it is that children initially begin to make this distinction. Olson and colleagues (Olson, 1977; Olson & Hildyard, 1983a, 1983b; Olson & Torrance, 1983; Robinson et al., 1983) have suggested that it is due to the effects of literacy. In oral language, what was meant has primacy over what was said; the words themselves are ephemeral. It is a well-established fact that adults' recall of a message is based on its semantic content rather than the exact words (Bransford, Barclay, & Franks, 1972). Written language, on the other hand, tends to reverse this emphasis. Writing preserves the surface structure of the language independently of what the author meant. Thus the experience of reading and writing, in which an utterance is preserved or frozen, may sensitize the child to the fact that the utterance itself has existence and meaning, somewhat independent of the meaning and intentions of the speaker or writer. Further, unlike conversational settings, with written language there is no ongoing interchange that allows for immediate clarification and correction. By its very nature, written language favors the literal; great care must be taken when writing to be clear and unambiguous (as the author of any technical paper knows) because readers, unlike listeners, have no recourse to the author when they fail to understand a text.

Thus, in addition to sensitizing the child to the existence of literal meaning, reading and writing may also sensitize the child to the possibility of ambiguous or unclear communication that would further emphasize the necessity of attending to literal meaning. Some suggestive evidence of this relationship has been provided by Bonitatibus and Flavell (1985). They found that first graders were better able to evaluate the adequacy of simple two-word directions if the experimenter wrote them legibly while they were being spoken rather than presented them only orally or with illegibly written versions. The authors argued that having the messages in written form emphasized their literal meanings, and this in turn aided evaluation. They further speculate that if experience with written language initially helps sensitize the child to literal meaning, then beginning readers may at first attend to literal meaning only when they can read the message. Generalization of this processing tendency to oral language may begin to appear only later. This hypothesis has yet to be tested. The hypothesized relationship between literacy, attention to literal meaning, and comprehension monitoring also suggests that people who do not know a written language system should have more difficulty with message evaluation (or at least the related notion of multiple interpretations of an utterance) than those that do, regardless of their age. Thus blind children, and deaf children using ASL (which has no written counterpart), should lag behind seeing or hearing children at the same cognitive developmental level in message evaluation or interpretation skills. One would expect similar phenomena from adults who are either illiterate or members of a preliterate culture.

In addition, it seems unlikely that once children become literate and develop the ability to scrutinize the literal meaning of an utterance, they will do so correctly and appropriately in all circumstances. Such factors as the difficulty of the verbal input, the goals of comprehension, and the type of problem (e.g., ambiguity vs. inconsistency with prior information) seem likely to affect children's and adults' comprehension monitoring. For example, studies using relatively complex paradigms in terms of the number of potential referents and the clarity with which the array was specified for the child tend to yield higher age norms for successful message evaluation than do studies using more simple, straightforward arrays (Patterson & Kister, 1981). Similarly, Markman (1977, 1979) used inconsistencies in prose passages rather than simple ambiguities and found that even 12-year-olds have difficulty correctly evaluating such messages. It would seem that an awareness of literal meaning is a necessary, but not always sufficient, condition for evaluating one's comprehension of verbal input.

An intriguing possibility is raised by the results of a recent study by Flavell, Green, and Flavell (1985). In this study second graders, sixth graders, and college students followed a two-part sequence of spatial directions (driving a toy car along roads that forked twice) and were asked to judge whether they had reached the destination intended by the direction giver. In some of the directions, the first step was referentially ambiguous, and although the second part was unambiguous in itself, it failed to clarify the initial ambiguity and left the intended destination uncertain. Two interesting results emerged. First, most subjects at all age levels could recall the initial uncertainty, even if they then went on to judge the directions on the whole adequate. Second, although there was significant improvement with age, even the college subjects were not perfect. This suggests that even some college students fail to take into account the effects of initial uncertainties for later, overall comprehension; and that they tend to overestimate their comprehension with the passage of time.

Through informal conversations with college students and professors, it has become clear that such phenomena are considered quite common. In a typical scenario, students listen to a lecture and experience a comprehension failure. They could ask a clarifying question, but often do not, primarily because of fear of looking foolish. (This is surprisingly similar to the behavior of young children in the referential communication paradigm: If the communication fails, it is not due to the message, it is because of the listener's inability to discern the speaker's intent.) By the time the teacher pauses and asks for questions, the uncertainty has been forgotten. A week later, students open their notebooks to study, and much to their dismay they realize that they have grossly overestimated their comprehension of the material. We are currently designing a study to test this: College students will read prose passages containing various types of problems. They will then assess their comprehension of the passage, and their attention to literal meaning will be assessed via a recognition measure. It is expected that subjects who fail to detect the problems will also gloss the literal meaning of the critical sentence(s), and wrongly accept disambiguated versions of the original passage.

Finally, I would like to speculate about some of the broader implications of learning to distinguish speaker's from literal meaning. An interesting contrast is found in children's moral development. According to Piaget (1948) until age 6 or 7, children are moral realists. That is, rules are taken literally; what is to be obeyed is the letter of the law, not its spirit. Somewhat later, children become moral rationalists. They realize that rules have some underlying intention, and it is this intention that is to be upheld. Similarly, when young children are asked to evaluate an act, they often base their judgments on the outcome of the act rather than on the actor's intentions; not until later do they begin to take the actor's motives into account. There is considerable controversy over whether and when this shift occurs; see Karniol (1978) for a review.

Although this may at first seem to contradict the literature on language development where initially intentions have primacy, closer examination indicates that such need not be the case. According to Piaget, moral realism has its basis in unilateral respect for and obedience to authority. Moral rationalism is the product of mutual respect and cooperation among individuals. Similarly, children who fail comprehension-monitoring tasks do so because they conflate a speaker's intentions with the meaning in the words, and assume that it is the listener's unilateral task to uncover what was meant. Children who successfully monitor their comprehension realize that it is more of a cooperative enterprise; it is not only the listener's task to attempt to comprehend the speaker's intention, the speaker also plays an important role in adequately expressing that intention.

In addition, with rules and morals, the most salient thing is a person's behavior. With language, it is the speaker's meaning. In both cases children seem to initially conflate two related aspects of behavior (what is said and what is meant; what is done and what is intended) and only later learn to differentiate them. Moral realists, like poor message-evaluators, feel that there is but one interpretation of a rule or sentence. More mature children realize that both rules and sentences are approximate representations of some underlying intention and that both the intention and the representation need to be attended to. This is strikingly similar to Piaget's notion of decentration. Children at first focus on one salient dimension or aspect of the situation. With development they "decenter" and become able to differentiate and attend to more than one. In conservation tasks, children learn to attend to both height and width; in class inclusion problems, they become capable of simultaneously representing roses as roses and as flowers; in moral development, they begin to attend to action and intention (or the letter of the law and its spirit); and in language development, they differentiate what is said from what is meant. Thus comprehension monitoring and attention to literal meaning may be part of a much broader developmental change, as Flavell (Chapter 13) suggests.

In conclusion, the data and ideas presented in this chapter suggest a number of things. First, it seems that the comprehension-monitoring abilities of children in the referential communication paradigm are based on the ability to differentiate and attend to what was said and its literal meaning as opposed to what the speaker meant by the utterance (speaker's meaning). Second, it is likely that the development of this ability is based, at least in part, on literacy. Third, the ability to attend to literal meaning is a necessary but not sufficient condition for comprehension monitoring; factors such as difficulty and goals of comprehension may exert strong effects on children's and adults' ability to evaluate communication. Finally, this ability can be seen as similar to other developments occurring at around the same age, and therefore may be part of a more global reorganization of the child's thought. That reorganization, it is suggested, is the child's acquisition of a theory of mind, a theory that specifies the thoughts and intentions of speakers, which may be adequately or ambiguously expressed by their words.

REFERENCES

Ackerman, B. P. (1981). Performative bias in children's interpretations of ambiguous referential communications. *Child Development, 52,* 1224–1230.

Beal, C. R., & Flavell, J. H. (1984). Development of the ability to distinguish communicative intention and literal message meaning. *Child Development, 55,* 920–928.

Bonitatibus, G. (1987, April). *The relationship between speaker variables and children's ability to evaluate and revise messages.* Paper presented at the conference of the Society for Research in Child Development, Baltimore, MD.

Bonitatibus, G. (1988). Comprehension monitoring and the apprehension of literal meaning. *Child Development, 59,* 60–70.

Bonitatibus, G., & Carrier, M. (1986). *The effect of explicitly marking a speaker's ambiguous intentions on children's ability to evaluate a message.* Unpublished manuscript, Saint Anselm College, Manchester, NH.

Bonitatibus, G., & Flavell, J. H. (1985). The effect of presenting a message in written form on young children's ability to evaluate its communication adequacy. *Developmental Psychology, 21,* 455–461.

Bransford, J. D., Barclay, J. R., & Franks, J. J. (1972). Sentence memory: a constructive versus interpretive approach. *Cognitive Psychology, 3,* 193–209.

Clark, H. H., & Clark, E. V. (1977). *Psychology and language.* New York: Harcourt Brace Jovanovich.

Donaldson, M. (1978). *Children's minds.* New York: Norton.

Flavell, J. H., Green, F. L., & Flavell, E. R. (1985). The road not taken: Understanding the implications of initial uncertainty in evaluating spatial directions. *Developmental Psychology, 21,* 207–216.

Flavell, J. H., Speer, J. R., Green, F. L., & August, D. L. (1981). The development of comprehension monitoring and knowledge about communication. *Monographs of the Society for Research in Child Development, 46,* (5, Serial No. 192).

Karniol, R. (1978). Children's use of intention cues in evaluating behavior *Psychological Bulletin, 85,* 76–85.

Markman, E. M. (1977). Realizing that you don't understand: A preliminary investigation. *Child Development, 48,* 986–992.

Markman, E. M. (1979). Realizing that you don't understand: Elementary school children's awareness of inconsistencies. *Child Development, 50,* 643–655.

Olson, D. R. (1977). From utterance to text: The bias of language in speech and writing. *Harvard Educational Review, 47,* 257–281.

Olson, D. R., & Hildyard, A. (1983a). Literacy and the comprehension and expression of literal meaning. In F. Coulmas & K. Ehlich (Eds.), *Writing in focus* (pp. 291–325). New York: Mouton.

Olson, D. R., & Hildyard, A. (1983b). Writing and literal meaning. In M. Martlew (Ed.), *The psychology of writing.* New York: Wiley.

Olson, D. R., & Torrance, N. (1983). Literacy and cognitive development: A conceptual transformation in the early school years. In S. Meadows (Ed.), *Developing thinking: Approaches to children's cognitive development.* London: Methuen.

Patterson, C. J., & Kister, M. C. (1981). The development of listener skills for referential communication. In W. P. Dickson (Ed.), *Children's oral communication skills* (pp. 143–166). New York: Academic Press.

Piaget, J. (1948). *The moral judgment of the child.* New York: Free Press.

Robinson, E. J. (1981). The child's understanding of inadequate messages and communication failure: A problem of ignorance or egocentrism? In W. P. Dickson (Ed.), *Children's oral communication skills* (pp. 167–188). New York: Academic Press.

Robinson, E., Goelman, H., & Olson D. R. (1983). Children's understanding of the relation between expressions (what was said) and intentions (what was meant). *British Journal of Developmental Psychology, 1,* 75–86.

Robinson, E. J., & Robinson, W. P. (1977a). Children's explanations of communication failure and the inadequacy of the misunderstood message. *Developmental Psychology*, *13*, 156–161.

Robinson, E. J., & Robinson, W. P. (1977b). Development in the understanding of the causes of success and failure in verbal communication. *Cognition*, *5*, 363–378.

Robinson E. J., & Robinson, W. P. (1978). The relationship between children's explanations of communication failure and their ability deliberately to give bad messages. *British Journal of Social and Clinical Psychology*, *17*, 219–225.

Shatz, M. (1983). Communication. In J. Flavell & E. Markman (Eds.), *Manual of child psychology: Cognitive development* (4th ed., Vol. 3, P. H. Mussen, General Ed., pp. 495–555). New York: Wiley.

Whitehurst, G. J., & Sonnenschein, S. (1978). The development of communication: Attribute variation leads to contrast failure. *Journal of Experimental Child Psychology*, *25*, 454–490.

Whitehurst, G. J., & Sonnenschein, S. (1981). The development of informative messages in referential communication: Knowing when versus knowing how. In W. P. Dickson (Ed.), *Children's oral communication skills* (pp. 127–142). New York: Academic Press.

Winograd, T. (1980). What does it mean to understand language? *Cognitive Science*, *4*, 209–241.

PART IV

Further theoretical implications of
children's concepts of mind

18

Assessing intention:
A computational model

THOMAS R. SHULTZ

Deciding whether an action, or outcome of an action, is intentional is often a major step in devising an explanation of the event (Lalljee & Abelson, 1983; Shultz, 1982). Intentional explanations have a different character than do explanations focusing on mistakes or accidents, and this distinction can have important implications for moral and legal evaluation of actions and outcomes (Shultz & Wright, 1985; Shultz, Wright, & Schleifer, 1986).

This chapter presents a computational model, JIA, that judges the intentionality of actions. The basic architecture of the model is explained, as is the knowledge representation scheme that it uses. Then the main features of the model are discussed in greater detail, and results for some sample problems are presented. Relations to other programs that generate or interpret plans or perceive actions are discussed. Limitations of the present program and likely future improvements are outlined, as are the advantages of both this particular project and the general strategy of implementing computational models of reasoning.

Purpose of the program

JIA was designed primarily to model the performance of young children in psychological experiments in which they are asked to decide whether a piece of behavior emitted by themselves or someone else, or an outcome of the behavior, was intended or not. In doing so, the program uses the same heuristics that children are presumed to use, including matching, valence, monitoring, and discounting (see section on objective heuristics and Poulin-Dubois & Shultz, Chapter 6). To account as well for what adults are able to do in this area, the program was extended to have the capacity to solve a variety of classic philosophical puzzles about judging intention involving multiple descriptions of actions and outcomes and deviant causal chains connecting them.

An example of one such puzzle is the case of the assassination of the Archduke Ferdinand of Austria by Gavrilo Princip, an incident widely considered to have triggered World War I. Princip enacted a plan to shoot and kill the Archduke, the presumptive heir to the Austrian empire, in order to hurt Austria and thus avenge his own country, Serbia, for Austrian oppression and interference. Searle (1983) presents this case as an example of the so-called *accordion effect*, in which multiple true descriptions can be made concerning actions in a complex plan. Like the folds of an accordion, the number of alternative true descriptions of an action can easily be expanded or contracted. In this case, correct answers to the question *What did Princip do?* could include *He pulled his finger, He fired a gun, He shot the Archduke, He killed the Archduke, He hurt Austria,* and so on.

The JIA program can be asked to assess the intentionality of any particular event, whether action or outcome, in a case. When asked to analyze whether the killing of the Archduke was intentional, it produced the following output:

> Concluded from rule 3.1
>   kill part.of.plan cf = 1
> Concluded from rule 3.2
>   kill caused.as.planned cf = 1
> Concluded from rule 3.3
>   kill intended cf = 1

That is, three successive conclusions were made by three different rules in the system. Rule 3.1 concluded that this outcome was part of the plan; rule 3.2, that it was caused as planned; and rule 3.3, that it was intended. Each such conclusion is believed by the system with a particular certainty factor (cf), which can range from -1, indicating definite falsity, to 1, indicating definite truth. In this case, the system drew each of the three conclusions with maximal certainty of their truth.

When asked whether a different outcome, the start of World War I, was intentional JIA reached a different set of conclusions:

> Concluded from rule 3.1
>   start part.of.plan cf = -1
> Concluded from rule 3.3
>   start intended cf = -1

That is, starting of the war was definitely not part of the plan (rule 3.1) and was definitely not intended (rule 3.3). How JIA reached these conclusions for the two different outcomes will become clearer as the system is described in greater detail.

Basic architecture of the model

The basic architecture of the JIA system is illustrated in Figure 18.1. The case or problem to be analyzed is presented in the form of two input net-

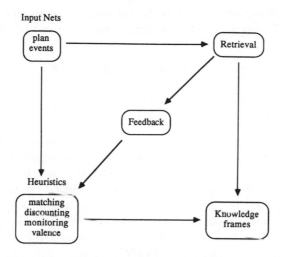

Figure 18.1. The basic architecture of the JIA system.

works, one representing the actor's plan and another representing the actual sequence of events. In addition, a particular event is singled out for analysis to determine whether or not it was intended.

The system can approach such a problem in either of two ways: by retrieving a previously computed answer from its knowledge frames, or by constructing a new answer based on application of its reasoning heuristics. It tries the retrieval strategy first. If retrieval yields an ambiguous answer or an unambiguous answer that is corrected by feedback from the program's user, then control is directed to the constructive strategy. Here, the various reasoning heuristics are applied. Matching the event (and the causal sequence by which it was produced) against the actor's plans will be attempted if any elements of the plan are known to the system. If the actor's plan is completely unknown, then the more objective heuristics of discounting, monitoring, and valence are applied. Sufficiently strong conclusions drawn from application of the heuristics are stored in the system's knowledge frames for later possible use by the retrieval strategies. Each of the central aspects of the system are described in more detail in the following sections.

Reasoning mechanisms

Most of the reasoning done by JIA is implemented in the form of a production system operating on the plan and event networks. A production system is made up of a set of if-then rules and an interpreter to process these rules. Each if-then rule, or production, specifies a set of antecedents and a set of conclusions. If the conjunction of the antecedents is true, the conclusions are drawn. Here is a sample production rule contained in JIA:

```
(rule 3.3
   (if (and (true? ?event 'part.of.plan)
            (true? ?event 'caused.as.planned))
      (conclude ?event 'intended 1)
      (conclude ?event 'intended −1)))
```

Rule 3.3 specifies that if the event in question was part of the actor's plan and was caused as planned, then it can be considered to have been intended; otherwise, the event can be considered to have been unintended. *True?* is a predicate procedure with two arguments: an event, which is bound to the variable *?event* and a proposition. The *True?* procedure retrieves the certainty factor associated with that event and proposition and returns *true* if that certainty factor is greater than .2 and less than or equal to 1, and otherwise returns *false*. *Conclude* is a procedure with three arguments: an event (bound to *?event*), a proposition, and a maximum certainty factor. *Conclude* updates the current certainty factor of the proposition taking into account both the certainty factor of propositions in the antecedents of the rule and the maximum certainty factor that is its third argument. It scales down the maximum certainty factor by the minimum certainty factor in the antecedents of the production rule and then, in turn, calls a procedure *cfcombine* that propagates certainty factors through the system. *Cfcombine* is a procedure that changes the value of its first argument, a prior certainty factor, by the value of its second argument, a new certainty factor. The amount of change is scaled down by the amount that the prior certainty factor could possibly change. This is basically the algorithm used to propagate certainty factors in the EMYCIN production system shell (van Melle, Scott, Bennett, & Peairs, 1981). This algorithm is in conformity with Bayesian mathematics under certain restricted assumptions (Wise & Henrion, 1985).

Production rules can contain any number of conjunctively connected antecedents and generate any number of conclusions (using *conclude* or other functions). Propositions can be assessed using any of a wide variety of certainty factor predicates. In addition to *true?*, the only certainty factor predicates used by JIA are *false?* which returns *true* only if the certainty factor is less than −.2 and greater than or equal to −1, and *untrue?*, which returns *true* only if the certainty factor is less than or equal to .2 and greater than or equal to −1.

The main task of the production system interpreter is to test the antecedents of the production rules to see which are satisfied and then to draw the appropriate conclusions. The interpreter used in JIA implements a so-called *agenda control structure* with production rules being grouped into *rule buckets*. There are five separate buckets for rules dealing with the retrieval strategy, heuristic selection, the matching heuristic, getting information relevant to the objective heuristics, and the objective heuristics. Control passes from one rule bucket to another based in large part on the firing of production rules dealing specifically with bucket selection. Within each rule bucket, control is based on forward-chaining through the rules in a linear, cyclic fashion. That is, starting with the first rule in a bucket, each rule in turn is examined to see if its conditions are satisfied. If they are, then the rule is fired and control returns to the first rule in that bucket. There is, in addition, a refractory principle, to the effect that a rule is fired no more than once with respect to a particular event.

This agenda control structure is very efficient because the interpreter does not have to examine the entire rule base on every cycle, only those unfired rules in the current bucket. Moreover, it has a certain psychological validity because the rules are grouped into natural task-oriented categories. The interested reader may consult Anderson (1983) for a well-reasoned argument that a combination of networks and production systems constitutes the right sort of architecture for modeling human cognition.

Knowledge representation

The basic structure for representing knowledge of plans and events in JIA is an (*agent action object*) triple. That is, each event or plan step is represented as an agent performing an action on or to a particular object. This simple format was found to be adequate for dealing with the cases of interest, but nothing much in the rest of the program hinges on this particular representation. It could be elaborated or extended, perhaps along the lines of Winston's (1980) frame-based *extensible relations*, with little substantive impact on the system described here (see section on limitations and future projects).

To represent an entire plan or a sequence of events, event triples are nodes in a network. The arcs that connect the nodes are asymmetric relations of two sorts: *by-means-of* relations and *effect-of* relations. The system attaches no importance to the difference between these two types of network relations.

The plan and events for the case of Gavrilo Princip are illustrated in Figures 18.2 and 18.3, respectively. Princip, the actor in this case, had a plan to avenge Serbia by-means-of hurting Austria. Austria was to be hurt by killing its Archduke, an event that was to be the effect-of (or to occur by-means-of) shooting the Archduke. Shooting the Archduke required a set of subplans including the getting, loading, aiming, and firing of a gun. Each triple on the end of an arrow's point represents a subplan for carry-

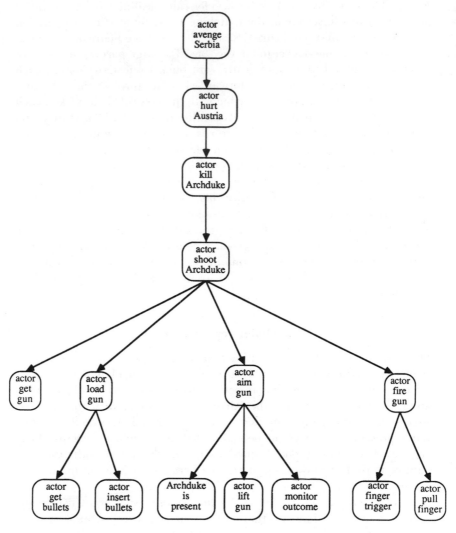

Figure 18.2. Plan net illustrating the *accordion effect*.

ing out the plan on the unpointed end of the arrow. In the case of multiple subplans or multiple causes, a strict left-to-right ordering is assumed. For example, the gun must be gotten before it is loaded, loaded before it is effectively aimed, and aimed before it is fired. In other words, the subplans of a plan are themselves connected by *successor links*, none of which are explicitly represented in the figures of this chapter. Princip's plan goes

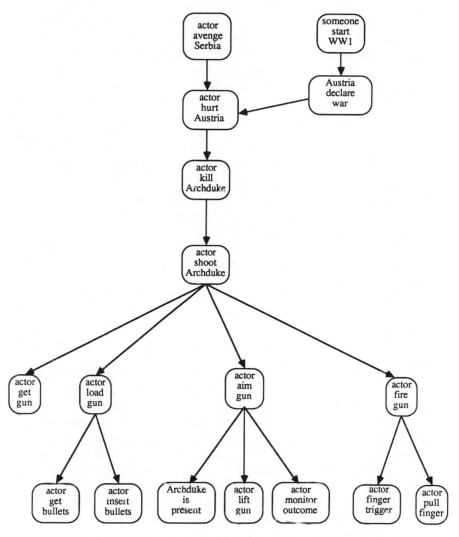

Figure 18.3. Events net illustrating the *accordion effect*.

on to specify further details of how loading, aiming, and firing the gun are to be done.

Hierarchical plans of this sort are assumed to expand downward only as more detail is needed. Such plans are further assumed to terminate with events that the system knows how to perform without further planning. The level of detail required will in general vary with both the nature of the actor and the nature of the task, but the philosophical notion of *basic action* may form a useful theoretical terminator for plans. Basic actions are essentially actions which are not performed by-means-of any other actions; they are just done (Danto, 1968; Goldman, 1970; Searle, 1983). Hence, they neither require nor permit further specification in terms of subplans. Moving one's finger is a good example of a basic action.

Intentions, or plan steps, may have conditions (Meiland, 1970), and these can also be represented as descendants, or subplans, of an intention. For example, the presence of the Archduke is a condition of the actor's aiming the gun. The type of an act token is given by the second and third terms in the triple, that is, the action followed by the object of the action. For example, the act type for the token (*actor insert bullets*) is (*insert bullets*). Whether an actor monitors (or needs to monitor) the relation between an action and outcome and whether an outcome produces a particular valence for an actor are represented by conventional triples.

In general, the network representation of plans used here is the sort produced by programs that generate hierarchical plans by means of theorem proving, or deductive retrieval (Fikes & Nilsson, 1971; McDermott, 1977; Sacerdoti, 1977; Tate, 1977; Wilkins, 1984). They also bear a strong resemblance to Goldman's (1970) *act diagrams* for the conceptual analysis of intentionality in complex cases, except that the nets used here are hierarchical (like the procedural nets of artificial intelligence planning programs) rather than linear.

Since the Princip case went much as planned, the representation of its events, presented in Figure 18.3, is nearly identical to the plan in Figure 18.2. The only difference is the occurrence of some unintended side effects of this Serbian partisan's having harmed Austria; namely, the declaration of war on Serbia by Austria causing a long sequence of other ultimatums, rejections, mobilizations, and declarations of war leading at some point to the start of World War I. Because events can be represented in the same notation as plans, the two can be compared, a fact that JIA's matching heuristic exploits. A constraint on the design of the plan and event nets is that they should have approximately equal levels of detail, although it is recognized that plans may be only vaguely known.

Psychological research by Wegner and Vallacher and their colleagues (Vallacher & Wegner, 1987; Wegner & Vallacher, 1986; Wegner, Vallacher, Macomber, Wood, & Arps, 1984) has shown that descriptions of one's own action converge on a particular level that enables the maintenance of the action up to capacity. This tends to restrict, though does not necessarily prevent, full expansion of the *accordion* of act descriptions. In general, their work suggests a somewhat more dynamic view of the action hierarchies discussed here.

Retrieval, learning, and feedback

As noted above, JIA first tries to determine the intentionality of an action outcome by retrieval from its knowledge frames. Evidence that human children try retrieval stategies before constructive strategies has been presented by Siegler & Shrager (1984) for the domain of arithmetic. In JIA, there is an *actions* frame with slots for *intended* and *unintended*. Every time an event token is found, with a sufficient degree of confidence, to be either intentional or unintentional via the heuristics, its action type is stored in the appropriate slot of the *actions* frame (unless it is present there already). This is the primary way that JIA learns. Tokens of particular action types, such as sneezing, may always be found to be unintentional. Tokens of other types, such as essay writing, may always be found to be intentional. It is reasonable to assume that systems with such experience will be able to classify immediately the intentionality of new tokens of these unambiguous types without any constructive computation. In contrast, tokens of many other action types may be found to be intended in some cases and unintended in others, thus always requiring constructive computation.

The retrieval strategy first looks to see whether the action type of the event token being analyzed is to be found in the *intended* and *unintended* slots of the actions frame. If it is present in one slot but not the other, JIA hazards the appropriate guess. If it is present in neither slot, or present in both slots, control is directed to the heuristics. If JIA does make a guess, but the program user knows this to be incorrect, the user can elect to give negative feedback to the system. In this case, the incorrect guess is withdrawn and control directed to the heuristics for further computation. It is not difficult to imagine the initial intentionality guesses of human observers to be corrected in similar fashion by people (often the actor) who know more about the event token and the plan underlying it than does the observer.

Heuristic selection

Once it has been decided to use constructive heuristics, JIA undertakes a decision about which ones to use. In conformity with the bias shown by human subjects (Shultz & Wells, 1985), it selects the matching heuristic whenever possible, that is, whenever at least some aspect of the actor's plan is known. Such is likely to be the case in judging one's own action outcomes and when another's plan is either stated publicly or constrained by context. If none of the actor's plan of action is known, JIA resorts to the objective heuristics. Because observers are, in general, much more likely to know their own than another person's plan, the matching heuristic will typically be invoked for self-observation and the objective heuristics for observation of others.

The matching heuristic

The essence of the matching heuristic is contained in rule 3.3. As noted above, this rule specifies that an event is intended only if it is part of the actor's plan and is caused as planned (Davidson, 1973; Goldman, 1970; Woodfield, 1976). To determine whether an event is part of actor's plan, a breadth-first search is undertaken, within the plan net, from the root or highest-level plan to the event in question. If that search can be successfully completed, then the event is indeed part of the plan; otherwise it is not a part of the plan. In breadth-first search, all nodes on one level are examined before any on the next level are considered. Nothing hinges on the fact that search in JIA is of this type; any of a number of other search strategies would work equally well. Breadth-first was chosen on the grounds that it is cautious and computationally quite simple.

   If the event was judged to be part of the plan, then the system attempts to determine whether it was caused as planned. To do this, it compares the portions of the plan and events nets from the event node down. Tversky's (1977) ratio model, which is supported by psychological evidence, is used to calculate the degree of similarity in these two portion nets. Basically, it computes the proportion of *by-means-of* and *effect-of* relations that the two portion nets have in common. This similarity metric is then scaled up by the vagueness of the plan: *degree of match = similarity + ((similarity * vagueness) * (1 − similarity))*. Two constraints governed the construction of this formula. One is that the increment should increase with both *similarity* and *vagueness*; the other is that the increment should not carry the value of *degree of match* over 1. Very preliminary pilot data suggest that this formula does predict subjects' ratings of *degree of match* from knowledge of *similarity* and *vagueness* with a high degree of accuracy, *r = .97*. *Plan vagueness* is, in turn, calculated as *1 − plan complexity*, where plan complexity is *depth of plan/depth of events*.

   As with human subjects (Shultz & Wells, 1985), JIA is relatively certain of any conclusions emerging from the matching heuristic. Thus, the maximum certainty factors specified in rule 3.3 are 1 and −1. Because the certainty factor of a conclusion is scaled down by the minimum certainty factor in the antecedents, the actual certainty factor for an intentional conclusion varies directly with the *degree of match* between the plan and events net portions. Although a strict interpretation of intentionality might demand a complete match between plan and events nets (Davidson, 1973; Goldman, 1970; Woodfield, 1976), JIA is able to compute and willing to consider matches that deviate from perfection. It may be that ordinary humans are as well, particularly in the case of imperfectly known plans.

Objective heuristics

When matching is not possible because the actor's plan is totally unknown, JIA, like human subjects (Shultz & Wells, 1985), attempts to employ the various objective heuristics. Because there is no plan net in these cases, all of the analysis focuses on the events net.

The valence heuristic specifies that outcomes that are positive for the actor are likely to be intended, whereas those that are negative for the actor are likely to be unintended. The program obtains valence information by undertaking a breadth-first search from a node of the form (*valence ? ?*) down to the event in question. Here the *?* symbolizes a one-place wild card. If this search is successful, then the adjective value is retrieved from the third slot of the event triple and translated into a numerical value which becomes the certainty factor of the valence proposition. If the search is unsuccessful, then the valence for the actor is unknown and the certainty factor of valence remains at the initialized level of 0.

The monitoring heuristic specifies that the event is likely to be intended if the actor monitors the relation between a basic action and the event, and likely to be unintended if no such monitoring occurs. JIA assesses monitoring by undertaking a breadth-first search from the event in question to any nodes of the form (*? monitor ?*) and (*? not.monitor ?*). If such a search is successful, the monitoring proposition receives a certainty factor of 1 or −1 as appropriate. An unsuccessful search leaves the certainty factor for monitoring at the initialized level of 0.

Evidence that children from 5 years of age and adults use valence and monitoring in their assessment of intentionality was provided in an experiment by Smith (1978). In contrast, 4-year-olds were found to consider all of the behaviors presented as intentional regardless of information on valence and monitoring. Interestingly, from Smith's description of the behavioral episodes, it is unlikely that his subjects could have been using the matching heuristic.

The discounting heuristic is a variant of Kelley's (1973) discounting principle. It specifies that internal causes, such as intentions, can be discounted insofar as sufficient external causes are perceived to be operational. There is a considerable amount of evidence, not all of it dealing with intentions, suggesting that discounting may be within the grasp of children as young as about 4 years (Lepper, Sagotsky, Dafoe, & Greene, 1982; Wells & Shultz, 1980). In JIA, if the event node has no descendants that are actions of the actor, then the certainty factor of the discounting proposition receives a value of 1. If all of the descendants of the event node are actions of the actor then the certainty factor of the discounting proposition receives a value of -1. Otherwise, this certainty factor retains its initialized value of 0.

Production rules employing propositions for these objective heuristics all have the same *intended* proposition in their conclusions. Once JIA decides to apply the objective heuristics, it applies them all, accumulating evidence either for or against intentionality by propagating the certainty factors in the manner described (see section on reasoning mechanisms).

Some sample output

Two sorts of cases have been presented to the system so far. One set contains problems from psychological experiments in which subjects (typically young children) have been asked to say whether a piece of behavior emitted by themselves or by someone else, or an outcome of such behavior, was intended or not. Most often, cases of this type are extremely simple, representable by very shallow nets of plans and events, so as to maximize the young child's chances of understanding and remembering the problem. The other sort of cases are rather more complicated, involving classic philosophical puzzles designed to cause difficulty for various theories of intention. Typically, they involve fairly deep nets of plans and events and what are called *deviant causal chains*, that is, chains somewhat different than what was intended. Only a few cases of each type are presented here.

One of the problems used by Shultz, Wells, and Sarda (1980) had the subject observing another child mistakenly pick up a dull coin after having been asked to pick up a shiny coin. The mistake was due to the actor's wearing a set of prism glasses that laterally distorted vision. The plan and events nets are each only one step deep, not requiring a graphical presentation. JIA, like most of the children in the experiment, uses the matching heuristic to conclude that the event of picking the dull coin was not intended:

> Concluded from rule 3.1
>   pick part.of.plan cf $= -1$
> Concluded from rule 3.3
>   pick intended cf $= -1$

Another example comes from the Shultz and Wells (1985) experiment in which access to information required by the various heuristics was more tightly controlled. The example involved the subject's observing another child who shot at a target without looking at the target, hit one color on the target, and lost his turn. Because this actor did not state his intention about which color he was trying to hit, the plan representation is nil. The events net is portrayed in Figure 18.4. Asked whether the event

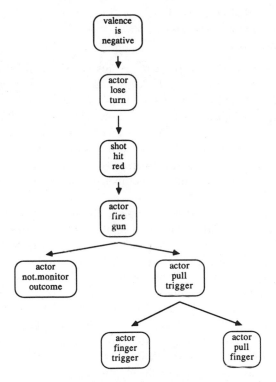

Figure 18.4. Events net for target shooting.

(*shot hit red*) was intended, the system uses the objective heuristics, first establishing certainty factor values for valence, monitoring, and discounting, and then propagating this evidence through the production rules of bucket 5. The evidence from valence and monitoring favored lack of intention, whereas the evidence from discounting favored the presence of intention. The final conclusion was weakly in favor of unintentionality, too weakly to learn anything about classifying the action type.

> Concluded from rule 4.1
>   hit valence[#] cf $= -0.6$
> Concluded from rule 4.3
>   hit monitor cf $= -1$
> Concluded from rule 4.5
>   hit discount cf $= -1$
> Concluded from rule 5.2
>   hit intended cf $= -0.24$
> Concluded from rule 5.4

hit intended cf = −.54
Concluded from rule 5.6
hit intended cf = −.24

JIA requires, somewhat arbitrarily at this point, an absolute cf of .7 or greater to store a conclusion in the knowledge frames. The proper level of this cf criterion should be established by further empirical research. Such research might well show that the criterion varies with task requirements to be correct versus have a quickly retrieved answer and, to some extent, with individual preferences for such options. In any case, JIA's rather wishy-washy results for this problem closely mirror those produced by children having access to conflicting objective information but no recourse to matching.

A final example from the psychological literature involves the subject's playing a card game against the experimenter (Shultz, 1980). Each player turns over one card at the same moment. If the colors of the two cards match, then the first player to slap the table wins all the exposed cards. If the colors do not match, any such slap is a mistake and results in losing all the exposed cards. There is, in other words, a condition on the intention of slapping the table, namely, that the colors of the cards should match. The plan net for each trick is represented in Figure 18.5. The events net for a particular trick is shown in Figure 18.6. Here, the child did a mistaken slap when the condition was not satisfied. Asked to judge the intentionality of this slap, JIA finds that although the slap was part of the actor's plan, the relevant part of the events net did not match that of the plan. Hence, the event was not intended, a conclusion also reached by nearly all children tested.

Concluded from rule 3.1
slap part.of.plan cf = 1
Concluded from rule 3.2
slap caused.as.planned cf = 0
Concluded from rule 3.3
slap intended cf = −1

One of the philosophical puzzles about intention has already been discussed, the *accordion effect*, as illustrated by the case of Gavrilo Princip (see section on purpose of the program, and Figs. 18.1 and 18.2). Such cases were considered puzzling because it was unclear how many actions had actually been performed and how the intentionality of each should be assessed. Goldman (1970) has convincingly argued for the conceptual separation of such expanded actions. And the knowledge representation scheme employed here allows for as much expansion as is desired.

Perhaps a more troublesome kind of puzzle has been that of deviant

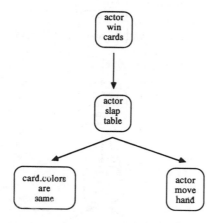

Figure 18.5. Plan net for a card game.

causal chains, in which an intended event is produced, although not quite in the planned manner. A case presented by Chisholm (1966) involved a person who in deciding to kill his uncle, became so upset that he was distracted from his driving and struck and killed a pedestrian. The interesting feature of this case is that the victim was later discovered to be the uncle. The puzzle derives from the fact that not only does the actor's intention match the outcome, but the intention causes the outcome. Yet because it does so in a deviant, unplanned way, most observers would probably consider the outcome to be unintentional. The plan net for this case consists of the single node (*actor kill uncle*). The events net is portrayed in Figure 18.7. When asked to analyze the event (*actor kill uncle*), JIA finds that although this event was part of the plan, it was not caused as planned, and thus was not intentional.

> Concluded from rule 3.1
>   kill part.of.plan cf = 1
> Concluded from rule 3.2
>   kill caused.as.planned cf = 0
> Concluded from rule 3.3
>   kill intended cf = −1

An even more puzzling case of a deviant causal chain is one discussed by Davidson (1973) and by Searle (1983). It involves an individual who tries to kill someone by shooting him. The shot misses but alarms a herd of wild pigs, which trample the victim to death. The relatively greater difficulty of this case derives from the fact that the plan became very detailed and was even enacted much as planned. Even so, the causal chain is prob-

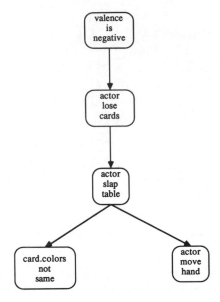

Figure 18.6. Events net for a card game.

ably deviant enough to make observers question the intentionality of the killing. The plan net and events net are presented in Figures 18.8 and 18.9, respectively.

Three different events from this case were presented to JIA for analysis. For (*victim cause-to-be dead*), the program concludes intentional, but at a level too uncertain to update the knowledge frames:

>   Concluded from rule 3.1
>   cause-to-be part.of.plan cf = 1
>   Concluded from rule 3.2
>   cause-to-be caused.as.planned cf = 0.55
>   Concluded from rule 3.3
>   cause-to-be intended cf = 0.55

Asked to analyze the event (*actor fire gun*), JIA concludes definitely intentional:

>   Concluded from rule 3.1
>   fire part.of.plan cf = 1
>   Concluded from rule 3.2
>   fire caused.as.planned cf = 1
>   Concluded from rule 3.3
>   fire intended cf = 1

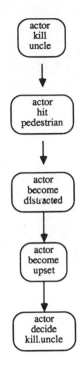

Figure 18.7. Events net for the uncle killing.

And the event (*pigs trample victim*) was found to be unintentional simply on the grounds that it was not part of the plan:

Concluded from rule 3.1
    trample part.of.plan cf = −1
Concluded from rule 3.3
    trample intended cf = −1

Relation to other programs

JIA may be considered to complement programs that generate plans (Fikes & Nilsson, 1971; McDermott, 1977; Sacerdoti, 1977; Tate, 1977; Wilkins, 1984), interpret plans (Schank & Abelson, 1977; Schmidt, Sridharan, & Goodson, 1978; Wilensky, 1978), or perceive actions (Thibadeau, 1986). Plan generators ordinarily start from a high-level goal and by deductive retrieval, break that goal down into subplans, stopping when the subplans reach a level that the output system knows how to perform. Plan interpreters start with low-level events and try to explain them by searching up

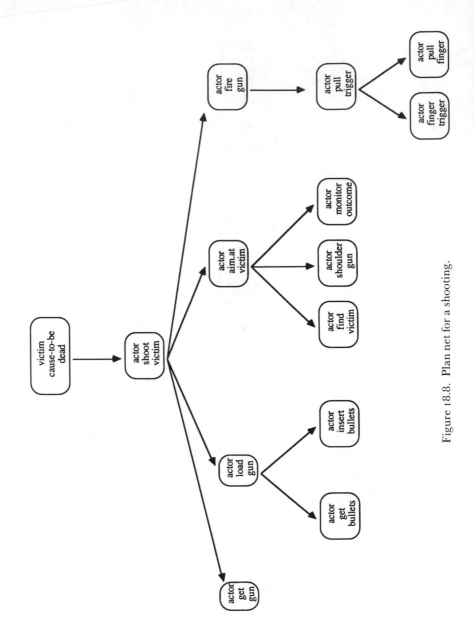

Figure 18.8. Plan net for a shooting.

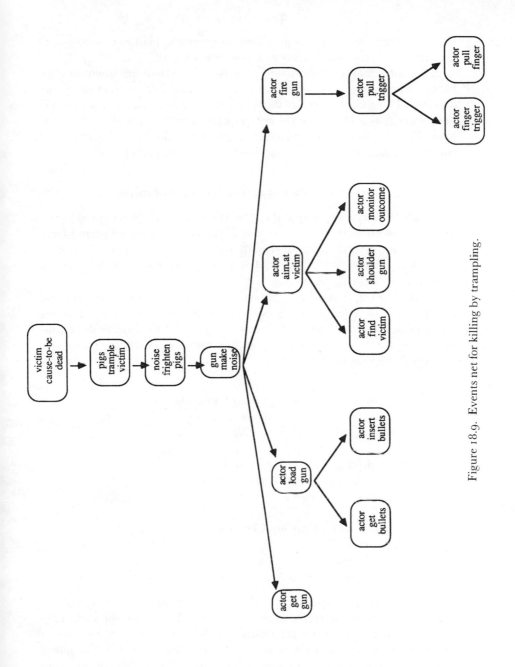

Figure 18.9. Events net for killing by trampling.

the net to some high-level plan. Often the search in plan interpretation is bidirectional with markers left at the nodes covered.

A new program by Thibadeau (1986) is designed to judge intentionality by considering only locally relevant actions and disregarding plans altogether. This might prove satisfactory for fairly basic actions, but it would not seem capable of solving the complex philosophical puzzles dealt with here. In the latter cases with their relatively deep nets, it is difficult to conceive of how to avoid the matching of plans against events.

Modeling other aspects of concept of mind

The question naturally arises about whether models like JIA could apply to other aspects of the concept of mind. Because the computational tools (production systems, frames, search) used here are so general, one is inclined to answer affirmatively. The proof, of course, would lie in the details of the models themselves.

A single example is a tiny production system designed to simulate the performance of a mature subject's understanding of the mental terms *remember* and *forget* (Wellman & Johnson, 1979). The following three production rules would appear to capture the essence of Wellman and Johnson's analysis of these terms.

```
(rule 1.3
   (if (and (true? ?event 'previous.knowledge)
            (true? ?event 'correct.retrieve))
      (conclude ?event 'remember 1)))
(rule 1.4
   (if (and (true? ?event 'previous.knowledge)
            (false? ?event 'correct.retrieve))
      (conclude ?event 'forget 1)))
(rule 1.5
   (if (false? ?event 'previous.knowledge)
      (begin
         (conclude ?event 'remember -1)
         (conclude ?event 'forget -1))))
```

Rule 1.3 specifies that if the subject had previous knowledge of the event and correctly retrieved it from memory, then he or she in fact remembered the event. Rule 1.4 similarly defines *forget* as the presence of previous knowledge and the absence of correct retrieval from memory. And rule 1.5 specifies that an absence of previous knowledge of the event implies that it can be neither remembered nor forgotten. Two other production rules were written to handle input and translation of information on the state of previous knowledge and the correctness of the retrieval.

Although Wellman and Johnson cautioned that their research did not identify reasoning mechanisms or processes, it is interesting that this small production system can, in fact, successfully crank out the responses of a mature thinker on their interview problems. Of course, a more complete and robust version of the model would specify additional details of how one judges the presence of previous knowledge and the correctness of retrieval. Even the toy model presented here does illustrate how reasoning mechanisms that are merely implicit in verbal theorizing can be made explicit as production rules. Further, the performance of young children, as described by Wellman and Johnson, could be simulated with a modified set of production rules that define *remember* in terms of successful performance, regardless of the status of previous knowledge. This would presumably entail the absence of the *previous.knowledge* proposition from all of the production rules. Once production rules for the various stages of performance were in place, the question of developmental change could be approached in a new light – that is, how to get from one set of production rules to another set (see section on limitations and future projects).

Undoubtedly, one of the major problems in the computational modeling of concepts of mind is that of representing the embedding of beliefs and other intentional states. A related problem is how to represent the differing beliefs of different individuals. These problems have not arisen either in the examples dealt with by JIA or in the toy model of understanding mental terms. They will arise, however, as modeling is extended to other aspects of concept of mind research. A general solution to this knowledge representation problem is discussed in the next section, on limitations and future projects.

Limitations and future projects

In its current implementation, JIA accepts plan and events nets as input. A more sophisticated program would start with natural language descriptions (or more likely a restricted version of natural language) and use some sort of language parser to construct these nets. A semantic parser is currently being developed (Shultz, 1987), based on that used by Winston (1980) in his work on reasoning by analogy. This parser will accept sentences in a restricted (*agent action object*) format and translate them into a frame-based semantic network representation. By representing these three terms, respectively, as a (*frame (slot (entry))*) relation with a unique label pointing to another, comment frame, it is possible to represent both Fillmore-type case relations (Fillmore, 1968) and embeddings of unlimited complexity. Each object, for example, could itself be an (*agent action object*) relation, as in *John believes that Henry is here*. And each such (*agent action object*) relation could have its own certainty factor and information about where it is embedded. Such a representation technique would not only handle embedded intentional states, but, in conjunction with the parser, would also allow for the more robust analysis of more natural input to the program. The production rule interpreter would be modified to communicate with these frames by implementing a more expressive rule structure in which each rule clause contains not only a certainty factor predicate but also a possibly embedded (*agent action object*) triple.

It might also be useful to combine JIA with plan-generating and plan-interpreting programs like those discussed in the section on relation to other programs. A plan generator could simulate the process leading to judging the intentionality of one's own actions; and a plan interpreter, the process leading to judging the intentionality of another's actions. These would be alternate ways of creating the plan nets that JIA needs. Adding an action perception program would increase the system's ability to deal with basic actions and with other low-level actions in the absence of plan information.

JIA could serve as a useful component of programs that make judgments of moral responsibility because intentionality is known to be a central aspect of such judgments (Shultz, 1986, 1987; Shultz & Wright, 1985; Shultz, Wright, & Schleifer, 1986).

The production rules that determine selection of retrieval versus constructive strategies could probably be somewhat more sophisticated. Psychological evidence collected by Reder (1985) suggests that humans do a sort of cost-benefit analysis of these strategies before selecting one of them.

Psychological evidence is needed with respect to a number of aspects of the current version of JIA. The setting of the certainty factor criterion for storage of conclusions has already been mentioned. It would also be useful to have a more precise specification of the certainty factors of conclusions in the various production rules. Current values reflect evidence that people are more certain of judgments based on matching rather than on the objective heuristics (Shultz & Wells, 1985), but the absolute values for any of these conclusions mainly reflect guessing on the part of the programmer. Work is currently under way on an algorithm that would dynamically modulate these certainty factors as a function of positive and negative feedback on the rule's success. Several of JIA's existing algorithms require psychological support including especially those that update certainty factors, assess plan complexity and vagueness, and match plans against events. In general, these algorithms produce quite sensible results, but more direct evidence that people do something similar would be welcome.

From the standpoint of developmental psychology one might well wonder about the origin of the heuristics and selection principles. As noted, about the only developmental change to have been reported in this area is the tendency for 3-year-olds, but not older children, to see all behaviors as intentional, at least when information is restricted to the objective heuristics. Such a developmental change could be simulated by a system that initially functions without, and subsequently constructs, the objective heuristics. Artificial intelligence research on construction of production rules is still quite primitive, but a number of promising mechanisms are receiving attention. Among these are induction (Mitchell, Utgoff, & Banerji, 1983), analogy (Anderson & Thompson, 1986; Winston, 1980), and compilation (Anderson, 1986). In induction, rules are learned by generalizing from positive and negative feedback. In analogy, they are constructed by altering similar, previously known rules. And in compilation, new rules are made by combining old ones that typically fire in sequence.

Consideration of the JIA program suggests two additional areas where psychological development might occur: learning that act tokens of particular act types are typically classified in a particular way, and the ability to deal with progressively deeper plans and event sequences. The latter development would presumably be related to the emergence of greater functional working memory (Case, Kurland, & Goldberg, 1982; Chi, 1977). It is noteworthy that both of these proposed developmental changes are quantitative, rather than qualitative.

Whether the tendency for actors to converge on particular levels of action description would have any implications for judging intentionality remains unclear (see section on knowledge representation). If there were such implications, this might represent another case of the importance of self-knowledge versus knowledge of others (see section on heuristic selection).

Lessons from the simulation

Apart from the above considerations, what was learned from doing this simulation? A major lesson was the construction of a set of procedures that can do matching of plans against event sequences. Before the simulation, there were no systematic ideas about how such matching could be done. Moreover, there was considerable doubt expressed at the Oxford workshop that matching was capable of solving the various philosophical puzzles about intentionality. Certainly, anything as primitive as the *equal?* function in LISP is not capable of handling deep nets of plans and events with multiple outcomes, successor links, approximate matching, and so on. But the present results show that a matching process that is generalized to deal with these complexities can do the job.

Other important lessons concern mechanisms for selecting and combining heuristics. As developmental psychologists have succeeded in demonstrating the presence of more and more cognitive structures in younger and younger children, the main developmental issue is now shifting to a concern with how these various structures are selected for use (Shultz, Fisher, Pratt, & Rulf, 1986; Siegler & Shrager, 1984). JIA contains an explicit model for heuristic selection, in terms of a production system with an agenda control structure and particular production rules that determine the program's flow depending on both the availability of relevant information and the direction of early conclusions. A related issue is how evidence from multiple selected heuristics might be combined, the mechanism here employing propagation of certainty factors over production rules having the same conclusion.

A minor lesson from the current project concerns how retrieval strategies might interact with strategies involving constructive computation. There may be many situations in which retrieval is tried first and constructive computation resorted to later if necessary, as in JIA. But the limitations and possible qualifications of this view may require further attention as discussed in previous paragraphs.

Advantages of computational modeling

The advantages of doing computational models in this area of early concepts of mind are undoubtedly much the same as in any other area. First, computational modeling forces theoretical precision. This is particularly true in terms of focusing attention on neglected issues and assumptions. And if the forced precision generates what seem like arbitrary decisions, these decisions can become ideas for future psychological research. Second, a computational approach provides the capability to deal with far larger working models than can be achieved in a single experiment. The importance of this is the ability to determine how parts of a large system interact with each other. And third, computational modeling tends to encourage theoretical unification of disparate phenomena. The basic reasoning mechanisms used in the present program, for example, are widely used for the simulation of psychological phenomena.

ACKNOWLEDGMENTS

This chapter is based on a paper presented to the Workshop on Children's Early Concept of Mind, St. John's College, University of Oxford, June 1986. This research was supported by the Natural Sciences and Engineering Research Council of Canada and by the Social Sciences and Humanities Research Council of Canada. I thank Andrew Woodfield for several insightful discussions of the problem of judging intention.

REFERENCES

Anderson, J. R. (1983). *The architecture of cognition.* Cambridge, MA: Harvard University Press.

Anderson, J. R. (1986). Knowledge compilation: The general learning mechanism. In R. Michalski, J. Carbonell, & T. Mitchell (Eds.), *Machine learning II.* Palo Alto, CA: Tioga.

Anderson, J. R., & Thompson, R. (June, 1986). *Use of analogy in a production system architecture.* Paper presented at the Workshop on Analogy and Similarity in Learning, University of Illinois at Urbana-Champaign.

Case, R., Kurland, D. M., & Goldberg, J. (1982). Operational efficiency and the growth of short-term memory span. *Journal of Experimental Child Psychology, 33,* 386–404.

Chi, M. T. H. (1977). Age differences in memory span. *Journal of Experimental Child Psychology, 23,* 266–281.

Chisholm, R. M. (1966). Freedom and action. In K. Lehrer (Ed.), *Freedom and determinism* (pp. 11–44). New York: Random House.

Danto, A. (1968). Basic actions. In A. R. White (Ed.), *The philosophy of action* (pp. 43–58). Oxford University Press.

Davidson, D. (1973). Freedom to act. In T. Honderich (Ed.), *Essays on freedom of action* (pp. 139–156). London: Routledge & Kegan Paul.

Feinberg, J. (1970). *Doing and deserving.* Princeton, NJ: Princeton University Press.

Fikes, R. E., & Nilsson, N. J. (1971). STRIPS: A new approach to the application of theorem proving to problem solving. *Artificial Intelligence, 2,* 189–208.

Fillmore, C. J. (1968). The case for case. In E. Bach & R. T. Harms (Eds.), *Universals in linguistic theory* (pp. 1–88). New York: Holt, Rinehart & Winston.

Goldman, A. I. (1970). *A theory of human action.* Princeton, NJ: Princeton University Press.

Kelley, H. H. (1973). The processes of causal attribution. *American Psychologist, 28,* 107–128.

Lalljee, M., & Abelson, R. P. (1983). The organization of explanations. In M. Hewstone (Ed.), *Attribution theory: Social and functional extensions* (pp. 65–80). Oxford: Blackwell Publisher.

Lepper, M. R., Sagotsky, G., Dafoe, J., & Greene, D. (1982). Consequences of superfluous social constraints: Effects of nominal contingencies on children's subsequent intrinsic interest. *Journal of Personality and Social Psychology, 42,* 51–65.

McDermott, D. (1977). Planning and acting. *Cognitive Science, 2,* 71–109.

Meiland, J. W. (1970). *The nature of intention.* London: Methuen.

Mitchell, T., Utgoff, P. E., & Banerji, R. (1983). Learning by experimentation: Acquiring and refining problem-solving heuristics. In R. S. Michalski, J. G. Carbonell, & T. M. Mitchell (Eds.), *Machine learning: An artificial intelligence approach* (pp. 163–190). Palo Alto, CA: Tioga.

Reder, L. (October, 1985). *Strategy-selection in question-answering.* Office of Naval Research, Technical Report No. ONR-85-2.

Sacerdoti, E. (1977). *A structure for plans and behavior.* New York: North Holland.

Schank, R. C., & Abelson, R. P. (1977). *Scripts, plans, goals, and understanding.* Hillsdale, NJ: Erlbaum.

Schmidt, C. F., Sridharan, N. S., & Goodson, J. L. (1978). The plan recognition problem: An intersection of psychology and artificial intelligence. *Artificial Intelligence, 11,* 45–83.

Searle, J. R. (1983). *Intentionality: An essay in the philosophy of mind.* Cambridge University Press.

Shultz, T. R. (1980). Development of the concept of intention. In W. A. Collins (Ed.), *Development of cognition, affect, and social relations. The Minnesota symposia on child psychology* (Vol. 13, pp. 131–164). Hillsdale, NJ: Erlbaum.

Shultz, T. R. (1982). Causal reasoning in the social and nonsocial realms. *Canadian Journal of Behavioural Science, 14,* 307–322.

Shultz, T. R. (1986, October). *A computational model of blaming.* Paper presented at the annual meeting of the Society for Experimental Social Psychology, Phoenix, AZ.

Shultz, T. R. (1987, April). *A computational model of causation, responsibility, blame, and punishment.* Paper presented at the meeting of the Society for Research in Child Development, Baltimore, MD.

Shultz, T. R., Fisher, G. W., Pratt, C. C., & Rulf, S. (1986). Selection of causal rules. *Child Development, 57,* 143–152.

Shultz, T. R., & Wells, D. (1985). Judging the intentionality of action-outcomes. *Developmental Psychology, 21,* 83–89.

Shultz, T. R., Wells, D., & Sarda, M. (1980). Development of the ability to distinguish intended actions from mistakes, reflexes, and passive movements. *British Journal of Social and Clinical Psychology, 19,* 301–310.

Shultz, T. R., & Wright, K. (1985). Concepts of negligence and intention in the assignment of moral responsibility. *Canadian Journal of Behavioural Science, 17,* 97–108.

Shultz, T. R., Wright, K., & Schleifer, M. (1986). Assignment of moral responsibility and punishment. *Child Development, 57,* 177–184.

Siegler, R. S., & Shrager, J. (1984). Strategy choices in addition and subtraction: How do children know what to do? In C. Sophian (Ed.), *Origins of cognitive skills: The eighteenth annual Carnegie symposium on cognition* (pp. 229–293). Hillsdale, NJ: Erlbaum.

Smith, M. C. (1978). Cognizing the behavior stream: The recognition of intentional action. *Child Development, 49,* 736–743.

Tate, A. (1977). Generating project networks. *Proceedings of the International Joint Conference on Artificial Intelligence, 5,* 888–893.

Thibadeau, R. (1986). Artificial perception of actions. *Cognitive Science, 10,* 117–149.

Tversky, A. (1977). Features of similarity. *Psychological Review, 84,* 327–352.

Vallacher, R. R., & Wegner, D. M. (1987). What do people think they're doing? Action identification and human behavior. *Psychological Review, 94,* 3–15.

van Melle, W., Scott, A. C., Bennett, J. S., & Peairs, M. A. S. (1981). *The EMYCIN manual.* Stanford University.

Wegner, D. M., & Vallacher, R. R. (1986). Action identification. In R. M.

Sorrentino & E. T. Higgins (Eds.), *Handbook of cognition and motivation: Foundations of social behavior* (pp. 550–582). New York: Guilford.

Wegner, D. M., Vallacher, R. R., Macomber, G., Wood, R., & Arps, K. (1984). The emergence of action. *Journal of Personality and Social Psychology*, *46*, 269–279.

Wellman, H. M., & Johnson, C. N. (1979). Understanding mental processes: A developmental study of *remember* and *forget*. *Child Development*, *50*, 79–88.

Wells, D., & Shultz, T. R. (1980). Developmental distinctions between behavior and judgment in the operation of the discounting principle. *Child Development*, *51*, 1307–1310.

Wilensky, R. (1978). Why John married Mary: Understanding stories involving recurring goals. *Cognitive Science*, *2*, 235–266.

Wilkins, D. E. (1984). Domain independent planning: Representation and plan generation. *Artificial Intelligence*, *22*, 269–301.

Winston, P. H. (1980, May). *Learning and reasoning by analogy: The details* M.I.T. Artificial Intelligence Laboratory Memo No. 520.

Wise, B. P., & Henrion, M. (1985, August). *A framework for comparing uncertain inference systems to probability*. Paper presented at the Workshop on Uncertainty and Probability in Artificial Intelligence, American Association of Artificial Intelligence, Los Angeles.

Woodfield, A. (1976). *Teleology*. Cambridge University Press.

19

Making judgments about thoughts and things

JAMES RUSSELL

Most of us believe that we have a more or less unique mental life set off from the physical world and from the mental lives of other people. Whether or not this is *just* a belief – just a piece of theory that may turn out under analysis to be muddled – or whether it is secure knowledge, it is certainly a belief whose origins psychology must explain.

In this chapter I shall consider the relation between two sets of considerations. I shall discuss four *necessary conditions* for distinguishing mental from nonmental entities, that is, for distinguishing a thinking subject from a world of enduring objects. In addition, I shall examine how children at different ages make judgments about mental entities and about these enduring objects, my general goal being to explain children's judgments by appeal to their understanding of the necessary conditions for distinguishing mental from physical objects.

The agentive condition

The first condition for distinguishing mental from physical realities, which I shall call the *agentive* condition, is derived from Kant. Imagine, in illustration, an individual who is *entirely* passive, who has no efferent capacities, not even the slightest eye movement. Additionally, he is never moved by anyone else. Every sequence of perceptual inputs that this person experienced would be world-determined. Now contrast this with a self-generated series of perceptions. Kant's example was the choice an active viewer has in looking at an object such as a house; one can, for example, begin with the ground floor and move up, or begin with the roof and move down. The sequence of perceptions is, in this case, viewer-generated. Kant contrasted this with the world-generated sequence of perceptions that a viewer experiences in standing by a river watching a ship sail upstream. If we are ever to experience an objective world, Kant argued, we must forge a division between these two kinds of perceptual sequence; and obviously this division is never going to be forged in an entirely passive perceiver.

The failure condition

The next necessary condition for distinguishing the mental from the nonmental is the *failure* condition, which is derived from Hegel and elaborated in James Mark Baldwin's (1906) concept of "refractoriness." Baldwin's examples of the importance of refractoriness were developmental – a baby turning to suck the nipple and being thwarted, a failure to grasp, and so on. These led to what Baldwin called, in his quaint terminology, the "embarrassments" out of which the first division between "interest" and "datum," or, in our terms, between intention and reality, is forged.

Now, it could be objected against the "necessity" of this condition, that the detection of refractoriness itself presupposes the distinction between intentions and things, because how can an individual be aware of a world resisting her intentions unless she can already "represent" these intentions? I think this objection relies on a very adult and intellectual notion of *intention*. If we stick with Baldwin's term *interest* we are probably on safer ground; for surely a week-old infant can want-the-nipple-and-want-it-now without "representing" this want to herself.

Both the agentive and the failure conditions carry a heavily Piagetian flavor; the agentive condition does much the same theoretical work as Piaget's distinction between the reversibility of action and the irreversibility of perception. Indeed, as I have mentioned elsewhere (Russell, 1978), it is no accident that in S. Körner's introduction to Kant's philosophy the terms *reversible* and *irreversible* are used to describe the distinction between self-generated and world-generated perceptual sequences (Körner, 1955, p. 85). The failure condition is surely reminiscent of Piaget's claim that accommodation after disequilibrium between scheme and outcome is the engine of sensorimotor development – *accommodation* being, in fact, Baldwin's term. Indeed, one of the things that it means to be broadly sympathetic to the Piagetian view of mental development is that one assumes, at least tacitly, that these two conditions have to be met by truly mental systems.

My treatment of the other two conditions will be rather different. Instead of simply regarding them as theoretical touchstones, I will introduce the conditions and then describe some of the empirical questions to which they give rise as well as some of the answers we now have to these questions. I will be doing this partly because the second two conditions seem to depend on the first two (although I shall not present arguments for this dependency), and partly because the second two suggest empirical issues in a more obvious way.

The asymmetry condition

The third condition is called the *asymmetry* condition because it concerns the asymmetrical relation that exists between things and our mental or "intentional" representations of them. This should be contrasted with the converse kind of asymmetry, *abstraction*, where we have one representation for a range of entities – "red" for strawberries, sunsets, and so forth.

The asymmetry of *intentionality* refers to the fact that one item can be represented in a number of ways: as "Amanda"; "an obstacle"; "something good to eat," and so on. In order to see the implications of this asymmetry, imagine an individual who is capable of acting in very many different ways, with the snag this time being that these actions are not really at his disposal because there is one particular action and only one particular action (or perhaps one attempt) for each different object that is encountered. These actions may indeed look richly planned and purposive (for instance, something resembling an Elizabethan courtier's bow to every motorbike); but to the extent that it is the *object* calling out the action rather than the individual choosing the action we do not truly have actions at all. This *symmetrical* relation between "thing" and "representation of it as actable on in a certain way" leaves no scope for any development of the notion of the independence of things from our representation of them.

Now an organism's merely *behaving* toward one item in a number of different ways does not necessarily imply any fulfillment of this condition. For the organism may *not*, in thus behaving, (a) know that it *is* the same item every time and (b) have intentional control over its behavior. I will expand on (b). Let us imagine, again, that depending on its biochemical state, an organism either (1) tries to eat, or (2) runs away from, or (3) tries to copulate with one item, while representing it as the same item each time. Here the behaviors are driven by, respectively, hunger, fear, and lust, and are therefore not intentional in my sense. To lapse once more into metaphor, the organism has no choice about how to represent this one item – as "good to eat," as "good to get away from," and so on.

Now consider, by way of contrast, a case where the passions are not in the foreground – a well-fed, calm, alert baby presented with a novel object. The baby seems to say through her behavior, "Now what can I do with *this*?" as she waves, then sucks, then bangs, then carefully releases the object, watching its journey to the floor. The baby is not "responding to" the item: She is finding out what it affords (Gibson, 1979). And in doing this she is doing something that is much more like choosing than it is like responding. Recall that Baldwin, and later Piaget, called infants' early proto-intentional behavior "*circular* reactions" – "circular" because they can go back and do it again if they *choose*.

Early landmarks in fulfilling the asymmetry condition

Although a baby of around 10 months of age may be able to apply a rich array of actions to an object, the range of actions is essentially determined by the physical properties of the object and by the immediate context. Thus, she will do basically bricklike things with her wooden bricks – stacking, sliding, perhaps banging. The role of the object – and thus the object as mentally represented – is as a determinate physical entity whose properties afford certain gross actions. There *is* the degree of choice that constitutes the asymmetry condition, but it is a physically constrained degree of choice.

A little later, however, and by some process we can as yet only describe, the child will become more or less free of this kind of determination by the object's properties, in the sense that she will choose the representation. The object will be pressed into service, so that what is in fact a brick becomes a "teacup," "a hat for teddy," or "the hamster's table" or whatever her interests require. I am resketching, therefore, the Vygotskian (1933/1976) picture of pretend play: The child applies her own meanings to objects and, while being able to appreciate the object's distinctive properties, (a) becomes free of simple determination by these properties (e.g., a ball used to practically *evoke* kicking); (b) makes a giant step in the divorcing of meaning from referent; and (c) learns about the refractoriness of objects at a higher level (e.g., you *could* pretend that a brick was a tablecloth, but the brick resists the attempt).

Note that the difference between the prepretense and the postpretense representations is not simply one of quantity. Whatever increase there is, I am arguing, is the effect of the mental change not the cause. The representations are different in kind, a difference on which Leslie (Chapter 2) has elaborated; the story being, roughly, that because the child can place perceptual representations of objects within mental quotation marks, the only thing that limits the number of representations she can construct for the object is her imagination – at least so long as the child is operating in the pretend mode. The advent of pretend or "symbolic" play is, therefore, one landmark in the continuing fulfillment of the asymmetry condition.

The next landmark is such because, for the first time, actions are not in the foreground. Actions are, we can say, physical orientations to objects and because they are, in some way, generated by mental representations, they have a mental source. However, this landmark concerns specifically *mental* orientations, and thus the asymmetry between an item in the world and the beliefs, hopes, fears, and so forth that we can have about it. Also we are dealing here not with individual things so much as with things grouped together in *situations*. Let us look first at the asymmetry between a situation and the myriad beliefs that can be entertained about it.

One of the principal acid tests for whether a child appreciates the asymmetry between situations and beliefs is whether he can appreciate how *false beliefs* are possible (see also Perner, Chapters 8 and 14). The *locus classicus* here is a study by Johnson and Maratsos (1977) in which the children were told an acted-out story in which Mary hides an object at place A but tells John that it is at place B, with the crucial question being about where John will look for the object. The predominant answer before 4 years of age is that he will look at place A – where the object really is – thereby evincing a failure to comprehend that there can be both true *and* false beliefs about a situation, veridical and nonveridical mental representations of it. After 4 years children can often not only say that John looks at place B, but will also judge that John *thinks* the object is at place B, but that Mary *knows* it is at place A.

In what sense are the 3-year-olds failing to appreciate the situation–beliefs asymmetry? They are doing so because if there is no recognition that any situation can, in principle, give rise to both true and false beliefs about it, then there will also be no recognition of *divergence* between what is the case and what is believed about it. There will be the assumption of a one-to-one relationship between situations and beliefs about them. I will now develop this thought a little.

My use of the asymmetry condition here owes a great deal (though not all: Russell, 1984a, pp. 251–254; Russell, 1984b) to John Flavell's (Chapter 13) deployment of his distinction between "Level 1" and "Level 2" thinking. Flavell describes what is, in the present terms, an assumption of symmetry between situations and beliefs as one of the symptoms of the Level 1 cognition that characterizes the thought of children under 4 years old. Only the Level 2 thinker can appreciate the "one–many" relation between a "content" (thing, situation, fact) and representations of it. So, in the present case, they cannot conceive that the content "object at B" can afford both the representation "at B" and "at A."

But there seems to be a missing step here in the attempt to explain the error. Strictly, the hypothesis can only predict that the young child will be unable to conceive of *both* "at B" and "at A" as possible representations: It cannot actually explain why "at B" is the one predominantly adopted. Why should the child not, for example, answer "at A" while believing that it really is at A, or why should she not just find the question unintelligible? Although I am not entirely confident that Flavell would endorse my version of his account, the extra step is to claim that the particular representation adopted is determined by a principle of *cognitive salience*. In this case, the fact that the object *is* at B is the salient fact, so "at B" is adopted while "at A" drops out. "Let us assume," writes Flavell, "that like their elders but probably to a greater degree, young children are primed to respond in terms of what is most cognitively salient – most 'up front' in consciousness – at a given moment" (Flavell, Flavell, & Green, 1983, p. 99). So the assumption is made – in keeping with the theme of the *continuing* difficulty with fulfilling the asymmetry condition I shall later develop – that both children and adults sometimes have their judgments overdetermined by cognitive saliency. The children's problems are just more obvious. What, for example, is adults' tendency to be overinfluenced by "vivid detail" (Nisbett & Ross, 1980) other than a case of cognitive saliency swamping cool reflection?

We can also observe difficulties with appreciating the asymmetry between a situation and mental representations of it in the area of emotion. A person who regarded the relation between situations and emotional reactions to them as symmetrical would possess an essentially S–R conception of emotional life; with situations calling out reactions in individuals rather as stimuli call out responses. Thus, a birthday party would inevitably evoke happiness, a canceled outing would inevitably evoke sadness, and so on. Now, as we know from the work of Paul Harris and others (e.g., Harris, Olthof, & Terwogt, 1981; and Harris & Gross, Chapter 15), younger children do indeed have this kind of behaviorist conception of emotional life, with the fully mentalistic conception only emerging slowly during middle childhood. This is most clearly seen in young children's difficulty with understanding how people might experience *ambivalent* emotions, how, that is, they can simultaneously have two kinds of emotional reactions to one situation – clearly an asymmetry problem.

But do these data on the late emergence of understanding emotional ambivalence not conflict with the Johnson and Maratsos (1977) data showing that children as young as 4 years are able to appreciate false beliefs? For *both* kinds of problem involve an appreciation of mental asymmetry. In fact, this conflict is not a serious one because there is evidence that children as young as 4 years do indeed have some burgeoning conception of the asymmetry between emotion and situation. First, as Harris has demonstrated (Harris, Donnelly, Guz, & Pitt-Watson, 1986), 4-year-olds can be encouraged to accept that emotional reactions might be concealed, that feeling and display of feeling may diverge. Second, it appears to be the case that, despite difficulty with ambivalence, quite young children can appreciate that different individuals may feel differently about one situation. Gnepp, McKee, and Domanic (1987) have recently shown that school-age children know that reactions to emotionally equivocal situations (such as having tomatoes for supper) will vary between individuals, depending on their likes and dislikes.

We have some evidence, then, that understanding the situation – mental representation asymmetry might emerge as early as 4 years of age. But what about an apparently more subtle asymmetry between *possible* situations and mental orientations to them? Thus, given the possible situation that the next Olympic Games will be held in Liverpool, we can believe it, hope it, fear it, neutrally envision it – whatever. It is convenient to refer to possible situations as "propositions" and usual to refer to the verbs that express different mental orientations to them as verbs of "propositional attitude."

A number of questions arise when we consider what children know about the proposition–mental orientation asymmetry. For instance: Is it the case that this asymmetry has to be more difficult to appreciate than the situation–mental representation asymmetry because a proposition is, as it were, one mental step "farther back" than an actual situation? The answer seems to be that in one area at least – the appreciation of "factive" verbs – it is no more difficult.

Factive verbs are those verbs, such as *know* and *realize*, that entail the truth of the propositions that they govern even when the verb is negated. Thus: "She did not know that Grusellier was ingratiating" implies that Grusellier was indeed ingratiating. If a child regards the relation between mental orientations and propositions as symmetrical, how will she be able to appreciate that some propositional attitude verbs entail the truth of the governed proposition and some do not? As Abbeduto and Rosenberg (1985) have recently shown, children below about 4 years of age do, indeed, fail to appreciate the status of factives and counterfactives (e.g., *wish* entails that the possible situation does *not* obtain). Their difficulty may take the form of overgeneralizing the scope of the negation of a factive verb to the complement. Thus, having been told "Mr. Jones did not know that the ball was blue," they will infer that the ball was *not* blue (see also Scoville & Gordon, 1980). This is exactly the kind of error one would expect from subjects who regard the relation between mental orientations and governed propositions as symmetrical: Negated mental verb means negative proposition. However, after 4 years – at least according to Abbeduto and Rosenberg's (1985) data – this kind of error is not made.

Research of our own has suggested that appreciation of proposition–mental orientation asymmetry soon comes to exert an influence on children's social cognition. After about 5 years of age, the occurrence of different kinds of propositional attitude verb in statements tends to determine the perceived *credibility* of that statement. In broad outline, we find that as children grow older they are less likely to judge as credible statements which make strong empirical claims by virtue of the propositional attitude verbs they contain and by virtue of whether they contain such verbs at all. Statements in the form "I know that p" "I'm sure that p" and "p" are more likely to be disbelieved than statements like "I think that p" and "I wish that p" (Russell & Haworth, 1987a). This is consistent with earlier data (Russell, 1984c) that children above about 6 years of age are likely to be more skeptical of objective statements (e.g., "I had eggs for breakfast") than of subjective statements (e.g., "I like eggs for breakfast"). The former make the stronger empirical claim.

But should we regard 4 years of age as a kind of developmental bridge, having crossed which the child must possess a secure grasp of the asymmetrical relationship between world states and mental states? It would be a mistake to do so. As I shall argue in the next section, difficulty with the asymmetry condition reappears when children are asked what it is appropriate to *say* about a situation.

A later landmark: Intensional versus extensional contexts

Recall that in Johnson and Maratsos's (1977) false belief task the children did not have to make judgments about *the correct form of words* to describe the protagonist's behavior and beliefs: They had to say where he would look or say where he thought the object was. In the task to be considered now, however, children are faced with the problem of how a protagonist's beliefs, behavior, and physical state should be *described* relative to a situation. And this time we are concerned not with clear errors but with whether the child's judgments about what it is appropriate to say about a situation match those of adults.

The kind of asymmetry to be appreciated here is that between a situation, on the one hand, and varieties of mentalistic and nonmentalistic descriptions of it, on the other. There are two modes in which situations can be regarded: in terms of the objects (including the people) referred to; and in terms of what a person playing a role within the situation would be in a position to say about it. Philosophers call the first mode *de re* and the second mode *de dicto*. Imagine, by way of illustration, that Jane has just borrowed John's car and that John knows she has. In this case we can surely say, "John thinks that Jane has borrowed his car." Further, suppose that Jane is allergic to cheese and John does *not* know this; might we then say, "John thinks that a person who is allergic to cheese has borrowed his car"? Well, maybe. Then what if we say, "John thinks: 'A person who is allergic to cheese has borrowed my car'"? This seems wrong because how could John mentally refer to her in these terms given his ignorance about her medical problem? And yet...one may say that still *in a sense* it is acceptable, unless the only way we can regard thinking is as a kind of literal talking to oneself. There is, therefore, an area of ambiguity about what is acceptable as a verbal characterization of thoughts. When quotation marks are used, then the *de dicto* mode seems to be appropriate to us. But when they are not, the situation is ambiguous and a *de re* reading *may* be acceptable.

It is in so-called *intensional* contexts that *de dicto* readings are appropriate. In the present intensional context we have a mental orientation verb (*think that, hope that,* etc.) governing a proposition, so the replacement of a term in the complement by a co-referential term (e.g., "Jane" by "a person . . .") *may* change the truth value of the whole sentence. These are contrasted with *extensional* contexts in which such replacement never results in a change of truth value because mental orientation verbs do not govern the proposition. We may, for example, use a *physical* orientation verb like *walk past*. In the case of "John walked past Jane" we can replace "Jane" by any true characterization of her that we like and the sentence will remain true or remain false. That is, extensional contexts invite *de re* readings. And yet . . . there is still a lurking ambiguity. Walking past need not be a mental activity, but what about *talking to* and *looking at*? So, apart from the clear case where we put thoughts into quotation marks and where we use physical verbs like *walk past*, there is normally some degree of choice about what mental orientation to take to a situation – a broadly mentalist one (*de dicto*) or a broadly realist one (*de re*). I do not wish to suggest, however, that this asymmetry is 1:2 (one situation to either a *de re* or a *de dicto* reading of it). It is, like the others, one:many, because there are as many *de dicto* readings of a situation as there are beliefs about it and as many *de re* readings of a situation as there are ways of describing it nonmentalistically.

Given this, asking whether children can understand the relationship between intensional and extensional contexts is a way of asking whether they can appreciate that one situation (e.g., a case of car-borrowing or of walking past somebody) affords both mind-relative and world-relative accounts of it. If children have an insufficient grasp of this asymmetry, their answers will be determined by cognitive saliency – by whatever the scenario or the question causes to be "most 'up front' in consciousness" at the time.

The first study I conducted on school-age children's appreciation of the difference between intensional and extensional contexts (Russell, 1987a) showed that young children often give *de re* readings where an adult would give a *de dicto* reading, and, less strongly, vice versa.

One of the intensional stories concerned George, who, while he is asleep, has his wristwatch stolen by a thief with curly red hair. Having established that they knew that George did not know what the thief looked like, the children are asked, "Can we say that George was thinking: 'I must find the man with the curly red hair who stole my watch'"? Of the 5-year-olds, around 98% said that we *could* say this, and even 63% of the 7-year-olds said that it was acceptable. That is, they gave a *de re* reading where an adult would surely have given a *de dicto* reading.

One of the extensional stories was about Jane, who, while playing in the street, was asked the way to the bus station by an old lady who, unbeknown to Jane, was her teacher's mother. Jane told her the way. The question was "Can we say that Jane was talking to her teacher's mother?" The *de re* reading is clearly acceptable here, for we can be said to be talking to somebody while lacking a good deal of knowledge about her. However, 42% of our 5-year-olds denied that we could say this. These children, I would argue, were influenced by the saliency of Jane's ignorance – hence the *de dicto* readings.

Although there are a number of qualifications to be entered about the data, by and large the proportion of inappropriate *de re* readings was very high and that of inappropriate *de dicto* readings was considerably lower, albeit still substantial. Where does the issue of cognitive saliency come in? My argument would be that one reason for the very high proportion of inappropriate *de re* readings of intensional contexts was that the question asked had highlighted the *object* (e.g., the thief). On the other hand, the number of inappropriate *de dicto* readings of extensional contexts was *relatively* low because the narrative did not sufficiently highlight the *uninformed nature of the protagonist's behavior* (e.g., that Jane did *not* know whom she was talking to).

Later studies (Russell & Haworth, 1987b) showed that when the narrative and the questions were modified so as to make the object less salient in the intensional stories and make the protagonist's lack of information more salient in the extensional stories, the proportion of misreadings decreased in the former case and increased in the latter. However, *de re* misreadings still continued to be the more common, suggesting it is objects rather than informational states that have the greater cognitive salience for children.

Stepping back a little, I suggest that future research in this area will illustrate that the gradual fulfillment of the asymmetry condition frees children from their earlier determination by the "surface" elements – the saliencies – when they think about people's thoughts about situations. Just as the infant learns that an object that is not visually salient (i.e., occluded) is still there, and just as the young child learns to withhold attention from the brickness of a brick when pretending it is a teacup, so the older child gains reflective control of her thinking, freeing it from determination by the obvious.

The perceptual field condition

The three conditions that I have introduced so far covered perception only insofar as it relates to action. However, the condition I now introduce concerns the ability to regard one's perceptual access to the world in a particular light – as more or less independent of action. I will first say why such a condition is needed.

The agentive, failure, and asymmetry conditions were all rooted in the appreciation that although action can determine mental representation, there is a point beyond which this is not possible. These conditions highlighted the tension, in our interaction with the world, between choice and constraint. Now, a person may well have some appreciation of these three conditions while having the following concept of perception. He may believe it is impossible for his perceptual experiences to *mislead* him about the current state of reality. For example, he may believe that what he sees always and inevitably corresponds to what he feels. None of the three action conditions cover this possibility. To know that it is *always possible* that our perceptions are not representing the world veridically is to appreciate that *perceptual appearance* is a middle term between *things* and *thoughts*. An individual who does not acknowledge this has failed to achieve the kind of division between mental and nonmental enjoyed by the normal adult.

To understand this condition, it is necessary to distinguish between two meanings of the term *perception* (for further distinctions and details, see Russell, 1987b). It may be useful to bear in mind that in the case of vision, perception of the first kind is relative to what James Gibson (1950) called the "visual world" and in the second it is relative to what Gibson called the "visual field." In taking perception in the first sense we concern ourselves with whether the organism succeeds or fails to pick up objective information in the world. Thus, the person either succeeds or fails to perceive that an object is three-dimensional, that it is supporting another object, that it is looming, and so on. In *this* sense of the word tiny babies are prodigiously successful "perceivers" (Gibson & Spelke, 1983). Indeed, we can even be said to succeed or fail to perceive the less formal features of the world – whether something is edible, or provides concealment, and so forth; a possibility covered in Gibson's (1979) concept of "affordances." Perception in this sense is *not* what we are concerned with in the perceptual field condition.

For perception in the second sense, the phenomenology is central, not the organism's successes and failures. The veridicality of a particular perceptual representation is irrelevant. We have, for instance, visual experiences when we see and auditory experiences when we hear, and it is possible to "bracket off" – to employ the phenomenologists' term – the question of whether these experiences correspond to something real. Given this, the essence of the perceptual field condition can be expressed by saying that it entails tacit knowledge that fields of perceptual experience are not true or false in themselves but are only *in the running for truth*. Illusion is never an impossibility. So a field of perceptual experience has to be *interpreted* and related, for example, to what has just happened to the perceiver.

How would somebody behave who lacked this conception? First, I suggest, he would sometimes naively trust every perceptual experience, believing that the visual field bears a kind of one-to-one relation to what is actually there (cf., the asymmetry condition). This is not the only possibility, however. To lack a conception of a perceptual field as interpretable – to fail to appreciate, for example, that to perceive what is really there the current visual field must be related to immediately preceding tactual perceptions – could also lead to a perceptual field being *ignored*. This is not at all the same as being *skeptical* about the information from one modality; rather, it is a simple failure to attend to one source of perceptual information if it *conflicts* with another source. I have argued elsewhere (Russell, 1987b) that we can make sense of infants' difficulties with object-permanence tasks by saying that they are overinclined to trust their visual fields as accurate representations of what is in the visual world; which leads them to fail to retrieve occluded objects. Conversely, when visual information conflicts with tactual information in occlusion by transparent screens, infants do not try to relate the two sources of perceptual information but ignore the visual and stubbornly attend to the tactual (Harris, 1974; Lockman & Ashmead, 1983).

I earlier mentioned pretend play as an example of the fulfillment of the asymmetry condition. However, because pretense often involves a kind of deliberately nonveridical perception of objects, it also serves as an excellent illustration of the fulfillment of the perceptual field condition in late infancy. Recall that Leslie's (Chapter 2) placement of pretense within general cognitive growth is based on the essentially Vygotskian idea that when operating in the pretend mode children put their perceptions within mental quotation marks, a process that Leslie calls the "decoupling" of perceptual representations. Now, this decoupling seems to involve something similar to the bracketing off of the possible truth or falsity of the perceptual representations, the treatment of a perceptual experience as being only in the running for truth – the perceptual field condition.

Appearance – reality judgments and the perceptual field condition

I hope it is evident by now that fulfilling the perceptual field condition can be regarded as the process of coming to treat perceptions as providing *appearances of reality*. Thus, failure to fulfill the perceptual field condition within one domain may take the form of a failure to draw adequately the appearance–reality distinction within that domain.

As research by Flavell and others has shown (Flavell, Chapter 13; Flavell, Flavell, & Green, 1983), children below what is fast becoming the "magic age of 4" answer as *phenomenists* when asked questions about the *real properties* of an object in an illusion-inducing situation, but are *intellectual realists* when asked about the *apparent identity* of an object. In the first case, for example, when asked what color a white card is "really, really" when it is placed behind a blue light filter, they say "blue." In the second case, when asked what a stone "egg" looks like "to your eyes" they say "a stone."

The account of this failure that is immediately suggested by my treatment of the perceptual field condition is the following: Children below 4 years lack reflective awareness of their visual fields as appearances of reality, with the result that any questions they are asked about their perceptions are not interpreted in the light of this fact but are simply answered in terms of whatever feature of their perceptual experience is the most salient. The principle of cognitive salience operates again. This in no way conflicts with Flavell's (Chapter 13) account of appearance–reality difficulties in terms of Level 1 thinking – as a failure to appreciate that one object can afford both "real" and "apparent" representations. In other words, to say the problem reflects lack of fulfillment of the asymmetry condition does not conflict with saying that it reflects lack of fulfillment of the perceptual field condition; because there is both a "mental representational" and a "perceptual" face to the problem. I would, however, say that because, in this case, children are being questioned about a visual illusion, about a perceptual anomaly, rather than about what somebody else thinks (as in the Johnson & Maratsos, 1977, experiment) the perceptual facet is primary. The difficulty here is with answering questions about one's own perceptual experiences, and so, perhaps, the first thing the child must get right is the fundamentally problematic nature of perception itself. This, it seems to me, is the central problem and unless it is solved, metacognitive moves (the achievement of Level 2 thinking/fulfilling the asymmetry condition) will not be effective.

My final task exactly parallels my task at a similar stage in the discussion of the asymmetry condition, where the concern was with children's characterization of *thoughts* rather than *things*. Having described a cognitive failure below 4 years of age in terms of the lack of fulfillment of a necessary condition for the mental versus nonmental distinction, I now illustrate how difficulties with this condition linger *beyond* 4 years in a different form. And as before, the tendency after 4 years is not to commit clear *errors* but to produce "readings" of questions that are at variance with the adult's readings. Another parallel between the "thought" questions and these "thing" questions involves their basic ambiguity. Earlier, I pointed out that a question about whether we can say that "John was thinking that a woman who is allergic to cheese borrowed his car" (when John does not know this fact about the borrower) is essentially ambiguous between a *de re* and a *de dicto* reading. Here, a question of the kind "What color is it?" is ambiguous between a realist and a phenomenist reading. I will call these questions "neutral" questions because they do not make explicit reference to appearance or to reality.

Some time ago Martin Braine (e.g., Braine & Shanks, 1965) demonstrated that although children can answer "looks?" and "really?" questions about visual illusions correctly when they are 5 years old, they continue to give phenomenist readings to neutral (or "ambiguous") questions that adults interpret in a realist fashion. Thus, when shown a straight stick leaning in a tank of water so that it looks bent by light refraction and asked whether it is straight or bent, they normally say that it is bent. This tendency is still found at age 7. In the present terms, the appearance of the materials is cognitively salient to a child in a way that it is not to an adult. (Note that this parallels Flavell's "property" questions, in which children's answers are phenomenist.)

It could be argued, however, that to claim that children and adults differ in this respect may be to read too much into the answers. The "social context" of the test may simply encourage the younger child, who is a more "context dependent" thinker, to give phenomenist readings. Compare the case of the conservation experiment. McGarrigle and Donaldson (1974) have pointed out that in the conservation experiment the experimenter may verbally refer to an underlying quantity, but she "behaviorally refers" to length, because this is what she manipulates before posing the question. Thus, in the Braine experiment the very presentation of the illusion is a kind of "behavioral reference" to appearance. This objection implies that the misreading is essentially a social phenomenon. Accordingly, if there were *social pressure* within the experiment to produce a realist rather than a phenomenist reading of the neutral question, children of this age should tend to abandon their phenomenist readings. If, on the other hand, the cognitive saliency of appearance is not the mere product of a social context, this pressure should have *no* effect. In particular, it should have no effect if the giving of appearance-based answers is a cognitive rather than a social phenomenon, as I have argued in my treatment of the perceptual field condition.

This question was addressed in a study of dyadic interaction between children who had been told to agree on one answer to a neutral question about a visual illusion (Russell & Haworth, 1988). The children were between 4½ and 7½ years of age. We employed four kinds of illusion (color, size, length, and brightness); and I will describe the procedure for color. To produce the first kind of social pressure (the "equal" condition), two children (of the same age and sex) sat before a group of white objects. One child wore green-tinted spectacles and one child wore red-tinted spectacles. They were asked the question "What color are these things on the table?" The experimenter emphasized that they should agree on one answer only and that they should only terminate (shouting "Ready!") when that answer had been agreed; after which she left the room and video-recording of the ensuing interaction began. Here the realist reading ("white") is clearly going to be a way out of an impasse – hence the "social pressure."

Within the second kind of social pressure (the "unequal" condition), one of the children wore tinted spectacles as before, but this time the partner's spectacles had clear lenses. In this way the phenomenist answer (e.g., "red") would be directly contradicted by the realist answer (i.e., "white") from the child with the nonillusory view. Would the child with the illusory view maintain her answer under these conditions? The situation in the other three illusions was exactly the same: Either each child had an equally illusory but conflicting view, or one child had an illusory view and the partner had a nonillusory view. The size illusion involved magnification, the length illusion involved the horizontal–vertical illusion, and the brightness illusion employed a black–white contrast effect (see Figure 19.1).

All the dyads experienced all four illusions, but each dyad only experienced one kind of social pressure. The number of phenomenist answers that were agreed could then be compared with those produced in three kinds of solo "control" condition: (a) Each child viewed the materials from one illusory perspective, (b) each child viewed the materials from two illusory perspectives, (c) each child viewed the materials from one illusory perspective and from a nonillusory perspective.

The results can be very easily reported: There was no effect of testing condition whatsoever. In the five conditions (two experimental, three control), around 60% of the answers were phenomenist at age $4\frac{1}{2}–5\frac{1}{2}$, around 40% at age $5\frac{1}{2}–6\frac{1}{2}$, and around 25% at age $6\frac{1}{2}–7\frac{1}{2}$. Phenomenist readings of neutral questions about the properties of objects are, therefore, robust – being undiminished by social pressure against them. Although negative findings must be interpreted with caution, the data do present a picture of a lingering but waning cognitive saliency of the phenomenal in the early school years. I interpret this as lack of reflective awareness of the visual field, as a symptom of the continuing difficulty with fulfilling the perceptual field condition for the mental versus nonmental division.

But, of course, we should not be patronizing about children's difficulties with this kind of reflection. If we had a perfect awareness of our visual fields, drawing and painting what we see would be a good deal easier than it is. One way, indeed, of regarding the history of the graphic arts is as the evolution of this awareness – as a symptom of the burgeoning self-consciousness of humankind.

APPARATUS (FOR 'EQUAL' CONDITION)

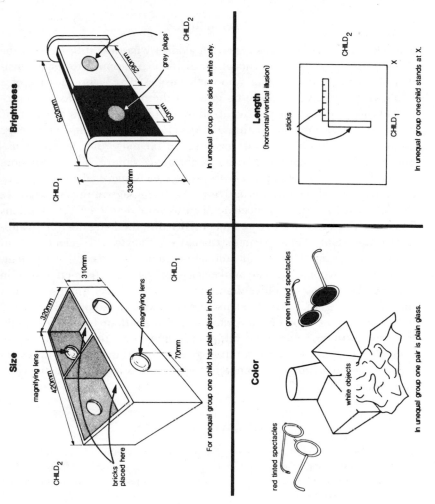

Size

CHILD₂

320mm

310mm

420mm

magnifying lens

magnifying lens

70mm

CHILD₁

bricks placed here

For unequal group one child has plain glass in both.

Brightness

620mm

CHILD₁

330mm

280mm

60mm

grey plugs

CHILD₂

In unequal group one side is white only.

Color

red tinted spectacles

green tinted spectacles

white objects

In unequal group one pair is plain glass.

Length
(horizontal/vertical illusion)

CHILD₂

sticks

X

CHILD₁

In unequal group one child stands at X.

Figure 19.1. Apparatus (for "equal" condition).

In conclusion

This chapter can be read as a caution against what might be dubbed the "magic age" approach to concept acquisition. As applied to the acquisition of mental concepts, this approach implies that before the age of 4 years, children have virtually no grasp of the mental as a distinct ontological category from the physical, and that after this age their grasp of the distinction is secure. Given this, the development of mental knowledge from 4 years to adulthood is regarded as no more than a rather uninteresting progression away from performance failure. The distinction, having been drawn, is applied with progressively more efficiency.

I have argued, as an alternative to the magic-age approach, that we should regard mental–physical dualism as implying a set of conditions for objective experience and judgment. Because these are abstract conditions rather than a set of particular behaviors, they can be seen to spread across many areas of mental life and across many periods of development. From this viewpoint, we can make sense of the very distinctive way in which children who are older than 4 years of age answer questions about thoughts (intensional versus extensional contexts) and about things (their nature as opposed to their appearance). Rather than trying to explain away the distinctive nature of children's judgments as the result of "social context" or "performance limitations," it is sometimes fruitful to regard them as symptoms of an incomplete cognitive division between thoughts and things.

ACKNOWLEDGMENTS

The research described here was carried out with the assistance of a grant from the Economic and Social Research Council (U.K.). I am very grateful to Paul Harris, David Olson, and Harriet Haworth for their useful comments on earlier drafts of this chapter.

REFERENCES

Abbeduto, L., & Rosenberg, S. (1985). Children's knowledge of the presuppositions of *know* and other cognitive verbs. *Journal of Child Language*, *12*, 621–641.

Baldwin, J. M. (1906). *Thought and things* (Vol. 1). London: Swann & Sonnenschein.

Braine, M. D. S., & Shanks, B. L. (1965). The conservation of shape property and a proposal about the origin of conservation. *Canadian Journal of Psychology*, *19*, 197–207.

Flavell, J. H., Flavell, E. R., & Green, F. L. (1983). Development of the appearance–reality distinction. *Cognitive Psychology*, *15*, 197–207.

Gibson, E. J., & Spelke, E. S. (1983). The development of perception. In P. Mussen (Ed.), *Handbook of child psychology* (Vol. 3). Vol. Ed.: J. H. Flavell & E. M. Markman. New York: John Wiley.

Gibson, J. J. (1950). *The perception of the visual world.* Boston: Houghton Mifflin.

Gibson, J. J. (1979). *The ecological approach to visual perception.* Boston: Houghton Mifflin.

Gnepp, J., McKee, E., & Domanic, J. A. (1987). Children's use of situational information to infer emotion: Understanding emotionally equivocal situations. *Developmental Psychology, 23,* 114–123.

Harris, P. L. (1974). Perseveration at a visibly empty space by young infants. *Journal of Experimental Child Psychology, 18,* 535–542.

Harris, P. L., Donnelly, K., Guz, G. R., & Pitt-Watson, R. (1986). Children's understanding of the distinction between real and apparent emotion. *Child Development, 57,* 895–909.

Harris, P. L., Olthof, T., & Terwogt, M. M. (1981). Children's knowledge of emotion. *Journal of Child Psychology and Psychiatry, 22,* 247–261.

Johnson, C. N., & Maratsos, M. P. (1977). The early comprehension of mental verbs: Think and know. *Child Development, 48,* 1743–1747.

Körner, S. (1955). *Kant.* Harmondsworth: Penguin.

Lockman, J. J., & Ashmead, D. H. (1983). Asynchronies in the development of manual behavior. In L. P. Lipsitt & C. K. Rovee-Coller (Eds.), *Advances in infancy research* (Vol. 2). New York: Ablex.

McGarrigle, J., & Donaldson, M. (1974). Conservation accidents. *Cognition, 3,* 341–350.

Nisbett, R. E., & Ross, L. (1980). *Human inference: Strategies and shortcomings of social judgment.* Englewood Cliffs, NJ: Prentice-Hall.

Russell, J. (1978). *The acquisition of knowledge.* London: Macmillan.

Russell, J. (1984a). *Explaining mental life: Some philosophical issues in psychology.* London: Macmillan.

Russell, J. (1984b). The subject–object division in language acquisition and ego development. *New Ideas in Psychology, 2,* 57–74.

Russell, J. (1984c). Should I believe you or what you say? Children's belief of children's statements. *Developmental Psychology, 20,* 64–82.

Russell, J. (1987a). "Can we say . . .?" Children's understanding of intensionality. *Cognition, 25,* 289–308.

Russell, J. (1987b). Reasons for believing that there is perceptual development in childhood. In J. Russell (Ed.), *Philosophical perspectives on developmental psychology.* Oxford: Blackwell Publisher.

Russell, J., & Haworth, H. M. (1987a). *The influence of propositional attitude verbs on children's belief of statements.* Manuscript submitted for publication.

Russell, J., & Haworth, H. M. (1987b). *The role of cognitive salience in children's misreadings of intensional and extensional contexts of utterance.* Manuscript submitted for publication.

Russell, J., & Haworth, H. M. (1988). Appearance versus reality in dyadic interaction: Evidence for a lingering phenomenism. *International Journal of Behavioral Development, 11,* 213–227.

Scoville, R. P., & Gordon, A. M. (1980). Children's understanding of factive presuppositions: An experiment and a review. *Journal of Child Language*, 7, 381–399.

Vygotsky, L. S., (1976). Play and its role in the mental development of the child. In J. S. Bruner, A. Jolly, & K. Sylva (Eds.), *Play: Its role in development and evolution*. Harmondsworth: Penguin. (Originally published in Russian, 1933).

20

Doubt and developing theories of mind

MICHAEL CHANDLER

The term *doubt* as it appears in the title to this chapter has two referents. The first concerns the role that uncertainty will be said to play in the formation of children's developing theories of mind. The second has to do with certain doubts of my own as to what is already known with certainty about this developmental process. Into this latter category go a string of doubts that emerged out of my ongoing efforts to document certain late-arriving cognitive competencies characteristic of adolescent youth caught up in the struggle to come to intellectual terms with the constructivistic or interpretive nature of the knowing enterprise. What became evident through the discussions and exchanges of papers out of which this volume grew is that, if certain of the accounts of much younger children's more fledgling theories of mind advanced by other contributors are interpretively correct, then there is little room and less need to pursue my original concerns, since a mature understanding of the constructivistic character of knowledge is already comfortably in place half a lifetime before adolescence ever gets under way.

Such claims, if true, carry the same significance for my own research program as did the debunking of phlogiston or the philosophers' stone for earlier investigators, off on their own fool's errand. Naturally, these prospects have prompted me to take a hard look at the evidence and argumentation put forward in support of the notion that the theories of mind circulating among typical 3- to 6-year-olds are actually equivalent in form, if not in content, to those characteristic of the average adult. What occupies the pages that follow includes, then, a series of reasons for doubting the authenticity of all claims to the effect that such young children are quick to imitate the theories of mind exercised by their elders. In making these points, I begin by discussing certain assumptions common to all those who attribute some kind of theory of mind to developing children, and then quickly go on to suggest why, despite what might otherwise appear to be a withholding attitude, I believe available evidence to support the view that young persons commonly acquire such theories well before they are usually thought to do so. Next, I will undertake to demonstrate that despite the importance of these initial accomplishments, preschoolers still do not demonstrate anything that can qualify as a constructive or interpretive theory of mind, an accomplishment that I will go on to argue is not fully in place until one's teenage years.

I. What is a theory of mind?

To have a theory of mind is to hold to a special sort of explanatory framework that interprets intentional behaviors as a partial consequence of the particular beliefs subscribed to by those whose actions are in question. Naturally, not everyone holds to this view. Some (young children and "lower" animals, for example) may harbor no explanatory systems of any sort, and others (usually social scientists of a certain behavioral bent), while holding to some explanatory framework, work hard to purge their thinking of anything that so clearly smacks of the mentalistic. Still, it is probably fair to say that theories of mind do form an integral part of the usual folk psychology according to which most persons assume that they and others govern their affairs and, consequently, that knowing who does and who does not subscribe to such views is a matter of practical as well as scientific importance. This chapter is about how such determinations are made.

Although there is no perfect consensus concerning how one might best sort out believers from disbelievers, any scheme for determining precisely who does and who does not subscribe to a theory of mind would, at a minimum, need to draw a careful distinction between the simple having of beliefs and the more complex matter of appreciating *that* such beliefs are actually had. Otherwise put, one would need to determine ways of separating the simple having of a representation of some actual state of the world and the weightier matter of representing such representations – of distinguishing first-order beliefs from higher-order beliefs about beliefs. What is one to say, for example, about the family dog that barks in a bid to be let outside, or the infant that holds up its arms in a way that tells us that it wants to be picked up? Are these simply expressions of first-order beliefs in action (i.e., does the dog merely "believe" that barking opens doors, and does the child simply think that giving the "high" sign will automatically result in its being picked up?), or are they rather something more on the order of "speech acts" (Searle, 1983), that can only be understood to work because the child and the dog both *believe* that their gestures are also *believed* by others to convey an agreed-upon meaning? Again, do young children or members of other species simply hold to beliefs or, rather, do they actually impute intentional states to self and others, and employ such beliefs about beliefs in the making of behavioral predictions (Premack & Woodrull, 1978)? Do they, in short, hold to some theory of mind?

Along with the other contributors to this volume, I will take it as a primitive assumption that, insofar as adult human beings are concerned, it is reasonable if not obligatory to imagine that they possess something as rich and powerful as a theory of mind, and that it is in terms of such theories that they understand and anticipate their own and others' behavior. This much agreement does not, however, begin to settle all of the remaining controversies concerning precisely when or how such accomplishments are imagined to come about; most of which reduce to the related questions of: (1) when, in the course of their development, do children first acquire anything that might qualify as a theory of mind; (2) assuming that mature theories of mind do not arrive in the world full-blown, how soon after their first appearance do such theories begin to resemble those held by adults; and (3) how many meaningfully different interim theories of mind separate those initial and final accomplishments? To anticipate my own answers to these questions, the conclusions I mean to defend are that children: (1) begin to acquire theories of mind a good deal sooner than is commonly imagined; (2) arrive at mature theories of mind at a considerably later point in development than is usually thought; and (3) evidence more intervening stages in this process than are generally supposed.

Whatever else might be said about them, it should be clear from the contrastive manner in which these claims are laid that they are intended to distance themselves from another more ecumenical view according to which the task of acquiring a theory of mind is said to begin later, to end sooner, and to be altogether less differentiated than I believe is warranted by the available evidence. According to this emerging, but I believe premature, consensus, most of the important progress that children are understood to make in approximating a mature theory of mind is assumed to both begin and end during the preschool and very early school-age years. The arguments to be developed in the following sections end up giving considerably less credit to such 4- to 6-year-olds and a good deal more to both still younger and older children. In order to see why such a redistribution of resources might be called for, some clearer statement of what I am describing as the consensus view is required.

The consensus view

The ecumenical view against which I wish to speak, like consensus claims more generally, is not advocated in all of its parts by any single investigator but must be patched together instead from the work of several different research groups that otherwise disagree about many of the particulars of their shared vision. Writ large, this mosaic account holds out that despite spontaneous references to and reliance on their own and others' beliefs, 2- and 3-year-olds actually lack any demonstrable theory of mind because they are thought to be incapable of representing the *differences* that divide their own or others' first-order beliefs. Despite the importance attached to this presumed shortfall, it is nevertheless seen to be quickly remedied, and by 3½ or 4 years of age the average child is held capable of entertaining contrastive notions of truth in such a way that one representation of reality can be judged demonstrably false relative to another. Children gifted with this new capacity are said to properly distinguish "seeing from believing" (Wellman, 1985), or "appearance from reality" (Flavell, Flavell, & Green, 1983), and, as a consequence, are said to possess not only *some* theory of mind but, more importantly, a constructivistic theory of mind. Although judged to be less sophisticated than the theories to which they will eventually come, the preliminary epistemic views of such preschoolers nevertheless are understood to be similar in *kind* to those counterpart theories held by their elders (Wellman, Chapter 4). Whenever further developments are envisioned (e.g., Feldman, Chapter 7; Perner, Chapter 14; Wellman, Chapter 4), such subsequent movements toward a more mature theory of mind are typically seen to involve a sequence of logical recursions (Broughton, 1981), in which second- or higher-order beliefs simply embed first-order beliefs, in a way similar to the serial stacking of subroutines within a computer program. Beyond such recursive moves, all other signs of progress toward a more fully adult theory of mind are read simply as evidence for a growth in "fluency" or "proficiency" and are taken as expressive of differences of the sort that typically divide "novices" from "experts" (Wellman, Chapter 4).

In the place of this consensus view, I want to promote an account of the process by means of which children come to employ a mature theory of mind that is a considerably less homogeneous and linear, and substantially more protracted and differentiated. In particular, I will begin by suggesting that the ability to explicitly register certain beliefs as false is less of a watershed in the acquisition of a theory of mind than it is often held out to be, and that the actual reasons for holding children to such a contrastive standard are more methodologic than substantive, primarily reflecting a wish to locate unimpeachable forms of evidence for competencies that are very likely already in place. Second, I will undertake to demonstrate that the cognitive competencies reflected in the mastery of various false belief and reality–appearance tasks are often considerably less complex than is generally supposed, and do not, as is generally maintained, signal the achievement of a constructivistic theory of mind. Finally, I will attempt to show that even the ability to recursively embed one intentional state within another still falls importantly short of, and fails to register, those critical differences that actually divide childish theories of mind from those more frankly constructivistic views commonly employed by adults. In what follows, I will take up these matters in turn, beginning with the front-end issue of *when* children first provide evidence of possessing an operative theory of mind.

II. When do "theories of mind" first come into evidence?

All answers to the question of when in the course of their development children first come into possession of anything that might resemble a theory of mind naturally depend both on exactly what having such a theory is understood to mean, and on what one is willing to take as evidence for the presence or absence of such a theory. Although both of these matters remain far from settled, there is at least a measure of indirect agreement among contributors to this literature as to what a theory of mind is *not*. Clearly, what is envisioned by those wishing to attribute theories of mind to young children are not theories of the formal sort that commonly fill up the pages of psychological texts. Because babes-in-arms, chimpanzees, and even rats are said by some to possess such theories, it is obvious that something much less wordy and explicit is had in mind. What is meant appears instead to be rather something more in the nature of a hypothetical construct or intervening variable, the existence of which needs to be inferred from the fact that the actual behavior of the individuals in question would be rendered incomprehensible without the assumption that they function with reference to some such theory. In this sense, explicit avowals of mentalistic beliefs are not required, and one can be accorded a theory of mind without having to claim as much for oneself. Instead, all that is necessary is that being said to have such a theory should provide a more parsimonious explanation of one's actions than do competing accounts that shy away from such mentalistic attributions. By this definition, then, lack of linguistic competence is no impediment to one's candidacy for possessing a theory of mind, and infant children and members of other species cannot be disqualified from having such theories solely on the grounds that they can't talk (Searle, 1983).

What are less generally agreed upon by those who have contributed to this literature are the sorts of behaviors that do need to be in place before one is justified in postulating such mentalistic theories. To appreciate why this ambiguous matter of standards remains as unsettled as it is, it will prove useful to begin by first standing back far enough to see the problem in some historical perspective.

As is commonly known, turn-of-the-century psychology grew out of an older philosophic tradition dominated by concerns over matters having to do with the status of beliefs, intentions, and desires. What eventually saved first comparative and then general psychology from continued domination by this earlier philosophic tradition was their decision to forego such mentalistic concerns in favor of something like Morgan's canon (Pylyshyn, 1978), which proscribes against all use of such mentalistic terms, unless doing otherwise is proven absolutely necessary. On these grounds, casual anthropomorphic assumptions about the mental states of nonhuman species were effectively ruled out of court and other more naturalistic accounts were substituted in their place. By extension, the same logic was also broadly applied by students of human psychology, who came to judge all professional lapses into such folk-psychological concepts as both imprudent and detrimental to the advance of serious scientific understanding. The point in mentioning all of this is to draw attention to the fact that there are honorable historical reasons for viewing any proposal to reintroduce such mental state terms into serious psychological discourse with more than a little suspicion. This has been especially the case among comparative psychologists, who have strong reasons for questioning whether any useful purpose can ever be served by representing other species as having theories of mind. Human psychology, however, has recently taken a rather different turn, and, with the advent of the modern cognitive revolution, it has once again become fashionable to think of the actions of adult human beings as being guided by systems of personal beliefs.

Out of this mixed heritage, two distinct but interacting lines of cognitive research have recently emerged. The first of these has been the responsibility of certain comparative psychologists (e.g., Premack & Woodruff, 1978) who, against strong opposition, have taken up the unpopular task of persuading their colleagues of the necessity of ascribing theories of mind to "lower" animals. The second has been the work of groups of developmental psychologists who have sought to provide answers to the more open question of *when*, in the usual ontogenetic course, the cautious withholding of mental state attributions to developing children is no longer defensible. Although the focus of the present chapter clearly falls on the second rather than the first of these matters, the two issues are sufficiently overlapping that it has often been assumed that the same evidentiary standards appropriate to the settling of one of these questions are equally applicable to efforts to answer the other. Contrary to such claims, it will be argued in the paragraphs that follow that the standard of proof appropriate to deciding the question of *whether* other species *ever* act in ways that require they be accorded something like a theory of mind are in fact poorly suited to the task of settling the quite different question of *when* the actions of children first require such an interpretation. On these and other grounds it will be suggested that the numerous claims to the effect that children younger than roughly 4 years of age lack theories of mind actually seriously underestimate the competence of still younger children, and do so as a partial function of the reliance of such claimants on measurement strategies and standards of proof better suited to the answering of other questions.

To warrant the claim that measurement strategies and evidencing standards originally conceived for the purpose of settling the either/or concerns of comparative psychologists are poorly suited to the purpose of determining when children first acquire theories of mind, it will prove useful to begin by first referring to the seminal paper by Premack and Woodruff (1978), in which these authors put forward evidence in support of their claim that the behavior of chimpanzees is uninterpretable unless it is supposed that chimpanzees have something like a theory of mind. Well aware of traditional sentiments supporting the notion that naturalistic accounts of animal behavior should never be abandoned in favor of the easier road of anthropomorphism (Pylyshyn, 1978), these authors nevertheless were persuaded by their own data that chimpanzees do, in fact, impute nonobservable mental states to self and others, and contrastively employ such mentalistic inferences in making behavioral predictions. Whether Premack and Woodruff successfully demonstrated their point, and consequently whether chimpanzees deserve to be categorized as having something one might loosely call a theory of mind, is an unsettled but much debated issue (e.g., Churchland & Churchland, 1978; Griffin, 1978) that is of only marginal relevance to the questions being pursued here. What are of more direct concern are the various methodologic considerations that their attempts to answer this either/or question brought to the surface.

Perhaps the clearest statement of the methodologic concerns identified by Premack and Woodruff was put forward in a commentary on this work by Dennett (1978), who argued that the minimally complex experimental paradigm necessary to successfully impute a theory of mind would need to demonstrate that: (1) C believes that E believes that p; (2) C believes that E desires that q; and (3) that C infers from his or her belief in (1) and (2) that E will do x. At least in the case of species that lack the capacity to clearly stipulate to (3), Dennett goes on to argue that it then becomes necessary to arrange things experimentally in such a way that: (4) C does y because; (5) C believes that if E does x, then unless C does y, C won't get something C wants or will get something C wants to avoid. All of this may sound unnecessarily elaborate, but the spirit of Dennett's list of minimal requirements is simply that (1) one should refrain from attributing a theory of mind to any organism whose own way of going about things can be just as easily understood without such mentalistic assumptions; and (2) that any candidate who is suspected of having such a theory of mind but cannot openly persuade us of this fact in his or her own words, must be set some behavioral task that makes the having or not having of such a theory

explicit. It is somewhat beside the present point that Dennett was not satisfied that Premack and Woodruff's research adequately met these minimal
demands. What is relevant is that others have adopted these standards as
constituting something of a "litmus test" (Wellman, Chapter 4) for the
existence of any theory of mind, and have employed some variation on
Dennett's minimally complex paradigm in their own efforts to settle the
rather different question of *when* such mentalistic theories are first
required to describe adequately the behaviors of growing children.

One further methodologic point that Premack and Woodruff's research
succeeded in burning into the conscience of subsequent contributors to
this field is that it might still prove premature to conclude that C actually
believes that E believes that p, if it should happen that p is coincidentally
true, or at least is assumed to be true by C. To see why this might be so, it
will be useful to consider in some detail an experimental paradigm introduced by Wimmer and Perner (1983), and intended by them as a further
guard against the possibility of mistakenly reading theories of mind into
the responses of children who have not as yet acquired them. Consider an
experimental setup involving a doll figure named Maxi, a chocolate bar,
two cabinets (A and B), and a script that has the chocolate originally
located in cabinet A but subsequently moved to cabinet B when Maxi is
out of the room and is in no position to appreciate this fact. I, as subject,
am privy to all of these details and am presumably in possession of the
correct first-order belief that the chocolate is now in cabinet B. Suppose,
now, as is not in fact the case in Wimmer and Perner's actual procedure,
that, like myself, Maxi has actually remained in the room and, like me,
has every reason also to know the chocolate is now in cabinet B.
Under these hypothetical circumstances, I am now asked to report, not on
what I believe to be the case, but rather on what I believe that Maxi believes about the location of the chocolate. Now it is a crucial point of distinction between my own first-order beliefs about actual states of affairs in
the world (in this case, where the chocolate is located) and my second-
order beliefs about Maxi's beliefs, that the accuracy or conditions of satisfaction for my beliefs regarding Maxi have only to do with whether or not
I am correct in figuring out what sorts of beliefs might be swimming
around in his head, and have absolutely nothing to do with the actual
location of the chocolate. That is, if Maxi was seriously mistaken regarding the current whereabouts of the chocolate, I would still be correct in
my second-order belief *about* him so long as I correctly knew in what sense
he was mistaken. Suppose further, then, under these circumstances, where
Maxi and I know the same thing, that I am asked, "Where does Maxi
think the chocolate is located?" and I respond by pointing to cabinet B.
Since under this experimental arrangement the same response that correctly expresses my own convictions about the true location of the choc-

olate also correctly expresses what is true about Maxi's beliefs, it follows that the diagnostic significance of my having pointed as I did is indeterminate because there is no way of knowing in whose behalf I am speaking. It would be charitable to conclude that an adult such as myself is capable of hearing the difference between questions that inquire about what I believe and what I believe Maxi believes, and you might well take my correct response as real but imperfect evidence that I do, in fact, have and am exercising a theory of mind. If, however, one is dealing with a young child, who it might be reasonable to suppose may not as yet be capable of entertaining second-order beliefs about beliefs, then continued uncertainty is warranted and the jury would need to remain out.

The obvious solution to this problem, which Wimmer and Perner actually incorporated into their original experimental design, is to change the location of the chocolate when Maxi isn't looking and thereby guarantee that the truth conditions for my own first-order beliefs and my second-order beliefs concerning Maxi's beliefs are actually different, thereby allowing me to point correctly to cabinet B in my own behalf and to the original cabinet A when giving "voice" to what I take to be true of Maxi. The procedural advantages of the second of these two experimental setups are obvious, and on this logic numerous investigators before (e.g., Chandler & Greenspan, 1974; Premack & Woodruff, 1978) and after have taken the higher road of questioning the evidentiary status of all claims about the mental lives of others that are coincidentally true about the beliefs of those persons laying such claims. On the basis of all that has just been said, it follows that even Dennett's "minimally complex experimental paradigm" is not sufficiently complicated by half, and that one should avoid ascribing theories of mind not only to those who systematically fail to use beliefs about the beliefs of others, but also to those who cannot employ another mistaken person's wrong beliefs as subgoals in their own planning strategies.

As if the foregoing were not already complicated enough to discourage anyone from ever attributing a theory of mind to others, still further interpretive snares await those who refuse to be sufficiently "naturalistic" in their claims. In addition, there appears to be afoot in human affairs what C. F. Lewis refers to as "the principle of charity," which enjoins us all to ascribe to others those beliefs that we would have in similar circumstances (Loar, 1981). On these grounds, which Premack and Woodruff (1978) alternatively refer to as the "empathy alternative," a given class of individuals might be characterologically incapable of entertaining anything like a theory of mind about others and yet still behave as though they did. At least this would be true in any context where the prospective beliefs of a subject and some protagonist could be assumed to be reasonably overlapping. Note that under this possibility, simply producing an experimental arrangement that guaranteed some separation between information *currently* available to a subject and some protagonist is not always enough to guarantee that one's own prior beliefs are not projected onto the other.

The upshot of all of these methodologic considerations is not that one can never demonstrate that certain persons do possess theories of mind, but rather that doing so with absolute certainty is devilishly difficult. It is unarguably the case, for example, that the individual who clearly and definitely expresses the belief that "Maxi believes that the chocolate is in cabinet A" when the chocolate is actually known by the respondent to be elsewhere, can be safely credited with having something like a theory of mind. It is just as clear, however, that children who make precisely the same claim, but only under the special condition that the candy is in fact exactly where Maxi should reasonably expect it to be, do not thereby automatically forfeit all claims to having a theory of mind. All kinds of competing interpretations are available that might lead one to expect that a child's first fledgling attempts at putting a theory of mind into practice might crumble when faced with the prospect of shifting truth conditions, without thereby justifying the decision to deny such an individual any and all claims to possessing any such theory. Although it continues to be true, then, that from a diagnostic point of view, any attribution of a false belief to others constitutes a more unimpeachable form of evidence in favor of that individual's having an operative theory of mind than does a similar attribution based on references to beliefs that are coincidentally true, the second is not invalid simply because it is more equivocal. If the goal one sets for oneself is only to avoid being duped into mistakenly attributing competencies to organisms that don't deserve as much (i.e., to avoid a type I error), then it is clear enough how one should proceed. It is equally clear, however, that certainty is a zero-sum game and that the strategy of escalating one's standards of proof in the hope of never being proven wrong is always at the expense of overlooking real competencies that remain unavoidably subject to some extravagant or hyperbolic brand of doubt.

In view of these competing prospects, it can be argued that comparative and developmental psychologists might reasonably elect to hold themselves to different standards on this matter. Because much of the real progress made in the study of other species has come about through a prudent disdain for all mentalistic concepts, there is an understandable reluctance on the part of such investigators to accept anything but the most demanding of evidentiary standards before awarding theories of mind to their animal subjects. A different posture would seem to suggest itself, however, to developmentalists who never seriously doubt that their subjects will all eventually come to something that might be called a theory of mind. I am not suggesting by this that bad evidence should be mistaken for good, but only that a demand for foolproof and incontrovertible answers that are totally resistant to all forms of deflationary redescription very likely represents a tougher-minded attitude than the situation warrants. Mistakes are to be had on both sides and the trick is not simply to find ways of avoiding only type 1 error, but somehow to appreciate the costs of both type 1 and type 2 errors and to set standards of proof that are respectful of both of these prospects.

By my own way of reckoning, the assumption that children a good deal younger than 4 years of age do, in fact, already possess a theory of mind is more in the running for truth than is the contrary and more incontrovertible conclusion that they are not. There is, for example, a great deal of evidence (Bretherton & Beeghly, 1982; Hood & Bloom, 1979; Johnson & Maratsos, 1977; Johnson & Wellman, 1980; Olson, Chapter 21, etc.) to suggest that children as young as 2½ or 3 years of age often employ a variety of mental state verbs, and do so in such ways as to convey their appreciation of various mental attitudes, stances, and epistemic states. It could be the case, of course, that in doing this they never really mean to comment on or "mention" the ways in which such intentional states differ from their own, but I personally find that extreme prospect rather far-fetched. Certainly there are those (e.g., Grice, 1957; Levinson, 1983; Searle, 1983) who would argue that intentional communication of any sort necessarily presupposes some explicit and definite representations of the representations of others.

Outside the restricted context of language usage, children as young as 2 also have been shown to expend considerable energy pointing out things that appear to have escaped the attention of others (Flavell, Flavell, Green, & Wilcox, 1980), presumably on the mentalistic assumption that the beliefs of others are shy of the particular bits of information one struggles to bring to their attention. Once again, some (e.g., Wimmer & Perner, 1983) would argue that any awareness that others simply lack certain informational details is importantly short of actually ascribing definite beliefs to them. As I will attempt to show in the following section, however, children as old as 5 or 6 regularly fail to do more with their theories of mind than note that some persons are less well informed than others, without consequently being held to lack the capacity to form beliefs about beliefs.

Comparable evidence could also be cited from other quarters to suggest that 2- and 3-year-olds also maintain beliefs about desires and other comparable intentional states. Only someone tightly in the grip of a philosophical theory could fail, for example, to imagine that 2-year-olds ("terrible 2"-year-olds), locked as they often are in battles of will over the indignities of being toilet-trained or sent off early to bed, are somehow incapable of representing the difference between their own desires and those of their parents. Nor could one not so indisposed fail to miss the point that games of pretense are constituted upon the ability to juggle simultaneously two

alternative representations of the world (Leslie, Chapter 2), or overlook the fact that the delaying tactics in which 3-year-olds are so expert
could hardly be accomplished without some clear grasp on the strategic
advantages of instilling false beliefs in others.

The point I would like to win by all of this is not that there exists proof
positive that such toddlers necessarily have operative theories of mind. I
mean only to imply that there is a strong enough possibility that they do,
to suggest that the reach of all of those who think otherwise may have ex-
ceeded their grasp. To the extent that such arguments are persuasive, and
you are prepared to entertain the notion that fledgling theories of mind
may be already in place well before the fourth year of life, then I will have
adequately prepared the way for the following section, in which I hope to
discount the common claim that the cognitive accomplishments of the
typical 4- to 6-year-old amount to the acquisition of a truly constructivistic
theory of mind.

III. Are all true theories of mind constructivistic theories of mind?

If, as the preceding section alleges, children much younger than $3\frac{1}{2}$ or 4
do, in fact, regularly behave in ways that warrant their being said to have
some prototheory of mind, and if, as a considerable body of carefully assembled evidence would suggest, such young persons cannot be relied
upon to pass standardized false belief measures, then it follows either: (1)
that, as implied earlier, such assessment strategies represent an unnecessarily cumbersome and demanding index of abilities that are already in
place; or (2) that at the developmental juncture in question, $3\frac{1}{2}$- or 4-
year-olds do acquire some new competency that goes beyond that required
for the initial framing of a theory of mind. Efforts to sort out this convoluted
matter, and to provide grounds for choosing between these alternatives
will, it is proposed, carry us some distance toward an answer to the second
of the orienting questions around which this chapter is organized: "How
soon after they first give evidence of having *some* theory of mind do the
theories of such children begin to take on the characters of those employed
by the average adult?"

The place to begin searching for an answer to this question would seem
to be with as clear an account as possible of precisely what it is that those
who promote the use of various false belief measures claim is demonstrated
whenever a child proves capable of definitely representing the falseness
relation that obtains between correct and incorrect beliefs. According to
Wimmer and Perner, who have done the most to bring these matters to
attention, children who clearly evidence an appreciation of the fact that
other persons sometimes subscribe to mistaken ideas, and can go on to

plan their own future actions relative to such false beliefs, unambiguously demonstrate by doing this that they hold to interpretive theories of mind – theories whose primary feature is that they allow those who hold to them to recognize that different people may attach conflicting truth values to one and the same proposition and, consequently, apprehend the very same content in different ways (Wimmer & Perner, 1983). Similarly, Flavell (Chapter 13), who reads the evidence in much the same way, and who consequently goes on to interpret children's successful handling of the Wimmer–Perner paradigm as an expression of what he describes as a "Level 2" cognitive accomplishment, also stresses that because such children can understand that others may construe the very same content in different or even contradictory-seeming ways, they must also implicitly conceive of the mind as an active processor or interpreter of reality.

Both Wimmer and Perner (1983) and Flavell (Chapter 13) go on to set this new accomplishment sharply apart from the presumptively earlier-arriving and simpler ability merely to represent another person's ignorance or lack of knowledge. For Flavell, this difference marks his well-publicized distinction between knowing that two persons may be in perceptual or intellectual contact with different informative content (Level 1), and knowing that they may *differently* construe the same facts (Level 2). Of greater significance for present purposes is that Wimmer and Perner see the simpler ability merely to represent another person's lack of knowledge as no evidence at all in favor of the proposition that one might have a theory of mind. Their claim is based on the argument that recognizing that someone else may be ignorant of facts known to oneself requires no sort of definite representation of a particular proposition, and by extension, no representation of the falseness relation between two contrastive propositions. It is in this sense, and on precisely these grounds, that they wish to claim that children younger than approximately 3½ or 4 lack theories of mind altogether.

The reason these claims appear not to be true, despite their interest value and the large amount of data offered in their support, and consequently the reason that 4-year-olds are not literally situated at the cusp of different possible interpretive worlds (Perner, Chapter 8) is that, contrary to what is generally supposed, the false belief tasks do not actually require subjects to appreciate that one and the same stimulus event can be construed as having more than a single meaning. Explaining why this might be so, and if it is, why this point should have otherwise escaped general notice, will require a fine-grained look at the actual task demand of the procedure employed by Wimmer and Perner.

To set the required contrast, it will be useful to recall that children as young as 2 years have regularly demonstrated their appreciation of the fact that other persons do not have eyes in the back of their heads (Flavell,

Flavell, Green, & Wilcox, 1980), and that those who are differently situated are understood to come away from what are ostensibly the "same" situations with quite different amounts of information (Flavell, Everett, Croft, & Flavell, 1981; Flavell, Shipstead, & Croft, 1978; Lempers, Flavell, & Flavell, 1977; Masangkay et al., 1974). Although the focus of attention in these earlier studies was on the threshold ability of 2- to 4-year-olds to recognize the epistemic relevance of accessing or not accessing particular factual details, such differences freely translate into the distinction between knowing and not knowing (Hogrefe, Wimmer, & Perner, 1986), and clearly suggest that by this early age children already have some grasp on the role that ignorance plays in the framing of beliefs. It is also noteworthy that in these several research demonstrations, the procedural route by means of which certain onlookers were gerrymandered into a position of relative ignorance was by guaranteeing that they were poorly placed to access the full informational payload automatically available to others better situated than themselves. Ignorance, then, under these experimental circumstances, was always an informational shutout, brought on by the bad fortune of being in the wrong place, even if at the right time.

In clear contrast to all of this experimental concern with spatial details, the typical paradigm for marking the onset of the ability to apprehend false beliefs has adopted a different and more narrative format, according to which persons who are continuously present throughout the full course of some temporally unfolding event are consequently placed in a privileged position relative to others who happen to be offstage at a moment critical to getting the full drift of what has transpired. In the Wimmer and Perner (1983) saga of the vanishing chocolate, for example, both Maxi and the subject are in a position to see the candy initially hidden in cabinet A, but only the subject is privy to the fact that in Maxi's absence the chocolate has ended up in a different location entirely. While I do not mean to minimize this difference, and will return to it in a later attempt to explain the difficulty most 2- and 3-year-olds have with such tasks, I do mean it to be obvious that these false belief measures, and the various other procedures meant to tap children's abilities to apprehend the distinction between seeing and not seeing, all share in the common feature of somehow engineering events in such a way that one person is better situated to receive all of the relevant information than is another who has the bad fortune to end up either in the wrong place or the right place at the wrong time. If, as I want to maintain, the only telling difference that divides these two sorts of measures has to do with whether they manipulate either *space* or *time* as a means of guaranteeing that some persons are better informed than others, then it should follow that the basic cognitive abilities necessary to master one of these tasks are no different from those required for success with the other. All other things then being equal, both should be passed at roughly the same chronological age and the average 2- to 3-year-old who clearly already appreciates that persons who are located in different places often end up being differently informed should also be able to master Wimmer and Perner's false belief task. Although the data say otherwise, unless other substantive differences between these two procedures can be brought to light, the safest conclusion is that there must be technical problems with such false belief tasks that make them difficult for what amount to uninteresting reasons. Candidate possibilities here include the fact that assessment procedures that require subjects to recover information spread out along some narrative dimension succeed in being difficult primarily by confusing young children, who are not otherwise noted for their ability to order and integrate details that crop up in different time frames (Feldman, Chapter 7).

Although not in response to the preceding concerns, Wimmer and Perner (1983) do attempt to distinguish further between measures sensitive to the possibility of false beliefs, and what might generally be called tests of privileged information, by arguing that situations that simply require the representation of another person's lack of knowledge do not require, as do their own measures, a definite representation of particular contrary-to-fact propositions. Despite such claims, it fails to be clear what sorts of knowledge could be assumed to characterize persons who happen to be shy of certain perceptual details easily available to others, unless it is some sort of definite belief that happens to be false. If, for example, I see, but you are unaware of, the monster creeping up on your blind side, then it would seem a strange use of the word *belief* to say that I believe you are in imminent danger and you believe nothing at all. Rather, it would appear that you have the definite but seriously mistaken notion that all is well, whereas I know something that not only is entirely different but something that puts the lie to your own unwarranted and dangerous false belief.

To the extent, then, that privileged information and false belief tasks both measure the same thing (i.e., that persons spatially or temporally separated from the whole truth are all flying partially blind), and to the degree that both imply a contrastive notion of truth, it would seem to follow that if passing a test of false beliefs is sufficient reason to suppose that some theory of mind is comfortably in place, then the same should also be said about the results of simpler measures demonstrating that even 2-year-olds appreciate that more information is better than less.

Is the grasp of false belief the proper mark of a constructivistic theory of mind?

Standard false belief paradigms of the sort just reanalyzed are not promoted simply as procedures for marking the transition between having and not having *some* theory of mind. They are also put forward as providing evidence in support of the claim that those who master them also grasp the constructive character essential to all interpretive acts of meaning making. This strong claim is based on the assumption that any individual who appreciates that the very "same" stimulus event can lend itself to two radically different readings is forced, as a result, to acknowledge the interpretive or meaning-generating nature of the knowing enterprise. Such a conclusion might be seen to follow if anything about such false belief measures did, in fact, expose two different observers to the self-same stimulus event, but nothing of this sort actually occurs. Two subjects, one of whom possesses complete and the other, incomplete, access to all relevant details in a particular narrative sequence, cannot be easily understood to operate with the "same" full deck. It seems instead, that the subjects in such false belief procedures end up knowing some fully elaborated thing that is quite different from the fragments of information available to their protagonists, who fall into error precisely because less than the full story is available to them. This does not imply, as Flavell (Chapter 13) suggests, that mastering a false belief task demonstrates an appreciation of the fact that one and the same reality can have many interpretations. Instead, all that is shown with certainty is the more pedestrian ability to acknowledge that different realities support different interpretations. None of this is meant to challenge the essential correctness of Flavell's Level 1–Level 2 distinction (Chapter 13), which contrasts the ability of 2- and 3-year-olds to apprehend that persons who are differently informed are driven to different conclusions with the later-arriving ability to apprehend that the very same content can be interpreted in different ways. What is asserted, however, is that the essential ability required to master false belief tasks is a Level 1 rather than a Level 2 competence.

The relevance of this point is brought home further by a comparison between the findings generated by standard false belief measures and another class of assessment procedures, which have their roots in the study of emerging role-taking competencies. Such measures, originally introduced by Flavell, Botkin, Fry, Wright, and Jarvis (1968), typically take the form of requiring the description of some stimulus event, from the perspective both of a subject that has seen it in its entirety and of someone who has witnessed only an abridged version of that same event. Although superficially similar to standard measures of false belief, such procedures are critically different in that they focus attention on a particular fragment of the total stimulus situation that, although common to all onlookers, takes on different significance depending upon the context of interpretation in which it is located. In the original Flavell et al. (1968) study, for example, subjects were asked to describe the significance of a dog that they and some protagonist *both* saw sitting beneath an apple tree, but that only they had observed previously chasing the boy into the tree. Similarly, both Chandler (Chandler, 1972; Chandler & Greenspan, 1974; Chandler & Helm, 1984) and Taylor (Taylor, Chapter 11) required subjects to offer their own interpretations of a cartoon drawing and to also speculate about what someone else who had only a keyhole view on a small corner of this same drawing might take it to be. Again, these latter tasks also bear a family resemblance to the false belief measure of Wimmer and Perner, but, like those of Flavell and his colleagues, also differ in that they specifi-cally inquire into how the *shared* content of the displays might be viewed by persons who are broadly or narrowly informed.

What is of particular note, then, in any comparison between this second class of role-taking measures and standard measures of false belief, is that everyone who has applied them has found that children do not typically pass such role-taking tasks until they are 6 or 7 years of age. These results are in sharp contrast to findings generalized by false belief measures that are commonly mastered by children as young as 3½ or 4. The apparent reason for this is that such role-taking tasks, but not the superficially similar measures of false belief, appear to index the ability of subjects to appreci-ate that one and the same stimulus event can generate different interpreta-tions as a function of the different histories of the onlookers involved (Taylor, Chapter 11). On this basis, it is argued again that an initial appreciation of the interpretive or meaning-generating character of the knowing enterprise is not a feature of early preschool thought, but rather puts in its first appearance during the school-age years.

IV. Are all theories of mind constructivistic theories of mind?

If successful, the arguments developed in preceding sections have not only persuaded you that children as young as 2 or 3 already have *some* theory of mind (section II) but have also brought into question the widely shared assumption that the ability to master successfully the requirements of standard false-belief tasks somehow requires a new set of second- and higher-order abilities not already entailed by an appreciation that more information is better than less (section III). Instead, the foregoing inter-pretive summary suggests that early-school-age but not still younger chil-dren do, in fact, arrive at some qualitatively different understanding of the process of belief entitlement, and do come to recognize – in a way not pre-viously true of them – that different persons not only may know different things but sometimes also may know the same thing in different ways. Clearly the work of Flavell et al. (1968), Chandler (Chandler, 1972; Chandler & Boyes, 1982; Chandler & Greenspan, 1974; Chandler & Helm, 1984), and Taylor (Chapter 11) argues in support of this new tran-sition. Similarly, Wellman (Chapter 4), who previously held out that theories of mind typical of 3-year-olds are "fundamentally akin" to those of adults, now also suggests that the distinction between "seeing" and "believing" is not fully forged until the grade-school years.

The effect of the interpretive rearrangement just outlined is to move the process by means of which children come to share in the folk psychology of their elders somewhat forward in developmental time and consequently closer to the adolescent period originally meant to be featured in this review. Still, early-school-age children are not adolescents, and if it is true that by 6 or 7 most young persons fully grasp the constructive character of the knowing process, then further talk about such accomplishments in still older children continues to remain a waste of space and time. In the place of this conclusion, what is put forward in the paragraphs that follow is that even though middle school children do, as Taylor (Chapter 11), Wellman (Chapter 4), and others have suggested, make important progress in wrenching total responsibility for meaning making out of the hands of the environment, their success in doing so continues to fall importantly short of what is required to interpret these accomplishments as expressive of a fully constructivistic theory of mind. In short, I still mean to persuade you that not until adolescence, do young persons come to participate fully in a genuinely constructivistic view of the knowing enterprise or to share fully in an adultlike theory of mind. To succeed in this agenda, three things are required. First, I must make a convincing case that the impressive accomplishments of middle school children still fall importantly short of the theories of mind routine among mature adults. Second, I must make a case that the theories of mind common to adults are something other than the theories of still younger persons simply raised by one or more recursive steps. That is, I will need to argue that cognitive maturity includes, but does not reduce to, the ability to entertain beliefs about beliefs regarding beliefs. Finally, abandoning any reliance on what it is not, something positive needs to be said about precisely what it is that is meant to distinguish the theories of mind of preadolescents from those characteristic of adolescents and still older persons. All of this begins in the following section with an account of what it is about simply knowing that different persons differently understand one and the same stimulus event that fails to render such an awareness an adequate demonstration of having come into possession of an unqualifiedly constructivistic theory of mind.

Is knowing that different persons find different meaning in the same event a sufficient demonstration of a constructivistic theory of mind?

In laying out the differences that divide the theories of mind characteristic of preschoolers and older children, Flavell (Chapter 13) usefully distinguishes between what he refers to as the assumptions of a one–one versus a one–many relationship between possible contents of the world and possible representations in the mind. In this way, he undertakes to distinguish between the simpler processes of seeing or not seeing, or knowing and not knowing, and any more sophisticated appreciation that under certain circumstances a self-same or singular object of knowledge can often be interpreted in *many* ways.

Not clearly explicated in this distinction are the potentially different ways in which a single event might fall into multiple interpretation. One could, for example, freely endorse the prospect that persons with different histories might find different meanings in the same event (Taylor, Chapter 11), and still easily conclude that all who strayed from the only possibly correct interpretation of such facts are simply wrong. The research of Clinchy and Mansfield (1985), of Enright and his colleagues (Enright & Lapsley, 1980; Enright, Lapsley, Franklin, & Steuck, 1984), and of Kuhn, Pennington, and Leadbeater (1983) suggests this is precisely what children in the middle school years actually do. That is, they fully anticipate that there may be a one–many relation between possible contents in the world and possible representations of such contents, without considering for a moment that more than one of these interpretations have any real legs to stand on. Instead, such preadolescents automatically assume that there are those who correctly grasp the one and only appropriate relation between actual facts and true beliefs and simply write off as misguided all those who see things otherwise. The upshot of all this research into "belief-discrepancy reasoning" is to underscore the point that merely knowing that a single stimulus event admits to more than a single interpretation is importantly short of recognizing the essentially constructivistic nature of the meaning-making enterprise.

How many times must a proposition be embedded before it qualifies as mature?

A popular way of regarding the course of cognitive development interprets any differences dividing more mature from less mature theories of mind as reducible to differences of the same order as those that otherwise separate metacommunications from more pedestrian communications, or theories from metatheories (Rogers, 1967). According to Perner and Wimmer (1985), for example, higher-order beliefs are simply lower-order beliefs raised to the next logical power. By this account, young preschoolers are said to be capable of first representing what poeple think about events, then representing what people think about other people's thoughts, and still later of representing what other people think about what still others think about their thoughts (Perner, Chapters 8 and 14). Although something like this is probably true in the same sense that "even fleas have lesser fleas upon their backs to bite them," only a minimum of real insight into the cognitive course can be extracted from the knowledge that "on and on and on it goes and so ad infinitum" (Broughton, 1981). The apparent reason that this is so, and the reason that "doubly embedded propositions" may be more complex without necessarily being more mature than single embedded ones, is that once an individual is capable of bracketing one thought within another there would seem to be no reason in principle why that mental product could not also be instantiated as the singular object of some new and seemingly "higher" order intentional state. If, for example, I know you hate, I can also hate it that you do, and can probably even hate myself for dwelling on such matters at all, without the necessity or even the possibility of simultaneously apprehending all the nested details of such an iterative sequence. This follows, as Bickhard (1978) points out, primarily because knowing is essentially a binary relationship between someone engaged in an act of knowing and a definite singular something being known, and this is so even when the object taken up for consideration can itself be unpacked for the different purpose of revealing its potentially compound nature. While, then, from a certain viewing posture, thought can be shown to have a hierarchical structure of varying depths, this analytic posture is not that of the usual knower, who instead frames all of his or her beliefs with reference to some essentially singular object of consideration. None of these assertions is meant to suggest that one cannot devise assessment procedures to measure accurately subjects' ability to unpack such nested thoughts or mentally to keep pace with ongoing iterative sequences. Nor is it suggested that the results of such tests will fail to show a rough correlation with chronological age. What is proposed, however, is that these matters will not prove to be the stuff that separates mature from immature theories of mind.

Something like this claim is indirectly acknowledged by Perner and Wimmer (1985), who remark that in certain competitive game situations, where alternating levels of recursive thought yield the same outcome, there is often no "strategic advantage" to higher over lower orders of reasoning. Under such circumstances, where delving into the recursive layers of competing mental states quickly ensnares one in a kind of empty infinite regress, subjects are often quick to grasp the futility of their situation and simply throw up their hands. Wisely, Perner and Wimmer recognize that such situations are poorly suited to reveal the number of recursive loops a given subject is capable of following, and consequently they carefully engineer experimental circumstances better calculated to provide a truer measure of this ability. Although there is no doubt that this can and has been done to good effect, it is not equally clear that doing so is an appropriate way of following the main channel of subsequent cognitive development. At least this will be the assumption pursued in the next and final section, which takes up the notion that the circular structure Perner and

Wimmer (1985) see in only a restricted class of competitive game situations is also characteristic of the great bulk of human affairs, about which it is true that no undoubtedly correct beliefs are available to be had.

Constructivistic versus quasi-constructivistic theories of mind

The license that has allowed investigators such as Flavell, Taylor and Wellman to read the theories of mind evidenced by primary school children as "constructivistic" or "interpretive" or "meaning-generating," and consequently as formally equivalent to our own adult outlook, is that by this stage in their development such children can be reliably shown to appreciate that what persons take away from any "common" experience is heavily dependent on their attitudes toward it. Such young-school-age children are said to recognize, according to Flavell (Chapter 13), that one's beliefs are at least a partial function of what one selectively perceives, understands, or remembers, and are known to depend, as Taylor (Chapter 11) has shown, on each individual's unique personal history. On similar grounds, Wellman (Chapter 4) describes children of this but not still younger ages as equating the mind with a sort of central information processor capable of actively interpreting rather than merely passively responding to its encounters with the environment. Without wishing to challenge the descriptive accuracy of these accounts, it should be pointed out that there nevertheless remain good reasons to suppose that the theories of mind subscribed to by middle school children still fall importantly short of being genuinely constructivistic; instead, they betray a persistent commitment to an earlier and considerably more realistic epistemology. On the strength of evidence in favor of the continued existence of such objectivistic views, it is argued that not until adolescence do young persons begin to understand that divergent views are not always or even primarily the consequence of correctable ignorance or personal bias, but come about instead as a function of all beliefs being inescapably relative to the framework of the entire knowledge constitutive enterprise. To clarify why this is said to be so, it will prove useful to begin by drawing distinctions between three contrasting ways in which beliefs can be understood to gain respectability or to fall into disrepute.

According to the first of these epistemic postures, widely associated with preschool children and other primitives, all beliefs are understood to have their origins in the external environment; are assumed to make their way into the mind by way of incorrigible sensory pathways; and, once in place, are thought to constitute mental structures that correspond, in a formal way, to structures of reality (Broughton, 1981). In terms of this naively realistic view – which Spence (1982) refers to as the "doctrine of immaculate perception" – becoming knowledgeable is the direct result of

passive visitation and is taken as the epistemological equivalent of having
been mugged by the facts. Consequently, anyone who is similarly situated
can be automatically expected to have been set upon by one and the same
truth. This is so because whatever eventually becomes knowledge is assumed to start out as a free-standing attribute of the environing world
and is simply thought to be pressed upon those who happen to be in
harm's way. As a result, any two persons who are similarly situated will
naturally end up with the same informational details identically embossed
on the recording equipment of their minds. Knowledge, then, for such preschoolers is understood to be a gift, a kind of door prize automatically
awarded to any and all who bother to show up for the facts. Doubts or uncertainties, to the extent that they can be said to exist at all, have only to
do with the prospects that persons may end up at the wrong place at the
wrong time and consequently fall into errors of oversight or omission.
Neither possibility is understood, however, to cast any serious doubts on
the ultimate possibility of knowing reality with absolute certainty (Enright et al., 1984). Serious uncertainty, or at least the kind of dubiousness
that might threaten to undermine the trustworthiness of any full complement of facts, consequently has no place in this early childhood world
(Mansfield & Clinchy, 1985).

With the advent of middle childhood, and with it all of the newly won
abilities to consider second- and higher-order beliefs already detailed in
preceding sections, a new class of retail, case-specific doubts come to attach
themselves to children's concrete convictions and cause them to waver in
their confidence that they know particular things with absolute certainty.
Case-specific doubts of this sort have their roots in the newly won realization that persons frequently approach the task of gathering new information trailing all of their older personal prejudices, and that these biases
– what Bacon called "idols of the mind" – seriously confound the possibility of gaining true or objective knowledge. Although such small-caliber,
retail doubts are sufficient to force the realization that single events in the
world can engender multiple and even contradictory representations
(what Flavell calls one–many rather than one–one relations), they are not
adequate to obligate those who recognize them to undertake a major over-
haul of the way in which they understand the basic epistemic relation, or
to force them to exchange their earlier realistic theories of mind for other,
more constructivistic, possibilities. The reason this is so is that all competing knowledge claims continue to be understood by such primary school
children as the product of simple and correctable illusions that can, in
principle, be set right. The recent research of Enright et al. (1984), Kuhn
et al. (1983), Mansfield and Clinchy (1985), and others (for a review, see
Chandler, in press) all lend support to the view that although children in
the middle school years fully understand that two people may earnestly

find different meanings in what are ostensibly the "same" facts, they are nevertheless equally confident that such conundrums automatically imply that at least one, and possibly both, of them is necessarily mistaken. Nothing, then, about such accomplishments appears to represent a radical departure from an earlier commitment to a realistic epistemology or would seem to suggest a shift to anything quite as toplofty as a constructivistic theory of mind.

In contrast to the less substantial claims offered in favor of the proposition that primary school children endorse a constructivistic theory of mind, the proposition that adolescents accomplish such a quantum leap is supported by a sizable body of research (for a review, see Chandler & Boyes, 1982), all of which suggests that they begin systematically to shift primary responsibility for the knowing process from the objects to the subjects of thought. Unlike their younger counterparts, such adolescent youths no longer hold out the prospect that all differences of opinion will eventually succumb to the authority of objective facts, and instead toy with the prospect that certain of the interpretive differences that divide people are endemic to the knowing process itself.

The costs associated with this clearly constructivistic move is a second and larger-caliber brand of generic doubts capable of promoting wholesale uncertainties that begin to call into radical question the prospect of any kind of trustworthy knowledge whatsoever. Such unassuageable generic doubts threaten for the first time to undermine the whole of the realistic epistemic enterprise, and if unchecked, may end up leaving no belief standing upon any other.

Long and impressive intellectual credentials can be offered to support the importance of any move in the direction of such a fully constructive epistemology. Descartes, for example, recognized that to deny there are determinate and unambiguous criteria for knowledge leads to "the dread of madness and chaos where nothing is fixed, where we can neither touch bottom nor support ourselves on the surface" (Bernstein, 1983, p. 18). Similarly, Hume said of himself that he became so wrought by what he perceived to be irreconcilable differences in human understanding that he was "ready to reject all belief and reason, and look upon no opinion ever as more probable or likely than another" (Hume, 1938, p. 267). Nor are those who are so troubled by such generic doubts all located in the distant past. Referring to what I have described elsewhere as the "prospect of epistemological loneliness" (Chandler, 1975), Feyerabend (1976) speaks of "epistemological anarchism"; MacIntyre (1981), of "metaphysical homelessness"; Rescher (1980), of "a loss of epistemic community"; and Douglas (1971), of "the specter of solipsism." Referring to the same sentiments, Berger and Luckman (1967) describe a "vertigo of relativism"; Sartre (1965), a "plurality of solitudes"; and Laing and Cooper (1964), a

"relativistic hall of mirrors." Tillich (1952) and Yalom (1980) talk of
"existential isolation," and Wittgenstein (1969), of an "epistemic privacy"
imposed by the fact that everyone occupies eternally separated solipsistic
worlds. In the face of such an impenetrable pluralism and the erosion of
any sense of definite standpoint (Arendt, 1961), Nietzsche (1956) talked of
the "weightlessness of all things," and Kundera (1984) spoke of "the unbearable lightness of being." All of this is seen by MacIntyre (1981) to
prompt a sense of "epistemological self-consciousness"; by Camus (1942),
to evoke a "nostalgia" for lost intersubjectivity; and by Bernstein (1983),
to be a source of "Cartesian anxiety," that is, an unrequited yearning for
some absolute foundation for certain knowledge.

The dangerous prospect that is raised, then, by the emergence of such
generic doubts is that diversity of opinion is intrinsic to the knowing process (Kurfiss, 1976); that the resulting plurality of available opinion is
nonreducible (Habermas, 1971); that rooted in the unavoidable necessity
of interpretation is a fundamental ambiguity in all knowledge (Sass &
Woolfolk, 1985); and that with the recognition of the essential subjectivity
of all truth the possibility of shareable and demonstrable knowledge may
have been irreparably destroyed (Douglas, 1971). If this is so, if what one
previously took to be evidence pointing unambiguously in one direction
now turns out to be susceptible to rival interpretation (MacIntyre, 1981);
if the best warrant for any belief is no better than a blind liking (Perry,
1970); and if all lived experience is unique (Tillich, 1952), then the possibility of shared belief breaks down irremediably and we all risk being per-
manently enclosed behind an impenetrable wall of our personal prejudices.

My point in mentioning all this is to draw attention to the significance
commonly attached to the shift from a realistic to a more constructivistic
epistemology, as well as to make a case that such preoccupation with the
ultimate decidability of competing knowledge claims is the business of
adolescents and young adults rather than early-school-age children. The
classic work of Perry (1970) and a whole literature better known to coun-
seling psychologists (i.e., Clinchy & Mansfield, 1985; Kitchener & King,
1981) lend strong support to this conclusion. None of this work is meant to
suggest that much younger children are unaware of the relativity of what
knowledge different people hold. What it does show to be novel to the
more constructivistic epistemology of the adolescent period, however, is
the potentially more disruptive recognition of the relativity of what knowledge is held to be. The effect of pulling on this small thread of insight is
eventually to unravel the whole epistemic fabric of middle childhood. So
long as the promise could be held out that competing knowledge claims
are subject to arbitration through eventual access to the truth, preadolescents were free to cling to their realistic epistemologic convictions. If,
however, all acts of knowledge acquisition come to be understood to be

inherently subjective, and if such interpretive acts of meaning making are thought to go so far as to intrude into the very criteria of knowledge, then all hope of obtaining absolute knowledge is irretrievably lost. This, in so many words, is the constructivistic platform of adolescents' newly emerging theory of mind, and its key plank is that it is impossible in principle to maintain any viable, certainty-preserving bridge between the realms of subjective experience and objective truth (Chandler, in press).

REFERENCES

Arendt, H. (1961). *Between past and future.* New York: Viking.

Berger, P., & Luckman, T. (1967). *The social construction of reality.* Harmondsworth: Penguin.

Bernstein, R. (1983). *Beyond objectivism and relativism.* Philadelphia: University of Pennsylvania Press.

Bickhard, M. H. (1978). The nature of developmental stages. *Human Development, 21,* 217–233.

Bretherton, I., & Beeghly, M. (1982). Talking about internal states: The acquisition of an explicit theory of mind. *Developmental Psychology, 18,* 906–921.

Broughton, J. M. (1981). Piaget's structural developmental psychology: 2. Logic and psychology. *Human Development, 24,* 195–224.

Camus, A. (1942). *The myth of Sisyphus.* Paris: Gallimard.

Chandler, M. J. (1972). Egocentrism in normal and pathological childhood development. In F. Monks, W. Hartup, & J. DeWitt (Eds.), *Determinants of behavioral development* (pp. 560–576). New York: Academic Press.

Chandler, M. J. (1975). Relativism and the problem of epistemological loneliness. *Human Development, 18,* 171–180.

Chandler, M. J. (in press). The Othello effect: An essay on the emergence and eclipse of skeptical doubt. *Human Development.*

Chandler, M. J., & Boyes, M. (1982). Social-cognitive development. In B. Wolman (Ed.), *Handbook of developmental psychology.* Englewood Cliffs, NJ: Prentice-Hall.

Chandler, M. J., & Greenspan, S. (1974). Ersatz egocentricism: A reply to H. Borke. *Developmental Psychology, 7,* 104–106.

Chandler, M. J., & Helm, D. (1984). Developmental changes in the contribution of shared experience to social role taking competence. *International Journal of Behavioral Development, 7,* 145–156.

Churchland, P. S., & Churchland, P. M. (1978). Commentary–cognition and consciousness in nonhuman species. *The Behavioral and Brain Sciences, 1,* 565–566.

Clinchy, B., & Mansfield, A. (1985, August). *Justifications offered by children to support positions on issues of "fact" and "opinion."* Paper presented at the Fifty-sixth Annual Meeting of the Eastern Psychological Association, Boston.

Dennett, D. C. (1978). Beliefs about beliefs. *The Behavioral and Brain Sciences, 1,* 568–570.

Douglas, J. (1971). Understanding everyday life. In J. Douglas (Ed.), *Understanding everyday life*. Hawthorne, NY: Aldine.

Enright, R., & Lapsley, D. (1980). Social role-taking: A review of the construct, measures, and measurement properties. *Review of Educational Research, 50*, 647–674.

Enright, R., Lapsley, D., Franklin, C., & Steuck, K. (1984). Longitudinal and cross-cultural validation of the belief-discrepancy reasoning construct. *Developmental Psychology, 20*, 143–149.

Feyerabend, P. (1976). *Against method*. Atlantic Highlands, NJ: Humanities.

Flavell, J. H., Botkin, P. T., Fry, C. L., Wright, J. W., & Jarvis, P. E. (1968). *The development of role taking and communication skills in children*. New York: Wiley.

Flavell, J. H., Everett, B. A., Croft, K., & Flavell, E. R. (1981). Young children's knowledge about visual perception: Further evidence for Level 1–Level 2 distinction. *Developmental Psychology, 17*, 99–103.

Flavell, J. H., Flavell, E. R., & Green, F. L. (1983). Development of the appearance–reality distinction. *Cognitive Psychology, 15*, 95–120.

Flavell, J. H., Flavell, E. R., Green, F. L., & Wilcox, S. A. (1980). Young children's knowledge about visual perception: Effect of observer's distance from target on perceptual clarity of target. *Developmental Psychology, 16*, 10–12.

Flavell, J. H., Shipstead, S. G., & Croft, K. (1978). Young children's knowledge about visual perception: Hiding objects from others. *Child Development, 49*, 1208–1211.

Grice, H. P. (1957). Meaning. *Philosophical Review, 66*, 377–388.

Griffin, D. (1978). Prospects for a cognitive ethology. *The Behavioral and Brain Sciences, 1*, 527–538.

Habermas, J. (1971). *Knowledge and human interests*. Boston: Beacon.

Hogrefe, G.-J., Wimmer, H. & Perner, J. (1986). Ignorance versus false belief: A developmental lag in attribution of epistemic states. *Child Development, 57*, 567–582.

Hood, L., & Bloom, L. (1979). What, when, and how about why: A longitudinal study of early expression of causality. *Monographs of the Society for Research in Child Development* (Serial No. 181).

Hume, D. (1938). *An abstract of a treatise of human nature*. Cambridge University Press.

Johnson, C. N., & Maratsos, M. P. (1977). Early comprehension of mental verbs: Think and know. *Child Development, 48*, 1743–1747.

Johnson, C. N., & Wellman, H. M. (1980). Children's developing understanding of mental verbs: Remember, know, and guess. *Child Development, 51*, 1095–1102.

Kitchener, K. S., & King, P. M. (1981). Reflective judgment: Concepts of justification and their relationship to age and education. *Journal of Applied Developmental Psychology, 2*, 89–116.

Kuhn, D., Pennington, N., & Leadbeater, B. (1983). Adult thinking in developmental perspective. In P. Baltes & O. Brim, Jr. (Eds.), *Life-span development and behavior* (Vol. 6). New York: Academic Press.

Kundera, M. (1984). *The unbearable lightness of being*. New York: Harper & Row.

Kurfiss, J. (1976). A neo-Piagetian analysis of Erikson's "Identity" period of late adolescent development. In S. Modgil & C. Modgil (Eds.), *Piagetian research: Compilation and commentary* (Vol. 5). Windsor, U.K.: NFER Press.

Laing, R. D., & Cooper, D. (1964). *Reason and violence*. London: Tavistock.

Lempers, J. D., Flavell, E. R., & Flavell, J. H. (1977). The development in very young children of tacit knowledge concerning visual perception. *Genetic Psychology Monographs, 95*, 3–53.

Levinson, S. C. (1983). *Pragmatics*. Cambridge University Press.

Loar, B. (1981). *Mind and meaning*. Cambridge University Press.

MacIntyre, A. (1981). *After virtue: A study in moral theory*. Notre Dame, IN: University of Notre Dame Press.

Mansfield, A., & Clinchy, B. (1985, April). A developmental study of natural epistemology. Paper presented at the biennial meeting of the Society for Research in Child Development. Toronto.

Masangkay, Z. S., McCluskey, K. A., McIntyre, C. W., Sims-Knight, J., Vaughn, B. E., & Flavell, J. H. (1974). The early development of inferences about the visual percepts of others. *Child Development, 45*, 357–366.

Nietzsche, F. (1956). *The birth of tragedy and the genealogy of morals*. New York: Doubleday. (Originally published in 1872).

Perner, J., & Wimmer, H. (1985). "John thinks that Mary thinks that . . .": Attribution of second order beliefs by 5- to 10-year-old children. *Journal of Experimental Child Psychology, 39*, 437–471.

Perry, W. G., Jr. (1970). *Forms of intellectual and ethical development in the college years*. New York: Academic Press.

Premack, D., & Woodruff, G. (1978). Does the chimpanzee have a theory of mind? *The Behavioral and Brain Sciences, 1*, 515–526.

Pylyshyn, Z. W. (1978). When is attribution of beliefs justified? *The Behavioral and Brain Sciences, 1*, 592–593.

Rescher, N. (1980). *Skepticism: A critical re-appraisal*. Oxford: Blackwell Publisher.

Rogers, H. (1967). *Theory of recursive functions and effective compatability*. New York: McGraw-Hill.

Sartre, J. P. (1965). *Being and nothingness*. New York: Philosophical Library.

Sass, L., & Woolfolk, R. (1985). *Psychoanalysis and the hermeneutic turn*. Unpublished paper.

Searle, J. (1983). *Intentionality*. Cambridge University Press.

Spence, D. (1982). *Narrative truth and historical truth: Meaning and interpretation in psychoanalysis*. New York: Norton.

Tillich, P. (1952). *The courage to be*. New Haven, CT: Yale University Press.

Wellman, H. M. (1985). The child's theory of mind: The development of concepts of cognition. In S. R. Yussen (Ed.), *The growth of reflection in children*. New York: Academic Press.

Wimmer, H., & Perner, J. (1983). Beliefs about beliefs: Representation and constraining function of wrong beliefs in young children's understanding of deception. *Cognition, 13*, 103–128.

Wittgenstein, L. (1969). *On certainty*. London: Blackwell Publisher.

Yalom, I. D. (1980). *Existential psychotherapy*. New York: Basic.

21

On the origins of beliefs and other intentional states in children

DAVID R. OLSON

At least since the time of Descartes, it has been common to think of people as *res cogitans*, things that think. Descartes wrote: "What is a thing which thinks? It is a thing which doubts, understands, [conceives], affirms, denies, wills, refuses, which also imagines and feels" (*Meditations*, II: Haldane & Ross, 1973, vol. 1, p. 153).

What for Descartes was a great discovery has become for us a "folk psychology," a set of accepted notions used to predict and explain the talk and action of oneself and others. That it is a folk psychology does not imply that it is false; but on the other hand, it does not assure us that it is true, that is, scientifically viable. Whether or not it is – that is, whether or not mental or representational states are to be treated as central to psychological explanation – remains a central problem in cognitive psychology. As is well known, the behaviorists – Ryle (1949) perhaps being a leading exponent – attempted to do away with the "ghost in the machine" while others, such as Searle (1983), regard intentionality as a "ground floor property of minds" (p. 26).

Philosophers of mind have debated these issues with conceptual subtlety and vigor but without resolution (otherwise it would not be philosophy). It is my purpose in this chapter to sketch one way in which the careful experimental study of children's understanding of intentional or mental states may help us thread a developmental course between the behaviorists, who eschew mental states, and the intentionalists, who espouse them.

Representational theories of mind

A central question, perhaps the central question, in cognitive science discourse is the role that "intentional states," that is, representational states including beliefs, desires, intentions, and sentiments, play in the explanation of behavior. Fodor (1985, p. 78) has recently provided a "guide" through the various stances that philosophers of mind have taken to these states in terms of their *ontologies*, that is, the structures and processes they are willing to countenance as *psychologically real*, psychologically real processes being those that figure directly in causing and organizing behavior. I shall emphasize only three stances to such states as they are of particular relevance to understanding the development of intentional states in children.

The first stance is simply to deny outright the psychological reality of mental states and hence their relevance to the explanation of behavior. Two psychological traditions, as different as they are in other ways from Ryle, have joined him in resolutely denying the validity of ascribing mental or representational states in the attempt to explain behavior. One of these was that begun by Skinner (1953), who claimed that the behavior of rats and pigeons could be explained without ascribing beliefs and desires to them. His solution was to see behavior in terms of its consequences, most notably in terms of reinforcement schedules, which made up part of the objective properties of the world. Behavior is then taken to be a direct function of these objective conditions. For Skinner, the rat does not entertain beliefs; it responds to or acts on the world in ways determined by the patterns of reinforcement, that is, the patterns of contingencies in the world.

The other was that initiated by Gibson, who, while maintaining some detachment from behaviorism, shuns mentalism. He wrote: "[Behaviorism's] influence is on the wane, no doubt, but a regression to mentalism would be worse" (1979, p. xiii). Gibson's (1972) central claim was that perception need not appeal to inference. He sustained this claim in a way similar to that used by Skinner (1953). He abandoned the notion that the stimulus be defined narrowly as the pattern of light falling on the retina at a particular instant of time. Rather, he characterized perception as the detection of higher-order structures of information in the environment. What humans do in seeing three-dimensional objects when looking at the two-dimensional display is, not to infer a third dimension but to detect sufficient of the information specifying a three-dimensional object to warrant seeing that object. These theories, in their different ways, offer an account of the perception of complex objects and the organization of complex behavior without appealing to mental states such as beliefs, desires, intentions, or to inferential operations on such representational states. Whether or not they succeed is, of course, very much a matter of controversy (see Pylyshyn, 1984).

The second stance is to regard mental states as part of a "folk psychology." This stance acknowledges the social and linguistic relevance of intentionalist talk but leaves open the question as to whether the mental states named in such talk directly refer to psychologically real entities and processes. Wittgenstein (1980) was, perhaps, among the first to cast doubt on the idea that mental terms simply referred to what are now called psychologically real events. He questioned whether the sentence "We all know

what phenomenon the word 'thinking' refers to" means anything more
than "We can all play the language game with the word 'think' " (1, §550).
His point is that the word *think* does not describe any particular mental
activity although it may express some internal activity; more generally, it
is a piece of social discourse.

Quine (1960) and Sellars (1963) and Rorty (1979) take the argument
a step further by pointing out that "belief" talk is theory talk. Accounts
of mental events are not direct reports obtained either through introspection or observation but ways of characterizing behavior from a theoretical
perspective. Such belief talk is parasitic on behavior; it is the attempt to
characterize action and talk by ascribing mental states to the actor or
speaker.

Quine (1960), for example, on the basis of his views about the indeter-
minacy of translation, claims that there is no "fact of the matter" involved
in the attribution of meanings to utterances *or* beliefs to people. He continues: "If we are limning the true and ultimate structure of reality, the
canonical scheme for us is the austere scheme that knows no quotation but
direct quotation and no propositional attitudes but only the physical con-
stitutions and behavior of organisms" (1960, p. 221). In a similar vein,
Dennett (1977) comments: "If one agrees . . . that it is the job of cognitive
psychology to map the psychologically real processes in people, then since
the ascription of belief and desire is only indirectly tied to such processes,
one might well say that beliefs and desires are not the proper objects of
study of cognitive psychology" (p. 278).

To a psychologist it requires effort to even consider denying the reality
of such mental states as believing and thinking. However, if we pay close
attention to the use of these terms rather than to the underlying processes
to which they purportedly refer, it becomes clear that such terms as *think*,
believe, *intend*, or *remember* do not refer to psychological states that are
invariant to their holder, but rather are devices used by speakers to
characterize the behavior of people or animals from the perspective *of the
speaker*. To say that children look into cookie jars because they believe
there are cookies in them, that the mouse ran down the maze because it
believes there to be cheese at the end, is the speaker's way of talking about
the child or the mouse; it has nothing, at least nothing much, to do with
what actually organized and propelled the relevant course of action.
Moreover, depending on the speaker's own mental state, the state of the
mouse or child will be characterized differently. If there is *no* cheese at *x*
we may say that the mouse thinks that the cheese is at *x* whereas if there *is*
some cheese there we may say it *knows* or *remembers* that the cheese is at *x*,
yet as far as the neurophysiological state of the mouse is concerned, it may
be identical in the two cases. Such arguments should convince one that
the mapping from cognitive concepts to "psychologically real" mental

states may be, to say the least, indirect. (See Olson & Astington, 1986, for an elaboration of this argument.)

Such ways of theoretically characterizing behavior in terms of "folk psychology," although of some relevance to linguistic practice and to social psychology, then, has no necessary relevance to the "realistic" explanation of behavior. Explanations that do appeal to such states assume a "ghost in the machine" (Ryle, 1949) or an "undischarged homunculus" (Dennett, 1978, chap. 1). Dennett continues that "wherever a theory relies on a formulation bearing the logical marks of intentionality, there a little man is concealed" (Dennett, 1978, p. 12). Dennett's view of the intentional concepts that make up folk psychology is that they are "instrumental," they are useful for characterizing behavior but must ultimately be explained in nonintentional terms. Other philosophers, notably Churchland (1986) and Stich (1983), urge that folk psychology simply be abandoned and replaced by more precise and predictive theoretical psychology.

The third stance, which I shall refer to as the "cognitivist" stance, acknowledges that representational states are real but restricts the reflexivity of these states. The "cognitive revolution" was, in large part, the attempt to explain behavior by appeal to representational states such as schemata and cognitive maps, which were seen as organizing action and underlying talk. The primary concern of such theories is to demonstrate that behavior is a function of representations of the world rather than of the world directly. If a desired object is at location x but the actor represents (roughly, believes) it to be at y, the behavior will be determined by the representational state rather than the actual state of the world. Furthermore, such representational states can be built into complex networks that support such mental activities as inference making.

A secondary concern is to determine the form of these representational codes, some writers claiming them to be propositional in form (Anderson, 1983; Pylyshyn, 1984); others, that they are image-like (Kosslyn, 1983; Shepard, 1984), others, that they are both (Paivio, 1971); and others, that they change form as a function of development (Bruner, 1966; Piaget, 1926). But being a realist about cognitive structures does not entail being a realist about such intentional states as beliefs, desires, intentions, and sentiments. Fodor (1981) makes the same point about functionalism: "Although functionalism tends, in general, to license realistic readings of psychological ascriptions, you need *more* than functionalism to license Realism about propositional attitudes" (p. 20).

An elaboration of the cognitive stance, the intentionalist stance, includes everything insisted upon in the cognitive stance, but adds that of being a realist about intentional states. Intentional states consist not only of representations of the world, the domain of the cognitivists, but also of "attitudes" to those representations. Consequently, behavior is a function, not only of propositional content, "that today is Saturday," but also of the holder's attitude to that content, that it is *believed*, *desired*, or *doubted*. Admitting these attitudes as part of the structure of mental representations is what is distinctive about the intentionalist stance.

The notion of "propositional attitude" comes from Russell, who noted, following Frege, the property of "opacity" that characterized these states. But the characterization of these states in terms of "intentionality" is usually traced further back to Brentano (1874/1960), who argued that such states are irreducibly mental. The most recent exponents of intentionalist theory, those of most relevance here, are Fodor (1978; 1981), Searle (1983), Pylyshyn (1984), and Rozeboom (1972), all of whom take a realist stance to intentional states. In such theories, mental states are simply brain states and function directly in the organization of behavior and talk. Searle, for example, says: "Intentionality is, so to speak, a ground floor property of the mind" (1983, p. 26). And for Fodor, intentionality is fundamental to the representational theory of mind.

The general schema for the representation of intentionality is that of a psychological predicate (or propositional attitude or psychological mode) which specifies a relation between a content expressed by a proposition and its holder, thus:

Subject	Attitude	Proposition
I	think	that today is Saturday
He	believes	that the chocolate is at A
	remembers	
	recognizes	
	pretends	
	imagines	
	construes	

The primary logical property of such psychological predicates is that of *opacity*. In the standard example, based on Quine, if the man in the brown hat is a spy, and if the man in the brown hat is named Ortcutt, then Ortcutt is a spy. In the case of propositional attitudes, such propositions have a use that is referentially opaque. One may believe that the man in the brown hat is a spy, but if one does not know that the man in the brown hat is Ortcutt, then, at least in the preferred sense, one will not believe that Ortcutt is a spy (Jackendoff, 1983). By means of such predicates one may refer to nonexisting things, such as "He believes in ghosts"; represent things as false, "He thinks that duck is a goose"; and represent things contrary to fact, "He is pretending that the bench is a horse," as Leslie (Chapter 2) has pointed out.

To be a realist about intentional states is to take these states to be intrinsic structures of behaving organisms. The justification for ascribing them is that one cannot make sense of behavior otherwise (Searle, 1983, p. 4; Pylyshyn, 1984, p. 26). A commonsensical or "folk" theory of mind brings those structures into reflective awareness, but such structures are assumed to be present, presumably "realized" in the neurophysiological structures of the brain, whether or not their holders are speakers of a language and whether or not their holders are aware of them. Thus, all of the above-mentioned theorists are willing to ascribe such international states to lower animals and, in some cases, computers. Fodor (1981, p. 192) claims that dogs hold beliefs: "You can, surely, believe that it's raining even if you don't speak a language at all." And Searle (1983, p. 5) adds: "Only someone in the grip of a philosophical theory would deny that babies can literally be said to want milk and that dogs want to be let out or believe that their master is at the door."

Writers such as Quine, of course, acknowledge the existence of these linguistic and logical properties. Their argument, rather, is about the relevance of these predicates to a psychological explanation, claiming that rather than referring to invariant psychological states of organisms, such predicates were part of a language game, a way of talking about or characterizing or construing others' talk and behavior, a part of social or "folk" psychology rather than of a realist theory of behavior. Some writers, such as Rorty (1979), argue that the whole ontological emphasis is misplaced; what is construed and what is a construal is to be resolved pragmatically: "such practices as the ascription of intentional states are justified by their social utility" (1979, p. 194).

What these theories lack, at least from the perspective of a developmentalist, is any acknowledgment that the "folk psychology" may only at a later stage of development become applicable to the developing child. Just how this could be is our next concern.

Children's intentional states

Just what are children acquiring when they develop a "theory of mind" – that is, the set of concepts, including belief, desire, and intention that they can use systematically in explaining the behavior of themselves and others? Are they acquiring nothing except a mistaken view of the organization of behavior analogous to beliefs in Santa Claus, ghosts, and demons, ideas that have nothing to do with reality, as a Skinner may suggest? Or are they acquiring a folk psychology, a kind of social psychology useful for talking and thinking about their own and others' behavior, yet without such intentional states actually playing a role in the organization of behavior, as a Quine may suggest? Or are children acquiring a set of concepts for explicitly representing intentional states that had, in fact, been represented in the child's mind/brain all along, as a Fodor or a Searle may suggest? Or, is it possible – and this is the view I shall urge – that children actually acquire the cognitive machinery that makes intentional state ascription literally true of them at a certain stage in development? That stage would correspond to the child's acquisition and use of a language for making statements, requests, and promises.

How can the careful empirical study of the origins of a "theory of mind" in children help to decide the issue of the ontological status of intentional states? Certainly not in any simple way, because the child may have beliefs but not a concept of a belief. It is even possible, I suppose, to have the concept without knowing a language in which such concepts could be expressed. Yet such an analysis may contribute to the ontological issue both methodologically and conceptually. Methodologically, empirical research on the origins of mental (or representational, or intentional) states in children provides a precisely articulated domain in which one can examine alternative theoretical possibilities. By posing just the right questions and by making just the right alterations in the environment, one can greatly narrow the gap between evidence and theoretical claims. Indeed, the evidence showing how children's talk and action become self-conscious and deliberate and how they become capable of separating beliefs from reality and intentions from expressions points to the significance of their acquisition of explicit knowledge about representational states, that is, their acquisition of a theory of mind.

Conceptually, the study of children offers a developmental perspective to the question of the reality of mental, representational states. The strategy is similar to that taken by Piaget in his examination of other cognitive systems such as space and number. By looking at children at a series of points in development, it may be possible to show that whereas the behavior of the youngest children can be adequately accounted for without ascribing intentional states, that of children with an appropriate level of linguistic sophistication cannot. Thus the behaviorists may be correct in denying the reality of beliefs and desires to infants, while the intentionalists may be correct in claiming the reality of beliefs and desires in older, linguistic children and adults. Moreover, it may be possible to see how a cultural form, a folk psychology, acquired by the child as a theory of mind, may be instrumental in making those mental states subject to awareness and deliberate control.

Here is one possibility within this developmental perspective. Intentional states are the product, first, of representing condition–action relations in the form of propositional representations, and later of representing those representations in the form of meta-representations. The first is achieved with the acquisition of language, the second, with the acquisition of a theory of mind. Roughly, before the acquisition of language, children's behavior may be most appropriately characterized in nonintentionalist terms. Once they acquire a language for stating propositions and for making requests and promises, their behavior may be characterized in intentionalist terms even if these intentional states are not subject to awareness or manipulation by their holders. And finally, when they acquire the concepts making up a theory of mind, they become meta-representational, and from that point on, their voluntary behavior is not only organized along intentionalist lines, these states become subject to awareness and deliberation – in a word, to thought. By taking our developmentalism seriously, we may be able to determine if and when behavior comes to be correctly characterized in intentionalist terms and when these intentional states become subject to reflection and manipulation. That is, we may be able to discover the conditions under which intentional states become psychologically real.

Let us attempt to spell out this developmentalist perspective more fully. In the first stage, for infants before the acquisition of a referential language, behavior may be characterized in terms of schemas or procedures that we may express as conditionals:

> If A do B
> If A then B

The former are procedures or habits, the latter are expectancies. Both are commonplace in behaviorist psychology. The first describes, among other things, the action of a thermostat: If condition A is met, it initiates procedure B; it continues until A is no longer met. The second describes an expectancy. An expectancy is taken by some to be identical to a belief. Wittgenstein (1958, §577) for one, did not do so. He attempted to distinguish two senses of expectancy. In one case, expecting someone to come would mean being surprised that he did not come and that would not, Wittgenstein says, "be called the description of a state of mind." In the other case of expecting someone, we mean that we are eagerly awaiting him, and that would be a description of a state of mind, an actual belief that he would come. Accounts phrased in terms of habits and expectancies make no appeal to such representational states as beliefs or desires.

It is important to introduce a caveat at this point, to avoid confusion. The states just described above as habits and expectancies may be represented by the theorist by propositions, just as they could be represented, if our science were sufficiently advanced, by mathematical equations. But this move clouds the issue of psychological reality. It is important to distinguish representations ascribed by the theorist in terms of his folk psychology, from the representations actually employed by the subject itself in managing its behavior.

The reason it is important to distinguish the ascriptions employed by an adult for "interpreting" the behavior of the child from the cognitive structures actually involved in regulating the behavior of the child is that development may consist precisely of the child's translating these habits and expectancies into a propositional form offered by a natural language. That is, in the course of acquiring a language to say things, ask for things, promise things, and the like, the child may simultaneously reorganize his habits and expectancies into the form of such intentional states as beliefs, desires, and intentions. If, therefore, intentional states are simply ascribed to young children, the primary device for explaining developmental change is preempted. Hence, it is important to distinguish what an adult may say about the actions of children, animals, and computers from the structures that actually organize and produce the behavior in question. That done, development may be viewed as a matter of the child's reorganizing habits and expectancies into propositional linguistic form and then again reorganizing those representational forms into the categories made available in the folk psychology. This would allow for the possibility that while representational states are a simple consequence of being a language-using creature, the structure of one's meta-representations, that is, one's theory of mind, may depend on the folk theory into which one is socialized.

The developmental scheme we end up with, then, has at least three distinct stages. The first is essentially behavioristic: Behavior is to be explained without recourse or appeal to intentional states. Ascriptions by observers of such states as "Baby thinks that mother going to leave" are entirely for the convenience and pleasure of the ascriber; they are not literally true. The second stage is, we may say, intentional. Children who have learned to talk, to make assertions and requests, may be credited with the corresponding intentional states: If they ask for x, they desire x, if they say that p, they think that p, and so on. But they do not, yet, think of their utterances and actions in terms of mental or representational states.

And finally, at the third stage, children acquire a theory of mind, a folk psychology, that permits them to think of their own and others' talk and actions in terms of mental states. When they begin to see their utterances as expressions of belief, for example, they begin to distinguish their beliefs from their utterances, to distinguish beliefs from reality, to store their beliefs as episodic representations of events rather than simply update their model of the world, and to make the other cognitive achievements that have been noted in children in their late preschool years.

This view is quite similar to that advanced by Sellars (1963) in his myth of our "Rylean ancestors." He asks us to imagine a stage in prehistory in which humans were limited to a Rylean language, a language that bore no marks of the mental, and then to imagine what would have to be added to allow the speakers of such a language to think of themselves and others as things that have mental states. He proposed two features: a metalanguage

for referring to meanings and truth, and, second, the development of theoretical discourse. With these two features, one could come up with a model
for overt speech as the product of some inner episode, such as inner speech.
Sellars continues:

> For once our fictitious ancestor ... has developed the theory that overt verbal
> behavior is the expression of thoughts, and taught his compatriots to make use of
> the theory in interpreting each other's behavior, it is but a short step to the use of
> this language in self-description. ...What began as a language with a purely
> theoretical use has gained a reporting role. (pp. 188–189)

Sellars does not commit himself as to whether or when our Rylean
ancestors came to hold beliefs; he is, rather, attempting to account for
when people come to think of themselves as holding those beliefs whether
or not they really do. They do so when they learn to apply to themselves
a social language, a language for talking about the talk and action of
others in terms of intentionality. Sellars is accounting for the rise of
self-consciousness, if you like.

The origins of beliefs and other intentional states, as I argued earlier,
may be tied to the acquisition of a language and its uses for stating propositions, issuing requests and commands, and making promises. This is
the view advanced by Vendler (1970), who notes the close ties between
saying something and thinking something. Rather than taking the conventional view that saying something is simply the expression of an already
available thought, he suggests that it is saying things that gives rise to
thinking things. This is how he put it:

> The problem is not: can we express in words whatever we can think? It is rather:
> can we think everything that we can say? I hazard a guess: speech is the primary
> phenomenon, thought is the derivative one. It is true that speech is the expression
> of thought, but it is also true, and I would like to say, more true, that thought is the
> suppression of speech. It is like typing or just touching the keys without pressing
> them. (p. 89)

If this is true, the beginnings of beliefs, and the beginnings of an awareness of those beliefs are both tied to the acquisition of language. The former
depends upon the acquisition of a language for formulating and expressing
propositions;[1] the latter depends on the acquisition of a metalanguage for
talking about those propositions.[2]

It is at the former stage, at the time of the acquisition of the ability to
say things, that children's perception and actions come to be organized in
terms of mental states such as beliefs and intentions, these beliefs and
intentions being simply the psychological counterparts of saying things.
At this point, such states are no longer merely part of the folk theory used

by theorists to talk about the behavior of humans, animals, and machines. The child now possesses the structures that can serve as the objects of higher-order representations. At this point the theorist can, correctly, be a realist about intentional states; from this point on, Fodor and Searle are correct about minds.

The development more relevant to the chapters in this volume revolves around the developments occurring at the latter stage, the stage at which children become conscious of the mental states of themselves and others. As a number of chapters show, children acquire an intentionalist vocabulary very early, about the time they acquire language generally – at least children in western cultures do – but its use is somewhat limited. They begin to use such talk in a more or less theoretical way at about 4 years of age to characterize both their own and others' talk and actions. Children begin to recognize that people say something because they think something or that they do something because they believe something.

It is at this third stage, I suggest, that children become deliberate and self-conscious; they come not only to think of themselves and others as holders of belief states, they also become capable of separating intention from action, intention from utterance, beliefs from reality, and the like. Tricks, secrets, and lies become possible.

Of course, it is possible that the behaviorists are right in denying the reality of intentional states; folk theory may be simply a useful fiction. It is also possible that the intentionalists, such as Searle and Fodor, are right in claiming that it is the very nature of brains of higher animals to be organized in terms of intentional states such as beliefs, desires, and intentions. On that view, the acquisition of language merely provides a means for expressing thought and the acquisition of a theory of mind is merely a language for describing, ascribing, and reflecting on preexisting mental states.

But it is also possible that intentional states are completely bound up in representing, or construing, or translating lower-order adaptive mechanisms including habits and expectancies into intentional form in the course of learning to say things, ask for things, and promise things – the mental states being simply the states implicated by those speech acts – and then acquiring the culture's metalanguage for talking about those putative states. It is the acquisition of this metalanguage that, I suggest, is central to the development of a theory of mind.

ACKNOWLEDGMENT

I am grateful to Christopher Olsen for saving me from dreadfully misrepresenting some contemporary philosophers if not others.

NOTES

1 Campbell and I (Olson & Campbell, 1987) have argued that the acquisition of a natural language is at the same time the acquisition of a language of thought.
2 Paul Harris (personal communication) asks why, if I would agree that atoms existed before their discovery and evolution occurred before the theory of evolution, I should not also agree that minds exist before the acquisition or invention of a theory of mind. In my view, minds are not brains. The brain, I would agree, existed even when it was believed to be a blood cooler. But mind, as a system of beliefs and desires, is a theoretical construction, analogous to the theory of spirits and demons or the theory of homunculi, which was invented to explain talk and behavior. It is not, in my view, the thing to be explained. Perhaps, as Dennett (1986) suggests, beliefs are analogous not to atoms and evolution, which exist independently of our knowledge of them, but to such social concepts as good and evil or rights and obligations, which are none the less real for their invented, contractual nature.

REFERENCES

Anderson, J. (1983). *The architecture of cognition*. Cambridge, MA: Harvard University Press.

Brentano, F. (1960). The distinction between mental and physical phenomena. In R. Chisholm (Ed.), *Realism and the background of phenomenology*. New York: Free Press. (Originally published in German, 1874).

Bruner, J. (1966). On cognitive growth. In J. Bruner, R. Olver, & P. Greenfield (Eds.), *Studies in cognitive growth*. New York: Wiley.

Churchland, P. S. (1986). *Neurophilosophy: Toward a unified science of the mind–brain*. Cambridge, MA: Bradford Books/MIT Press.

Dennett, D. (1977). Critical notice. *Mind*, 86, 265–280.

Dennett, D. (1978). *Brainstorms*. Montgomery, VT: Bradford Books.

Dennett, D. (1986). Julian Jaynes's software archeology. *Canadian Psychology*, 27 (2), 149–154.

Descartes, R. (1973). *The philosophical works of Descartes* (E. Haldane & G. Ross, Trans. & Eds.). Cambridge University Press.

Fodor, J. A. (1978). Propositional attitudes. *Monist*, 61, 501–523.

Fodor, J. A. (1981). *Representations*. Cambridge, MA: Bradford Books/MIT Press.

Fodor, J. A. (1985). Fodor's guide to mental representation: The intelligent auntie's vade-mecum. *Mind*, 94, 76–100.

Gibson, J. (1972). A theory of direct visual perception. In J. Royce & W. Rozeboom (Eds.), *The psychology of knowing*. New York: Gordon & Breach.

Gibson, J. (1979). *The ecological approach to visual perception*. Boston: Houghton Mifflin.

Jackendoff, R. (1983). *Semantics and cognition*. Cambridge, MA: Bradford Books/ MIT Press.

Kosslyn, S. (1983). *Ghosts in the mind's machine: Creating and using images in the brain.* New York: Norton.

Olson, D., & Astington, J. (1986, October). *Talking about texts: How literacy contributes to thought.* Paper presented at the 11th Annual Boston University Conference on Language Development, Boston, MA.

Olson, D., & Campbell, R. (1987, April). *On the ascription of mental states to young computers.* Paper presented at the Conference on Computers, Cognition and Epistemology, Aarhus, Denmark.

Paivio, A. (1971). *Imagery and verbal processes.* New York: Holt, Rinehart & Winston.

Piaget, J. (1926). *Language and thought of the child* (M. Gabain, Trans.). London: Routledge & Kegan Paul.

Pylyshyn, Z. (1984). *Computation and cognition: Toward a foundation for cognitive science.* Cambridge, MA: Bradford Books/MIT Press.

Quine, W. (1960). *Word and object.* Cambridge, MA: MIT Press.

Rorty, R. (1979). *Philosophy and the mirror of nature.* Princeton, NJ: Princeton University Press.

Rozeboom, W. (1972). Problems in the psycho-philosophy of knowledge. In J. Royce & W. Rozeboom (Eds.), *The psychology of knowing.* New York: Gordon & Breach.

Ryle, G. (1949). *The concept of mind.* London: Hutchinson.

Searle, J. (1983). *Intentionality: An essay in the philosophy of mind.* Cambridge University Press.

Sellars, W. (1963). *Science, perception and reality.* London: Routledge & Kegan Paul.

Shepard, R. (1984). Ecological constraints on internal representation: Resonant kinematics of perceiving, imagining, thinking and dreaming. *Psychological Review, 91,* 417–447.

Skinner, B. (1953). *Science and human behavior.* New York: Macmillan.

Stich, S. (1983). *From folk psychology to cognitive science.* Cambridge, MA: Bradford Books/MIT Press.

Vendler, Z. (1970). Say what you think. In J. L. Cowan (Ed.), *Studies in thought and language.* Tucson: University of Arizona Press.

Wittgenstein, L. (1958). *Philosophical investigations* (G. E. M. Anscombe, Trans.). Oxford: Blackwell Publisher.

Wittgenstein, L. (1980). *Remarks on the philosophy of psychology* (G. E. M. Anscombe, Trans.; G. E. M. Anscombe & G. H. von Wright, Eds.). Oxford: Blackwell Publisher.

Name index

Subject index